Rhetorical Writing Habits

University of Nevada, Reno

Adapted from Carol Lea Clark's
Praxis: A Brief Rhetoric, 3rd edition

Contributing Editors:
Leslie Anglesey
Brady Edwards
Derrian Goebel
E. Jann Harris
Tom Hertweck
Maureen McBride
Melissa Nicolas
Blake Watson
Citlalin Xochime

FOUNTAINHEAD
PRESS

Our green initiatives include:

Electronic Products
We deliver products in non-paper form whenever possible. This includes pdf downloadables, flash drives, & CDs.

Electronic Samples
We use Xample, a new electronic sampling system. Instructor samples are sent via a personalized web page that links to pdf downloads.

FSC Certified Printers
All of our printers are certified by the Forest Service Council which promotes environmentally and socially responsible management of the world's forests. This program allows consumer groups, individual consumers, and businesses to work together hand-in-hand to promote responsible use of the world's forests as a renewable and sustainable resource.

Recycled Paper
Most of our products are printed on a minimum of 30% post-consumer waste recycled paper.

Support of Green Causes
When we do print, we donate a portion of our revenue to green causes. Listed below are a few of the organizations that have received donations from Fountainhead Press. We welcome your feedback and suggestions for contributions, as we are always searching for worthy initiatives.
Rainforest 2 Reef
Environmental Working Group

Cover Designer: Johanna Lopez

Design: Ellie Moore
Developmental Editor: Amy Salisbury-Werhane

Some photos provided by Shutterstock.

Books may be purchased for educational purposes.

For information, please call or write:

> 1-800-586-0330
> Fountainhead Press
> Southlake, TX 76092

> Web site: www.fountainheadpress.com
> E-mail: customerservice@fountainheadpress.com

ISBN: 978-1-68036-797-3
Printed in the United States of America

Welcome

As a student in ENG 101 or 113, you are preparing yourself for a successful career in college and beyond by developing the skills necessary to think and express ideas clearly. Your work this semester will prepare you for the research-based writing course (ENG 102 or 114) you will be taking after successful completion of this course, and ENG 101/113 will also help you better understand that successful writing comes from thoughtful revision of ideas across multiple drafts. In ENG 101/113 you will be working in a small-classroom setting with peers whom you will have an opportunity to get to know better in ways you may not in other courses, all with a textbook that has been custom-designed to facilitate the best possible user experience.

Rhetorical Writing Habits was carefully chosen for ENG 101/113 because it focuses on the rhetorical tools you will need to successfully navigate communication (both oral and written) throughout your time at UNR and beyond. In fancy rhetorical terms, these tools fall under the category of *techne*; you can think of them as powerful techniques that facilitate your ability to be an effective communicator. In ENG 102/114, you will learn how to deploy *techne* in the service of *kairos*—another fancy term that concerns itself with the time, place, occasion, and circumstances of rhetorical acts. Combined, ENG 101/113 and ENG 102/114 provide you with the skills and habits of minds you will find necessary for your work across the university. And 21st century employers want and need employees who are skilled rhetoricians, i.e., employees who can think and write clearly, responding to the needs of their various audiences.

If you should have any questions—about this course or otherwise—do not hesitate to ask your instructor.

Best wishes for a successful semester!

The Core Writing Program

The Core Writing Program at UNR, housed in the Department of English, offers a series of first-year writing courses designed to meet the needs of incoming students. ENG 101/113 develops your writing process and rhetorical awareness (*techne*) in preparation for ENG 102/114, as well as introduces you to Silver Core Objective 1 (CO1): Effective Composition & Communication and Silver Core Objective 3 (CO3): Critical Analysis and Use of Information. Both CO1 and CO3 are the foundation for ENG 102, and both objectives will be developed and integrated in your future course work.

Silver Core Objective 1: Effective Composition & Communication

Brief Description: Students will be able to effectively compose written, oral, and multimedia texts for a variety of scholarly, professional, and creative purposes.

Silver Core Objective 3: Critical Analysis and Use of Information

Brief Description: Students will be critical consumers of information, able to engage in systematic research processes, frame questions, read critically, and apply observational and experimental approaches to obtain information.

Student Learning Outcomes (SLOs)

The Silver Core objectives represent the large pieces of the Core Curriculum that all UNR students are expected to meet. In order to make these large categories more legible, each Core Curriculum course you take at UNR will also outline smaller, specific outcomes that, when taken together, meet the goals of the Core Curriculum. These smaller outcomes are usually called "Student Learning Outcomes" or "SLOs."

The SLOs for ENG 101/113 state that after successful completion, you will be able to:

1. Recognize, articulate, and respond to a variety of rhetorical contexts;

2. Practice strategies for purposeful, concrete development of topics, for example, by using writing to record, explore, organize, and communicate;

3. Interpret, analyze, discuss, and evaluate a variety of readings;

4. Use multiple drafts and peer review to improve own texts;

5. Use generating, organizing, revising, and editing strategies that are appropriate to specific writing situations;

6. Use reflection to examine personal experience, expertise, writing process, and sources;

7. Write understandable, efficient sentences;

8. Control general conventions of usage, spelling, grammar, and punctuation in standard written English.

In addition to the above outcomes, ENG 113 provides extra practice with, and dedicated instruction in, English language fluency.

Overview of ENG 101/113

ENG 101/113 represents the English course that most first-year students initially take at UNR. This course is designed to teach you to use an intentional writing process to address a variety of writing tasks. ENG 101/113 prepares you to successfully complete ENG 102/114 as well as to respond to writing situations you will encounter in the Silver Core and your major; however, this course does not meet Silver Core requirements. Only ENG 102/114 satisfies the foundational elements of CO1 and CO3 required by the Silver Core Curriculum.

In ENG 101/113 you will practice critical reading and academic writing strategies (*techne*) that contribute to a solid foundation for the communication experiences you will encounter in ENG 102/114 and beyond. At UNR, ENG 101/113 is taught as a portfolio course; however, we offer flexibility to instructors regarding what these portfolios look like (e.g., midterm and final portfolio, process portfolio, showcase portfolio). Your instructor will explain what type of portfolio you will be asked to complete for your particular section.

Writing as a Process

You can expect to write 16-20 pages of polished prose in ENG 101/113. "Polished prose" is writing that has gone through multiple stages of the writing process, including:

Prewriting/Planning—You will consider conceptual groundwork as well as strategize about how you will address an assignment prompt. This phase may include prewriting strategies such as freewrites, clustering/mapping, reading and/or research, class discussions, or writing center visits.

Drafting—You will take your writing through multiple stages, not simply submitting your first attempts. Multiple drafts may be achieved through portfolio requirements.

Revising—You will consider higher order concerns such as organization, purpose/focus, development, and integration of supporting texts/documents after an initial draft has been composed. Polished prose should integrate feedback from peers, instructors, and/or writing center staff.

Editing & Proofreading—Editing will focus on later order concerns such as sentence-level correctness, academic tone, refining word choice, standard academic English, and convention usage. You will proofread for accuracy before submitting polished prose.

Core Writing Program and English Department Offices

The Core Writing Program office is located in Frandsen Humanities, room 131 (FH 131), and is open Monday through Friday from 8:00 a.m. to 5:00 p.m. Frandsen Humanities also houses the offices for the program's instructors. All of those teaching for the Core Writing Program have mailboxes in FH 127. Contacts for program and relevant departmental representatives include:

Core Writing Program (FH 131):   784-6709

English Department (FH 119):   784-6689

Course Placement Policies and Procedures

The Core Writing Program (CWP) maintains an offering of courses that are meant to serve your abilities appropriately. To that end, the CWP allows you to work at a level that best matches your skills at the time of matriculation.

Standard Placement Policy

For your initial placement into the Core Writing Program, UNR used your ACT or SAT scores (whichever was higher if you took both examinations). If you are an international student, please contact the registrar's office (775) 784-4700 (option 2) or mynevada@unr.edu for more information about your placement.

Course	Old SAT Verbal/Critical Reading	New SAT EBRW (March 2016 and After)	ACT	Alternative Route
ENG 098	≤430	≤410	≤17	N/A
ENG 100J	440–500	420–470	18–20	N/A
ENG 101	510–670	480–650	21–29	Pass ENG 098
ENG 102	680 and above	660 and above	≥30	Pass ENG 100J or Pass ENG 101 or Pass ENG 101 CBE

You must complete ENG 102/114 to satisfy the Core Curriculum requirement. Typically, you will take ENG 101/113 during your first semester and ENG 102/114 during your second semester. For more information on placement, please see the Core Writing Website: https://www.unr.edu/english/core-writing

Contents

Chapter 1: Defining Rhetoric   1
*Praxis in Action: "Why Rhetoric Is Important in My Writing" by Meaghan
    Elliott   1*

What Is Rhetoric?   2
Rhetoric and Power   3
Selected Definitions of Rhetoric   4
Activity 1.1 • Historical Usage of the Word "Rhetoric"   5
Are We All Greeks?   5
Activity 1.2 • Contemporary Usage of the Word "Rhetoric"   7
Visual Map of Meanings for the Word Rhetoric   7
Activity 1.3 • Explore the Visual Map of the Word *Rhetoric*   7
Reading 1.1 • "'Columbusing': The Art of Discovering Something that
    is Not New" by Brenda Salinas   8
Activity 1.4 • Analyzing Columbusing as an Argument   11

Rhetorical Argument   11
Types of Argument   12

Aristotle's Three Appeals   13
Reading 1.2 • "Microsoft Just Laid Off Thousands of Employees
    With a Hilariously Bad Memo" by Kevin Roose   15
Activity 1.5 • Discuss Microsoft's Memo Laying Off Employees   20
Reading 1.3 • "The Sleepover Question" by Amy Schalet   20
Activity 1.6 • Analyze "The Sleepover Question"   23

Become Part of the Academic Conversation   23
The Burkean Parlor   25
Activity 1.7 • Joining the Conversation   25

Collaborative Groups Help Students Enter the Academic Conversation   26

Why Study Rhetoric?   27

Activity 1.8 • How Do You Use Rhetoric?   28

Rhetorical Arguments Stand the Test of Time   28

Reading 1.4 • "Text of the Gettysburg Address" by Abraham Lincoln   28

Activity 1.9 • Paraphrase the Gettysburg Address   29

Activity 1.10 • Comment on Your Classmate's Paraphrase of the Gettysburg Address   29

Respond to Visual Rhetoric   29

Activity 1.11 • Decoding Clothing Choices as Visual Rhetoric   31

Chapter Exercises

Activity 1.12 • Keep a Commonplace Book   31

Activity 1.13 • Create Your Own Blog   33

Chapter 2: Responding Rhetorically   35

Praxis in Action: "Why I Annotate Readings" by Isidro Zepeda   35

Thinking Critically, Reading Rhetorically   36

Activity 2.1 • Think about Critical Reading   37

Reading 2.1 • "Do You Know How Your Mascara is Made?" by Arna Cohen   37

Activity 2.2 • Analyze "Do You Know How Your Mascara is Made?"   47

Activity 2.3 • Why Is Activity 2.2 Critical Reading?   48

Ways of Reading Rhetorically   48

Checklist of Essential Elements in an Argument   50

Reading 2.2 • "The Web Means the End of Forgetting" by Jeffrey Rosen   51

Activity 2.4 • Discuss "The Web Means the End of Forgetting"   57

Activity 2.5 • Apply the Checklist of Essential Elements in an Argument   58

Activity 2.6 • What Is the Current State of Identity Protection in Social Networking Sites?   58

Close Reading of a Text   58

Checklist for Close Reading of a Text   61

Reading 2.3 • "The Point When Science Becomes Publicity" by James Hamblin, M.D.   62

Activity 2.7 • Apply Close Reading to a Text   66

Activity 2.8 • Discuss "The Point When Science Becomes Publicity"   66

The Rhetorical Triangle   66

Activity 2.9 • Apply the Rhetorical Triangle   67

Activity 2.10 • Write a Summary   68

Respond to Multimedia   68

Reading 2.4 • "'Flawless' Excerpt" by Beyoncé and Chimamanda Ngozi Adichie   69

Activity 2.11 • Respond to Song Lyrics   70

Activity 2.12 • Consider a Song as an Argument   70

Respond to Visual Rhetoric   70

Activity 2.13 • Interpret Advertisements   72

Activity 2.14 • Find Advertisements with Effective Arguments   73

Reading 2.5 • "Why Has Godzilla Grown?" by Lisa Wade   73

Activity 2.15 • Consider Shock Value in Today's Cartoon Characters   75

Interaction between Texts and Images   75

Reading 2.6 • "All-Star Rockers Salute Buddy Holly" by Andy Greene   76

Activity 2.16 • Analyze Interaction between Texts and Images   76

Reading 2.7 • "How to Make a Kindle Cover from a Hollowed Out Hardback Book" by Justin Meyers   77

Activity 2.17 • Write and Illustrate Instructions   80

Activity 2.18 • Summarize the Argument in Your Illustrations   80

Chapter Exercises

Activity 2.19 • Write on Your Blog   80

Activity 2.20 • Write in Your Commonplace Book   81

Chapter 3: Persuading Rhetorically   83

Praxis in Action: "If You Want to Write Well, Then Read" by Amber Lea Clark   83

Discover the *Kairos*—The Opening for Argument   84

Use *Kairos* to Make Your Own Argument   84

Reading 3.1 • "I Have a Dream" by Dr. Martin Luther King, Jr.   86

Activity 3.1 • Use Microsoft's Comment Feature to Annotate a Text   91

Activity 3.2 • Discuss "I Have a Dream"   91

Activity 3.3 • Identify the *Kairos*   92

Activity 3.4 • Analyze an Audience   92

Aristotle's Persuasive Appeals   93

Arguments from *Logos*   93

Reading 3.2 • "Executions Should Be Televised" by Zachary B. Shemtob and David Lat   94

Activity 3.5 • Analyze an Argument from *Logos*   96

Activity 3.6 • Find an Argument from *Logos*   96

Deductive Reasoning   97

Activity 3.7 • Develop a Deductive Argument   98

Inductive Reasoning   98

Activity 3.8 • Develop an Inductive Argument   99

Logical Fallacies   99

Activity 3.9 • Identify Logical Fallacies   103

Activity 3.10 • Create Examples of Logical Fallacies   103

Arguments from *Pathos*   103

Reading 3.3 • "People for Sale" by E. Benjamin Skinner   104

Activity 3.11 • Write about an Argument from *Pathos*   109

Activity 3.12 • Analyze an Argument from *Pathos*   109

Activity 3.13 • Find an Argument from *Pathos*   109

Arguments from *Ethos*   109

Reading 3.4 • "Alien Life Coming Slowly into View" by Ray Jayawardhana   110

Activity 3.14 • Analyzing an Argument from *Ethos*   113

Activity 3.15 • Find an Argument from *Ethos*   113

Combining *Ethos, Pathos,* and *Logos*   113

Activity 3.16 • Identify *Ethos*, *Pathos*, and *Logos*   114

Photos Heighten *Ethos*   114

Activity 3.17 • Locate a Photo that Presents an Argument from *Logos*, *Ethos*, or *Pathos*   115

Chapter Exercises

Activity 3.18 • *Logos* Activity: Write a Letter to the Editor   115

Activity 3.19 • *Pathos* Activity: Portray an Emotion in a Collage   116

Activity 3.20 • *Ethos* Activity: Create a Professional LinkedIn Page   116

Activity 3.21 • Write a Rhetorical Analysis   118

Activity 3.22 • Reflect on Your Rhetorical Analysis   119

Activity 3.23 • Write on Your Blog   119

Activity 3.24 • Write in Your Commonplace Book   119

Chapter 4: Inventing Rhetorically   121
Praxis in Action: "My Invention Strategies" by Jenelle Clausen   121

Aristotle's Classification of Rhetoric   122

The Five Canons of Rhetoric   122

The Modern Writing Process Overview   123

Prewriting (Inventing)   123

Drafting   124

Revising   124

Editing and Polishing   124

Activity 4.1 • Compare the Five Canons of Rhetoric and the Modern Writing Process   125

Stasis Theory   126

Using Stasis Questions   129

Stasis Theory and *Kairos*   131

Activity 4.2 • Identify the Defense in a Television or Film Courtroom Drama   132

Activity 4.3 • Use Stasis Theory to Explore Your Topic   132

Activity 4.4 • Evaluate a Public Debate   132

The $300 House Casebook   133

Casebook Reading 1 • "The $300 House: A Hands-On Lab for Reverse Innovation?" by Vijay Govindarajan and Christian Sakar   133

Casebook Reading 2 • "Hands Off Our Houses" by Matias Echanove and Rahul Srivastava   135

Casebook Reading 3 • "The $300 House: A Hands-On Approach to a Wicked Problem" by Vijay Govindarajan with Christian Sakar   138

Casebook Reading 4 • "A $300 Idea that Is Priceless" from Schumpeter, column in the *Economist*   141

Activity 4.5 • Use Stasis Questions to Analyze the $300 House Casebook   143

Activity 4.6 • Persuasive Essay about the $300 House Casebook, Utilizing Stasis Theory   143

Activity 4.7 • Comment on Your Essay about the $300 House   144

Other Invention Strategies   144

Freewriting   144

Invisible Freewriting   145

Focused Freewriting   145

Listing/Brainstorming   145

Clustering   146

Activity 4.8 • Try Different Prewriting Techniques   147

Activity 4.9 • Organize or Arrange Your Prewriting   147

Reading 4.1 • "Take a Leap into Writing" by Craig Wynne   147

Activity 4.10 • Consider "Take a Leap into Writing"   149

Activity 4.11 • Focused Freewriting   150

Artistic and Inartistic Proofs   150

Activity 4.12 • Begin with What You Know   151

Develop Artistic Proofs through Observation   151

Activity 4.13 • Observation Exercise to Develop Artistic Proofs   152

Reading 4.2 • "Porsche Macan S: Is This Compact Crossover Barbie's Dream Car?" by Dan Neil   153

Activity 4.14 • Find Artistic and Inartistic Proofs in a Reading   156

Activity 4.15 • Develop Criteria for Reviews   157

Activity 4.16 • Write a Product Review   157

Reading 4.3 • *"Guardians of the Galaxy*'s Happy Satire of the Sad Origin Story" by Katie Kilkenny   157

Activity 4.17 • Discuss Review of *Guardians of the Galaxy*   160

Activity 4.18 • Develop Criteria for Film Reviews   160

Activity 4.19 • Write a Film Review   161

Activity 4.20 • Reflect on Your Film Review   162

Chapter Exercises

Activity 4.21 • Write on Your Blog   162

Activity 4.22 • Write in Your Commonplace Book   162

Chapter 5: Writing Rhetorically   163
Praxis in Action: "How I Write" by Amy Brumfield   163

Enter the Conversation Through Writing   164

Respond to the Rhetorical Situation   165

Reading 5.1 • "Can Social Media Make Us Better Writers?" by Laura Klocinski   166

Activity 5.1 • Tailor Your Social Media Message   167

Activity 5.2 • Write a Blog Post about Writing   168

Activity 5.3 • Comment on Your Blog Post   168

Reading 5.2 • "Laws Protecting Women From Upskirt Photo Assaults Fall Short" by Holly Kearl   168

Activity 5.4 • Discuss "Laws Protecting Women From Upskirt Photo Assaults Fall Short"   170

Activity 5.5 • A Logical Fallacy in Upskirt Laws?   171

Activity 5.6 • What Is the Rhetorical Situation of an Op-Ed?   171

Activity 5.7 • Write an Op-Ed Argument   171

Activity 5.8 • Freewrite about Your Op-Ed Essay   174

The Research-Based Argument Essay   174

Reading 5.3 • "Student Research Paper, 'Understanding the Effects of Mass Media's Portrayals of Black Women and Adolescents on Self-Image'" by Cherish Green   175

Activity 5.9 • Discuss "Understanding the Effects of Mass Media's Portrayals of Black Women and Adolescents on Self-Image"   180

The Sky Is Falling Casebook   180

Casebook Reading 1 • "Vindication for Entrepreneurs Watching Sky: Yes, It Can Fall" by William J. Broad   181

Casebook Reading 2 • "B612 Foundation Releases Video at Seattle Museum of Flight Earth Day Event Showing Evidence of 26 Multi-Kiloton Asteroid Impacts Since 2001" from B612 Foundation Press Release   184

Casebook Reading 3 • "NASA Near Earth Object Program: Target Earth"   186

Activity 5.10 • Summarize Information from Casebook   188

Write an Argumentative Essay   189

Toulmin Model   189

Activity 5.11 • Develop a Toulmin Argument for The Sky Is Falling Casebook   190

Rogerian Model   190

Activity 5.12 • Develop a Rogerian Argument for The Sky is Falling Casebook   191

General Modern Format   191

Activity 5.13 • Develop a General Modern Format Argument for The Sky is Falling Casebook   192

Activity 5.14 • Write a Research-Based Essay Utilizing The Sky is Falling Casebook   193

Activity 5.15 • Freewrite about "The Sky is Falling" Essay   193

Write a Thesis Statement   193

Compose an Introduction   196

    Reading 5.4 • "How I Write an Introduction" by Natalie Gorup   198

    Reading 5.5 "The Truth about Writer's Block" by Judith Johnson   199

    Activity 5.16 • Discuss "The Truth about Writer's Block"   202

Support Your Ideas with Source Materials   202

Support Your Thesis   203

Answer Opposing Arguments   203

Vary Your Strategies or Patterns of Development   204

Include Effective Transitions   204

Write a Conclusion   206

Consider Elements of Page Design   206

Choose Evocative Photos to Illustrate Essays   208

    Reading 5.6 • "How I Create a Multimedia Presentation" by Jason Tham   209

Including Images in Your Projects: Copyright Implications   211

Chapter Exercises

    Activity 5.17 • Write a Research-Based Argument Paper   212

    Activity 5.18 • Freewrite about Your Research Paper   213

    Activity 5.19 • Write on Your Blog   213

    Activity 5.20 • Write in Your Commonplace Book   213

Chapter 6: Revising Rhetorically   215

Praxis in Action: "How I Revise" by Sarah Gray   215

Revision Is Part of the Writing Process   216

Begin Revision by Rereading   216

    Reading 6.1 • "Shitty First Drafts" by Anne Lamott   217

    Activity 6.1 • Discussing "Shitty First Drafts"   220

Qualities of Effective Writing   220

Keep It Simple   220

Rely on Everyday Words   221

Use Precise Words   222

Be Concise   223

Use Action Verbs   224

Fill in the Gaps   225

Speak Directly   225

Strengthen Your Voice   226

Activity 6.2 • Apply Qualities of Effective Writing   228

Activity 6.3 • Share Your Own Grammar Cartoon   228

Activity 6.4 • When You Reeeaaallly Want to Describe Something   229

Remember to Proofread   230

Reading 6.2 • "Grammar Girl's Top Ten Grammar Myths" by Mignon Fogarty   230

Reading 6.3 • "Top Ten Distractions for Writers, or Any Job Really" by Sam Scham   233

Activity 6.5 • Write a List of Your Writing Habits   235

Gain Feedback by Peer Editing   235

When Your Essay Is Being Reviewed   235

When You Are the Reviewer   236

Independent Reviewing   236

Sample Questions for Peer Review   237

Overall Content   237

Paragraph Development   237

Word Choice and Sentence Structure   238

Activity 6.6 • Peer Editing   238

Examples of Annotated Student Essays   238

Rhetorical Analysis Assignment   238

Short Op-Ed Argument   242

Short Research Paper in MLA Style   245

Research Paper in APA Style   251

Additional Research Paper in APA Style   258

Chapter Exercises

Activity 6.7 • Write on Your Blog   267

Activity 6.8 • Write in Your Commonplace Book   267

Chapter 7: Researching Rhetorically   269

Praxis in Action: "How I Research" by Rosalie Krenger   269

Research Provides Inartistic Proofs   270

You Do Research Every Day   271

Primary and Secondary Research   272

Reading 7.1 • "Bringing History to Life with Primary Sources" by Alexander L. Ames   274

Reading 7.2 • "What Does It Mean to Drink Like a Woman?" by Shanna Farrell   275

Activity 7.1 • Analyze "What Does It Mean to Drink Like a Woman?"   279

Interviews   279

Activity 7.2 • Reconstruct Interview Questions for "What Does It Mean to Drink Like a Woman?"   281

Activity 7.3 • Write Interview Questions   282

Activity 7.4 • Summarize Your Interview   282

Activity 7.5 • Write a Profile of a Person   282

Surveys   283

Activity 7.6 • Conduct a Survey   283

Secondary Research Sources Expected by Professors   284

Employ Computerized Library Catalogs   286

Types of Computerized Searches   287

Activity 7.7 • Locate Books on Your Topic   288

Utilize Electronic Library Resources   288

Activity 7.8 • Locate Newspaper and Magazine Articles   288

Find Internet Information   289

Indexing Projects   290

Google Books   291

Scholarly Journal Articles   291

Government Documents   292

Activity 7.9 • Find a Journal Article in Google Scholar   292

Activity 7.10 • Compare and Contrast Media   292

Make a Research Plan   293

Evaluate Sources   295

Activity 7.11 • Locate and Evaluate a Source   297

Activity 7.12 • Evaluate a Website   297

Activity 7.13 • Prepare an Annotated Bibliography   297

Sample Annotated Bibliography in MLA Style   298

Sample Annotated Bibliography in APA Style   299

Research Casebook on Climate Change   301

Casebook Reading 1 • "One in Four in U.S. Are Solidly Skeptical of Global Warming" by Lydia Saad   302

Casebook Reading 2 • "IPCC: Greenhouse Gas Emissions Accelerate Despite Reduction Efforts" from press release by IPCC   307

Casebook Reading 3 • "Scientists Warn of Rising Oceans as Antarctic
    Ice Melts" by Justin Gillis and Kenneth Chang   310
Synthesizing Casebook Sources   312
    Activity 7.14 • Discuss the Casebook on Climate Change   313
    Activity 7.15 • Develop a Working Thesis on Climate Change   313
    Activity 7.16 • Collect More Information about Climate Change   314
    Activity 7.17 • Write a Short Essay about Climate Change   314

Avoid Plagiarism   314
    Reading 7.3 • "Anatomy of a Fake Quotation" by Megan
        McArdle   315
    Activity 7.18 • Discuss "Anatomy of a Fake Quotation"   318

Chapter Exercises
    Activity 7.19 • Write on Your Blog   318
    Activity 7.20 • Write in Your Commonplace Book   318

Appendix: Citing Sources   319
Evolving Formats of Document Citation   320
When You Have a Choice of Electronic Source Format, Choose a PDF   321
MLA Style   322
    Bibliographic Documentation   322
    Key Changes in MLA's 8th Edition   323
    The Core Elements   323
    MLA Parenthetical (In-text) Documentation   332
APA Style   333
    Bibliographic Documentation   334
    APA Parenthetical (In-text) Documentation   337

Acknowledgments   339

Student Forms and Worksheets   341

Index   375

chapter 1

Defining Rhetoric

Praxis in Action

Why Rhetoric Is Important in My Writing

Meaghan Elliott
Ph.D. student in
Composition & Rhetoric
University of New Hampshire

Here is a partial list of the things I needed to write today:

- An email to someone in my field asking her questions for a seminar paper I'm writing
- A lesson plan I intend to use for my students in this week's class
- An email to a family member
- Text messages to a friend in the hospital
- A reading response for a doctoral course I'm taking
- A grocery list for my boyfriend
- This short essay about rhetoric

All of these are rhetoric. Rhetoric is inescapable because we use it every time we use words to address an audience. Rhetoric gives us tools for deciding how to be successful in any given situation, and it acknowledges that words and languages were designed for people to communicate with each other. People think, we feel, we judge others. In each of these actions, we have *logos*, *pathos*, and *ethos*. Rhetoric is what makes us human.

In the list I provided, I have seven different scenarios with seven different audiences. In each one, I judge (sometimes consciously, sometimes unconsciously) how effectively to present myself and my message. This means no two pieces of writing will look or sound the same. We make rhetorical judgments based on to whom we are speaking and what we know about our audience, and these judgments affect the way we write each document.

Rhetoric is important because it helps us get work done in the world, and it helps us organize how we interact with the places and people around us. This is a field older than Aristotle but still as relevant as it has ever been. Without my careful use of rhetoric, my lesson plans would fall flat, my family member may be insulted, and my boyfriend might bring home Brussels sprouts instead of broccoli. I hate Brussels sprouts. We use rhetoric all the time, whether we know it or not. But knowing about rhetoric and knowing how to use it effectively and creatively makes us better at it. I couldn't get through my day without it.

What Is Rhetoric?

You have probably heard someone say of a politician's speech, "Oh, that's just rhetoric," meaning the politician's words are empty verbiage or hot air. The politician is attempting to sound impressive while saying nothing that has real meaning. Or perhaps the politician is making promises listeners believe he or she has no intention of keeping. The use of rhetoric in speeches—both bad speeches and good ones—is only the most visible use of rhetoric.

Rhetoric happens all around us, every day. Rhetoric is a persuasive language act—whether accomplished by speech, written texts, or images. It is the video footage of a demonstration on YouTube. It is the headlines on blog articles. It is the *Declaration of Independence.* Sam Leith explains,

> Rhetoric is language at play—language plus. It is what persuades and cajoles, inspires and bamboozles, thrills and misdirects. It causes criminals to be convicted, and then frees those criminals on appeal. It causes governments to rise and fall, best men to be ever after shunned by their friends' brides, and perfectly sensible adults to march with steady purpose toward machine guns [. . .]
>
> It is made of ringing truths and vital declarations. It is a way in which our shared assumptions and understandings are applied to new situations, and the language of history is channeled, revitalized, and given fresh power in each successive age.[1]

Your parents and teachers have used rhetoric on you since you first understood the words "yes" and "no." And you've been using it right back to them, whenever you want to persuade them to let you do something that is contrary to their stance on a topic.

The word *praxis* (the title of this book) can be translated as "process" or "practice." Aristotle, the great Greek rhetorician, employed the term in a special way to mean practical reasoning for which the goal was action. To be practical in the Aristotelian sense is a little different from what being practical means today. It indicates the ability to apply abstract theory to concrete situations and, thus, to move from theory to action. Moreover, praxis embodies a creative element that raises it above the mundane or merely pragmatic. Therefore, "practicing rhetoric" is not practice in the sense of rehearsal. Rather, it is performing, or applying, or acting out rhetoric—taking theory and turning it into action.

Rhetoric has been studied in an organized manner since the days of the ancient Greeks and Romans. The elites of both countries studied persuasive argument out of necessity. Their democratic systems of government required that citizens

1. Leith, Sam. *Words Like Loaded Pistols: Rhetoric from Aristotle to Obama.* Basic, 2012, p. 6.

be able to argue persuasively in public, since there were no attorneys or professional politicians.

Today, rhetoric is still used in courts of law and political forums, but it is also studied in academia because it causes us to examine critically our own as well as others' ideas. Persuasive argument compels us to consider conflicting claims, to evaluate evidence, and to clarify our thoughts. We know that even wise, well-intentioned people don't always agree, so we consider others' ideas respectfully. After one person presents a persuasive argument, either orally or in writing, others respond to that argument with support, modification, or contradiction. Then, in turn, more individuals counter with their own versions, and thus, the interchange becomes a conversation.

Rhetoric and Power

Aristotle defined rhetoric as "the faculty of discovering, in a given instance, the available means of persuasion," which we might paraphrase as the power to see the means of persuasion available in any given situation. Each part of this definition is important. Rhetoric is power. The person who is able to speak eloquently, choosing the most suitable arguments about a topic for a specific audience in a particular situation, is the person most likely to persuade. In both Greece and Rome, the primary use of rhetoric was oratory—persuasion through public speaking. However, the texts of many famous speeches were studied as models by students, and prominent rhetoricians wrote treatises and handbooks for teaching rhetoric. To Greeks and Romans, a person who could use rhetoric effectively was a person of influence and power because he could persuade his audience to action. The effective orator could win court cases; the effective orator could influence the passage or failure of laws; the effective orator could send a nation to war or negotiate peace.

Skill with rhetoric has conveyed power through the ages, though in our contemporary world, rhetoric is often displayed in written text such as a book, newspaper or magazine article, or scientific report, rather than presented as a speech. Persuasive communication also can be expressed visually, as an illustration that accompanies a text or a cartoon that conveys its own message. Indeed, in our highly visual society, with television, movies, video games, and the Internet, images can often persuade more powerfully than words alone.

Using rhetoric effectively means being able to interpret the rhetoric we are presented with in our everyday lives. Knowledge of persuasive communication or rhetoric empowers us to present our views and persuade others to modify their ideas. By changing ideas, rhetoric leads to action. By influencing actions, rhetoric affects society.

Selected Definitions of Rhetoric

Aristotle, 350 BCE—Rhetoric is "the faculty of discovering, in a given instance, the available means of persuasion."

Cicero, 90 BCE—Rhetoric is "speech designed to persuade" and "eloquence based on the rules of art."

Quintilian, 95 CE—Rhetoric is "the science of speaking well."

Augustine of Hippo, ca. 426 CE—Rhetoric is "the art of persuading people to accept something, whether it is true or false."

Anonymous, ca. 1490–1495—Rhetoric is "the science which refreshes the hungry, renders the mute articulate, makes the blind see, and teaches one to avoid every lingual ineptitude."

Heinrich Cornelius Agrippa, 1531—Rhetoric is "nothing other than an art of flatter, adulation, and, as some say more audaciously, lying, in that, if it cannot persuade others through the truth of the case, it does so by means of deceitful speech."

Hoyt Hudson, 1923—Rhetoric is effective persuasion. "In this sense, plainly, the man who speaks most persuasively uses the most, or certainly the best, rhetoric; and the man whom we censure for inflation of style and strained effects is suffering not from too much rhetoric, but from a lack of it."

I. A. Richards, 1936—Rhetoric is "a study of misunderstanding and its remedies."

Sister Miriam Joseph, 1937—Rhetoric is "the art of communicating thought from one mind to another, the adaptation of language to circumstance."

Kenneth Burke, 1950—Rhetoric is, "the use of words by human agents to form attitudes or to induce actions in other human agents."

Gerard A. Hauser, 2002—"Rhetoric, as an area of study, is concerned with how humans use symbols, especially language, to reach agreement that permits coordinated effort of some sort."

Activity 1.1 • Historical Usage of the Word "Rhetoric"

Read through the list of historical definitions of the word "rhetoric," and choose one that you find interesting. In a discussion, compare your chosen definition with those of your classmates.

Explore

Are We All Greeks?

As Americans, we owe an immense debt to ancient Greek civilization. Our laws, our democratic form of government, our literature, and our art have their roots in ancient Athens. Earlier generations of Americans and Western Europeans who often studied Latin and Greek may have had a clearer understanding of the direct connections between our culture and Athens of the fourth and fifth centuries BCE. Indeed, the English poet Percy Bysshe Shelley famously said, "We are all Greeks" because of the essential influence of ancient Greek culture upon Western civilization. However, even translated into twenty-first-century American English, the linkage is still there.

Something quite amazing happened in Athens, around 500 BCE. Instead of being invaded by a foreign country who appointed a puppet ruler or experiencing a coup in which a strong man seized power, the people peaceably chose to put in place a direct democracy. Attica (with its capital Athens) was not the only city-state to have a democracy, but it was the most successful. During the golden age of Greece, from roughly 500 BCE to 300 BCE, art, architecture, and literature thrived.

500 BCE

Direct or radical democracy meant all male citizens of Attica over the age of 20 could vote in the Assembly, the policy-making body of the city-state. They did not elect senators or representatives as we do today. Each of these men *voted directly*. Moreover, they could settle differences with fellow citizens by suing in the law courts. Out of 250,000 to 300,000 residents in Attica, some 30,000 were citizens. Amazingly, it was not unusual for 10,000 of these eligible men to vote in the Assembly. The law courts had juries of 500 or more. Imagine trying to speak to an audience of 10,000 people without modern loudspeakers. Even with the wonderful acoustics in Greek theatres, it would have been a challenge.

Ordinary citizens were required to speak in the Assembly or the courts to promote laws or defend themselves from lawsuits, since there were no attorneys or professional politicians. Certainly, speaking before such large audiences necessitated special skills acquired only through extensive training and practice. Many sought out teachers to help them learn how to speak persuasively, and, indeed, training in rhetoric became the primary method of education for the elite young men (and even a few women).

The earliest teachers of the verbal persuasive skills we now call rhetoric were Sophists who migrated to Athens from Sicily and other Greek states. Some of their viewpoints were curiously modern—for example, some argued that knowledge is relative and that pure truth does not exist. However, they became known for teaching their pupils to persuade an audience to think whatever they wanted them to think. Sophists such as Gorgias often presented entertainment speeches during which they would argue, on the spur of the moment, any topic raised by the audience, just to show they were able to construct effective arguments for any subject.

Claiming the Sophists' rhetoric could be employed to manipulate the masses for good or ill, and that rhetoricians used it irresponsibly, Plato coined the term, *rhetorike*—from which we take the term, "rhetoric"—as a criticism of the Sophists. Ironically, Plato demonstrates excellent rhetorical techniques himself when he condemns rhetoric by arguing that only the elite who are educated in philosophy are suited to rule, not the rhetoricians. Aristotle, Plato's student, took a more moderate viewpoint toward rhetoric. Indeed, he was the first philosopher to classify rhetoric as a tool for practical debate with general audiences. His book *On Rhetoric* (though it was probably lecture notes possibly combined with student responses rather than a manuscript intended for publication) is the single most important text that establishes rhetoric as a system of persuasive communication.

Athens, even in its glory days, seethed with controversy and bickering over the many inefficiencies of democracy. Men trained in rhetoric executed two coups, the Tyranny of the Four Hundred in 411 BCE and the Tyranny of the Thirty in 404 BCE, neither of which was an improvement; after each coup, democracy returned. Moreover, Athenians fought wars with Persia (the Battle of Marathon in 490 BCE and the Battle of Thermopylae in 480 BCE) and Sparta (the Peloponnesian War in 431–404 BCE and the Corinthian War of 395–387 BCE). Finally, the armies of Philip II of Macedonia defeated Athens at the Battle of Chaeronea in 338 BCE, ending Athenian independence. Despite coups and wars, democracy remained in place in Athens for nearly 200 years.

If Americans might be called Greeks because our country is based on Greek traditions, this does not mean that rhetoric does not appear in all cultures. True, one might say that all civilizations have some sort of persuasive negotiation process; but profound differences exist between cultures in terms of what verbal strategies are considered persuasive. Indeed, disparity in expectations and the actions of individuals and groups from different traditions can be a cause of strife in any culture.

Activity 1.2 • Contemporary Usage of the Word "Rhetoric"

Explore

Find at least two recent but different examples involving uses of the word "rhetoric." For example, search your local newspaper for an example of how the word "rhetoric" is being used. A search of the *Dallas Morning News* for the word "rhetoric" led to a story about citizen efforts to clean up a neglected area of town: "He now hopes for help to finally fill the gap between rhetoric and reality." Or ask a friend, fellow employee, or a family member to tell you what the word "rhetoric" means, and write down what they say. Discuss your examples in your small group, and present the best ones to the class.

Visual Map of Meanings for the Word "Rhetoric"

The word map for the word "rhetoric" shown in Figure 1.1 on the next page has branches for different meanings of the word, with some branches splitting again to display subtle subsets of connotation. It was created by a website, *Visual Thesaurus* (www.visualthesaurus.com), which computes visual word maps for any word inputted in its search box. The idea is that words lead to branches that lead to more words, inspiring users to think of language in new ways.

If you recreate the rhetoric word map at the *Visual Thesaurus* site and place your cursor over any of the circles connecting the branches, a small box will pop up that defines that connection. One of these connection boxes is visible in Figure 1.1. Notice it says, "using language effectively to please or persuade." This is the branch of the visual map that is closest to the meaning of "rhetoric" as used in this book. The other branches illustrate other contemporary uses of the word.

Activity 1.3 • Explore the Visual Map of the Word "Rhetoric"

Explore

In your small group, choose one of the five branches of words in the visual map of the word "rhetoric." Go to one or more good dictionaries and explore the meanings of the words in that branch. A good place to start would be the *Oxford English Dictionary (OED)*, which your college library may offer online. The *OED* offers intricate analyses of the histories of word meanings. Report to the class what you find out about the words on your particular branch.

Figure 1.1 • Word Map for "Rhetoric"

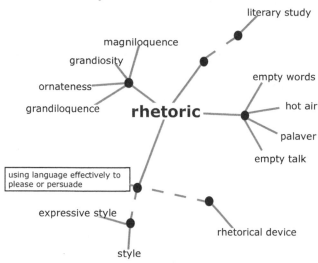

Have you bought hummus or coconut water at the grocery store? Worn a henna tattoo? Then you may have participated in Columbusing, the art of "discovering" something, usually from another culture, that is not new. The term echoes Columbus's "discovery" of the New World, which had long been inhabited by non-Europeans.

Brenda Salinas writes about Columbusing in this article published on NPR.com.

There isn't anything inherently wrong about eating hummus or getting a henna tattoo, argues Salinas. She attempts to persuade you that the problem is the stripping of cultural context from the item, in effect, engaging in cultural appropriation. To the Latinos who grew up eating empanadas, for example, it can feel like theft when Buzzfeed raves about "a hand pie, a little foldover pie that you can fit in your hand. They have flaky crusts and can be sweet or savory."

As you read Salinas's article, think about occasions when you may have engaged in Columbusing.

"Columbusing": The Art of Discovering Something that is Not New
by Brenda Salinas

If you've danced to an Afrobeat-heavy pop song, dipped hummus, sipped coconut water, participated in a Desi-inspired color run or sported a henna tattoo, then you've Columbused something.

Columbusing is when you "discover" something that's existed forever. Just that it's existed outside your own culture, nationality, race or even, say, your neighborhood. Bonus points if you tell all your friends about it.

Why not? In our immigrant-rich cities, the whole world is at our doorsteps.

Sometimes, though, Columbusing can feel icky. When is cultural appropriation a healthy byproduct of globalization and when is it a problem?

All the Rage

Buzzfeed Food published an article asking, "Have you heard about the new kind of pie that's *all the rage* lately?" It's a hand pie, a little foldover pie that you can fit in your hand. They have flaky crusts and can be sweet or savory. You know, exactly like an empanada, a Latin American culinary staple.

On face value, it seems stupid to get worked up over an empanada. I mean, it's just a pastry, right? But "discovering" empanadas on Pinterest and calling them "hand pies" strips empanadas of their cultural context. To all the people who grew up eating empanadas, it can feel like theft.

In this promotional photo shot, TV star Jennie Garth sprays the crowd with orange at the Shout Color Throw on June 21 at Dodger Stadium in Los Angeles. Events like this one are being held in Europe and the United States, but most organizers don't mention that these events are inspired by the Hindu festival of Holi—but stripped of religious meaning.

Photo Credit: Jeff Lewis/AP Images for SC Johnson

Feeling Overlooked

When it comes to our culinary traditions, Latinos are used to feeling robbed.

Latino activists spoke out in May when Chipotle announced plans to print original stories by famous writers on its paper goods and failed to include any Mexican-Americans or Latinos on the roster. The American-owned chain can profit from Mexican culture while overlooking the harsh reality of how Latinos have been treated in this country.

A man sprays colored dye on people dancing during Holi celebrations in India in 2012. Holi, the Hindu festival of colors, also heralds the coming of spring—a detail that partiers at the Shout Color Throw might miss.

Photo Credit: Rajesh Kumar Singh/AP

On Cinco de Mayo, chef Anthony Bourdain asked why Americans love Mexican food, drugs, alcohol and cheap labor but ignore the violence that happens across the border. "Despite our ridiculously hypocritical attitudes towards immigration," writes Bourdain, "we demand that Mexicans cook a large percentage of the food we eat, grow the ingredients we need to make that food, clean our houses, mow our lawns, wash our dishes, look after our children."

It's frustrating when even the staunchest anti-immigration activists regularly eat Mexican food. It seems like a paradox to relish your fajitas while believing the line cook should get deported.

Admittedly, cultural appropriation is an integral and vital part of American history. And one day, empanadas might become as American as pizza (yes, I appreciate the irony of that statement). But the day when Latinos are considered as American as Italian-Americans, well, that feels further away.

Why It Hurts

The condolence prize for being an outsider is that you can take solace in the cultural traditions that make you unique. When outsiders use tweezers to pick out the discrete parts of your culture that are worthy of their attention, it feels like a violation. Empanadas are trendy, cumbia is trendy, but Latinas are still not trendy.

Code Switch blogger Gene Demby writes, "It's much harder now to patrol the ramparts of our cultures, to distinguish between the appreciators and appropriators. Just who gets to play in which cultural sandboxes? Who gets to be the bouncer at the velvet rope?"

Playing Explorer

Of course, there is no bouncer, but we can be careful not to Columbus other culture's traditions. Before you make reservations at the hottest fusion restaurant or book an alternative healing therapy, ask yourself a few questions:

Who is providing this good or service for me?

Am I engaging with them in a thoughtful manner?

Am I learning about this culture?

Are people from this culture benefiting from my spending money here?

Are they being hurt by my spending money here?

It is best to enter a new, ethnic experience with consideration, curiosity and respect. That doesn't mean you have to act or look the part of a dour-faced anthropologist or an ultra-earnest tourist. You can go outside your comfort zone and learn about the completely different worlds that coexist within your city. If you're adventurous, you can explore the entire world without leaving the country and without needing a passport.

Just remember, it's great to love a different culture and its artifacts, as long as you love the people too.

Activity 1.4 • Analyzing Columbusing as an Argument

Collaborate

" 'Columbusing': The Art of Discovering Something that Is Not New" is a rhetorical document because the author is attempting to persuade her audience to believe something. In a group, use these review questions to discuss what Salinas is arguing.

1. What does Salinas want her audience to do differently? How does she define Columbusing? What does it have to do with Columbus?

2. Make a list of the examples Salinas gives of Columbusing. Then, make a list of other Columbusing items or activities you have bought or engaged in. Share your group's list with the class.

3. What does Salinas say we can do to avoid Columbusing other cultures' traditions? Do you agree that these are good suggestions? Why or why not? Discuss these questions in your group, and share your thoughts with the class.

Rhetorical Argument

Often, in our culture, the word *argument* is taken to mean a disagreement or even a fight, with raised voices, rash words, and hurt feelings. We have the perception of an argument as something that leads to victory or defeat, winners or losers. A *rhetorical argument,* however, is the carefully crafted presentation of a viewpoint or position on a topic and the giving of thoughts, ideas, and opinions along with reasons for their support. The persuasive strength of an argument rests upon the rhetorical skills of the rhetor (the speaker or the writer) in utilizing the tools of language to persuade a particular audience.

Types of Argument

Academic arguments can be divided into several different categories, depending upon the extent of the writer's desire to persuade and the scope of the conversational exchange.

1. Makes a point. One type of argument simply makes a point about a topic. The article in this chapter, " 'Columbusing': The Art of Discovering Something that Is Not New," argues, for example, that buying hummus or getting a henna tattoo is Columbusing, which labels as new something ancient from another culture. To do so strips the cultural context from things or activities. The subtext of the article suggests Columbusing is a bad thing and should be avoided. If the author of this type of argument offers sufficient evidence to back up the thesis, no one is likely to disagree, except to say, perhaps, the author is overreacting or the point the author makes is not important.

2. Aims to persuade. A second type of argument involves a controversial issue, and the writer's aim is to persuade the audience to change its stance on the matter. For the writer, the ideal result would be that members of the audience alter their positions to coincide with the writer's viewpoint. In this second type of argument, it is essential that the writer offer the complete structure of thesis, evidence, possible opposing viewpoints which are discussed and countered, and a conclusion. "The Sleepover Question," another reading in this chapter, presents this kind of argument. The author, who has conducted research in both America and Holland, argues the controversial position that if American parents would adopt more liberal attitudes toward their children's sexuality, like the parents in Holland, "the transition into adulthood need not be so painful for parents or children." A reading in Chapter 3, "Executions Should Be Televised," offers a more extreme version of this type of argument. Either executions are televised or they aren't, and the writer advocates that they should be.

3. Tries to find common ground. A third type of argument emphasizes multiple perspectives and viewpoints and tries to find common ground participants can agree upon. In Chapter 4, several readings are collected

in a casebook called "The $300 House." The *Harvard Business Review* initiated a design competition called The $300 House, which was intended to spark inclusive argument with the aim of gathering ideas about how to build inexpensive but adequate homes for the poor in the world's slums. One of the readings, "Hands Off Our Houses," opposes the design competition, saying that bringing $300 houses into the slums of Mumbai is not the answer to the housing problem. However, the author of "The $300 House: A Hands-On Approach to a Wicked Problem," attempts to find common ground with the authors of "Hands Off Our Houses" by saying he agrees housing for the poor is a complex problem "that can't be fixed with a clever shack alone."

In Chapter 5, Rogerian (or common ground) argument, named after psychologist Carl Rogers, is discussed and outlined. Rogerian argument has four elements: introduction, common ground and common arguments, a position or argument, and a positive statement of how the position could, at least in some instances, benefit the opposition.

These three types of arguments represent points in a spectrum, and all persuasive texts may not neatly fit into one of the three categories. A crucial thing to remember, though, is that all arguments involve the presentation of a line of reasoning about a topic or an issue—a thesis, hypothesis, or claim—and the support of that reasoning with evidence.

Aristotle's Three Appeals

Aristotle identified three appeals (see Figure 1.2 on the following page) or three ways to persuade an audience, and we are still using these today, though often without using the Greek terms to identify the means of persuasion.

Ethos—The rhetor persuades by means of his or her character or credibility. In oratory, the speaker projects an air of confidence and authority. In writing, *ethos* is conveyed by the writer's qualifications or the authorities cited and also by the quality of the writing.

Pathos—The rhetor persuades by playing upon the listener's (or reader's) emotions. He or she may refer to children, death, disaster, injustice, or other topics that arouse pity, fear, or other emotions.

Logos—The rhetor persuades by using reasoning and evidence. Arguments based on *logos* employ deductive or inductive reasoning.

Figure 1.2 • Aristotle's Three Appeals

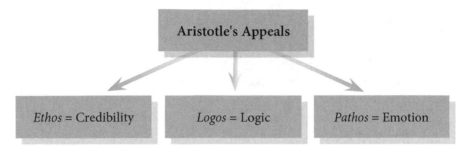

Although a good argument will contain at least traces of all three appeals, skilled rhetors analyze their audiences to determine which of the three will be most persuasive for that particular audience. Then, they construct arguments that emphasize that particular appeal.

In addition, a knowledgeable rhetor considers the time, place, audience, topic, and other aspects of the occasion for writing or speaking to determine the *kairos*, or opportune moment for the argument (see Figure 1.3). This factor or critical moment both provides and limits opportunities for appeals suitable to that moment. For example, someone giving a commencement address has certain opportunities and constraints. Likewise, an attorney writing a last-minute appeal for someone on death row has a very different set of options.

Figure 1.3 • *Kairos*

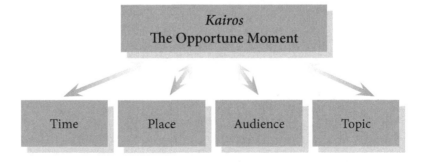

Microsoft Just Laid Off Thousands of Employees With a Hilariously Bad Memo

by Kevin Roose

Typically, when you're a top executive at a major corporation that is laying off more than 10 percent of your workforce, you say a few things to the newly jobless. Like "sorry." Or "thank you for your many years of service." Or even "we hate doing this, but it's necessary to help the company survive."

What you don't do is bury the news of the layoffs in the 11th paragraph of a long, rambling corporate strategy memo.

And yet, this was Microsoft honcho Stephen Elop's preferred method for announcing to his employees today that 12,500 of them were being laid off. (18,000 are being laid off companywide; Elop, the former head of Nokia, oversees the company's devices unit, which was hardest hit by the layoffs.)

Kevin Roose's essay, "Microsoft Just Laid Off Thousands of Employees With a Hilariously Bad Memo" illustrates the dangers of not considering kairos. *When Stephen Elop needed to lay off more than 10 percent of Microsoft workers under his supervision, Elop did not say anything one might expect—like "sorry," or "I regret," or "thank you for your service." In a memo to the affected employees, he did not even get around to the news of layoff until the eleventh paragraph.*

If Elop had considered the kairos *of the situation, then he would have realized his audience would not be interested in all the planning information he crowded into the memo. They would want to know the bad news, if it had to be told, near the beginning of the memo. Elop, as Roose reveals in his analysis of the memo, was more interested in his corporate strategy than in what his audience at that time and place needed or wanted to hear.*

The essay was published in New York Magazine.

How bad was Elop's job-axing memo? Really, really bad. It's so bad that I can't even really convey its badness. I just have to show you.

Here's how it starts:

> Hello there,

Hello there? *Hello there?* Out of all the possible "you're losing your job" greetings, you chose the one that sounds like the start to a bad OKCupid message? "Hello there" isn't how you announce layoffs; it's what you

Stephen Elop, lead-burier.

Photo Credit: Josh Edelson/AFP/Getty Images

say right before you ask, "What's a girl like you doing on a site like this? ;)" It's the fedora of greetings.

Anyway, carry on. Let's hear the bad news:

> Microsoft's strategy is focused on productivity and our desire to help people "do more." As the Microsoft Devices Group, our role is to light up this strategy for people. We are the team creating the hardware that showcases the finest of Microsoft's digital work and digital life experiences, and we will be the confluence of the best of Microsoft's applications, operating systems and cloud services.

Wait, what does this have to do with layoffs?

> To align with Microsoft's strategy, we plan to focus our efforts. Given the wide range of device experiences, we must concentrate on the areas where we can add the most value. The roots of this company and our future are in productivity and helping people get things done. Our fundamental focus—for phones, Surface, for meetings with devices like PPI, Xbox hardware and new areas of innovation—is to build on that strength. While our direction in the majority of our teams is largely unchanging, we have had an opportunity to plan carefully about the alignment of phones within Microsoft as the transferring Nokia team continues with its integration process.

Oh, I get it. This is the warm-up. You're giving me a few minutes to sit down, compose myself, grab the Kleenex. Now you're going to drop the hammer.

> **It is particularly important to recognize that the role of phones within Microsoft is different than it was within Nokia. Whereas the hardware business of phones within Nokia was an end unto itself, within Microsoft all our devices are intended to embody the finest of Microsoft's digital work and digital life experiences, while accruing value to Microsoft's overall strategy. Our device strategy must reflect Microsoft's strategy and must be accomplished within an appropriate financial envelope. Therefore, we plan to make some changes.**

"Financial envelope"? You don't literally keep all of Microsoft's cash in a big envelope, do you? Anyway, "changes." I know what that's supposed to mean. Now, please, give it to me straight: tell me I'm fired.

We will be particularly focused on making the market for Windows Phone. In the near term, we plan to drive Windows Phone volume by targeting the more affordable smartphone segments, which are the fastest growing segments of the market, with Lumia. In addition to the portfolio already planned, we plan to deliver additional lower-cost Lumia devices by shifting select future Nokia X designs and products to Windows Phone devices. We expect to make this shift immediately while continuing to sell and support existing Nokia X products.

To win in the higher price segments, we will focus on delivering great breakthrough products in alignment with major milestones ahead from both the Windows team and the Applications and Services Group. We will ensure that the very best experiences and scenarios from across the company will be showcased on our products. We plan to take advantage of innovation from the Windows team, like Universal Windows Apps, to continue to enrich the Windows application ecosystem. And in the very lowest price ranges, we plan to run our first phones business for maximum efficiency with a smaller team.

WTF. Is this some kind of joke? DO I HAVE A JOB OR NOT?

We expect these changes to have an impact to our team structure. With our focus, we plan to consolidate the former Smart Devices and Mobile Phones business units into one phone business unit that is responsible for all of our phone efforts. Under the plan, the phone business unit will be led by Jo Harlow with key members from both the Smart Devices and Mobile Phones teams in the management team. This team will be responsible for the success of our Lumia products, the transition of select future Nokia X products to Lumia and for the ongoing operation of the first phone business.

I AM GNAWING ON MY MOUSE PAD IN ANGER. ALL I WANT TO KNOW IS WHETHER I NEED TO START SELLING MY PLASMA TO MAKE RENT NEXT MONTH. PLEASE TELL ME THIS BIT OF INFORMATION.

As part of the effort, we plan to select the appropriate business model approach for our sales markets while continuing to offer our products in all markets with a strong focus on maintaining business continuity. We will determine each market approach based on local market dynamics, our ability to profitably deliver

local variants, current Lumia momentum and the strategic importance of the market to Microsoft. This will all be balanced
with our overall capability to invest.

Our phone engineering efforts are expected to be concentrated in
Salo, Finland (for future, high-end Lumia products) and Tampere,
Finland (for more affordable devices). We plan to develop the supporting technologies in both locations. We plan to ramp down engineering work in Oulu. While we plan to reduce the engineering in
Beijing and San Diego, both sites will continue to have supporting
roles, including affordable devices in Beijing and supporting specific US requirements in San Diego. Espoo and Lund are planned
to continue to be focused on application software development.

Blah blah blah I don't even care anymore. You have numbed me to the af-
flictions of mankind with phrases like "business continuity" and "market dynamics." And now you're probably going to use some crazy euphemism, like
"streamline," to tell me I'm fired. Go ahead.

We plan to right-size our manufacturing operations to align to the
new strategy and take advantage of integration opportunities. We expect to focus phone production mainly in Hanoi, with some production to continue in Beijing and Dongguan. We plan to shift other Microsoft manufacturing and repair operations to Manaus and Reynosa
respectively, and start a phased exit from Komaron, Hungary.

"Right-size"! "Phased exit"! Oh, you are so killing this. You get an extra snack
ration at CEO summer camp.

In short, we will focus on driving Lumia volume in the areas where
we are already successful today in order to make the market for
Windows Phone. With more speed, we will build on our success in
the affordable smartphone space with new products offering more
differentiation. We'll focus on acquiring new customers in the markets where Microsoft's services and products are most concentrated. And, we'll continue building momentum around applications.

Life is empty. All that remains is dust.

We plan that this would result in an estimated reduction of 12,500
factory direct and professional employees over the next year.

These decisions are difficult for the team, and we plan to support departing team members' with severance benefits.

There it is, finally. In paragraph 11. I would react more strongly to the news that I'm laid off, but my synapses are no longer firing properly. The badness of this email has rewired my brain's circuitry. All I understand now is business-school jargon. And death. Sweet death.

More broadly across the Devices team, we will continue our efforts to bring iconic tablets to market in ways that complement our OEM partners, power the next generation of meetings & collaboration devices and thoughtfully expand Windows with new interaction models. With a set of changes already implemented earlier this year in these teams, this means there will be limited change for the Surface, Xbox hardware, PPI/meetings or next generation teams.

We recognize these planned changes are broad and have very difficult implications for many of our team members. We will work to provide as much clarity and information as possible. Today and over the coming weeks leaders across the organization will hold town halls, host information sharing sessions and provide more details on the intranet.

Oh, good. Because if it's one thing I need right now, it's more details.

The team transferring from Nokia and the teams that have been part of Microsoft have each experienced a number of remarkable changes these last few years. We operate in a competitive industry that moves rapidly, and change is necessary. As difficult as some of our changes are today, this direction deliberately aligns our work with the cross company efforts that Satya has described in his recent emails. Collectively, the clarity, focus and alignment across the company, and the opportunity to deliver the results of that work into the hands of people, will allow us to increase our success in the future.

Regards,

"Regards?" Really? We started at OKCupid stalker, and you're ending at "over-eager candidate for summer internship?" Well, okay. Sure. Whatever. Not like it matters.

Stephen

Collaborate

Activity 1.5 • **Discuss Microsoft's Memo Laying Off Employees**

In a small group, discuss Stephen Elop's memo to employees who were being laid off and Roose's colorful commentary.

1. What would you think if you received such a memo? How is Elop ignoring *kairos* in his memo? Reread the section earlier in the chapter in which *kairos* is discussed, and then decide with your group how Elop fails to take *kairos* into consideration in writing his memo. Report to the class.

2. Discuss what employees would have preferred to hear from Elop, assuming they must be laid off. Share your conclusions with the class.

Reading 1.3

This selection by Amy Schalet was first published in The New York Times. *"The Sleepover Question" hazards an argument that many Americans—or at least American parents—may find controversial. Backed by her credentials as a professor of sociology, Schalet cites research from 130 interviews, both in the United States and the Netherlands, and tackles the issue of whether or not American parents should allow their adolescent children to have sex in the family home. Pay particular attention, for she shows how to argue a subject that is not only controversial but often ignored.*

The Sleepover Question
by Amy Schalet

NOT under my roof. That's the attitude most American parents have toward teenagers and their sex lives. Squeamishness and concern describe most parents' approach to their offspring's carnality. We don't want them doing it—whatever "it" is!—in our homes. Not surprisingly, teenage sex is a source of conflict in many American families.

Would Americans increase peace in family life and strengthen family bonds if they adopted more accepting attitudes about sex and what's allowable under the family roof? I've interviewed 130 people, all white, middle class and not particularly religious, as part of a study of teenage sex and family life here and in the Netherlands. My look into cultural differences suggests family life might be much improved, for all, if Americans had more open ideas about teenage sex. The question of who sleeps where when a teenager brings a boyfriend or girlfriend home for the night fits within the larger world of culturally divergent ideas about teenage sex, lust and capacity for love.

Kimberly and Natalie dramatize the cultural differences in the way young women experience their sexuality. (I have changed their names to protect confidentiality.) Kimberly, a 16-year-old American, never received sex education at home. "God, no! No, no! That's not going to happen," she told me. She'd like to tell her parents that she and her boyfriend are having sex, but she believes it is easier for her parents not to know because the truth would "shatter" their image of her as their "little princess."

Natalie, who is also 16 but Dutch, didn't tell her parents immediately when she first had intercourse with her boyfriend of three months. But, soon after, she says, she was so happy, she wanted to share the good news. Initially her father was upset and worried about his daughter and his honor. "Talk to him," his wife advised Natalie; after she did, her father made peace with the change. Essentially Natalie and her family negotiated a life change together and figured out, as a family, how to adjust to changed circumstance.

Respecting what she understood as her family's "don't ask, don't tell" policy, Kimberly only slept with her boyfriend at his house, when no one was home. She enjoyed being close to her boyfriend but did not like having to keep an important part of her life secret from her parents. In contrast, Natalie and her boyfriend enjoyed time and a new closeness with her family; the fact that her parents knew and approved of her boyfriend seemed a source of pleasure.

The difference in their experiences stems from divergent cultural ideas about sex and what responsible parents ought to do about it. Here, we see teenagers as helpless victims beset by raging hormones and believe parents should protect them from urges they cannot control. Matters aren't helped by the stereotype that all boys want the same thing, and all girls want love and cuddling. This compounds the burden on parents to steer teenage children away from relationships that will do more harm than good.

The Dutch parents I interviewed regard teenagers, girls and boys, as capable of falling in love, and of reasonably assessing their own readiness for sex. Dutch parents like Natalie's talk to their children about sex and its unintended consequences and urge them to use contraceptives and practice safe sex.

Cultural differences about teenage sex are more complicated than clichéd images of puritanical Americans and permissive Europeans. Normalizing ideas about teenage sex in fact allows the Dutch to exert *more* control over their children. Most of the parents I interviewed actively discouraged promiscuous behavior. And Dutch teenagers often reinforced what we see as 1950s-style mores: eager to win approval, they bring up their partners in conversation, introduce them to their parents and help them make favorable impressions.

Some Dutch teenagers went so far as to express their ideas about sex and love in self-consciously traditional terms; one Dutch boy said the advantage of spending the night with a partner was that it was "Like Mom and Dad, like when you're married, you also wake up next to the person you love."

Normalizing teenage sex under the family roof opens the way for more responsible sex education. In a national survey, 7 of 10 Dutch girls reported that by the time they were 16, their parents had talked to them about pregnancy and contraception. It seems these conversations helped teenagers prepare, responsibly, for active sex lives: 6 of 10 Dutch girls said they were on the pill when they first had intercourse. Widespread use of oral contraceptives contributes to low teenage pregnancy rates—more than 4 times lower in the Netherlands than in the United States.

Obviously sleepovers aren't a direct route to family happiness. But even the most traditional parents can appreciate the virtue of having their children be comfortable bringing a girlfriend or boyfriend home, rather than have them sneak around.

Unlike the American teenagers I interviewed, who said they felt they had to split their burgeoning sexual selves from their family roles, the Dutch teens had a chance to integrate different parts of themselves into their family life. When children feel safe enough to tell parents what they are doing and feeling, presumably it's that much easier for them to ask for help. This allows parents to have more influence, to control through connection.

Sexual maturation is awkward and difficult. The Dutch experience suggests that it is possible for families to stay connected when teenagers start having sex, and that if they do, the transition into adulthood need not be so painful for parents or children.

Activity 1.6 • Analyze "The Sleepover Question"

In a group, discuss these review questions about the emphasis of *logos* in "The Sleepover Question."

1. Can you paraphrase the logic of the argument? How does emotion (*pathos*) play a role in resistance to this argument?

2. What do you think about the "not under my roof" approach to a parent controlling a teen's sexuality versus the Dutch approach of allowing a teen's partner to sleep over?

3. How do stereotypes play against the argument for a more open approach to teen sex in America? How much of parents' discomfort with their teen potentially having sex is guided by how their parents treated the subject when they were teens?

4. In the article, the writer discusses the link between the use of oral contraceptives and lower teen pregnancy rates but does not mention the risk of STDs or condom use. Is it irresponsible of the author not to discuss the risk of STDs and sex, especially when she is willing to discuss teen pregnancy? Does it feel like an incomplete argument without discussing STDs?

After you've discussed these questions as a group, individually reflect on what you would say in a letter to the editor about this article.

Become Part of the Academic Conversation

As a student, you are asked to comment on or analyze texts others have written. In effect, you are expected to join academic conversations that are already in progress. How do you do that? How do you know what kind of response is appropriate? Have you ever entered a party where everyone is talking excitedly? Most likely, you paused near the doorway to get a sense of who was there and what they were discussing before you decided who to talk to and what to say. Or, have you become part of a Facebook group or a listserv discussion group? If so, you know it is a good idea to "lurk" for a while before asking questions or contributing a remark. Writing an academic paper involves a similar process. You read about a subject until you have a good grasp of the points authorities are debating. Then you find a way to integrate your own ideas about that subject with the ideas of others and create an informed contribution to the conversation.

For example, the following students' introductions to movie reviews demonstrate they not only understand the films and have interesting things to say about them;

their writing also displays knowledge of what others have written about the films, whether the students agree with those evaluations or not.

▮   Roger Ebert claims that audience members who haven't seen the first two *Lord of the Rings* films (Peter Jackson, 2001, 2002) will likely "be adrift during the early passages of [the third] film's 200 minutes." But then again, Ebert continues, "to be adrift occasionally during this nine-hour saga comes with the territory" (par. 3). Ebert, though, misses one crucial fact regarding *Lord of the Rings: The Return of the King* (2003). This third installment opens with a flashback intended to familiarize new spectators about what happened in the previous two films. Within these five minutes, the audience discovers how Gollum (Andy Serkis) came to be corrupt through the destructive power of the Ring. The viewer, therefore, will not necessarily be "adrift," as Ebert claims, since the lighting, setting, and sound in the opening of *The Return of the King* show the lighter, more peaceful world before Gollum finds the ring, compared to the darker, more sinister world thereafter.

▮   "It's hard to resist a satire, even when it wobbles, that insists the most unbelievable parts are the most true" (*Rolling Stone* par. 1). This is Peter Travers's overarching view of Grant Heslov's satire, *The Men Who Stare at Goats* (2009). Travers is correct here; after all, *Goats's* opening title card, which reads, "More of this is real than you would believe," humorously teases the viewer that some of the film's most "unbelievable parts" will, in fact, offer the most truth. We experience this via Bill Wilson's (Ewan McGregor) interview of an ex "psy-ops" soldier, when Wilson's life spirals out of control, and all the other far-fetched actions presenting "reality." But again, it is the film's opening—specifically, its setting, camera movements and angles, dialogue, effects, and ambient noise—that sets the foundation for an unbelievably realistic satire.[2]

In both of these introductions, the students quote reviews by professional film critics and respond to the critics' opinions. Moreover, the students continue their arguments by using the critics' ideas as springboards for their own arguments. These two short examples indicate these students have learned how to counter positions advocated by authorities without losing their own voices. If the rest of their essays continue as they have begun, the students will have written essays

---

2. Marshall, Kelli. "Entering a Conversation, Teaching the Academic Essay." *Unmuzzled Thoughts about Teaching and Pop Culture,* Tumblr, 23 Oct. 2010, kellirmarshall.tumblr.com/post/1391060136/entering-a-conversation-teaching-the-academic.

to which others can reply, thus continuing the conversation. Later in this text-book, you will have your own chance to enter the conversation of film reviews by reviewing a favorite movie of your own.

The Burkean Parlor

Kenneth Burke, philosopher and rhetorician, described the "unending con-versation" that surrounds each of us. To do academic research, we must en-ter the conversation of people who already know the topic and have dis-cussed part or all of it before we are even aware the topic exists. Burke wrote,

> Imagine that you enter a parlor. You come late. When you arrive, others have long preceded you, and they are engaged in a heated discussion, a discussion too heated for them to pause and tell you exactly what it is about. In fact, the discussion had already be-gun long before any of them got there, so that no one present is qualified to retrace for you all the steps that had gone before. You listen for a while, until you decide that you have caught the tenor of the argument; then you put in your oar. Someone answers; you answer him; another comes to your defense; another aligns him-self against you, to either the embarrassment or gratification of your opponent, depending upon the quality of your ally's assis-tance. However, the discussion is interminable. The hour grows late, you must depart. And you do depart, with the discussion still vigorously in progress.[3]

Activity 1.7 • Joining the Conversation

Collaborate

Divide into groups of five or six members. Have one member of each group leave the room for five to ten minutes. Meanwhile, each group selects a topic and begins con-versing about it. When the excluded member of the group returns, the group simply continues their conversation. When the excluded member figures out what the con-versation is, he or she can join it by making a comment or asking a question.

After a few minutes, have each of the excluded group members tell the class what it was like to enter a conversation after it had already started. As a class, discuss how this is similar to what you experience when you research an academic topic and write about it.

---

3. Burke, Kenneth. *The Philosophy of Literary Form: Studies in Symbolic Action.* U of California, 1967, pp. 110-11.

Collaborative Groups Help Students Enter the Academic Conversation

Likely, your writing class will include collaborative group work as part of the mix of activities, along with lecture, class discussion, and in-class writing. You may wonder why there is so much talk in a writing class, which is a good question. Use of collaborative groups is based on extensive research, which shows that students who work in small groups as part of their courses tend to learn more and retain the knowledge longer than students who are not asked to work in groups. Also, research shows students who participate in collaborative group work generally are more satisfied with the course. Groups give students a chance to apply knowledge they have learned and provide a change of pace from lectures or other class activities. There are several types of groups, and your class may include one or all of them.

- **Informal, one-time pairs or groups.** After presenting some material, your instructor may ask you to turn to the person next to you and discuss the topic or answer a question.

- **Ongoing small classroom groups.** Usually, these groups work together for a significant part of the semester, and your instructor may assign roles to members of the group such as recorder, facilitator, editor, and spokesperson. Often, the roles will rotate, so everyone has a chance to try out each job. Your instructor may give you a job description for each role or train the class in the tasks for each role.

- **Task groups.** These groups are formed to write a report, complete a project, or do some other task together. These groups meet several times, often outside of class. The products of these groups are usually graded, and your instructor will often require members to rate each other on their performance.

- **Peer editing groups.** When you have completed a draft of an essay or other text, your instructor may ask you to exchange papers in pairs or within small groups. You will be asked to read your classmate's paper carefully and make comments, either on a peer editing form or on the paper itself. Likewise, your classmate will read and make comments on your paper. Then, when your paper is returned, you can make revisions based on your classmate's comments.

An added benefit to the use of collaborative groups in writing classes is that students can help each other figure out what the ongoing conversation is for a particular topic or issue before writing about it. Also, groups provide a forum where students can practice making comments that are part of that conversation.

Why Study Rhetoric?

Rhetoric, or persuasive communication, happens all around us every day, in conversation at the grocery store, in blogs, on television, and in the classroom. We Americans constantly air our opinions about almost everything. Sometimes it is to convince others to share our opinions, and sometimes the reason is to engage in a dialogue that will help us understand the world around us, and sometimes it is to persuade others to action.

Argument is essential to human interaction and to society, for it is through the interplay of ideas in argument that we discover answers to problems, try out new ideas, shape scientific experiments, communicate with family members, recruit others to join a team, and work out any of the multitude of human interactions essential for society to function. When issues are complex, arguments do not result in immediate persuasion of the audience; rather, argument is part of an ongoing conversation between concerned parties who seek resolution, rather than speedy answers.

Rhetoric provides a useful framework for looking at the world, as well as for evaluating and initiating communications. In the modern world, writing and communicating persuasively is a necessary skill. Those who can present effective arguments in writing are, in the business world, often the ones who are promoted. In addition, those who are able to evaluate the arguments presented to them, whether by politicians, advertisers, or even family members, are less likely to be swayed by logical fallacies or ill-supported research.

Also, writing rhetorically is a tool with sometimes surprising uses. Research shows that we are more likely to remember material we have written about rather than simply memorized. Also, through the process of writing, writers often find that they initiate ideas and connections between ideas that they might not otherwise have found. Thus, writing may lead to new discoveries.

Rhetoric is a part of our everyday lives. When we're in a conversation with someone, we use rhetoric on a conscious or subconscious level. If you go to class wearing the T-shirt of your favorite musician or band, you're ultimately sending a rhetorical message identifying yourself as a fan of that artist or group.

If you've ever written a profile on a dating site, you've used rhetorical principles to convince an audience of potential partners to contact you or to write you back if you have chosen to make the first contact. You build *ethos* by talking about yourself in order to build credibility among potential partners, and you establish *pathos* when you talk about an interest that is shared by a potential mate.

Being able to use the tools of rhetoric effectively gives you the power to control your communication—both incoming and outgoing—and to affect your environment in a positive way.

Collaborate

Activity 1.8 • How Do You Use Rhetoric?

In your small group, make a list of five ways that you use rhetoric in your everyday lives. Then, create a list of five ways studying rhetoric could make a difference in your lives. As a class, compare the lists.

Rhetorical Arguments Stand the Test of Time

Abraham Lincoln's Gettysburg Address is the short speech that the president delivered at the site of the Battle of Gettysburg where, four months previously, the Union Army defeated Confederate forces. His was not the only talk that day at the dedication of the Soldiers' National Cemetery, but it is the only one remembered. In just over two minutes, he was able to reframe the Civil War not just as a victory for the North but as a "new birth of freedom" for all Americans. Now, during the 150th anniversary of the Civil War, is a good time to remember Lincoln's rhetoric—in terms of both the content and the style of his speech.

Reading 1.4

Though no actual recording exists of Abraham Lincoln giving the speech, you can listen to others reading it aloud if you search on the Internet for "recording of Gettysburg Address." Listen to the speech, noting the phrase "Four score and seven years ago," which is so famous that Americans know instantly, when it is quoted by orators or writers, that it is a reference to Lincoln. Consider what arguments the president makes in his speech. Think about their relevance today.

Text of the Gettysburg Address
by Abraham Lincoln

Four score and seven years ago, our fathers brought forth on this continent, a new nation, conceived in Liberty and dedicated to the proposition that all men are created equal.

Now we are engaged in a great civil war, testing whether that nation, or any nation so conceived and so dedicated, can long endure. We are met on a great battlefield of that war. We have come to dedicate a portion of that field, as a final resting place for those who here gave their lives that that nation might live. It is altogether fitting and proper that we should do this.

But, in a larger sense, we cannot dedicate—we cannot consecrate—we cannot hallow—this ground. The brave men, living and dead, who struggled here, have consecrated it, far above our poor power to add or detract. The world will little note, nor long remember what we say here, but it can never forget what they did here. It is for us the living, rather, to be dedicated here to the unfinished work which they who fought here have thus far so nobly advanced. It is rather for us to be here dedicated to the great task remaining before us—that from these honored dead we take increased devotion to that cause for which they gave the last full measure of devotion—that we here highly resolve that these dead shall not have died in vain—that this nation, under God, shall have a new birth of freedom—and that government of the people, by the people, for the people, shall not perish from the earth.

Activity 1.9 • Paraphrase the Gettysburg Address

Rephrase each sentence of the Gettysburg Address in your own words, putting it in twenty-first century wording rather than Lincoln's ceremonial, nineteenth-century phrasing. In a paraphrase, the text does not become shorter; it is recreated in different words. This is a useful technique in helping you understand a text. It is also helpful when you are writing an analysis of a text because you can use your paraphrase rather than long, block quotes. Remember, though, when you are writing an essay, you must cite a paraphrase in the text and also include it in your list of references.

Activity 1.10 • Comment on Your Classmate's Paraphrase of the Gettysburg Address

In your small group, trade your paraphrase of the Gettysburg Address with the paraphrase of the person next to you. Read through the document carefully, looking for how well your partner paraphrased, rather than commented on, Lincoln's words. Mark each place where a comment or analysis appears. Give the paper back to the author for revision, if needed.

Why might it be useful to paraphrase a document rather than analyze or comment on it?

Respond to Visual Rhetoric

To the ancient Greeks and Romans, rhetoric largely involved verbal skills—the use of words to persuade an audience. But rhetoricians were also aware that how something was said was sometimes as important as what was said, so they also studied the use of visual cues such as gestures and tone of voice to deliver oral arguments. Today, concern with gestures and other visual cues used to persuade an audience is encompassed in visual rhetoric, which could be defined as the use of images or other visual elements as argument.

Supreme Court Justice Ruth Bader Ginsburg, for example, wears different jabots, or collars, with her black robe to visually communicate her opinion of different court decisions. In this, she differs from the other justices who tend to wear similar collars, no matter their stance on a court ruling.

In an interview with Katie Couric, Justice Ginsberg decoded her jabots. She wears a studded black velvet collar when she issues a dissenting opinion about a court ruling. She wears her favorite, a white beaded jabot from South Africa, when she is not trying to send a message. When she wants to signal her agreement with the majority court opinion, she wears a beaded gold lace jabot.

As a student, you can train yourself to be aware of visual clues expressed in clothing choices such as messages on T-shirts, colors of men's ties, or women's preferences of jeans or dresses.

Ruth Bader Ginsberg's dissent jabot.

The favorite jabot from Cape Town, South Africa.

The majority opinion collar.

Activity 1.11 • Decoding Clothing Choices as Visual Rhetoric

In a small group, review these discussion questions in consideration of Supreme Court Justice Ruth Bader Ginsberg's choice of jabots or collars.

1.　Search the internet using the keywords "Ruth Bader Ginsberg jabot." What other jabots do you find? What do you think of her choices to indicate her agreement or dissent with the court decision on a case?

2.　Discuss your own clothing choices in your small group. Are you making a rhetorical statement when you choose your clothes for work, class, or leisure time? How so?

3.　Find an example of a rhetorical clothing choice on the Internet or in a magazine or newspaper. Bring it to class and explain to your group what the person is conveying with his or her clothing. Choose your group's most interesting example and present it to the class.

Activity 1.12 • Keep a Commonplace Book

Ancient rhetoricians performed speeches with little warning, often to advertise their services as teachers of rhetoric. Thus, they frequently memorized arguments about specific topics that could be adapted to the audience and situation on a moment's notice. They called these memorized arguments "commonplaces." Commonplace books are an outgrowth of the Greek concept of commonplaces, but they are a little different. They became popular in the Middle Ages as notebooks in which individuals would write down quotes or ideas about a particular topic. These notations might later be used to generate an idea for a composition. In more modern times, people have created commonplace books in the form of scrapbooks in which they collect quotes as well as drawings and clippings. Thus, they become a record of a person's intellectual life and can be saved for later reference.

For this class, take a notebook, perhaps one with a colorful or interesting cover, and keep notes, quotes, vocabulary words, and clippings related to the topics discussed in class. As your instructor directs, this commonplace book may be graded as evidence of class participation, or it may be a private journal. Take a look at the commonplace books shown here for ideas. Be creative and enjoy adapting this ancient journal form to record ideas that interest you.

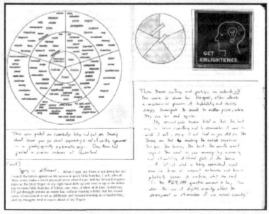

For thousands of years, people have been keeping commonplace books, a kind of journal or diary in which the author includes quotes, drawings, and images.

Activity 1.13 • **Create Your Own Blog**

Create your own blog by using a blog platform site such as *Tumblr, Blogger, WordPress,* or *LiveJournal* to create and publish it. Read the help screens for instructions on how to create your blog. Your design choices should reflect your personality. Keep in mind, though, that you are building an "academic self," so all the topics you write about should be of an academic nature and in an academic tone. Some students decide to have two blogs, one for their friends and one for professional networking, so you may want to do this, especially if you already have a blog.

During this class, you'll use the blog to explore different aspects of each chapter in the textbook (and other topics that your instructor directs). You can also blog about other topics related to your writing this semester, and you can link to other blogs that you think your readers would find interesting.

After you have created the look of your blog, write a first entry in which you introduce yourself to your readers. You might include your major, your college, and something interesting that might attract readers to your blog.

This student's blog incorporates some pictures in her entry about her favorite memory. She also designed the blog with a personal title and category tabs.

chapter 2
Responding Rhetorically

Why I Annotate Readings

Isidro Zepeda
M.A. in English Composition and
Applied Linguistics & TESL
California State University, San
Bernardino

Annotations are maps that detail our journeys through texts. My annotations are not random; instead, they show my responses to a text. As I engage the words of a text with my own words, complex ideas become more accessible to me. My words leave my footprints on the text.

When I annotate, I converse with voices that have traveled similar paths before me, and this activity allows my own ideas to flourish. These ideas are possessed with more than pleasure; they have a purpose that completes a specific task I have set forth to accomplish. For me, annotations are not simply notes on a text—they are marks demonstrating how my ideas interact with other authors' ideas to produce

something new, even if it is just another idea. Our annotations also describe our uniqueness, since they represent how we view and interpret the world.

To annotate means to experience, at a more intimate level, the relationship between text and reader. The annotation process allows the reader to merge with the text—to become an active voice within the margins. In its most simplistic function, annotations help us keep track of all the ideas, connections, and realizations we have during our conversations with texts.

Later, when I am composing my own essay or article, and I wish to utilize quotes or paraphrases from a text I have annotated, the footprints of my words immediately draw me to the portions of the other text I previously found important. Then my annotations can lead to more than a voice in the margins. The words of my new text can engage the annotated text in a conversation of ideas.

Thinking Critically, Reading Rhetorically

Today we study texts to encourage students to develop the critical thinking skills essential for understanding the scientific method and for making effective judgments in the workplace and in civil life. This student-centered emphasis would have seemed strange to ancient Greek and Roman rhetoricians and their students. They believed that a rhetor's skill was best developed by honoring the skills of those who excelled in the past. Therefore, a large part of the educational process involved having students study the texts of well-regarded speeches, memorize and recite them, and model new compositions based on those speeches' approaches to topics and language style. As Isocrates explained,

> Since language is of such a nature that it is possible to discourse on the same subject matter in many different ways—to represent the great as lowly or invest the little with grandeur, to recount the things of old in a new manner or set forth events of recent date in an old fashion—it follows that one must not shun the subjects upon which others have composed before, but must try to compose better than they. ("Panegyricus")

Thus, students in ancient Greece or Rome would have been presented with a text, often read aloud by a teacher, and they would be asked to transcribe or copy it down with the idea that they would internalize the skills of the master rhetor who had originally given the speech. Then, they would be asked to write about the same subject in a way that built upon what they had learned from the master text but incorporated their own personal attitudes or perspectives.

Today, rather than being asked to model new compositions based upon the techniques of classic texts, students are asked to read texts carefully and then to engage in critical thinking and discussion about those texts.

Critical thinking involves considering issues thoughtfully and independently. Critical thinkers do not believe facts or opinions just because they are published—whether in newspapers, textbooks, on television, or on the Internet. Nor do they focus upon just understanding or memorizing information, as in facts and figures. Critical thinkers examine the reasoning behind the information in front of them, looking for premises and considering the inferences drawn from those premises. They are able to think for themselves, making logical connections between ideas, seeing cause and effect relationships, and using information to solve problems.

Activity 2.1 • Think about Critical Reading

Compose

Freewrite for five minutes about a controversial issue about which you have a strong opinion. Consider why you believe what you do about this issue. What outside influences or sources have influenced your position? In what ways has the opposing side also influenced what you believe about the issue?

After you finish freewriting, look back at what you have written and consider the social (other people, articles, videos, etc.) nature of the sources that have influenced you. In your group or as a class, discuss the influences—not the particular issues themselves—that have affected your opinion. How have you decided what to believe?

Reading rhetorically makes use of critical thinking skills, but it also involves looking at texts as arguments and evaluating them for validity, adequacy of evidence, and presence of bias. Moreover, reading rhetorically involves having a knowledge of rhetoric and specialized Greek terms such as *logos, pathos, ethos,* and *kairos*—words that were defined briefly in Chapter 1 and will be discussed more extensively in Chapter 3. Practice reading rhetorically as you read the following article.

Reading 2.1

Do You Know How Your Mascara is Made?

by Arna Cohen

Customers grabbing a late-morning cup of coffee in downtown Brussels caught a strange sight two years ago. Suddenly, across the street, on the grounds of the European Commission, there were rabbits everywhere.

Some seemed to emerge from nearby bushes. Others slipped out from behind city walls as pedestrians stopped to watch and curious faces peered down from office windows. And then,

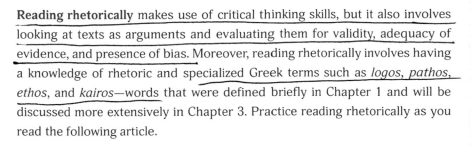

Worldwide, activists protest the use of laboratory animals to test cosmetics, according to "Do You Know How Your Mascara is Made?" The article has a tag line that reads, "Across the globe, countless animals continue to suffer in painful tests simply to bring new skin creams, hair dyes, and other nonessential cosmetics to market. But the cruelty-free campaign is leading the charge to ban cosmetic animal testing worldwide by engaging consumers and companies, rewriting laws, and advancing the science of safety testing."

The article was printed in All Animals, *a publication of the Humane Society. The magazine aims to bring to the public stories about the Humane Society and the humane movement.*

Arna Cohen, the author, is online editor and producer for the Companion Animals Division, Humane Society of the U.S.

right there on an open stretch of sidewalk, on a Wednesday in June, those rabbits began to dance.

As a happy burst of music piped out over a nearby sound system—"Saturday night, I feel the air is getting hot"—27 advocates in white rabbit costumes stepped, hopped, clapped, and spun in unison. Reporters snapped photos. A few onlookers began to move with the song. And atop a stone wall, two women unfurled a large white banner: "350,000 Petition for EU Cosmetics to be Cruelty-Free in 2013."

The flash mob gathered to shine a spotlight on the issue of cosmetics animal testing in the European Union—one white rabbit representing each member country. "It attracted quite a lot of attention, as you might imagine," says Wendy Higgins, remembering a round of applause as the dancing concluded. The local media even asked for an encore, to capture more footage.

Immediately afterward, Humane Society International and Lush cosmetics company delivered stack upon stack of signatures to the European health commissioner, calling on him to support a March 2013 ban on the sale of animal-tested cosmetics.

"It was quite an emotional event, I have to say. I had a tear in my eye," says Higgins, HSI European communications director." This had a real sense of meaning, and it was such a joyful event. But all of us knew, for animals in laboratories being tested on for cosmetics, there is no joy. There is no happy moment. And we were there, speaking up for them."

The eventually successful petition was one in a series of rapid-fire victories achieved recently by HSI and The HSUS's Be Cruelty-Free Campaign. Last year alone, Israel banned the sale of all newly animal-tested cosmetics, India prohibited animal tests of cosmetics within its borders, and China announced that it will no longer require animal testing for domestically manufactured nonmedicated cosmetics. In South Korea, the government invested more than $150 million to establish the country's first nonanimal testing center, further committing to accept alternative methods for safety assurance of medicated cosmetics such as sunscreens and anti-wrinkle creams.

Progress has been most striking in the European Union: Five months after those white rabbits danced their jig in Belgium, the health commissioner stated he would fully implement the March 2013 ban on the import and sale of cosmetics newly tested on animals or containing ingredients tested on animals, regardless of where such tests are conducted. With an EU testing ban already in place since 2009, the 2013 sales ban marked the final piece in a 20-year struggle by advocates to remove cruelty from the beauty equation there, and the domino that is knocking down barriers worldwide, says Troy Seidle, HSI director of research and toxicology.

"With the EU closing its doors to animal-tested cosmetics, the beginning of the end of global cosmetics cruelty is within our grasp. It is a major moral milestone in the history of ending cosmetics animal testing."

Pascaline Clerc, HSUS senior director of animal research issues, adds that the EU decision has wider implications for animal testing of noncosmetic products such as paint, coffee sweeteners, and household cleaners. "This is the first step in replacing animals used for toxicity testing in general. People can see that it can be done."

An animated bunny is taken from the wild and imprisoned in a research laboratory. He is locked in a full-body restraint system and a chemical is applied to his eyes, which blister and turn red.

A rabbit-costumed flash mob marches toward EU headquarters in Brussels in June 2012, bearing 350,000 signatures against cosmetics animal testing. Exposing the cruelty behind the beauty industry has been the focus of intense efforts by the animal protection movement for decades, marked by boycotts, protests, petitions, and extraordinary levels of consumer participation.

Photo Credit: Virginia Mayo/Associated Press

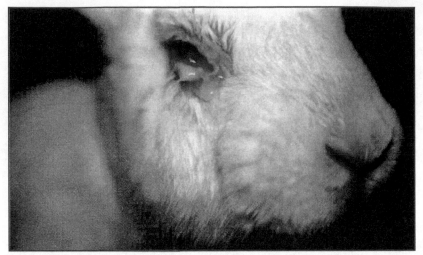

Pain-filled lives and deaths are the fate of rabbits and other animals used for cosmetics test-ing. Alternative methods are gaining traction thanks to a growing recognition that animal tests are poor predictors of how substances will affect people.

Photo Credit: PETA

Bright Eyes, a video created by HSI partner Choose Cruelty Free Australia, is based on a true story (with creative license: Unlike the animated speci-men, laboratory rabbits are not obtained from the wild; they're purpose-bred for research). For 70 years, rabbits have been the go-to animal for the Draize eye irritation test the video depicts. They spend their short lives undergoing the procedure without anesthetic before being killed when no longer "useful."

The Draize test is only one in a litany of toxicity tests performed on animals, each more horrifying than the last. In the acute oral toxicity test, the nee-dle of a syringe is forced down the throat of a rat and a massive dose of the test substance injected into her stomach to determine the amount that causes death. The animal can experience diarrhea, convulsions, bleeding from the mouth, seizures, and paralysis. The same procedure is used to as-sess smaller amounts in repeated dose toxicity tests, which last daily for one to three months or longer.

In carcinogenicity tests, rats and mice are exposed to substances daily for up to two years to see if they develop tumors; reproductive toxicity tests involve daily exposure of pregnant rats and up to two generation of pups, often by force-feeding (a method that seems doubly unnecessary given that most personal care products are applied to the skin). Even tests that aren't measuring fatal doses ultimately end in death, notes Catherine Willett, HSUS director of regulatory toxicology, risk assessment, and alternatives:

"Oftentimes you need to kill the animal to see what has actually happened at the microscopic level." Typical killing methods include asphyxiation, neck-breaking, and decapitation.

A dubious science underpins the physical and psychological suffering endured by animals in laboratories, as results of tests done on rodents and rabbits are poor predictors of a substance's effect on humans. Spurred by widening acknowledgment of these limitations, scientists are increasingly focused on developing state-of-the-art, human-relevant, animal-free alternatives.

The days of the Draize test, for one, look to be numbered. Many governments approve the use of cow or chicken corneas left over from the meat industry for certain types of eye irritancy tests. The next generation of tests will use human cells, such as a new artificial cornea under development by Japanese researchers that could ultimately replace rabbits entirely. Preliminary evaluations of the tissue have obtained results that more closely predict effects on human eyes than animal tests have.

Meanwhile, the number of rabbits used in skin irritation and corrosion tests is being reduced thanks to computer modeling analyses and other techniques. Skin cells can be grown in petri dishes, says Willett: "You add two or three different kinds of cells to an artificial scaffold, and they start to form tissues that look and behave just like living tissues"—imitating skin on body parts as varied as the nose, trachea, and lungs. And Procter & Gamble scientists recently developed the first nonanimal method for skin allergy testing; chemicals are assessed in test tubes for their allergic reactivity according to the amount of depletion they cause in proteins known as peptides.

As critical as these developments are, an emerging body of research is seeking to transcend such one-on-one test replacements with a more exhaustive approach that focuses on predicting chemical pathways in the human body. "Where does the chemical enter the body? How does it enter the body?" says Willett: "Does it bind to a receptor and cause a cascade of things to happen in the cell? Does it chemically modify a protein?

"And you can actually map this out from many different kinds of chemicals that cause different kinds of reactions," she continues. "You can actually get a pretty decent idea of what a chemical is going to do based on the biological pathway it affects. It's a completely different way of thinking about testing than has ever been done before. People who know about this are very excited about it."

Governments have embraced the changes, with agencies such as the FDA, EPA, and Department of Defense investing in complex computer models, "organs on a chip," and other technologies, says Willett. "Similar investment is being made around the world, in the European Union, Japan, Brazil, Korea, and elsewhere."

Where alternative testing methods are not available, companies can create new cosmetics by choosing among thousands of ingredients that have been tested in the past and proven to be safe.

Taken together, these options provide a counter argument to industry claims that animal testing is the only possible way to assess safety. "Now that we've had the technical progress, the politicians have become—well, they've lost sympathy," says Seidle.

The EU import and sales ban was the initial focus of the Be-Cruelty Free Campaign, a global push to rewrite laws, train technicians in alternative testing methods, and engage consumers and corporations. Stalled for years, an EU testing ban was originally passed in 1993, with a five-year phase-in period, but the cosmetics industry managed to secure delay after delay, claiming that it needed more time to replace animals in testing. Finally, in 2009, all animal testing of finished cosmetics and their ingredients was prohibited within EU borders; a ban on sales of products animal-tested elsewhere was slated to go into effect in 2013.

But in 2012, it again appeared that the cosmetics industry might impede progress. So HSI delivered the European health commissioner a large Valentine's Day card from singer Leona Lewis, asking him to have a heart for animals. They held meetings with policymakers. They asked European citizens to send postcards in support. And then, immediately following the purposely upbeat, positive white rabbit event, they brought 350,000 signatures to that pivotal June meeting, including ones from celebrities such as Ricky Gervais, Kesha, Sir Roger Moore, and Chrissie Hynde.

"Even though only two HSI lobbyists were allowed into the meeting, they weren't in that room alone," Higgins says. "They said that when they stepped into that room, they felt the hands of those 350,000 people on their shoulders, spurring them on. And that's what it's all about. That's what all of the petition-collecting was all about, was that moment where we could say: We're watching. Europe is waiting for you to do this."

Nine months later, they had their ban. "We probably would have been look-ing at more delays if our campaign hadn't been there to really hold the EU's feet to the flame," says Seidle.

With the mission accomplished in Europe, the Be Cruelty-Free Campaign is working to achieve similar progress in other lucrative sales markets: Brazil, South Korea, Russia. In India, dedicated personnel hired with funds from a Lush grant recruited Bollywood stars and thousands of consumers to help HSI pressure officials to replace animal tests with alternative methods in the country's regulations of cosmetics manufacturing. "We went as far as we could with the Bureau of Indian Standards," says Seidle, "and from there we engaged some lead members of parliament and really just ratcheted up the heat with a very high-impact public campaign, which got the drug control-ler's attention, and he personally went in with our letter in hand and said, 'Yes, we're just going to do this; get it done.'"

In June, HSI launched Be Cruelty-Free China, turning its focus to a criti-cal battleground where the government has required all cosmetics for sale, both domestically produced and imported, to be safety-tested on animals in government laboratories, and where in recent years the lure of huge prof-its—$24 billion spent on cosmetics and personal care items in 2012—has proven irresistible to Mary Kay and other companies that had been cruelty-free for decades.

Decisions by these companies to surrender their principles have outraged their customers. When Urban Decay, a popular cruelty-free company, an-nounced that it would sell in China, thousands expressed anger through email, social media, and online petitions, prompting company executives to reverse course.

Seeking to bring this element of popular pressure to bear on the govern-ment, HSI partnered with three Chinese organizations, "one that's very con-nected politically, one that's very media-wise, and one that's a youth social media organization," says Seidle. Advocates began spreading the cruelty-free message on the Chinese social media platform Weibo, with more than 500 million users, while press releases began naming companies that refuse to sell in China because of the testing policy.

"We've been actively disseminating information to the Chinese consumers for the first time ever," says Seidle. "No one has ever done that before, to explain this is how your cosmetics are being tested; this is what's involved;

this is what the idea of cruelty-free means." The European Union health commissioner applied additional leverage, meeting with Chinese officials to discuss animal testing as a barrier to trade.

A significant breakthrough came in November, when the China Food and Drug Administration announced that it would allow domestic cosmetics manufacturers to opt out of mandatory animal testing in favor of using previously collected ingredient safety data and possibly alternative test methods accepted by EU regulators—allowing Chinese goods to be sold in the world's largest cosmetics market. The Institute for In Vitro Sciences is now training Chinese scientists in alternative methods, thanks to an $80,000 grant from HSI, The HSUS, and the Human Toxicology Project Consortium.

The change comes into force in June and doesn't yet apply to imported cosmetics or to "special-use" products like hair dyes, sunscreens, and antiperspirants. But in meetings with HSI, the CFDA has indicated that, after the change has been implemented and assessed, it may be extended to the other categories. Companies are still free to continue animal testing if they so choose, so HSI's next focus will be to persuade regulators to ban the tests altogether.

In small ways, consumers have shown their approval of the government's change of heart. In Dalian, a port city in northeast China, animal advocates adorned with rabbit ears held several events that attracted 2,700 people, hundreds of whom signed HSI's Be Cruelty-Free China pledge and a petition supporting the government's plans. A tiny percentage of a huge populace, but notable in a nation not known for freedom of expression.

In the U.S., the state of cosmetics testing is somewhat of a different story. Even with the availability of cutting-edge technology, even with years of safety data on thousands of chemicals, even with no legal requirements that cosmetics be tested on animals, many American companies continue the practice in part because it's what they've always done.

Fear of lawsuits is a factor in their conservatism, says The HSUS's Willett. In our litigious society," people will sue the company and they will sue the FDA. Not only do you have to convince the regulators that the method you used to evaluate your chemical was sound, but you have to make it legally defensible. Because animal tests are the historical measure that we've used, people feel that they're on safer ground."

And profit sings its siren song. The bulk of animal testing these days is done in the lucrative field of anti-aging products that claim to reduce wrinkles, lighten brown spots, or lift sagging skin. The chemical ingredients in these treatments affect the body's structure, thus pushing them into the category of over-the-counter drugs and, if an ingredient has never been used before, making it subject to mandatory animal testing (see "What's in a Name," p. 20).

"It's so sad that these animals are dying for . . . the myth that we can hold back the march of time," says Lush ethics director Hilary Jones." Companies sell that myth and sell us these miracle ingredients that disappear two or three months later, to be replaced by a new miracle ingredient, all of them tested on animals."

With a strong industry lobby keeping a legislative ban on animal testing a nonstarter, the Be Cruelty-Free Campaign's focus in the U.S. has been on public education. According to a 2013 poll, a majority of Americans oppose animal testing of cosmetics, and they actually feel safer if alternatives are used instead. But even so, consumers here simply aren't as engaged, or informed, as they have been in the EU, says The HSUS's Clerc. "When we started this campaign, people were surprised that animal testing was still around. They thought we had moved beyond that."

Reaching out especially to a new generation concerned about what they put in and on their bodies, the campaign engages music, television, and film stars to spread the message through Twitter and public service announcements. It recently teamed with Miss DC 2013 Bindhu Pamarthi, who announced she was willing to compete barefaced in the Miss America 2014 pageant if it would draw attention to her platform of ending cosmetics animal testing. Although Pamarthi didn't ultimately compete barefaced and didn't ultimately win the crown, she did get a Facebook shout-out from R.E.I.G.N., the pageant's makeup partner, which honored her "thought provoking platform" and called her "a beyond beauty inspiration to us all."

The campaign also partners with bloggers who search out cruelty-free cosmetics and personal care products, doing intensive detective work on manufacturers before making recommendations. On Jen Mathews's My Beauty Bunny blog, every item is tested on staff members before being recommended to readers. Today, the blog receives 100,000 views a month, while 140,000 people follow along on Facebook. But Mathews's reach extends beyond the known numbers, with the blog winning multiple awards and featured in magazines and on television, radio, and websites.

Mathews began supporting animal welfare in college. "I was one of those college students who was posting things on billboards all over campus and the faculty were constantly taking them down." She would put animal rights fliers in her bill payment envelopes, "doing everything I could, grass roots, to get the message out. [. . .] Now I'm able to take that to the Web."

While Mathews's mission is to show consumers that cruelty-free beauty products are high quality, affordable, and widely available, Clerc focuses within the industry, seeking examples to share with companies that want to adopt humane business models. The strategy, she says, "is to find those companies that have done the right thing from the beginning and prove they can still be profitable; they can innovate without animal testing."

One such company is Biao, whose laboratory evaluates skin care compounds for safety using technology such as gene chips that allow mass in vitro cell testing. Founder Nicole Baldwin's entrepreneurial journey began as a little girl, when she suffered serious burns on her face, neck, and chest after upsetting a pot of boiling water on herself. Her grandmother, who was a nurse at the time, created a treatment from botanicals and other natural products, using formulas that had been passed down to her from her own mother.

Years later, when Baldwin was stationed with the U.S. Army in Afghanistan, her skin suffered again, this time from stress, dust, and the extreme temperatures of the arid desert climate. When none of the commercial products she tried provided relief, Baldwin decided to develop her own skincare line. Returning home to Houston after her tour, she became a licensed aesthetician.

A second tour of duty took Baldwin back to Afghanistan, where, using her grandmother's remedies and her own experience as inspiration, she began to create face and body treatments formulated with sustainable organic plant oils and extracts. She named the line Biao—an acronym for "beautiful inside and out"—as a tribute to her grandmother, whose care healed not just Baldwin's skin but her self-esteem and confidence. "I am following in her footsteps," Baldwin said in an interview with ABC News, "and I'm very glad that at 81 years old she's able to see me do this."

Baldwin attributes her cruelty-free philosophy to her relationship with her childhood pet, a German shepherd abandoned by his previous owners. After she saved Spicy from choking on a chicken bone, Baldwin says he "followed behind me everywhere. When I would awake for school, he would be in . . . my bedroom door. . . . When I would ask him to get me a newspaper, he would go get it. . . . I discovered that animals were so similar to humans. Spicy knew that I had saved his life." Experiencing this kind of bond, Baldwin couldn't fathom subjecting an animal to the cruelty of testing.

Prai Beauty, a skincare company founded in 1999 by HSUS board member Cathy Kangas, shares its cruelty-free status as a key component of its sales pitch on the home shopping networks where it sells in the U.S. and six countries. Kangas says a survey following the product launch found that "the most overwhelming thing that excited [customers] . . . was it being cruelty-free. It really mattered to 72 percent of all of our customers."

The financial success of Prai, with $30 million in annual sales, and other companies founded on humane principles, such as Paul Mitchell, Aubrey Organics, and Burt's Bees, clearly demonstrates that cruelty-free can be good business—business that the cosmetics industry can no longer profitably ignore. "Companies that are still testing on animals will soon lose money and market shares," notes Clerc. And now, the stakes are even higher for those selling in countries that have taken a stand against animal testing. "Those companies will see those markets slipping away from them if they don't move away from animal testing rapidly."

Activity 2.2 • Analyze "Do You Know How Your Mascara is Made?"

Collaborate

In your small group, discuss the following questions, and then report your group's opinion(s) to the class.

1. After reading "Do You Know How Your Mascara is Made?" identify the problem the author is concerned with.

2. What is the author arguing in the article?

3. What evidence of animal testing does the author offer? Is it sufficient to support the argument?

4. What laws or changed laws does the author mention that lend credibility to the argument?

5. Does the argument appeal primarily to *ethos, pathos,* or *logos*? How so?

6. Who published the article? Does the organization have a particular bias?

Compose

Activity 2.3 • Why Is Activity 2.2 Critical Reading?

After your group completes Activity 2.2, freewrite for five minutes about the questions you answered in your group in response to Activity 2.2. What do those questions ask you to do that is reading critically?

Ways of Reading Rhetorically

Reading theorist Louise Rosenblatt suggests a technique for analyzing written texts—particularly those with few visual cues other than words on paper or a computer screen. She says that we take the pattern of verbal signs left by the author and use them to recreate the text, not in the exact way the author perceived the text, but guided by it.

So, as we read, there is a constant stream of response to the text. However, Rosenblatt says that even as the reader is recreating the text, he or she is also reacting to it. Thus, there are two interacting streams of response involved as the person moves through the text. The reader, rather than being a passive receptor for the author's text, actually participates in the creative process during reading.

However, we read differently depending on the text and the occasion. For example, if you take a paperback novel on an airplane trip, you probably read simply for entertainment and to pass the time in the air. If you read *King Lear* for a literature class, you read for the plot, characterization, and other elements that you know will be discussed in class. If you read a chapter in your chemistry textbook before an exam, you are focusing on remembering concepts and details that might be on the test. Reading as a writer is another type of reading. You examine the text with an eye for the choices the writer made when crafting the text, such as whether the writer begins with a narrative introduction, a quote from a noted authority, or a startling statement. You notice, for example, what people are mentioned in the text, either as authorities or participants in activities.

Rosenblatt also makes a useful distinction between two main kinds of reading—aesthetic reading and efferent reading.[1] In **aesthetic reading**, the reader is most interested in what happens "during the reading event, as he fixes his attention on the actual experience he is living through," according to Rosen-

---

1. Rosenblatt, Louise Michelle. "Efferent and Aesthetic Reading." *The Reader, the Text, the Poem: The Transactional Theory of the Literary Work.* Carbondale, IL: Southern Illinois UP, 1994. 22-47. Print.

blatt. Readers focus upon the ideas, images, and story of the text that evoke an aesthetic experience in the moment of reading. **Efferent readers**, in contrast, read to learn from the text, and, thus, according to Rosenblatt, "concentrate on the information, the concepts, the guides to action, that will be left with him when the reading is over."

Reading rhetorically is efferent reading, focusing not on the experience of reading but on the information the text conveys and upon the way an argument is established and supported in a text. Some arguments are written in an engaging style that is a pleasure to read, while others are written in a highly emotional tone that arouses a visceral response in the reader. A text that inspires aesthetic reading must sometimes be read several times in order for the reader to focus on the structure of the argument beneath the creative language.

Some theorists say that critical thinking is "thinking about thinking" or "reasoning about reasoning," and that is exactly what reading rhetorically involves—reasoning about whether or not a text presents a reasoned argument. A good way to begin reading rhetorically is to be aware of the essential elements of an argument and identify these elements in the text you are evaluating.

The elements of an argument include a debatable issue, clearly stated, for which an audience is to be persuaded. Without an issue, a text may be simply informative, rather than persuasive. Those individuals or groups holding a position may be considered biased toward that position. For example, the reading in this chapter, "Do You Know How Your Mascara is Made?" was published by the Humane Society and expresses a clear argument against the use of animals for testing cosmetics. Because the Humane Society has a stated agenda about animal rights, the article should not, then, be the only source cited in an academic essay about the issue of animal testing in the production of cosmetics. An argument about this issue, put forward in academic writing, should be backed by additional reliable evidence from sources that are unbiased—independent articles not written by the Humane Society. The use of biased sources for support evidence can lead to a biased argument. Moreover, to be fair and complete, an argument must contain an acknowledgment of opposing argument(s). Otherwise, the reader may be left with unanswered questions about why alternatives are not considered. And finally, a well-written argument features a conclusion, which may include a call to action.

See the Checklist of Essential Elements in an Argument on the next page.

Checklist of Essential Elements in an Argument

☑ **A debatable issue.** By definition, for a text to be an argument, there must be at least two sides that can be asserted and supported.

☑ **A clearly stated position, claim statement, or thesis.** Arguments assert different kinds of claims, such as taking a position on an issue of fact, asserting a cause and effect relationship, declaring the value of some entity, or advocating for a solution to a problem; but, in each case, after you read the argument, you should be able to restate or summarize the position, claim, or thesis in one or two sentences.

☑ **An audience.** To evaluate an argument, you need to know the original intended audience or place of publication, so that you can decide if the argument takes into account the audience's attitudes, background, and other factors. Ask yourself, for example, if the writer is assuming too much or too little background knowledge on the part of the audience or if the writer is using language that assumes the reader's agreement on the issue when that assumption is not warranted.

☑ **Evidence from reliable sources.** Quotes, statistics, and other evidence should be credited to reputable sources, even if your text is not a document that offers academic-style citations. The evidence should be sufficient to support the author's position or thesis.

☑ **Acknowledgment of the opposing argument.** A good rhetorician does not ignore any potential weaknesses in the argument. It is better to acknowledge points in favor of the opposing argument and then, if possible, refute the opposition's strong points than it is to allow an audience to poke holes in an argument.

☑ **A conclusion and/or call to action.** An argument can be concluded in a variety of effective ways, but it is important to note that it does, indeed, conclude. The conclusion can be a call to action on the part of the audience, but it should not be the beginning of an additional argument that is not supported by the evidence presented.

The Web Means the End of Forgetting

by Jeffrey Rosen

Several years ago, Stacy Snyder was a fairly typical 25-year-old college student training to be a teacher. That all changed forever when she did something that she probably thought was harmless fun—she posted a photo of herself on a social network site. In this article published in The New York Times, *Jeffrey Rosen uses Snyder's case to illustrate how notions of privacy are changing because of the ever-growing presence and popularity of social networking sites. What is even more alarming, according to Rosen, is that photos and information, once posted on the web, are there forever. The web does not forget, and this lack of forgetting is changing society's ability to forgive and forget.*

You may enjoy posting status updates about your life on a Facebook or Twitter account; however, with employers increasingly conducting background checks on such sites, it's very important to be careful about what you choose to post. This includes status updates, photographs, and videos. If you read the following article carefully, you may never look at social networking sites quite the same again.

Four years ago, Stacy Snyder, then a 25-year-old teacher in training at Conestoga Valley High School in Lancaster, Pa., posted a photo on her MySpace page that showed her at a party wearing a pirate hat and drinking from a plastic cup, with the caption "Drunken Pirate." After discovering the page, her supervisor at the high school told her the photo was "unprofessional," and the dean of Millersville University School of Education, where Snyder was enrolled, said she was promoting drinking in virtual view of her underage students. As a result, days before Snyder's scheduled graduation, the university denied her a teaching degree. Snyder sued, arguing that the university had violated her First Amendment rights by penalizing her for her (perfectly legal) after-hours behavior. But in 2008, a federal district judge rejected the claim, saying that because Snyder was a public employee whose photo didn't relate to matters of public concern, her "Drunken Pirate" post was not protected speech.

When historians of the future look back on the perils of the early digital age, Stacy Snyder may well be an icon. The problem she faced is only one example of a challenge that, in big and small ways, is confronting millions of people around the globe: how best to live our lives in a world where the Internet records everything and forgets nothing—where every online photo, status update, Twitter post and blog entry by and about us can be stored forever. With websites like LOL Facebook Moments, which collects and shares embarrassing personal revelations from Facebook users, ill-advised photos and online chatter are coming back to haunt people months or years after the fact.

Examples are proliferating daily: there was the 16-year-old British girl who was fired from her office job for complaining on Facebook, "I'm so totally bored!!"; there was the 66-year-old Canadian psychotherapist who tried to enter the United States but was turned away at the border—and barred permanently from visiting the country—after a border guard's Internet search found that the therapist had written an article in a philosophy journal describing his experiments 30 years ago with LSD. According to a recent survey by Microsoft, 75 percent of U.S. recruiters and human-resource professionals report that their companies require them to do online research about candidates, and many use a range of sites when scrutinizing applicants—including search engines, social networking sites, photo- and video-sharing sites, personal websites and blogs, Twitter and online gaming sites. Seventy percent of U.S. recruiters report that they have rejected candidates because of information found online, like photos and discussion-board conversations and membership in controversial groups.

Technological advances, of course, have often presented new threats to privacy. In 1890, in perhaps the most famous article on privacy ever written, Samuel Warren and Louis Brandeis complained that because of new technology—like the Kodak camera and the tabloid press—"gossip is no longer the resource of the idle and of the vicious but has become a trade." But the mild society gossip of the Gilded Age pales before the volume of revelations contained in the photos, video and chatter on social media sites and elsewhere across the Internet. Facebook, which surpassed MySpace in 2008 as the largest social-networking site, now has nearly 500 million members, or 22 percent of all Internet users, who spend more than 500 billion minutes a month on the site. Facebook users share more than 25 billion pieces of content each month (including news stories, blog posts and photos), and the average user creates 70 pieces of content a month. There are more than 100 million registered Twitter users, and the Library of Congress recently announced that it will be acquiring—and permanently storing—the entire archive of public Twitter posts since 2006.

In Brandeis's day—and until recently, in ours—you had to be a celebrity to be gossiped about in public: today all of us are learning to expect the scrutiny that used to be reserved for the famous and the infamous. A 26-year-old Manhattan woman told *The New York Times* that she was afraid of being tagged in online photos because it might reveal that she wears only two outfits when out on the town—a Lynyrd Skynyrd T-shirt or a basic black dress. "You have movie-star issues," she said, "and you're just a person."

We've known for years that the web allows for unprecedented voyeurism, exhibitionism and inadvertent indiscretion, but we are only beginning to understand the costs of an age in which so much of what we say, and of what others say about us, goes into our permanent—and public—digital files. The fact that the Internet never seems to forget is threatening, at an almost existential level, our ability to control our identities; to preserve the option of reinventing ourselves and starting anew; to overcome our checkered pasts.

In a recent book, "Delete: The Virtue of Forgetting in the Digital Age," the cyberscholar Viktor Mayer-Schönberger cites Stacy Snyder's case as a reminder of the importance of "societal forgetting." By "erasing external memories," he says in the book, "our society accepts that human beings evolve over time, that we have the capacity to learn from past experiences and adjust our behavior." In traditional societies, where missteps are observed but not necessarily recorded, the limits of human memory ensure that people's sins are eventually forgotten. By contrast, Mayer-Schönberger notes, a society in which everything is recorded "will forever tether us to all our past actions, making it impossible, in practice, to escape them." He concludes that "without some form of forgetting, forgiving becomes a difficult undertaking."

It's often said that we live in a permissive era, one with infinite second chances. But the truth is that for a great many people, the permanent memory bank of the web increasingly means there are no second chances—no opportunities to escape a scarlet letter in your digital past. Now the worst thing you've done is often the first thing everyone knows about you.

The Crisis—and the Solution?

Concern about these developments has intensified this year, as Facebook took steps to make the digital profiles of its users generally more public than private. Last December, the company announced that parts of user profiles that had previously been private—including every user's friends, relationship status and family relations—would become public and accessible to other users. Then in April, Facebook introduced an interactive system called Open Graph that can share your profile information and friends with the Facebook partner sites you visit.

What followed was an avalanche of criticism from users, privacy regulators and advocates around the world. Four Democratic senators—Charles Schumer of New York, Michael Bennet of Colorado, Mark Begich of Alaska and Al Franken of Minnesota—wrote to the chief executive of Facebook,

Mark Zuckerberg, expressing concern about the "instant personalization" feature and the new privacy settings. In May, Facebook responded to all the criticism by introducing a new set of privacy controls that the company said would make it easier for users to understand what kind of information they were sharing in various contexts.

Facebook's partial retreat has not quieted the desire to do something about an urgent problem. All around the world, political leaders, scholars and citizens are searching for responses to the challenge of preserving control of our identities in a digital world that never forgets. Are the most promising solutions going to be technological? Legislative? Judicial? Ethical? A result of shifting social norms and cultural expectations? Or some mix of the above? Alex Türk, the French data protection commissioner, has called for a "constitutional right to oblivion" that would allow citizens to maintain a greater degree of anonymity online and in public places. In Argentina, the writers Alejandro Tortolini and Enrique Quagliano have started a campaign to "reinvent forgetting on the Internet," exploring a range of political and technological ways of making data disappear. In February, the European Union helped finance a campaign called "Think B4 U post!" that urges young people to consider the "potential consequences" of publishing photos of themselves or their friends without "thinking carefully" and asking permission. And in the United States, a group of technologists, legal scholars and cyberthinkers are exploring ways of recreating the possibility of digital forgetting. These approaches share the common goal of reconstructing a form of control over our identities: the ability to reinvent ourselves, to escape our pasts and to improve the selves that we present to the world. [. . .]

In the near future, Internet searches for images are likely to be combined with social-network aggregator search engines, like today's Spokeo and Pipl, which combine data from online sources—including political contributions, blog posts, YouTube videos, web comments, real estate listings and photo albums. Increasingly these aggregator sites will rank people's public and private reputations. In the Web 3.0 world, Michael Fertik, a Harvard Law School graduate, predicts people will be rated, assessed and scored based not on their creditworthiness but on their trustworthiness as good parents, good dates, good employees, good baby sitters or good insurance risks.

One legal option for responding to online setbacks to your reputation is to sue under current law. There's already a sharp rise in lawsuits known as Twittergation—that is, suits to force websites to remove slanderous or false posts. Last year, Courtney Love was sued for libel by the fashion designer Boudoir Queen for supposedly slanderous comments posted on Twitter, on Love's MySpace page and on the designer's online market-place-feedback page. But even if you win a U.S. libel lawsuit, the website doesn't have to take the offending material down any more than a newspaper that has lost a libel suit has to remove the offending content from its archive.

Some scholars, therefore, have proposed creating new legal rights to force websites to remove false or slanderous statements. Cass Sunstein, the Obama administration's regulatory czar, suggests in his new book, "On Rumors," that there might be "a general right to demand retraction after a clear demonstration that a statement is both false and damaging." (If a newspaper or blogger refuses to post a retraction, they might be liable for damages.) Sunstein adds that websites might be required to take down false postings after receiving notice that they are false—an approach modeled on the Digital Millennium Copyright Act, which requires websites to remove content that supposedly infringes intellectual property rights after receiving a complaint.

As Stacy Snyder's "Drunken Pirate" photo suggests, however, many people aren't worried about false information posted by others—they're worried about true information they've posted about themselves when it is taken out of context or given undue weight. And defamation law doesn't apply to true information or statements of opinion. Some legal scholars want to expand the ability to sue over true but embarrassing violations of privacy—although it appears to be a quixotic goal.

Daniel Solove, a George Washington University law professor and author of the book, *The Future of Reputation*, says that laws forbidding people to breach confidences could be expanded to allow you to sue your Facebook friends if they share your embarrassing photos or posts in violation of your privacy settings. Expanding legal rights in this way, however, would run up against the First Amendment rights of others. Invoking the right to free speech, the U.S. Supreme Court has already held that the media can't be prohibited from publishing the name of a rape victim that they obtained from public records. Generally, American judges hold that if you disclose something to a few people, you can't stop them from sharing the information with the rest of the world.

That's one reason that the most promising solutions to the problem of embarrassing but true information online may be not legal but technological ones. Instead of suing after the damage is done (or hiring a firm to clean up our messes), we need to explore ways of preemptively making the offending words or pictures disappear.

Zuckerberg said in January to the founder of the publication TechCrunch that Facebook had an obligation to reflect "current social norms" that favored exposure over privacy. "People have really gotten comfortable not only sharing more information and different kinds but more openly and with more people, and that social norm is just something that has evolved over time," he said.

However, norms are already developing to recreate off-the-record spaces in public, with no photos, Twitter posts or blogging allowed. Milk and Honey, an exclusive bar on Manhattan's Lower East Side, requires potential members to sign an agreement promising not to blog about the bar's goings on or to post photos on social-networking sites, and other bars and nightclubs are adopting similar policies. I've been at dinners recently where someone has requested, in all seriousness, "Please don't tweet this"—a custom that is likely to spread.

But what happens when people transgress those norms, using Twitter or tagging photos in ways that cause us serious embarrassment? Can we imagine a world in which new norms develop that make it easier for people to forgive and forget one another's digital sins? [. . .]

Perhaps society will become more forgiving of drunken Facebook pictures in the way Samuel Gosling, the University of Texas, Austin, psychology professor says he expects it might. And some may welcome the end of the segmented self, on the grounds that it will discourage bad behavior and hypocrisy: it's harder to have clandestine affairs when you're broadcasting your every move on Facebook, Twitter and Foursquare. But a humane society values privacy, because it allows people to cultivate different aspects of their personalities in different contexts; and at the moment, the enforced merging of identities that used to be separate is leaving many casualties in its wake. Stacy Snyder couldn't reconcile her "aspiring-teacher self" with her "having-a-few-drinks self": even the impression, correct or not, that she had a drink in a pirate hat at an off-campus party was enough to derail her teaching career.

That doesn't mean, however, that it had to derail her life. After taking down her MySpace profile, Snyder is understandably trying to maintain her privacy: her lawyer told me in a recent interview that she is now working in human resources; she did not respond to a request for comment. But her success as a human being who can change and evolve, learning from her mistakes and growing in wisdom, has nothing to do with the digital file she can never entirely escape. Our character, ultimately, can't be judged by strangers on the basis of our Facebook or Google profiles; it can be judged by only those who know us and have time to evaluate our strengths and weaknesses, face to face and in context, with insight and understanding. In the meantime, as all of us stumble over the challenges of living in a world without forgetting, we need to learn new forms of empathy, new ways of defining ourselves without reference to what others say about us and new ways of forgiving one another for the digital trails that will follow us forever.

Activity 2.4 • Discuss "The Web Means the End of Forgetting"

Explore

In your small group, discuss the following questions, and then report your group's opinion(s) to the class.

1. What is the significance of the article's title?

2. What does Rosen mean when he suggests that in the future Stacy Snyder may be an icon?

3. What is the main point in Rosen's essay? What is he arguing?

4. Does Rosen offer sufficient evidence to make you take his argument seriously? Why or why not?

5. Are you a member of any social networking sites? What can you do in order to protect your reputation?

6. A woman interviewed in the article said, in regard to being tagged in online photos, "you have movie-star issues—and you're just a person." If you are a member of any social networking sites, do you tag friends in photos? Is it important to be careful about this? Why or why not?

Collaborate

Activity 2.5 • **Apply the Checklist of Essential Elements in an Argument**

Apply the Checklist of Essential Elements in an Argument (discussed on p. 50) to "The Web Means the End of Forgetting" or another text that your instructor specifies. In your group or individually, check off the following elements and be prepared to explain your selections.

- A debatable issue
- A clearly stated position, claim statement or thesis
- An audience
- Evidence from reliable sources
- Acknowledgment of the opposing argument
- A conclusion and/or call to action

Explore

Activity 2.6 • **What Is the Current State of Identity Protection in Social Networking Sites?**

In your group, explore news, watchdog, and government sites to see if any new laws or other protections have been implemented to safeguard individuals posting personal information on the web. Report what you learn to the class.

Close Reading of a Text

Rhetorical reading involves careful and patient attention to the text, even reading the text several times. Following are several strategies for close reading rhetorically. You do not need to use all of the reading strategies suggested for each essay you read, but as you begin to read rhetorically, you should try all of the strategies at least once to see which ones supplement your natural reading and learning style.

1. Learn about the author. Knowing whether an author is a biologist, a professional writer, or a politician can guide your expectations of the essay. If you are reading in a magazine or journal, you can often discover information in the contributor's notes at the beginning or end of the essay or at the beginning or end of the magazine. Many books have a dust jacket or a page giving a short biography of the author. As you learn about the author, jot down any impressions you may have about the author's purpose in writing the essay. Does the author have an obvious agenda in promoting a certain viewpoint on the topic?

2. **Skim the text.** Once you've gotten to know the author a little, it is helpful to read the essay quickly and superficially by reading the introduction, the first sentence in every paragraph, and the conclusion. Read quickly. When you skim a text, you are not trying to understand it. You are preparing for the more careful read that will follow. If the essay tells a story, skimming will give you a good sense of the chronology of the story. When is the story taking place? How much time seems to pass? If the essay is argumentative, skimming will provide knowledge of the basic structure of the argument and will introduce you to the main points of support. If the essay is primarily informative, you will learn some of the important distinctions and classifications the author uses to organize the information.

   It may be interesting to note whether you can get the gist of the reading by skimming. Has the writer provided topic sentences for paragraphs or sections? If so, the writer is trying to make his or her message easily accessible.

3. **Explore your own knowledge and beliefs on the subject.** Make a list of what you already know about the topic of the text. Then, make a list of what you believe about this topic. Finally, make a note beside each entry that marks where that information or belief came from.

4. **Reflect on the topic.** The final step before reading is reflecting on what you expect from the essay before you begin a careful reading. What does the title lead you to expect from the essay? Does your quick glance at the essay seem to support the title? How do you feel about the essay so far? Does it anger you, interest you, bore you? Do you think you have any experience that relates to the essay? Will your experience and the author's experience lead you to the same conclusions? One effective way to reflect is to freewrite on the topic of the essay. Exploring what you know before you embark on a careful reading of the essay can deepen your responses.

5. **Annotate.** Read the essay slowly, thinking about what meaning the author is trying to convey. It is a good idea to annotate as you read, particularly points that seem important and/or raise questions in your mind. If you don't want to write in your text, try photocopying assigned essays so you can annotate them. You'll probably develop your own system of annotation as you begin to use this technique more often, but here are some basic guidelines to help you begin your annotations.

▌ Underline sentences, phrases, and words that seem important to the essay.

▌ Circle words you don't know but think you understand from the context. You can look them up later to see if the dictionary definition matches the definition you assumed from the context.

▌ Write questions in the margins. If the margins aren't large enough to write a complete question, a couple of words to remind you of what you were thinking and a question mark will do. You can also write brief comments in the margins, again just a few words to remind you of your thoughts.

▌ Number or put check marks in the margin by major points. Careful annotation of each point in the margin will help you later if you choose to outline.

▌ Use arrows, lines, and symbols in the margins to connect ideas in the essay that seem related or depend on each other.

▌ Note transitions, sentence structures, examples, topic sentences, and other rhetorical moves that seem particularly effective in the essay by writing a brief comment or an exclamation mark in the margin next to the underlined text.

See Figure 2.1 on page 65 for an example of an annotated article.

6. Outline. An excellent way to distill the meaning of a text is to create an informal outline of the argument. If, as part of annotating the essay, you jot down the main subject of each paragraph in the margin, this will allow you to see the organization of the essay and outline it easily. An outline should list the focus of the essay and track how that focus unfolds paragraph by paragraph. If you are outlining a narrative essay, the outline will probably follow the chronology of the events. Outlining an informative essay, you might find that the outline tracks the steps of a process or reveals divisions and classifications. Outlining an argumentative essay, you'll probably find your outline works to prove a thesis by making statements which support that thesis, raising objections and refuting them, or, perhaps, proposing solutions to solve a problem.

7. Freewrite about the text. Another way to distill the meaning of a text after you have read it carefully is to lay the essay aside and freewrite for a few minutes about the content and purpose of the essay. If you have not tried freewriting before, it is easy. You simply put your pen to

the paper, focus the topic in your mind, and write whatever comes to mind about the topic for a set period of time, perhaps five minutes. If you cannot think of anything to write, you write, "I can't think of anything to write," and then you continue writing what is in your mind. You may find it helpful to begin your freewriting by writing, "This essay is about . . ." and continue writing, explaining to yourself what you think the essay is about.

8.   Summarize the text. Write a summary of what you consider to be the primary meaning of the text. Your summary should answer certain questions about claims, support, purpose, and audience.

   ▌ What is the author of the essay trying to show or prove (claim)?

   ▌ What does the writer use to convince me that he or she is well informed or right (support)?

   ▌ Why did the writer choose to write this essay (purpose)?

   ▌ Who is the author addressing or writing for (audience)?

To write a clear summary, you have to understand the essay. You might test your understanding by reading the essay again and deciding whether your summary is accurate. Writing summaries helps you understand your assignments and prepares you for the numerous summaries you will complete.

Checklist for Close Reading of a Text

☑ Learn about the author.

☑ Skim the text.

☑ Explore your knowledge and beliefs on the subject.

☑ Reflect on the topic.

☑ Annotate the text.

☑ Outline the text.

☑ Freewrite about the text

☑ Summarize the text.

Reading 2.3

Have you read health-scare articles like "If You've Ever Eaten Pizza, You'll Want to Read About the Toxin That Is Pretty Certainly Ravaging Us From the Bowels Outward" or "This Common Household Item Is Definitely Killing You, Says a New Study"? Can you trust the information presented by such sensationalized articles? Maybe not. According to the Atlantic *article, "The Point When Science Becomes Publicity," the actual studies that are the basis of such articles may blur the distinction between a possible association and a definite connection. Moreover, psychology professor Petroc Sumner traced the source of numerous extreme articles to press releases written by public relations departments of the researchers' own universities rather than to the news media or the researchers themselves.*

James Hamblin, M.D., the article's author, is a senior editor at the Atlantic, *where he writes a health column.*

The Point When Science Becomes Publicity

by James Hamblin, M.D.

One of the sources of academic disdain for popular health media is its reputation for sensationalism and exaggeration. "If You've Ever Eaten Pizza, You'll Want to Read About the Toxin That Is Pretty Certainly Ravaging Us From the Bowels Outward" or "This Common Household Item Is Definitely Killing You, Says a New Study"—when the actual study only posited that a "possible association may potentially exist" between, say, exposure to antibacterial soap and liver disease in a handful of mice who were exposed to more antibacterial soap than any human could ever dream of using, even if they washed their hands literally every time they went to the bathroom.

Petroc Sumner, a professor of psychology at Cardiff University in Wales, has been trying to pinpoint exactly where exaggeration in science reporting comes from. At what level, in the ladder from lab data to news headline, are most inaccuracies introduced?

Yesterday Sumner and colleagues published some important research in the journal BMJ that found that a majority of exaggeration in health stories was traced not to the news outlet, but to the press release—the statement issued by the university's publicity department.

"The framing of health-related information in the national and international media has complex and potentially powerful impacts on healthcare utilization and other health-related behavior," Sumner and colleagues write. "Although it is common to blame media outlets and their journalists for news perceived as exaggerated, sensationalized, or alarmist, most of the inflation detected in our study did not occur de novo in the media but was already present in the text of the press releases."

The goal of a press release around a scientific study is to draw attention from the media, and that attention is supposed to be good for the university, and for the scientists who did the work. Ideally the endpoint of that press release would be the simple spread of seeds of knowledge and wisdom; but it's about attention and prestige and, thereby, money. Major universities employ publicists who work full time to make scientific studies sound engaging and amazing. Those publicists email the press releases to people like me, asking me to cover the story because "my readers" will "love it." And I want to write about health research and help people experience "love" for things. I do!

Across 668 news stories about health science, the Cardiff researchers compared the original academic papers to their news reports. They counted exaggeration and distortion as any instance of implying causation when there was only correlation, implying meaning to humans when the study was only in animals, or giving direct advice about health behavior that was not present in the study. They found evidence of exaggeration in 58 to 86 percent of stories when the press release contained similar exaggeration. When the press release was staid and made no such errors, the rates of exaggeration in the news stories dropped to between 10 and 18 percent.

Even the degree of exaggeration between press releases and news stories was broadly similar.

Sumner and colleagues say they would not shift liability to press officers, but rather to academics. "Most press releases issued by universities are drafted in dialogue between scientists and press officers and are not released without the approval of scientists," the researchers write, "and thus most of the responsibility for exaggeration must lie with the scientific authors."

In an accompanying editorial in the journal, Ben Goldacre, author of the book *Bad Science,* noted that bad news tends to generate more coverage than good and that less rigorous observational studies tend to generate more coverage than robust clinical trials, probably due to the applicability of the subject matter to lay readers.

Guidelines for best practices already exist among academic journals and institutional press officers, he notes, "but these are routinely ignored." So Goldacre corroborates Sumner's argument for accountability: that academics should be held responsible for what's said in the universities' press releases that publicize said academics' research. The press releases will often be read much more widely than the actual journal article, yet many academics take little to no interest in them. Instead, writing an accurate press release should be considered part of the scientific publication process.

"This is not a peripheral matter," writes Goldacre, citing research that has found that media coverage has important effects on people's health behaviors and healthcare utilization, and even on subsequent academic research.

He notes that Sumner was "generous" to avoid naming particular offenders in this study. But Sumner did share with me some of the less egregious examples by email. In one case, a journal article read[,] "This observational study found significant associations between use of antidepressant drugs and adverse outcomes in people aged 65 and older with depression." The press release went on to read[,] "New antidepressants increase risks for elderly." There are of course many reasons why taking antidepressants would be associated with worse outcomes. For example, people with worse symptoms to begin with are more likely to take antidepressants.

"It is very common for this type of thing to happen," said Sumner, "probably partly because the causal phrases are shorter and just sound better. There may be no intention to change the meaning."

There is also, almost always, an implied causal relationship when reporting on a correlation. Every time we note a correlation in anything we publish on this site, at least one of our fair commenters will jump to point out that correlation is not causation. That comment may as well just auto-populate on any article that involves science. Which is fine—even though we're deliberate in not mistaking the relationships for causal—because why even report on a correlation if you don't mean to imply in some way that there is a chance there could be causation?

I asked Sumner how he felt about the press release for his study, because I thought that would be kind of funny.

"We were happy with our press release," he said. "It seemed to stick closely to the article and not claim causal relationships, for example, where we had not."

Appropriately reported scientific claims are a necessary but not sufficient condition in cultivating informed health consumers, but misleading claims are sufficient to do harm. Since many such claims originate within universities, Sumner writes, the scientific community has the ability to improve this situation. But the problem is bigger than a lack of communication between publicists and scientists. The blame for all of this exaggeration is most accurately traced back, according to the researchers, to an "increasing culture of university competition and self-promotion, interacting with the increasing pressures on journalists to do more with less time."

In his ivory tower, in his ivory cap and gown, the academic removes his ivory spectacles just long enough to shake his head at the journalists who are trying to understand his research. The headlines and tweets are wretched misappropriations. Wretched! The ink-stained journalists shake their ink-stained heads in time at the detached academics, at the irrelevance of work written in jargon behind giant paywalls where it will be read by not more than five to seven people, including the nuclear families of the researchers. The families members who, when the subject of the latest journal article comes up at dinner, politely excuse themselves.

But the divide is narrowing every day.

"Our findings may seem like bad news, but we prefer to view them positively," Sumner and colleagues conclude. "If the majority of exaggeration occurs within academic establishments, then the academic community has the opportunity to make an important difference to the quality of biomedical and health-related news."

Figure 2.1 • Example of Close Reading Annotation

The Web Means the End of Forgetting
by Jeffrey Rosen

Four years ago, Stacy Snyder, then a 25-year-old teacher in training at Conestoga Valley High School in Lancaster, Pa., posted a photo on her MySpace page that showed her at a party wearing a pirate hat and drinking from a plastic cup, with the caption "Drunken Pirate." After discovering the page, her supervisor at the high school told her the photo was "unprofessional," and the dean of Millersville University School of Education, where Snyder was enrolled, said she was promoting drinking in virtual view of her underage students. As a result, days before Snyder's scheduled graduation, the university denied her a teaching degree. Snyder sued, arguing that the university had violated her First Amendment rights by penalizing her for her (perfectly legal) after-hours behavior. But in 2008, a federal district judge rejected the claim, saying that because Snyder was a public employee whose photo didn't relate to matters of public concern, her "Drunken Pirate" post was not protected speech.

When historians of the future look back on the perils of the early digital age, Stacy Snyder may well be an icon. The problem she faced is only one example of a challenge that, in big and small ways, is confronting millions of people around the globe: how best to live our lives in a world where the Internet records everything and forgets nothing—where every online photo, status update, Twitter post and blog entry by and about us can be stored forever. With websites like LOL Facebook Moments, which collects and shares embarrassing personal revelations from Facebook users, ill-advised photos and online chatter are coming back to haunt people months or years after the fact.

Reading 2.2

Several years ago, Stacy Snyder was a fairly typical 25-year-old college student training to be a teacher. That all changed forever when she did something that she probably thought was harmless fun—she posted a photo of herself on a social network site. In this article published in The New York Times, Jeffrey Rosen uses Snyder's case to illustrate how notions of privacy are changing because of the ever-growing presence and popularity of social networking sites. What is even more alarming, according to Rosen, is that photos and information, once posted on the web, are there forever. The web does not forget, and this lack of forgetting is changing society's ability to forgive and forget.

You may enjoy posting status updates about your life on a Facebook or Twitter account; however, with employers increasingly conducting background checks on such sites, it's very important to be careful about what you choose to post. This includes status updates, photographs, and videos. If you read the following article carefully, you may never look at social networking sites quite the same again.

Handwritten annotations:
- The problem
- She was a teacher even during off hours
- Snyder argued for her 1st amendment rights.
- information once posted, is forever.
- But Snyder misunderstood 1st amendment rights
- We can no longer rely on the assumption of privacy

Compose

Activity 2.7 • **Apply Close Reading to a Text**

Apply the eight steps of close reading to "The Point When Science Becomes Publicity" or another reading that your instructor specifies. Review the annotation example in Figure 2.1 to begin. Next, make a copy of the text, so that you can annotate it. Then answer these questions in a small group or individually.

1. What can you learn about the author by reading a headnote or doing a search on Google or Wikipedia? Explain briefly.

2. Skim the text of the reading. What did you learn about the purpose of the text?

3. Briefly explain your own knowledge or beliefs about the subject.

4. Reflect on the topic before you read it thoroughly. What does the title lead you to expect? How do you feel about the text so far? Freewrite for five minutes, and then summarize your freewriting in a few coherent sentences.

5. Annotate then outline the essay, then freewrite for five minutes before summarizing the text. Follow the instructions on pp. 59–61 for each step.

Explore

Activity 2.8 • **Discuss "The Point When Science Becomes Publicity"**

According to James Hamblin, articles published in popular health media often sensationalize scientific findings. Use these questions to inform your discussion of "The Point When Science Becomes Publicity" in a small group.

1. What do you think is the source of the sensationalism in this article?

2. In effect, university publicity departments misuse rhetoric to attract reporters' attention. According to Hamblin's argument, why do they do this? Why is it a misuse of rhetoric?

3. Identify one of the examples Hamblin gives of sensationalized health news.

4. In your group, brainstorm other articles you may have read that sensationalize health news. Alternatively, find examples on the Internet. Report the most interesting ones to the class.

The Rhetorical Triangle

When reading a text or listening to a speech, keep in mind the three parts of the rhetorical triangle—writer, audience, and subject (see Figure 2.2). Each of these can be framed as a question.

Figure 2.2 • The Rhetorical Triangle

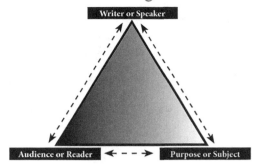

- Who is the **writer**? What is the impression the writer wants to make on the audience? What does the writer do to establish credibility (*ethos*)? How does the writer create common ground with the audience?

- Who is the **intended audience**? How would a logical appeal influence the audience? An ethical appeal? An emotional appeal? What does the audience anticipate in terms of organization and format of the presentation or paper? What is the extent of their knowledge about the subject, and do they have prejudices or preferences?

- What is the **purpose** of the communication? In the case of an argument, the purpose is to persuade. Is that the case with this reading? Is it clear what the writer wants to persuade the audience to believe or to do? Is the request phrased in a logical manner?

Activity 2.9 • **Apply the Rhetorical Triangle**

Explore

For each of the readings presented thus far in the textbook, identify the speaker, the audience, and the purpose. Then, analyze how each of those elements affects the content of the reading.

- "'Columbusing': The Art of Discovering Something that Is Not New," Chapter 1, p. 8.

- "Microsoft Just Laid Off Thousands of Employees with a Hilariously Bad Memo," Chapter 1, p. 15.

- "The Sleepover Question," Chapter 1, p. 20.

- "The Gettysburg Address," Chapter 1, p. 28.

- "Do You Know How Your Mascara is Made?" Chapter 2, p. 37.

- "The Web Means the End of Forgetting," Chapter 2, p. 51.

- "The Point When Science Becomes Publicity," Chapter 2, p. 62.

Compose

Activity 2.10 • **Write a Summary**

Summarizing is an excellent technique to use when preparing for an exam or researching for an essay. It allows you to discern the main points of a text to see what is beneficial for you to know for the exam or paper.

With a classmate, search for an article from a newspaper or magazine that presents a strong argument. Read the article, and list the main points individually. After you've listed the main points, put them into paragraph form.

Beware of the temptation to add your own analysis of what the text is saying. For example, if you are summarizing a scientist's article on global warming, you need to be careful not to reveal your personal opinion about whether or not global warming is occurring or whether or not human actions are to blame. In this assignment, you summarize only. You do not argue or analyze.

When you're finished, compare your summary with that of your partner.

Respond to Multimedia

Increasingly, young "politically minded viewers" are plugging into YouTube, Facebook, and comedy shows like *The Daily Show* and other alternative media instead of traditional news outlets. According to a *New York Times* article, surveys and interviews during the 2008 presidential election indicate that "younger voters tend to be not just consumers of news and current events but conduits as well—sending out emailed links and videos to friends and their social networks. And in turn, they rely on friends and online connections for news to come to them." **Word of mouth** (via email) is replacing traditional media as the major news filter, at least for young viewers. Moreover, in this new process, "viewers" or "writers of email" move seamlessly back and forth between email, text-messaging, television viewing, and Internet surfing, appreciating and sharing the choicest rhetorical pieces with others. "We're talking about a generation that doesn't just like seeing the video in addition to the story—they expect it," said Danny Shea, 23, the associate media editor for *The Huffington Post* (huffingtonpost.com). "And they'll find it elsewhere if you don't give it to them, and then that's the link that's going to be passed around over email and instant message." This multistream, cross-platform method of communication among younger viewers/readers is a fertile forum for rhetorical analysis.

Actually, the lines between oral, written, and visual "texts" have always been somewhat blurred. Speeches delivered orally in person or on television have a visual component, as the audience sees the speaker present the text. A written text is also, in a sense, visual because the audience's mind must process the little squiggles of ink on paper or on the computer screen into words. A visual text such as an advertisement or cartoon often includes written text, and, even if it does not, the image will inspire thoughts that are often distilled into language for expression. Reasonably, many of the same techniques used to analyze written and oral texts also can be applied to visual media (cartoons, advertisements, television, etc.).

Excerpt from "Flawless"

by Beyoncé and Chimamanda Ngozi Adichie

We teach girls to shrink themselves

To make themselves smaller

We say to girls,

"You can have ambition

But not too much

You should aim to be successful

But not too successful

Otherwise you will threaten the man."

Because I am female

I am expected to aspire to marriage

I am expected to make my life choices

Always keeping in mind that

Marriage is the most important

Now marriage can be a source of

Joy and love and mutual support

But why do we teach girls to aspire to marriage

And we don't teach boys the same?

We raise girls to see each other as competitors

Not for jobs or for accomplishments

Which I think can be a good thing

But for the attention of men

We teach girls that they cannot be sexual beings

In the way that boys are

Feminist: the person who believes in the social

Political, and economic equality of the sexes

Reading 2.4

"Flawless," the hit song from Beyoncé's fifth studio album, includes the voice of Nigerian novelist Chimamanda Ngozi Adichie delivering an excerpt from her 2012 TEDx Talk, "We Should All be Feminists." Beyoncé Giselle Knowles-Carter is a Grammy-award-winning singer, songwriter, and actress.

Adichie is the author of the acclaimed 2013 novel Americanah, *that Carolyn Kellogg of the* Los Angles Times *calls "a smart and surprisingly funny take on race and gender in contemporary society." Adichie was awarded a MacArthur "Genius" Fellowship in 2008 after the publication of her novel,* Half a Yellow Sun, *which is set during Nigeria's Biafran War. Kellogg praises the inclusion of Adichie's excerpt in the middle of Beyoncé's song.*

Explore

Activity 2.11 • Respond to Song Lyrics

In a small group or on your own, explore these discussion questions in response to the excerpt from "Flawless" by Beyoncé and Chimamanda Ngozi Adichie.

1. What does Chimamanda Ngozi Adichie's excerpt (from her *TEDx Talk* "We Should All be Feminists") say about what society teaches girls? What does the message in the excerpt have to do with being a feminist?

2. On the Internet, locate the complete lyrics for Beyoncé's song "Flawless" and/or listen to the complete song. How do Beyonce's own lyrics compliment Adichie's excerpt?

3. What argument is Beyoncé making in her song "Flawless"?

4. What do you think of including a non-singing element such as this excerpt in the middle of a popular song? Does it add to or detract from the song's effect?

Collaborate

Activity 2.12 • Consider a Song as an Argument

In your small group, explore the Internet for a song that seems to make an argument, and answer the following questions. Share your findings with the class.

1. What message is the artist/group trying to transmit with the song?

2. What are some lyrics that help to support this message?

3. How would you describe the musical style of the song? In what ways does the style of singing and instrumentation help convey the rhetorical argument?

Respond to Visual Rhetoric

Methods of analyzing visual rhetoric draw upon several theoretical traditions. In art criticism, viewers may look for symbolism in an image or consider what meaning the artist was trying to convey. Semiotics views images as having intertextuality, as similar images come to have similar meanings, and those meanings may create similar emotions in the viewer. Rhetoricians, as you might expect, consider the argument that an image may present to a viewer. They think about how the subject of the image is presented in relation to other elements in the visual, how the image is cropped, and what types of lighting and colors are present. Rhetoricians also pay particular attention to the interplay between the visual image and any text that may appear with the image and how the two together construct an argument.

Courtesy BMW premium advertising

In the BMW advertisement shown above, for example, a beautiful blonde-haired young woman is presented without clothes and lying down with her hair artfully arranged in waves. *Salon* magazine reprinted a copy of the BMW advertisement, pointing out that, "in small print scrawled across her bare shoulder, it reads: 'You know you're not the first.' As your eyes drift to the bottom of the advertisement—and the top of her chest—you learn that it's an advertisement for BMW's premium selection of used cars."

Of course, sexual appeal has been used for decades to sell a whole range of products. However, what do you think is BMW's argument here? *Salon* thinks the ad is implying, "Used cars, used women" and that the ad gives a "whole new meaning" to BMW's slogan, printed in the ad: "Sheer Driving Pleasure."

The image that appears on the next page, surprisingly, isn't advertising a car. No, it is selling a community college, West Hills College, capitalizing on the idea that with all the money you would save by going to a community college, you could buy a nice car.

Two years at West Hills College: $600
vs.
Two years at a UC school: $28,000
Why not spend $27,400 on something else?

Courtesy West Hills College

Explore

Activity 2.13 • Interpret Advertisements

On your own, explore the rhetorical implications of the two advertisements referenced in this section using these discussion questions.

1. What is the symbolism of the beautiful young woman (presumably naked) posed as she is in the BMW advertisement?

2. What meaning do you think the tag line, "You know you're not the first," adds to the image? Then, when you realize that the image is an ad for BMW used cars, does your interpretation of this tag line's meaning change?

3. What are the creators of the West Hills College advertisement trying to say by showing the image of the student sitting on the car?

4. The use of fonts is another important element in transmitting a message in an advertisement. In the West Hills College ad, why are the words "and save" written in a different font and inserted with the caret?

5. As a college student, would you be convinced by the West Hills advertisement? Why or why not? What elements exist in the ad that would or would not convince you to attend the college mentioned?

6. Do you find the BMW advertisement amusing, objectionable, or appealing? Does it make you want to buy a used BMW?

Activity 2.14 • Find Advertisements with Effective Arguments

Collaborate

Bring to class an advertisement that you think makes an effective argument. It can be torn from a magazine or downloaded from the Internet. In your small group, evaluate each advertisement for its effectiveness in selling something, and choose the one with the most successful argument. Present your choice to the class along with an explanation of why you think it is effective.

Reading 2.5

Why Has Godzilla Grown?

by Lisa Wade

Recently, the Internet chuckled at the visual below. It shows that, since Godzilla made his first movie appearance in 1954, he has tripled in size.

Kris Holt, at PolicyMic, suggests that his enlargement is in response to growing skylines. She writes:

> As time has passed, buildings have grown ever taller too. If Godzilla had stayed the same height throughout its entire existence, it would be much less imposing on a modern cityscape.

This seems plausible. Buildings have gotten taller and so, to preserve the original feel, Godzilla would have to grow too.

Why has Godzilla grown over the years? One possible explanation is that buildings have grown taller, and Godzilla has grown to keep up. However, Godzilla has grown at a faster rate than skyscrapers, as you can see from the graphs "Godzilla Through the Years" and "History of the World's Tallest Skyscrapers." The most recent Godzilla is three times the size of the original, while today's tallest skyscraper is much less than three times the size of the Empire State Building, the tallest building at the time of the original Godzilla.

According to an article in Sociological Images *by professor Lisa Wade, the best explanation is that the flood of advertising spawned by the Internet has resulted in advertisers resorting to shock value. The article quotes media guru Sut Jhally asking, "So overwhelming has the commercial takeover of culture become, that it has now become a problem for advertisers who now worry about clutter and noise. That is, how do you make your ads stand out from the commercial impressions that people are exposed to?"*

You make Godzilla stand out by making her disproportionally large. Though the article doesn't use the term "visual rhetoric," that's what it is talking about. In today's media climate, for something, even Godzilla, to make a medial splash, it has to be bigger, weirder, more violent, or more gorgeous.

Godzilla through the Years

| 50 Meters | 55 Meters | 80 Meters | 100 Meters | 120-150 Meters |
| 1954-1975, 2001 | 1999-2000, 2002-2003 | 1984-1989 | 1991-1995, 2004 | 2014 |

But rising buildings can't be the only explanation. According to this graphic, the tallest building at the time of Gozilla's debut was the Empire State Building, rising to 381 meters. The tallest building in the world today is (still) the Burj Khalifa. At 828 meters, it's more than twice as tall as the Empire State Building, but it's far from three times as tall, or 1,143 meters.

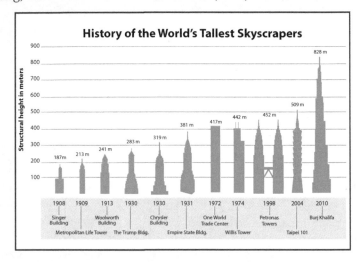

Is there an alternate explanation? Here's one hypothesis.

In 1971, the average American was exposed to about 500 advertisements per day. Today, because of the Internet, they are exposed to over 5,000. Every. Day.

Media critic Sut Jhally argues that the flood of advertising has forced marketers to shift strategies. Specifically, he says

So overwhelming has the commercial takeover of culture become, that it has now become a problem for advertisers who now worry about clutter and noise. That is, how do you make your ads stand out from the commercial impressions that people are exposed to.

One strategy has been to ratchet up shock value. "You need to get eyeballs. You need to be loud," said Kevin Kay, Spike's programming chief.

So, to increase shock value, everything is being made more extreme. Compared to the early '90s, before the Internet was a fixture in most homes and businesses, advertising—and I'm guessing media in general—has gotten more extreme in lots of ways. Things are sexier, more violent, more gorgeous, more satirical, and weirder.

So, Godzilla because, eyeballs.

Explore

Activity 2.15 • Consider Shock Value in Today's Cartoon Characters

After you read Wade's article, discuss the following in your group.

1. What argument does sociology professor Lisa Wade make about the growth of Godzilla's size in advertisements over the years?

2. If you accept Wade's argument, what does it have to do with visual rhetoric?

3. What other cartoon characters in advertisements or other media also have grown or otherwise changed because of a response to the pressure to stand out from the clutter and noise of today's media world?

4. How have other cartoon characters been altered for shock value?

Interaction between Texts and Images

Many of the texts we encounter in everyday life—in newspapers, magazines, and on the Internet—are not texts in isolation but texts combined with images. Indeed, when readers first glance at one of these media, likely their attention is caught first by photos, then by headlines. Only after being engaged by these attention-getting visual elements (for headlines are visual elements as well as written) are readers likely to focus on the written text. Student writers today, like professionals, have access to the use of visual elements in their compositions, and adding photos can not only catch the reader's attention but also emphasize particular points of an argument or create an overall mood.

Reading 2.6

Take a look at the images in this Rolling Stone *article by Andy Greene. Greene writes about a tribute record on Buddy Holly called* Rave *that several famous musical artists contributed to. Think about how Greene's choice of text and image pairings affect the rhetorical impact of the article.*

All-Star Rockers Salute Buddy Holly
by Andy Greene

All-Star Rockers Salute Buddy Holly

McCartney, Cee Lo, the Black Keys, Kid Rock and more cut killer covers disc

NOT FADE AWAY
Holly in 1950. McCartney and Cee Lo recorded new songs commemorating Holly's 75th birthday.

When Buddy Holly died in a plane crash in 1959, he was just 22 years old and had been writing and recording songs for only about two years. But that music—including immortal hits like "Not Fade Away" and "Peggy Sue"—has had an incalculable impact on rock history. "He was a major influence on the Beatles," Paul McCartney told Rolling Stone recently. "John and I spent hours trying to work out how to play the opening riff to "That'll Be the Day," and we were truly blessed by the heavens the day we figured it out. It was the first song John, George and I ever recorded."

A half-century later, McCartney has returned to Holly's catalog, cutting a smoking rendition of "It's So Easy." It's one of 19 newly recorded Holly covers—by an all-star lineup including the Black Keys, My Morning Jacket, Kid Rock Fiona Apple, Patti Smith, and Lou Reed—for the tribute

disc *Rave on Buddy Holly*, spearheaded by Randall Poster, music supervisor of movies such as *The Royal Tenenbaums* and *I'm Not There*. "We wanted to commemorate Buddy's 75th birthday," Poster says. "I've used a lot of his songs in movies, and they're so powerful and so ripe for interpretation."

Florence and the Machine cut a New Orleans-flavored version of "Not Fade Away" while on tour in the Big Easy last year. "My grandmother took me to the musical *Buddy: The Buddy Holly Story* when I was a kid, and it changed my life," says singer Florence Welch. "When we were in New Orleans, we decided

it would be good to use the environment around us, so we brought in local Cajun musicians." Cee Lo Green tackled the relatively obscure "You're So Square (Baby, I Don't Care)." "We wanted to keep the rockabilly intact," he says. "But we broadened it and gave it a bit of something unique to me. There's something Americana about it, something country and something African."
Smith selected "Words of Love." "During the song she talks in Spanish and is sort of channeling [Holly's widow] Maria Elena Holly," says Poster. "It's so romantic and so novel. More times than not, we were just overwhelmed by the power of the renditions that we received." Despite Holly's extremely brief career, Poster thinks the set could have been even longer: "There's probably a half-dozen more songs we could have done. If I had more time and more of a budget, I would have kept on going."   ANDY GREENE

Explore

Activity 2.16 • Analyze Interaction between Texts and Images

Read the article, "All-Star Rockers Salute Buddy Holly," by Andy Greene, published in *Rolling Stone* magazine. Look at how the images and layout work together, and respond to these questions on your own.

1. What rhetorical purpose do the photos of these musicians achieve in relation to the article? Hint: think about the *ethos* (credibility, reputation, power) of these particular musicians, especially when they appear together on the page.

2. Consider the way the text is wrapped around the pictures. In particular, notice how this layout suggests a close relationship between Buddy Holly, Paul McCartney, and Cee Lo Green. What does this layout signify?

How to Make a Kindle Cover from a Hollowed Out Hardback Book

by Justin Meyers

Kindle users love reading. But let's face it—nothing compares to the feel of a book is in your hands.

Sure, Amazon's Kindle makes it possible to read more books, clears up a lot of shelf space, fits snugly in anyone's baggage and can actually be cheaper in the long run. But each reading feels the same. The only difference is the words you read and your reaction to them.

The author of the following article explains why you would want to make a Kindle cover out of an old book instead of buying a new Kindle cover. What does the article say are the drawbacks of the Kindle? Think about it. These instructions are an argument, saying in text and photos that as wonderful as the Kindle is, it does not satisfy the needs of a reader to touch and smell a book. The author attempts to rectify the Kindle's shortcomings through these instructions for making a cover out of a book.

Notice also how the author uses photos to illustrate his text. If you had just the text and no photos, following the instructions would be much more difficult.

You begin to miss that sometimes rough feel of a hardback book, along with the slick, almost slippery design of a paperback. Each book seems to have a smell of its own, something unique. And getting your hands dirty with ink from the finely written words was half the journey.

The Kindle erases that part of your reading experience. It feels the same, smells the same and even looks the same. Instead of turning pages, which is different sizes, thicknesses and colors from book to book, you're pressing the same button over and over again. In some ways, reading a classic on your Kindle actually devalues its adventure. But the eBook reader is convenient, practically weightless and serves up immediate literature consumption.

So where's the compromise?

Well, you can have the best of both worlds—sort of . . .

[Twitter user] @ebonical has crafted the perfect Kindle case—out of a hard-cover book. Kindle cases can be expensive, so making a homemade Kindle cover is the perfect weekend project. And chances are you already have the perfect book for your Kindle collecting dust on your bookshelf. If not, you'll need to shop the local bookstores.

"I decided to carve out the pages of a printed book and thus complete the poetic circle of digital book readers destroying the printed word.

"Getting the right book turned out to be harder than I thought as most hard-cover books are designed to be a particular size and variance is slight. Too small and the edges would be brittle. Too large and it would just become a hassle and ruin the point of having the small digital reader in the first place. With some time spent scouring thrift shops and second hand book stalls I managed, with some luck, to find what seemed to be the right book."

So, then how do you actually make the Kindle book cover?

STEP 1 Gather the Materials

- Your perfectly-sized hardcover book
- Hobby PVA glue (polyvinyl acetate) or Elmer's white glue
- Paintbrush
- Scalpel, box cutter or other sharp utility knife
- Ruler
- Pencil
- More books (for use as weights)

STEP 2 Crafting Your Kindle Case

Getting your book ready for your Kindle is an easy process, though a lengthy one.

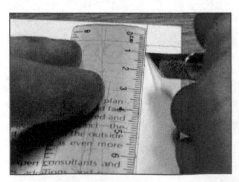

You begin by choosing where you want your hole to start. Once you have your spot picked, you use the paintbrush to spread the glue onto the edges of the pages where the hole will be cut. Use your extra books to weigh it down during the drying process.

When dry, open the book back up to your cho- sen starting point. Use the ruler and pen- cil to mark your hole the size of the Kindle. Once all marked, use your utility knife to start cutting on the outline. It's probably best to use your ruler as a

straight edge to help guide the blade along, for a better, straighter cut. This is the lon- gest step, because you have a lot to cut through. The time will vary depending on how deep your book is. I wouldn't recom- mend *War and Peace*.

Once you've gotten all the way to the back cover, the rest is easy. Just clean up the edges of your cuts as best you can, then use your paintbrush again to spread some glue along the cut edges.

TIP: When choosing your first page to cut, it's good to actually save it for later. Don't cut with the rest of them. When you have your hole fully cut open

and have applied the glue, apply an- other thin line on the top border of your actual first page cut (essentially, the second page). Then close the book and add the weights to the top and let dry. Saving the first page helps reduce the chance of you accidentally gluing unwanted pages to cut ones, causing you to have to cut the pages you didn't want to cut to open the hole back up. Saving your first page makes it premeditated.

After fully dried, open it up and cut the final page (first page) to open the hole up. Then, you'll need to let it dry again, with the book open. After dried, that's it. You're done!

Activity 2.17 • **Write and Illustrate Instructions**

Write and illustrate your own set of instructions for an activity that includes an argument.

For example, during a lawn party at the White House, First Lady Michelle Obama served Carrot Lemonade to children who gave the drink rave reviews. Such a recipe could include an introduction explaining that creating healthy adaptations of popular foods and drinks for children only works if they taste good. Or, you might write instructions for how to remove geotags from photos before posting them on Facebook or other social networking sites.

In your instructions, you could explain that this process prevents people you don't know from learning where you took the picture—and possibly learning where you live if you took it at home. Your argument would be that it is important to protect your privacy when you post photos on the Internet.

Try out your instructions on a friend, so you are sure you have included all the necessary steps and illustrated them adequately. Don't forget to include a brief statement of your argument, as does the writer of the Kindle cover article.

Activity 2.18 • **Summarize the Argument in Your Illustrations**

Write one or more sentences summarizing your argument in the illustrations you wrote for Activity 2.17. For example, the author of "How to Make a Kindle Book Cover from a Hollowed Out Hardback Book" is arguing in his instructions that the Kindle is wonderful but does not completely satisfy the desire of a reader to touch and smell a book.

Activity 2.19 • **Write on Your Blog**

Read an article on the Internet related to a topic in which you're interested. Make sure the article has a substantial amount of text and related images. In your blog, discuss how the text and the images both contribute to the article's rhetorical message. Include the title of the article, the author, the name of the publication or web page, and a link to the article.

Activity 2.20 • **Write in Your Commonplace Book**

Compose

What do you read for fun? Magazines, blogs, books? Do you engage in what Louise Rosenblatt calls "aesthetic reading"? (See the section titled, "Ways of Reading Rhetorically") Write down a quote in your commonplace book from something that you have read for fun. First, reflect about what the quote means to you. Then, comment about why it is important to read things for fun and how that experience is different than reading to learn.

c h a p t e r   3

Persuading Rhetorically

Praxis in Action

If You Want to Write Well, Then Read

Amber Lea Clark, M.L.S. Student in Liberal Studies, Southern Methodist University

"Readers make the best writers." I can't tell you how many times my instructors have said those words. As I have become a reader, I have learned that this is true. Reading teaches me about the construction of stories and arguments. In a movie or TV show, I almost instantly know who did it or who not to trust based on previous movies or TV shows I've watched. The same goes for analyzing arguments. Through reading critically, I have learned to see when an author is trying to convince me by manipulating my feelings versus persuading me by providing all of the facts. I can distinguish between fair representation of an issue, embellishment of truth, and bitter sarcasm. Every text needs to be taken with a grain of salt, slowly simmered, and thought about before the final evaluation can be made.

This chapter provides sample essays that illustrate different types of rhetorical arguments or appeals—arguments from *ethos* (credibility), *pathos* (emotion), or *logos* (logic). I encourage you to read them carefully. What do you see? How has each writer used his or her credibility, your emotions, or logic to reach you—the audience? How would each essay be different if the author had chosen to emphasize a different appeal, or would that even be possible?

Sentence structure, word use, and argument construction—the ability to perform each of these writing tasks effectively comes from more than just the practice we get from completing an assignment. It comes from analyzing others' arguments—my classmates' and published authors'. It comes from thinking critically as I read. Does this convince me? What is the author using for sources? Is this logical or a logical fallacy? Had I not read how other writers construct their arguments, I would never have become a better writer. Start now; become a reader.

Discover the *Kairos*–The Opening for Argument

Kairos is a Greek word often translated as the right or opportune moment to do something, though it has no exact English translation. The first recorded

use of the word *kairos* is in Homer's *Iliad*, where it appears as an adjective referring to an arrow striking the "deadliest spot" on the human body. When the word appears again later in Greek writing as a noun—a *kairos*—it retains this essential meaning as an opening or aperture. Twelve bronze axes with ring openings for wooden shanks are positioned in a line, so archers can practice by aiming at the *kai-*

Ancient Greek archer   *ros* or ring opening, with the arrow passing down the line, through

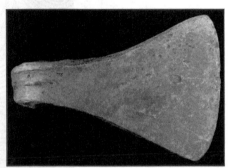

each ax. Clearly, launching an arrow through the *kairos* of twelve axes placed a yard apart required strength, training, practice, and a precise visual and muscle awareness of place. When people today say, "I saw my opening, and I took it," they are conveying this meaning of *kairos* as an opening, combined with the idea of *kairos* as an opportunity.[1]

Ancient bronze ax with a ring hole for a wooden shank

Each time a rhetor (a speaker or writer) constructs an argument, he or she is working within the context of a certain moment, a particular time and place, that come together in a unique opportunity or opening for action—a *kairos*. A *kairos* both constrains and enables what a rhetor can say or write effectively in a particular situation. So, to compose the most effective text, a rhetor must do more than develop a thesis or statement of the main idea that takes a position about the subject—he or she must discover the *kairos* of the argument and its ramifications. What opportunities does the *kairos* present for making a persuasive argument, and what restrictions may be wise in consideration of the audience or occasion?

Use Kairos to Make Your Own Argument

Consider the following suggestions for determining the kairotic moment for your argument—the opening of sensitivity where you can shoot your metaphoric arrow.

▌   **Consider timeliness.** What is going on right now with the issue, and how can you emphasize that in an argument? For example, if you are writing

---

1. Rickert, Thomas. "Invention in the Wild: On Locating *Kairos* in Space-Time." *The Locations of Composition*, edited by Christopher J. Keller and Christian R. Weisser, SUNY, 2007, pp. 72-73.

about the death penalty, choose to write about the current cases on death row or the most recent person to be executed. Or, if your topic is about the unemployed exhausting their government benefits and you have, yourself, recently become unemployed, you can use your own experience as an illustration of the problem.

- **Know your audience.** What are the characteristics of the audience? Do they agree with your position on the issue or not? What is their educational level and the extent of their knowledge about the subject? For example, if you are writing about immigration policy reform, does your audience believe there is a need for reform? Do they have personal experience with illegal or legal immigrants? You can judge the amount of background information you need to provide based upon the characteristics of your audience. Also, the most important members of the audience, so far as an argument is concerned, are not those who already agree with you but those who are neutral or even slightly opposed to your position but willing to listen. Be careful not to phrase your argument in ways that are insulting to people who do not agree with you, for if you do so, they will stop listening to you.

- **Find a place to stand.** In the reading that follows, Dr. Martin Luther King, Jr. stood in front of the Lincoln Memorial as he gave his famous speech, "I Have a Dream." This location greatly impacts the speech and increases King's *ethos*, which we discuss in more detail below. You can make a similar rhetorical move, for example, if you live in a border community because you stand, metaphorically and physically, at an important juncture for issues such as immigration, free trade, and national security.

When Dr. Martin Luther King, Jr., gave his "I Have a Dream" speech, his words were carefully crafted to take into consideration the setting in front of the Lincoln Memorial. He said, "Five score years ago, a great American, in whose symbolic shadow we stand today, signed the Emancipation Proclamation." The words "five score" recall the "four score and seven years ago" of President Abraham Lincoln's words in the Gettysburg Address. And King also pointed out that he and his audience that day stood in the "symbolic shadow" of the president who signed the Emancipation Proclamation. In these ways, he made use of Lincoln's shadow to legitimize what he was saying about civil rights.

In other ways, however, the *kairos* of the moment limited what he could say. His audience included both the thousands of people in front of him who were dedicated to the cause of racial equality and also the audience of those millions watching on television who may or may not have agreed with his message.

Thus, the tone of his message needed to be subtly measured not to antagonize those among his audience, particularly the television audience, who may have opposed aspects of the civil rights movement such as school integration. However, he spoke to let both his supporters and his opponents know, "The whirlwinds of revolt will continue to shake the foundations of our nation until the bright day of justice emerges." Yes, King advocated nonviolent demonstrations, but they were demonstrations nonetheless; he was putting opponents on notice that the disruptions caused by demonstrations would continue "until justice emerges." King consistently took the high road while maintaining the power of the kairotic moment when he spoke. This is one reason why his words continue to be studied decades after his death.

Reading 3.1

Dr. Martin Luther King, Jr. delivered this speech on August 28, 1963, at the Lincoln Memorial in Washington, D.C., as part of the March on Washington for Jobs and Freedom. A Baptist minister, King received the Nobel Peace Prize in 1964 for his efforts to end racial discrimination through nonviolent means. He was assassinated in 1968.

I Have a Dream

by Dr. Martin Luther King, Jr.

I am happy to join with you today in what will go down in history as the greatest demonstration for freedom in the history of our nation.

Five score years ago, a great American, in whose symbolic shadow we stand today, signed the Emancipation Proclamation. This momentous decree came as a great beacon light of hope to millions of Negro slaves who had been seared in the flames of withering injustice. It came as a joyous daybreak to end the long night of their captivity.

But one hundred years later, the Negro still is not free. One hundred years later, the life of the Negro is still sadly crippled by the manacles of segregation and the chains of discrimination. One hundred years later, the Negro lives on a lonely island of poverty in the midst of a vast ocean of material prosperity. One hundred years later, the Negro is still languished in the corners of American soci-ety and finds himself an exile in his own land. And so we've come here today to dramatize a shameful condition.

In a sense we've come to our nation's capital to cash a check. When the architects of our republic wrote the magnificent words of the Constitution and the Declaration of Independence, they were signing a promissory note to which every American was to fall heir. This note was a promise that all men, yes, black men as well as white men, would be guaranteed the "unalienable Rights" of "Life, Liberty and the pursuit of Happiness." It is obvious today that America has defaulted on this promissory note, insofar as her citizens of color are concerned. Instead of honoring this sacred obligation, America has given the Negro people a bad check, a check which has come back marked "insufficient funds."

But we refuse to believe that the bank of justice is bankrupt. We refuse to believe that there are insufficient funds in the great vaults of opportunity of this nation. And so, we've come to cash this check, a check that will give us upon demand the riches of freedom and the security of justice.

We have also come to this hallowed spot to remind America of the fierce urgency of Now. This is no time to engage in the luxury of cooling off or to take the tranquilizing drug of gradualism. Now is the time to make real the promises of democracy. Now is the time to rise from the dark and desolate valley of segregation to the sunlit path of racial justice. Now is the time to lift our nation from the quicksands of racial injustice to the solid rock of brotherhood. Now is the time to make justice a reality for all of God's children.

It would be fatal for the nation to overlook the urgency of the moment. This sweltering summer of the Negro's legitimate discontent will not pass until there is an invigorating autumn of freedom and equality. Nineteen sixty-three is not an end, but a beginning. And those who hope that the Negro needed to blow off steam and will now be content will have a rude awakening if the nation returns to business as usual. And there will be neither rest nor tranquility in America until the Negro is granted his citizenship rights. The whirlwinds of revolt will continue to shake the foundations of our nation until the bright day of justice emerges.

But there is something that I must say to my people, who stand on the warm threshold which leads into the palace of justice: In the process of gaining our rightful place, we must not be guilty of wrongful deeds. Let us not seek to satisfy our thirst for freedom by drinking from the cup of bitterness and hatred. We must forever conduct our struggle on the high plane of dignity and discipline. We must not allow our creative protest to degenerate into physical violence. Again and again, we must rise to the majestic heights of meeting physical force with soul force.

The marvelous new militancy which has engulfed the Negro community must not lead us to a distrust of all white people, for many of our white brothers, as evidenced by their presence here today, have come to realize that their destiny is tied up with our destiny. And they have come to realize that their freedom is inextricably bound to our freedom.

> We cannot walk alone.
> And as we walk, we must make the pledge that we shall always
> march ahead.
> We cannot turn back.

There are those who are asking the devotees of civil rights, "When will you be satisfied?" We can never be satisfied as long as the Negro is the victim of the unspeakable horrors of police brutality. We can never be satisfied as long as our bodies, heavy with the fatigue of travel, cannot gain lodging in the motels of the highways and the hotels of the cities. We cannot be satisfied as long as the negro's basic mobility is from a smaller ghetto to a larger one. We can never be satisfied as long as our children are stripped of their selfhood and robbed of their dignity by a sign stating: "For Whites Only." We cannot be satisfied as long as a Negro in Mississippi cannot vote and a Negro in New York believes he has nothing for which to vote. No, no, we are not satisfied, and we will not be satisfied until "justice rolls down like waters, and righteousness like a mighty stream."[1]

I am not unmindful that some of you have come here out of great trials and tribulations. Some of you have come fresh from narrow jail cells. And some of you have come from areas where your quest—quest for freedom left you battered by the storms of persecution and staggered by the winds of police brutality. You have been the veterans of creative suffering. Continue to work with the faith that unearned suffering is redemptive. Go back to Mississippi, go back to Alabama, go back to South Carolina, go back to Georgia, go back to Louisiana, go back to the slums and ghettos of our northern cities, knowing that somehow this situation can and will be changed.

Let us not wallow in the valley of despair, I say to you today, my friends.

And so even though we face the difficulties of today and tomorrow, I still have a dream. It is a dream deeply rooted in the American dream.

I have a dream that one day this nation will rise up and live out the true meaning of its creed: "We hold these truths to be self-evident, that all men are created equal."

I have a dream that one day on the red hills of Georgia, the sons of former slaves and the sons of former slave owners will be able to sit down together at the table of brotherhood.

I have a dream that one day even the state of Mississippi, a state sweltering with the heat of injustice, sweltering with the heat of oppression, will be transformed into an oasis of freedom and justice.

I have a dream that my four little children will one day live in a nation where they will not be judged by the color of their skin but by the content of their character.

I have a dream today!

I have a dream that one day, down in Alabama, with its vicious racists, with its governor having his lips dripping with the words of "interposition" and "nullification"—one day right there in Alabama little black boys and black girls will be able to join hands with little white boys and white girls as sisters and brothers.

I have a dream today!

I have a dream that one day every valley shall be exalted, and every hill and mountain shall be made low, the rough places will be made plain, and the crooked places will be made straight; "and the glory of the Lord shall be revealed and all flesh shall see it together."[2]

This is our hope, and this is the faith that I go back to the South with.

With this faith, we will be able to hew out of the mountain of despair a stone of hope. With this faith, we will be able to transform the jangling discords of our nation into a beautiful symphony of brotherhood. With this faith, we will be able to work together, to pray together, to struggle together, to go to jail together, to stand up for freedom together, knowing that we will be free one day.

And this will be the day—this will be the day when all of God's children will be able to sing with new meaning:

> My country 'tis of thee, sweet land of liberty, of thee I sing.
> Land where my fathers died, land of the Pilgrim's pride,
> From every mountainside, let freedom <u>ring</u>!
> And if America is to be a great nation, this must become true.
> And so let freedom ring from the prodigious hilltops of New Hampshire.
> Let freedom ring from the mighty mountains of New York.
> Let freedom ring from the heightening Alleghenies of
>   Pennsylvania.
> Let freedom ring from the snow-capped Rockies of Colorado.
> Let freedom ring from the curvaceous slopes of California.
> But not only that:
> Let freedom ring from Stone Mountain of Georgia.
> Let freedom ring from Lookout Mountain of Tennessee.
> Let freedom ring from every hill and molehill of Mississippi.
> From every mountainside, let freedom ring.

And when this happens, when we allow freedom to ring, when we let it ring from every village and every hamlet, from every state and every city, we will be able to speed up that day when all of God's children, black men and white men, Jews and Gentiles, Protestants and Catholics, will be able to join hands and sing in the words of the old Negro spiritual:

> Free at last! Free at last!
> Thank God Almighty, we are free at last![3]

[1] Amos 5:24 (rendered precisely in The American Standard Version of the Holy Bible)

[2] Isaiah 40:4–5 (King James Version of the Holy Bible). Quotation marks are excluded from part of this moment in the text because King's rendering of Isaiah 40:4 does not precisely follow the KJV version from which he quotes (e.g., "hill" and "mountain" are reversed in the KJV). King's rendering of Isaiah 40:5, however, is precisely quoted from the KJV.

[3] "Free at Last" from *American Negro Songs* by J. W. Work.

Activity 3.1 • Use Microsoft's Comment Feature to Annotate a Text

Compose

If you download Dr. Martin Luther King, Jr.'s speech from *American Rhetoric* (www.americanrhetoric.com), you can make use of Microsoft's Comment feature to annotate the speech with your comments, as is done in the example below. In Microsoft Word, highlight the text you want to annotate, go to the "Insert" pull-down menu, and select "Comment." A box will appear where you can enter your comment.

I am happy to join with you today in what will go down in history as the greatest demonstration for freedom in the history of our nation.

Five score years ago, a great American, in whose symbolic shadow we stand today, signed the Emancipation Proclamation. This momentous decree came as a great beacon light of hope to millions of Negro slaves who had been seared in the flames of withering injustice. It came as a joyous daybreak to end the long night of their captivity.

Comment [1]: Reference to Lincoln's Gettysburg Address

But one hundred years later, the Negro still is not free. One hundred years later, the life of the Negro is still sadly crippled by the manacles of segregation and that chains of discrimination. One hundred years later, the Negro lives on a lonely island of poverty in the midst of a vast ocean of material prosperity. One hundred years later, the Negro is

Activity 3.2 • Discuss "I Have a Dream"

Collaborate

Read the "I Have a Dream" speech by Dr. Martin Luther King, Jr., and, if possible, watch the speech. It is archived at *AmericanRhetoric.com*, where it is listed as the most requested speech and is #1 in the website's list of the top 100 American speeches.

Discuss the *kairos* of Dr. King's speech. What was the occasion? Who was his audience, both present and absent? What were the issues he spoke about?

How did Dr. King take advantage of the *kairos* of the situation in the wording of his speech?

Why do you think the speech continues to be so popular and influential?

Activity 3.3 • Identify the *Kairos*

Identifying the *kairos* in Dr. Martin Luther King, Jr.'s speech in front of the Lincoln Memorial is easy. In some speeches, however, identifying the *kairos* is more difficult. Every speech and every text has a *kairos*, but some rhetors are better at identifying it and utilizing it than others. Identify the *kairos* in the following readings that have appeared thus far in the text. Then discuss in your group how the writer or speaker does or does not utilize *kairos* to maximum effect.

- " 'Columbusing': The Art of Discovering Something that is Not New," Chapter 1, p. 8.

- "Microsoft Just Laid Off Thousands of Employees with a Hilariously Bad Memo," Chapter 1, p. 15.

- "The Sleepover Question," Chapter 1, p. 20.

- "Do You Know How Your Mascara is Made?" Chapter 2, p. 37.

- "The Web Means the End of Forgetting," Chapter 2, p. 51.

- "The Point When Science Becomes Publicity," Chapter 2, p. 62.

- "Why Has Godzilla Grown?" Chapter 2, p. 73.

Activity 3.4 • Analyze an Audience

Select a group that you do not belong to, and analyze it as a potential audience. To begin your analysis, you might locate a blog on the Internet that advocates a point of view different from your own. For example, if you agree with theories about climate change, read a blog frequented by those who do not share your perspectives. If you are a Democrat, look for an Independent or Republican blog. Find a yoga blog if you are a football fan. Read a week's worth of blog entries, and write a one-page analysis, including the answers to these questions.

1. What are the two or three issues of primary interest to the group? What is the group's general position on each issue?

2. Who are these people? Where do they live? What is their educational level?

3. What is the extent of their knowledge about the issues of primary interest? Are they familiar with the evidence, or do they just repeat opinions?

Aristotle's Persuasive Appeals

Some theorists associate the rhetorical triangle directly with Aristotle's **appeals** (or proofs): *ethos, pathos,* and *logos*. **Ethos** refers to the writer's (or speaker's) credibility; **pathos** refers to emotion used to sway the audience; and, finally, **logos** refers to the writer's purpose (or subject), for an effective argument will include evidence and other supporting details to back up the author's claims.

Aristotle wrote:

> Of those proofs that are furnished through the speech there are three kinds. Some reside in the character [*ethos*] of the speaker, some in a certain disposition [*pathos*] of the audience and some in the speech itself, through its demonstrating or seeming to demonstrate [*logos*].

Contemporary theorist Wayne C. Booth said something similar:

> The common ingredient that I find in all writing that I admire—excluding for now novels, plays, and poems—is something that I shall reluctantly call the rhetorical stance, a stance which depends upon discovering and maintaining in any writing situation a proper balance among the three elements that are at work in any communicative effort: the available arguments about the subject itself [*logos*], the interests and peculiarities of the audience [*pathos*], and the voice, the implied character of the speaker [*ethos*].

Arguments from *Logos*

Logos, or reason, was Aristotle's favorite of the three persuasive appeals, and he bemoaned the fact that humans could not be persuaded through reason alone, indeed that they sometimes chose emotion over reason. Aristotle also used the term *logos* to mean rational discourse. To appeal to *logos* means to organize an argument with a clear claim or thesis, supported by logical reasons that are presented in a well-organized manner that is internally consistent. It can also mean the use of facts and statistics as evidence. However, *logos* without elements of *pathos* and *ethos* can be dry, hard to understand, and boring.

Consider the following logical argument that advocates televising executions.

Reading 3.2

In this opinion piece published in The New York Times, *Zachary B. Shemtob and David Lat argue what they know is going to be an unpopular position in the United States—that executions should be televised. Shemtob is an assistant professor of criminal justice at Connecticut State University, and Lat is a former federal prosecutor who also founded a legal blog,* Above the Law. *They reason, "democracy demands maximum accountability and transparency." Knowing that their position contradicts present policy, they carefully address possible objections to their position, such as the idea that executions are too gruesome to put on television.*

Executions Should Be Televised

by Zachary B. Shemtob and David Lat

[In July of 2011], Georgia conducted its third execution of the year. This would have passed relatively unnoticed if not for a controversy surrounding its video-taping. Lawyers for the condemned inmate, Andrew Grant DeYoung, had persuaded a judge to allow the recording of his last moments as part of an effort to obtain evidence on whether lethal injection caused unnecessary suffering.

Though he argued for videotaping, one of Mr. DeYoung's defense lawyers, Brian Kammer, spoke out against releasing the footage to the public. "It's a horrible thing that Andrew DeYoung had to go through," Mr. Kammer said, "and it's not for the public to see that."

We respectfully disagree. Executions in the United States ought to be made public.

Right now, executions are generally open only to the press and a few select witnesses. For the rest of us, the vague contours are provided in the morning paper. Yet a functioning democracy demands maximum accountability and transparency. As long as executions remain behind closed doors, those are impossible. The people should have the right to see what is being done in their name and with their tax dollars.

This is particularly relevant given the current debate on whether specific methods of lethal injection constitute cruel and unusual punishment and therefore violate the Constitution.

There is a dramatic difference between reading or hearing of such an event and observing it through image and sound. (This is obvious to those who saw the footage of Saddam Hussein's hanging in 2006 or the death of Neda Agha-Soltan during the protests in Iran in 2009.) We are not calling for opening executions completely to the public—conducting them before a live crowd—but rather for broadcasting them live or recording them for future release, on the Web or TV.

When another Georgia inmate, Roy Blankenship, was executed in June, the prisoner jerked his head, grimaced, gasped and lurched, according to a medical expert's affidavit. The *Atlanta Journal-Constitution* reported that Mr. DeYoung, executed in the same manner, "showed no violent signs in death." Voters should not have to rely on media accounts to understand what takes place when a man is put to death.

Cameras record legislative sessions and presidential debates, and courtrooms are allowing greater television access. When he was an Illinois state senator, President Obama successfully pressed for the videotaping of homicide interrogations and confessions. The most serious penalty of all surely demands equal if not greater scrutiny.

Opponents of our proposal offer many objections. State lawyers argued that making Mr. DeYoung's execution public raised safety concerns. While rioting and pickpocketing occasionally marred executions in the public square in the 18th and 19th centuries, modern security and technology obviate this concern. Little would change in the death chamber; the faces of witnesses and executioners could be edited out, for privacy reasons, before a video was released.

Of greater concern is the possibility that broadcasting executions could have a numbing effect. Douglas A. Berman, a law professor, fears that people might come to equate human executions with putting pets to sleep. Yet this seems overstated. While public indifference might result over time, the initial broadcasts would undoubtedly get attention and stir debate.

Still others say that broadcasting an execution would offer an unbalanced picture—making the condemned seem helpless and sympathetic, while keeping the victims of the crime out of the picture. But this is beside the point: the defendant is being executed precisely because a jury found that his crimes were so heinous that he deserved to die.

Ultimately the main opposition to our idea seems to flow from an unthinking disgust—a sense that public executions are archaic, noxious, even barbarous. Albert Camus related in his essay "Reflections on the Guillotine" that viewing executions turned him against capital punishment. The legal scholar John D. Bessler suggests that public executions might have the same effect on the public today; Sister Helen Prejean, the death penalty abolitionist, has urged just such a strategy.

That is not our view. We leave open the possibility that making executions public could strengthen support for them; undecided viewers might find them less disturbing than anticipated.

Like many of our fellow citizens, we are deeply conflicted about the death penalty and how it has been administered. Our focus is on accountability and openness. As Justice John Paul Stevens wrote in *Baze v. Rees*, a 2008 case involving a challenge to lethal injection, capital punishment is too often "the product of habit and inattention rather than an acceptable deliberative process that weighs the costs and risks of administering that penalty against its identifiable benefits."

A democracy demands a citizenry as informed as possible about the costs and benefits of society's ultimate punishment.

Collaborate

Activity 3.5 • Analyze an Argument from *Logos*

In your small group, discuss the following points, and prepare to present and defend your responses to the class.

1. Go over the Checklist of Essential Elements in an Argument (Chapter 2, p. 50), and decide if the authors of this article fulfill each one.

2. Shemtob and Lat present a logical argument about why executions should be televised. Ignoring your own reaction to their editorial, outline the main points.

3. Explain how the authors handle their audience's possible emotional objections to their argument.

4. What is your reaction to the argument that executions should be televised? Did reading and evaluating the article cause you to see the issue differently? If so, in what way?

Explore

Activity 3.6 • Find an Argument from *Logos*

Find an essay or article in print or on the Internet that uses *logos* as its primary appeal. Make a copy, and bring it to class. In your small group, discuss the texts the group members brought in, and decide which one contains the strongest argument based on *logos*. Describe the argument for the class.

Deductive Reasoning

Aristotle was the first person in Western culture to write systematically about logic, and he is credited with developing and promoting syllogistic or **deductive reasoning** in which statements are combined to draw a **conclusion**. He wrote that "a statement is persuasive and credible either because it is directly self-evident or because it appears to be proved from other statements that are so." This logical structure is called a **syllogism**, in which premises lead to a conclusion. The following is perhaps the most famous syllogism:

Major premise: All humans are mortal.

Minor premise: Socrates is human.

Conclusion: Socrates is mortal.

The **major premise** is a general statement accepted by everyone that makes an observation about all people. The second statement of the syllogism is the **minor premise**, which makes a statement about a particular case within the class of all people. Comparison of the two premises, the general class of "all humans" and the particular case of "Socrates" within the class of "all humans" leads to the conclusion that Socrates also fits in the class "mortal," and therefore his death is unavoidable. Thus, the logic moves from the general to the particular.

Similarly, if you try the pumpkin bread at one Starbucks and like it, you may infer that you will like the pumpkin bread at another Starbucks. The argument would look like this:

Major premise: Food products at Starbucks are standardized from one Starbucks to another.

Minor premise: You like the pumpkin bread at one Starbucks.

Conclusion: You will like the pumpkin bread at another Starbucks.

Often in deductive reasoning, one of the premises is not stated, resulting in what is called a truncated syllogism or **enthymeme**.

For example, in the above syllogism about pumpkin bread, an enthymeme might leave out the major premise, "Food products at Starbucks are standardized from one Starbucks to another." In that case, the syllogism could be shortened to this:

Enthymeme:	If you like the pumpkin bread at one Starbucks, you will like it at another Starbucks.

However, if your major premise is wrong (whether it is stated or not) because the owner of one Starbucks substitutes an inferior stock of pumpkin bread, then your conclusion is wrong.

An enthymeme also relies upon common experience between speaker and audience. If your audience has never tasted pumpkin bread at Starbucks, then they are less likely to believe your enthymeme.

Deductive reasoning is dependent upon the validity of each premise; otherwise the syllogism does not hold true. If the major premise that food products are standardized at all Starbucks franchises does not hold true, then the argument is not valid. A good deductive argument is known as a valid argument and is such that if all its premises are true, then its conclusion must be true. Indeed, for a deductive argument to be valid, it must be absolutely impossible for both its premises to be true and its conclusion to be false.

Collaborate

Activity 3.7 • Develop a Deductive Argument

In your small group, develop a deductive argument by creating a major premise, a minor premise, and a conclusion for a topic of your group's choice. Present the argument to the class.

Inductive Reasoning

Aristotle identified another way to move logically between premises, which he called "the progress from particulars to universals." Later logicians labeled this type of logic **inductive reasoning**. Inductive arguments are based on probability. Even if an inductive argument's premises are true, that doesn't establish with 100 percent certainty that its conclusions are true. Even the best inductive argument falls short of deductive validity.

Consider the following examples of inductive reasoning:

Particular statement:	Milk does not spoil as quickly if kept cold.
General statement:	All perishable foods do not spoil as quickly if kept cold.

Particular statement:	Microwaves cook popcorn more quickly than conventional heat.
General statement:	All foods cook more quickly in a microwave.

In the first example, inductive reasoning works well because cold tends to pro-long the useable life of most perishable foods. The second example is more problematic. While it is true that popcorn cooks more quickly in a microwave oven, the peculiarities of microwave interaction with food molecules does not produce a uniform effect on all food stuffs. Rice, for example, does not cook much, if any, faster in a microwave than it does on a stovetop. Also, whole eggs may explode if cooked in their shells.

A good inductive argument is known as a strong (or "cogent") inductive argu-ment. It is such that if the premises are true, the conclusion is likely to be true.

Activity 3.8 • Develop an Inductive Argument

In your small group, develop an inductive argument by creating a particular state-ment and a general statement for a topic of your group's choice. Present the argu-ment to the class. Be sure that your inductive argument is strong or "cogent."

Collaborate

Logical Fallacies

Generally speaking, a **logical fallacy** is an error in reasoning, as opposed to a factual error, which is simply being wrong about the facts. A **deductive fallacy** (sometimes called a *formal fallacy*) is a deductive argument that has premises that are all true, but they lead to a false conclusion, making it an invalid argu-ment. An **inductive fallacy** (sometimes called an *informal fallacy*) appears to be an inductive argument, but the premises do not provide enough support for the conclusion to be probable. Some logical fallacies are more common than others and, thus, have been labeled and defined. Following are a few of the most well-known types.

Ad hominem (Latin for "to the man") arguments attempt to discredit a point of view through personal attacks upon the person who has that point of view. These arguments are not relevant to the actual issue because the character of the person that holds a view says nothing about the truth of that viewpoint.

> *Example*: Noam Chomsky is a liberal activist who opposes Ameri-can intervention in other countries. Noam Chomsky's theory of

transformational grammar, which suggests that humans have an innate ability to learn language, is ridiculous.

Non sequitur (Latin for "it does not follow") arguments have conclusions that do not follow from the premises. Usually, the author has left out a step in the logic, expecting the reader to make the leap over the gap.

Example: Well, look at the size of this administration building; it is obvious this university does not need more funding.

Either/or or **false dichotomy** arguments force an either/or choice when, in reality, more options are available. Issues are presented as being either black or white.

Example: With all the budget cuts, we either raise tuition or massively increase class size.

Red herring arguments avoid the issue and attempt to distract with a side issue.

Example: Why do you question my private life issues when we have social problems with which to deal?

Ad populum (Latin for "appeal to the people") arguments appeal to popularity. If a lot of people believe it, it must be true.

Example: Why shouldn't I cheat on this exam? Everyone else cheats.

Ad vericundiam (Latin for "argument from that which is improper") arguments appeal to an irrelevant authority.

Example: If the President of Harvard says it is a good idea, then we should follow suit. Or, That is how we have always done it.

Begging the question arguments simply assume that a point of view is true because the truth of the premise is assumed. Simply assuming a premise is true does not amount to evidence that it *is* true.

Example: A woman's place is in the home; therefore, women should not work.

Confusing cause and effect is a common problem with scientific studies in which the fact that two events are correlated implies that one causes the other.

Example: Obese people drink a lot of diet soda; therefore, diet soda causes obesity.

Post hoc (from the Latin phrase *Post hoc, ergo proper hoc,* or "after this, therefore because of this") is a fallacy that concludes that one event caused another just because one occurred before the other.

Example: The Great Depression caused World War II.

In a **straw man** fallacy, a position of an opponent is exaggerated or weakened, so that it is easier for the opponent to argue against it.

Example: Pro-choice advocates believe in murdering unborn children.

A **slippery slope** argument asserts that one event will inevitably lead to another event.

Example: This Dilbert cartoon:

DILBERT © 2008 Scott Adams. Used by permission of UNIVERSAL UCLICK. All rights reserved.

Table 3.1 • Descriptions and Examples of Logical Fallacies

Fallacy	The Error in Reasoning	Example
Ad populum	When we attempt to persuade people by arguing our position is reasonable because so many other people are doing it or agree with it.	"Why shouldn't I cheat on this exam? Everyone else cheats."

Fallacy	The Error in Reasoning	Example
Ad vericundiam	An appeal to persuasion based on higher authority or tradition.	"If the president of Harvard says it is a good idea, then we should follow suit." Or, "That is how we have always done it."
Begging the question	When a speaker presumes certain things are facts when they have not yet been proven to be truthful.	"Oh, everyone knows that we are all Christians."
Confusing cause and effect	A common problem with scientific studies in which the fact that two events are correlated implies that one causes the other.	"Obese people drink a lot of diet soda; therefore, diet soda causes obesity."
Either/or	Presents two options and declares that one of them must be correct while the other must be incorrect.	"We either raise tuition or massively increase class size."
Non sequitur	When you make an unwarranted move from one idea to the next.	"Well, look at the size of this administration building; it is obvious this university does not need more funding."
Post hoc	Assumes that because one event happened after another, then the preceding event caused the event that followed.	"Every time Sheila goes to a game with us, our team loses. She is bad luck."
Red herring	When a speaker introduces an irrelevant issue or piece of evidence to divert attention from the subject of the speech.	"Why do you question my private life issues, when we have social problems with which to deal?"
Slippery slope	Assumes that once an action begins it will follow, undeterred, to an eventual and inevitable conclusion.	"If we let the government dictate where we can pray, soon the government will tell us we cannot pray."

Activity 3.9 • Identify Logical Fallacies

Explore

Match the following types of logical fallacies with the examples below.

Types:

Ad hominem	*Post hoc*
Begging the question	Straw man
Confusing cause and effect	Slippery slope

Examples:

1. Legalization of medical marijuana will lead to increased marijuana use by the general population.

2. Twenty-one is the best age limit for drinking because people do not mature until they are 21.

3. If you teach birth control methods, more teenage girls will get pregnant.

4. The culture wars of the 1960s were a result of parents being unable to control their children after the post–World War II baby boom.

5. Al Gore claims that climate change is a dangerous trend. Al Gore is a liberal. Therefore, there is no climate change.

6. Immigration reform advocates want to separate families and children.

Activity 3.10 • Create Examples of Logical Fallacies

Collaborate

In your small group, work through the chart of logical fallacies above and create a new example for each type of fallacy. Then report to the class, one fallacy at a time, with the instructor making a list of each group's examples on the chalk board. Discuss any examples that are not clear cases of a particular fallacy.

Arguments from *Pathos*

Pathos makes use of emotion to persuade an audience.

Aristotle wrote:

> Proofs from the disposition of the audience are produced whenever they are induced by the speech into an emotional state. We do not give judgment in the same way when aggrieved and when pleased, in sympathy and in revulsion.

Effective rhetors know their audiences, particularly what emotions they hold that are relevant to the issue under consideration. What motivates them? What are their fears, their hopes, their desires, and their doubts? If the audience has the same emotions as you do, fine. However, if they do not already hold those emotions, you need to bring them to share the hurt, the anger, or the joy that will persuade them to share your viewpoint—through the stories you tell, the statistics you cite, and the reasoning you offer.

For example, when Dr. Martin Luther King, Jr., in his "I Have a Dream" speech referred to the "hallowed spot" of the Lincoln Memorial, he was appealing to his audience's feelings of patriotism and reverence for the accomplishments of President Lincoln. Subtly, he was also garnering this emotion toward Lincoln in contemporary support of civil rights. Lincoln had issued the Emancipation Proclamation that declared all slaves to be free, yet, according to King, America had not lived up to Lincoln's promise.

Reading 3.3

E. Benjamin Skinner has written on a wide range of topics. His articles have appeared in News-week International, Travel and Leisure, *and other magazines. This essay was adapted from* A Crime So Monstrous: Face-to-Face with Modern-Day Slavery *and appeared in* Foreign Policy.

People for Sale
by E. Benjamin Skinner

Most people imagine that slavery died in the nineteenth century. Since 1810, more than a dozen international conventions banning the slave trade have been signed. Yet today there are more slaves than at any time in human history.

And if you're going to buy one in five hours, you'd better get a move on. First, hail a taxi to JFK International Airport and hop on a direct flight to Port-au-Prince, Haiti. The flight takes three hours. After landing, take a tap-tap, a flatbed pickup retrofitted with benches and a canopy, three-quarters of the way up Route de Delmas, the capital's main street. There, on a side street, you will find a group of men standing in front of Le Réseau (the Network) barbershop. As you approach, a man steps forward: "Are you looking to get a person?"

Meet Benavil Lebhom. He smiles easily. He has a trim mustache and wears a multicolored striped golf shirt, a gold chain, and Doc Martens knockoffs. Benavil is a courtier, or broker. He holds an official real estate license and calls himself an employment agent. Two-thirds of the employees he places are child slaves. The total number of Haitian children in bondage in their own country stands at 300,000. They are restavèks, the "stay-withs," as they are euphemistically known in Creole. Forced, unpaid, they work in captivity from before dawn until night. Benavil and thousands of other formal and informal traffickers lure these children from desperately impoverished rural parents with promises of free schooling and a better life.

The negotiation to buy a child slave might sound a bit like this:

"How quickly do you think it would be possible to bring a child in? Somebody who could clean and cook?" you ask. "I don't have a very big place; I have a small apartment. But I'm wondering how much that would cost? And how quickly?"

"Three days," Benavil responds.

"And you could bring the child here?" you inquire. "Or are there children here already?"

"I don't have any here in Port-au-Prince right now," says Benavil, his eyes widening at the thought of a foreign client. "I would go out to the countryside."

You ask about additional expenses. "Would I have to pay for transportation?"

"Bon," says Benavil. "A hundred U.S."

Smelling a rip-off, you press him, "And that's just for transportation?"

"Transportation would be about 100 Haitian," says Benavil, "because you'd have to get out there. Plus, [hotel and] food on the trip. Five hundred gourdes"—around $13.

"OK, 500 Haitian," you say.

Now you ask the big question: "And what would your fee be?" Benavil's eyes narrow as he determines how much he can take you for.

"A hundred. American."

"That seems like a lot," you say, with a smile so as not to kill the deal. "Could you bring down your fee to 50 U.S.?"

Benavil pauses. But only for effect. He knows he's still got you for much more than a Haitian would pay. "Oui," he says with a smile.

But the deal isn't done. Benavil leans in close. "This is a rather delicate question. Is this someone you want as just a worker? Or also someone who will be a 'partner'? You understand what I mean?"

You don't blink at being asked if you want the child for sex. "Is it possible to have someone who could be both?"

"Oui!" Benavil responds enthusiastically.

If you're interested in taking your purchase back to the United States, Benavil tells you that he can "arrange" the proper papers to make it look as though you've adopted the child.

He offers you a 13-year-old girl.

"That's a little bit old," you say.

"I know of another girl who's 12. Then ones that are 10, 11," he responds.

The negotiation is finished, and you tell Benavil not to make any moves without further word from you. You have successfully arranged to buy a human being for 50 bucks.

It would be nice if that conversation were fictional. It is not. I recorded it in October 2005 as part of four years of research into slavery on five continents. In the popular consciousness, "slavery" has come to be little more than just a metaphor for undue hardship. Investment bankers routinely refer to themselves as "high-paid wage slaves." Human rights activists may call $1-an-hour sweatshop laborers slaves, regardless of the fact that they are paid and can often walk away from the job.

The reality of slavery is far different. Slavery exists today on an unprecedented scale. In Africa, tens of thousands are chattel slaves, seized in war or tucked away for generations. Across Europe, Asia, and the Americas, traffickers have forced as many as 2 million into prostitution or labor. In South Asia, which has the highest concentration of slaves on the planet, nearly 10 million languish in bondage, unable to leave their captors until they pay off "debts," legal fictions that in many cases are generations old.

Few in the developed world have a grasp of the enormity of modern-day slavery. Fewer still are doing anything to combat it. . . . Between 2000 and 2006, the U.S. Justice Department increased human trafficking prosecutions from 3 to 32, and convictions from 10 to 98. By the end of 2006, 27 states had passed anti-trafficking laws. Yet, during the same period, the United States liberated only about 2 percent of its own modern-day slaves. As many as 17,500 new slaves continue to enter bondage in the United States every year . . . Many feel that sex slavery is particularly revolting—and it is. I saw it firsthand. In a Bucharest brothel, I was offered a mentally handicapped suicidal girl in exchange for a used car. But for every woman or child enslaved in commercial sex, there are some 15 men, women, and children enslaved in other fields, such as domestic work or agricultural labor.

Save for the fact that he is male, Gonoo Lal Kol typifies the average slave of our modern age. (At his request, I have changed his name.) Like a majority of the world's slaves, Gonoo is in debt bondage in South Asia. In his case, in an Indian quarry. Like most slaves, Gonoo is illiterate and unaware of the Indian laws that ban his bondage and provide for sanctions against his master. His story, told to me near his four-foot-high stone and grass hutch, represents the other side of the "Indian Miracle."

Gonoo lives in Lohagara Dhal, a forgotten corner of Uttar Pradesh, a north Indian state that contains 8 percent of the world's poor. I met him one evening in December 2005 as he walked with two dozen other laborers in tattered and filthy clothes. Behind them was the quarry. In that pit, Gonoo, a member of the historically outcast Kol tribe, worked with his family 14 hours a day. His tools were a hammer and a pike. His hands were covered in calluses, his fingertips worn away.

Gonoo's master is a tall, stout, surly contractor named Ramesh Garg. He makes his money by enslaving entire families forced to work for no pay beyond alcohol, grain, and subsistence expenses. Slavery scholar Kevin Bales estimates that a slave in the 19th-century American South had to work 20 years to recoup his or her purchase price. Gonoo and the other slaves earn a profit for Garg in two years.

Every single man, woman, and child in Lohagara Dhal is a slave. But, in theory at least, Garg neither bought nor owns them. The seed of Gonoo's slavery, for instance, was a loan of 62 cents. In 1958 his grandfather borrowed that amount from the owner of a farm where he worked. Three generations and three slave masters later, Gonoo's family remains in bondage.

Recently, many bold, underfunded groups have taken up the challenge of tearing out the roots of slavery. Some gained fame through dramatic slave rescues. Most learned that freeing slaves is impossible unless the slaves themselves choose to be free. Among the Kol of Uttar Pradesh, for instance, an organization called Pragati Gramodyog Sansthan (PGS)—the Progressive Institute for Village Enterprises—has helped hundreds of families break the grip of the quarry contractors.

The psychological, social, and economic bonds of slavery run deep, and for governments to be truly effective in eradicating slavery, they must partner with groups that can offer slaves a way to pull themselves up from bondage. One way to do that is to replicate the work of grassroots organizations such as the India-based MSEMVS (Society for Human Development and Women's Empowerment). In 1996 the group launched free transitional schools where children who had been enslaved learned skills and acquired enough literacy to move on to formal schooling. The group also targeted mothers, providing them with training and start-up materials for microenterprises. . . . In recent years, the United States has shown an increasing willingness to help fund these kinds of organizations, one encouraging sign that the message may be getting through.

For four years, I encountered dozens of enslaved people, several of whom traffickers like Benavil actually offered to sell to me. I did not pay for a human life anywhere. And, with one exception, I always withheld action to save any one person, in the hope that my research would later help to save many more. At times, that still feels like an excuse for cowardice. But the hard work of real emancipation can't be the burden of a select few. For thousands of slaves, grassroots groups like PGS and MSEMVS can help bring freedom. Until governments define slavery in appropriately concise terms, prosecute the crime aggressively in all its forms, and encourage groups that empower slaves to free themselves, however, millions more will remain in bondage. And our collective promise of abolition will continue to mean nothing at all.

Activity 3.11 • Write about an Argument from *Pathos*

After reading Skinner's essay on slavery, reread the passage in which he negotiated to buy a child slave. Then freewrite for five minutes about how that negotiation made you feel.

Activity 3.12 • Analyze an Argument from *Pathos*

Most people feel emotional when they read about a child in distress, and Skinner further highlights that emotional effect by putting this particular episode in dialogue, always a point of emphasis in an essay. Discuss these questions in your small group.

1. Do you think Skinner deliberately appealed to *pathos* in this part of his essay?

2. List other areas where the essay evokes an emotional response. Consider why, and freewrite on the feelings and beliefs that are brought into play on your own. Discuss with your group your responses and how you think the author knew you would probably react this way.

3. Although much of Skinner's argument relies on *pathos*, he also provides statistics and references to authorities to bolster his argument. Identify the paragraphs which provide statistics or other evidence that would qualify as *logos*.

Activity 3.13 • Find an Argument from *Pathos*

Find an essay or article in print or on the Internet that uses *pathos* or emotion as its primary appeal. Make a copy and bring it to class. In your small group, discuss the texts that the group members brought in, and decide which one contains the strongest argument based on *pathos*. Describe the argument for the class.

Arguments from *Ethos*

No exact translation exists in English for the word *ethos*, but it can be loosely translated as the credibility of the speaker. This credibility generates good will which colors all the arguments, examples, and quotes the rhetor utilizes in his or her text. Rhetors can enhance their credibility by providing evidence of intelligence, virtue, and goodwill and diminish it by seeming petty, dishonest, and mean-spirited. In addition, a speaker or writer can enhance his or her own credibility by incorporating references to quotes or the actions of authorities or leaders.

Aristotle wrote:

> Proofs from character [*ethos*] are produced, whenever the speech is given in such a way as to render the speaker worthy of

credence—we more readily and sooner believe reasonable men on all matters in general and absolutely on questions where precision is impossible and two views can be maintained.

For example, Dr. Martin Luther King, Jr., pointed out in his "I Have a Dream" speech, that, according to the framers of the Constitution and the Declaration of Independence, "unalienable Rights" of "Life, Liberty and the pursuit of Happiness" apply equally to black men and white men. He was, in effect, borrowing the *ethos* of Thomas Jefferson and the framers of the Constitution in support of the unalienable rights of black people.

Consider the following article and how the author's credibility or *ethos* enhances the appeal of his arguments.

Reading 3.4

Ray Jayawardhana, the author of "Alien Life Coming Slowly into View," which was originally published in The New York Times, *is a professor of astronomy and astrophysics at the University of Toronto. He is also the author of* Strange New Worlds: The Search for Alien Planets and Life Beyond Our Solar System.

Alien Life Coming Slowly into View

by Ray Jayawardhana

I remember the first time the concept of another world entered my mind. It was during a walk with my father in our garden in Sri Lanka. He pointed to the Moon and told me that people had walked on it. I was astonished: Suddenly that bright light became a place that one could visit.

Schoolchildren may feel a similar sense of wonder when they see pictures of a Martian landscape or Saturn's rings. And soon their views of alien worlds may not be confined to the planets in our own solar system.

After millenniums of musings and a century of failed attempts, astronomers first detected an exoplanet, a planet orbiting a normal star other than the Sun, in 1995. Now they are finding hundreds of such worlds each year. Last month, NASA announced that 1,235 new possible planets had been observed by Kepler, a telescope on a space satellite. Six of the planets that Kepler found circle one star, and the orbits of five of them would fit within that of Mercury, the closest planet to our Sun.

By timing the passages of these five planets across their sun's visage—which provides confirmation of their planetary nature—we can witness their graceful dance with one another, choreographed by gravity. These discoveries remind us that nature is often richer and more wondrous than our imagination. The diversity of alien worlds has surprised us and challenged our preconceptions many times over.

It is quite a change from merely 20 years ago, when we knew for sure of just one planetary system: ours. The pace of discovery, supported by new instruments and missions and innovative strategies by planet seekers, has been astounding.

What's more, from measurements of their masses and sizes, we can infer what some of these worlds are made of: gases, ice or rocks. Astronomers have been able to take the temperature of planets around other stars, first with telescopes in space but more recently with ground-based instruments, as my collaborators and I have done.

Two and a half years ago, we even managed to capture the first direct pictures of alien worlds. There is something about a photo of an alien planet—even if it only appears as a faint dot next to a bright, overexposed star—that makes it "real." Given that stars shine like floodlights next to the planetary embers huddled around them, success required painstaking efforts and clever innovations. One essential tool is adaptive optics technology, which, in effect, takes the twinkle out of the stars, thus providing sharper images from telescopes on the ground than would otherwise be possible.

At the crux of this grand pursuit is one basic question: Is our warm, wet, rocky world, teeming with life, the exception or the norm? It is an important question for every one of us, not just for scientists. It seems absurd, if not arrogant, to think that ours is the only life-bearing world in the galaxy, given hundreds of billions of other suns, the apparent ubiquity of planets, and the cosmic abundance of life's ingredients. It may be that life is fairly common, but that "intelligent" life is rare.

Of course, the vast majority of the extra-solar worlds discovered to date are quite unlike our own: many are gas giants, and some are boiling hot while others endure everlasting chills. Just a handful are close in size to our planet, and only a few of those may be rocky like the Earth, rather than gaseous like Jupiter or icy like Neptune.

But within the next few years, astronomers expect to find dozens of alien earths that are roughly the size of our planet. Some of them will likely be in the so-called habitable zone, where the temperatures are just right for liquid water. The discovery of "Earth twins," with conditions similar to what we find here, will inevitably bring questions about alien life to the forefront.

Detecting signs of life elsewhere will not be easy, but it may well occur in my lifetime, if not during the next decade. Given the daunting distances between the stars, the real-life version will almost certainly be a lot less sensational than the movies depicting alien invasions or crash-landing spaceships.

The evidence may be circumstantial at first—say, spectral bar codes of interesting molecules like oxygen, ozone, methane and water—and leave room for alternative interpretations. It may take years of additional data-gathering, and perhaps the construction of new telescopes, to satisfy our doubts. Besides, we won't know whether such "biosignatures" are an indication of slime or civilization. Most people will likely move on to other, more immediate concerns of life here on Earth while scientists get down to work.

If, on the other hand, an alien radio signal were to be detected, that would constitute a more clear-cut and exciting moment. Even if the contents of the message remained elusive for decades, we would know that there was someone "intelligent" at the other end. The search for extraterrestrial intelligence with radio telescopes has come of age recently, 50 years after the first feeble attempt. The construction of the Allen Telescope Array on an arid plateau in northern California greatly expands the number of star systems from which astronomers could detect signals.

However it arrives, the first definitive evidence of life elsewhere will mark a turning point in our intellectual history, perhaps only rivaled by Copernicus's heliocentric theory or Darwin's theory of evolution. If life can spring up on two planets independently, why not on a thousand or even a billion others? The ramifications of finding out for sure that ours isn't the only inhabited world are likely to be felt, over time, in many areas of human thought and endeavor—from biology and philosophy to religion and art.

Some people worry that discovering life elsewhere, especially if it turns out to be in possession of incredible technology, will make us feel small and insignificant. They seem concerned that it will constitute a horrific blow to our collective ego.

I happen to be an optimist. It may take decades after the initial indications of alien life for scientists to gather enough evidence to be certain or to decipher a signal of artificial origin. The full ramifications of the discovery may not be felt for generations, giving us plenty of time to get used to the presence of our galactic neighbors. Besides, knowing that we are not alone just might be the kick in the pants we need to grow up as a species.

Activity 3.14 • Analyzing an Argument from *Ethos*

Collaborate

Ray Jayawardhana draws upon the *ethos* of his position as a professor of astronomy and astrophysics to formulate a convincing argument for the strong possibility of the existence of alien life. In your group, discuss how Jayawardhana's profession increases the credibility of his argument.

1. How do you think this essay would compare to essays by people with greater credentials who argue that no alien life exists? What kinds of additional evidence could Jayawardhana have offered that would strengthen his argument?

2. Is Jayawardhana appealing to *pathos* with his opening narrative? What effect does he want to have on his audience by describing this childhood memory?

Activity 3.15 • Find an Argument from *Ethos*

Explore

Find an essay or article in print or on the Internet that uses *ethos* or the credibility of the author as its primary appeal. Make a copy and bring it to class. In your small group, discuss the texts that the group members brought in, and decide which contains the strongest argument based on *ethos*. Describe the argument for the class.

Combining *Ethos, Pathos,* and *Logos*

The *ethos, pathos,* and *logos* appeals are equally important and merit equal attention in the writing process. No text is purely based on one of the three appeals, though more of the argument in a particular text may be based on one appeal rather than another. In each writing situation, however, an effective rhetor will think about how each plays into the structure of the argument.

Today, for example, a public speaker's effectiveness is influenced by his or her ability to use a teleprompter, or, if one is not available, to memorize a speech well enough so he or she can speak without frequently referring to notes. If a speaker's eyes flit from left to right across the text of a teleprompter, it shows on television. This reduces the credibility, or *ethos,* of the speaker, no matter how well the other appeals are executed in the speech. The equivalent of strong public speaking skills for a written text would be to produce a document that is essentially free from grammatical errors, spell-checked, and printed on good paper stock with the correct margins and type size. If the document does not look professional, it will lose credibility or *ethos* no matter what it says.

To give another example, E. Benjamin Skinner's essay, "People for Sale," relies on the highly emotional image of a child being sold into slavery for its major appeal. However, if you read back through the essay, you will see that it has a clear thesis, which could be stated as the following: Slavery exists in the present time, even in the United States, and it is not even that difficult to buy a slave. The essay is well organized and offers a variety of evidence, including statistics and first-person observation. *Logos* may not stand out as the primary appeal in Skinner's essay, but it is nevertheless strong in its appeal to *logos*.

If you want to develop your writing skills, it is essential that you pay attention to each of Aristotle's appeals—*ethos*, *pathos*, and *logos*.

Compose

Activity 3.16 • Identify *Ethos, Pathos,* and *Logos*

Choose one of the texts in Chapters 1, 2, or 3, and identify in your small group the *ethos, pathos,* and *logos* of the particular text. Then discuss how the three appeals together are used by the author to produce an effective essay. Alternatively, discuss which of the appeals is weak in the particular essay and how that affects the effectiveness of the essay.

Photos Heighten *Ethos*

Caitlyn Jenner, formerly Bruce Jenner, asserted her visual *ethos* as a transgender woman when she accepted the Arthur Ashe Courage Award at the ESPY Awards in Los Angeles in July 2015. News outlets worldwide carried videos or photos of Jenner wearing a stunning white Versace gown as she received a standing ovation from some of sport's greatest stars and celebrities. The same month, further enhancing Jenner's *ethos* as a transgender woman, *Vanity Fair* featured her on its cover in a traditionally female pose, wearing a glamorous white swimsuit. The

Caitlyn Jenner wore a feminine Versace evening gown at the ESPY Awards.
Photo Credit: Getty Images.

A transgender woman posted her own magazine "cover" on the Internet.
Photo Credit: Tumblr/ missinginanus

Vanity Fair cover received both praise and criticism, with some bloggers saying Jenner's photos perpetuated white female beauty stereotypes. However, other transgender women were inspired to create their own "covers" and post them on the Internet. Thus, having a "cover" photo became a new way for transgender women to establish their gender *ethos*.

Activity 3.17 • Locate a Photo that Presents an Argument from *Logos*, *Ethos*, or *Pathos*

Explore

Locate and print or photocopy a photo that presents an argument from *logos*, *ethos*, or *pathos*. In one sentence, state the photo's argument, identifying whether it is from *logos*, *ethos*, or *pathos*. Bring the photo and your sentence to class, and share them with your group. Then the group will select one photo and sentence to present to the class.

Activity 3.18 • *Logos* Activity: Write a Letter to the Editor

Compose

In the following letter to the editor of *The Baltimore Sun* (published in the Readers Respond section), the author takes exception to the new city policy of equipping police officers with body cameras. The cameras are not being deployed as a crime deterrent but rather to collect data to be used in lawsuits alleging police brutality and misconduct.

Be Prudent with Police Cameras

Though I understand the rush to hold police officers accountable for their behavior, I do not understand placing body cameras on all cops ("Police Body Cameras Will Yield Important Data, Baltimore Task Force Says," Feb. 21 [2015]). This would be like putting every citizen who commits a crime on supervised probation. It is not necessary for all folks, but some need the extra incentive to remain lawful.

I suggest we treat cops like society in general. If one's behavior merits extra scrutiny, then by all means place a camera on him or her. If, however, an officer is honoring the oath and not acting outside of legal authority, leave him or her alone. The cost to place a camera on thousands of police officers is not a great way to spend tax dollars.

I believe this rational response is more prudent than an overreaction. I also believe that facts, not emotion, should dictate how we react to issues that matter.

Mike Snyder, Havre de Grace

---

1. Choose one of your favorite newspapers or magazines and write a letter to the editor. Express your opinion about an issue profiled in a recent article published in the periodical, as the writer does in the above sample letter to the editor, or about a recent editorial or op-ed. Your letter does not need to be long, but you need to make your argument clear and support it with specific examples.

(continued on next page)

2. After you have written your letter to the editor, write a paragraph describing your target publication, what you have written in your letter, and why your letter is an illustration of *logos*. Turn in your paragraph with your letter to the editor.

Explore

Activity 3.19 • *Pathos* Activity: Portray an Emotion in a Collage

Think of an emotion that you've been feeling lately and that you are willing to explore. Create a collage to express that emotion. Use these criteria.

▌ You can create your collage with cut and paste paper or you can create it through a computer program.

▌ Have little white space. Use colors with emotional connotations (blue for calm, for example).

▌ Have at least three images. You can find these on the Internet or in magazines, or take your own photos.

▌ Before you begin your collage, write down the emotion you are trying to explore, and describe how you plan to represent it. In other words, make a plan, even though you will likely deviate from it.

▌ When you finish, write a paragraph describing the experience of creating the collage. Turn your paragraph in with your collage.

Compose

Activity 3.20 • *Ethos* Activity: Create a Professional LinkedIn Page

LinkedIn, the world's largest professional network, provides a unique opportunity for aspiring professionals. Using several basic steps, you can create a page on LinkedIn that projects your professional *ethos*—the "you" that you want others in your field to see—so you can find opportunities and make meaningful connections with other LinkedIn participants.

Stephanie Laszik, a M.A. student and instructor at the University of Texas at Tyler shares these tips for creating your own LinkedIn page.

* * *

(continued on next page)

Remember that LinkedIn is a social media network in which both employers and employees create user profiles and establish professional connections. LinkedIn provides users with the opportunity to present their educational and professional accolades, seek and post potential jobs, follow companies and employees of companies, maintain supportive professional relationships, and network with other users in similar professions.

For this assignment, create a professional-looking LinkedIn page similar to the one shown here. Discuss in your small group what information and photos you want to use on a page intended for networking with others in your professional field. In effect, you are creating an *ethos* for yourself by these choices.

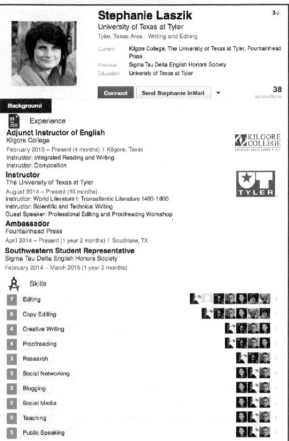

- Access LinkedIn at www.LinkedIn.com and complete the free registration using a reliable email account and password.

- Be sure to include a professional head shot as your identity photo. This is often the first component potential employers and connections will see when they browse LinkedIn.

- The key to a strong LinkedIn profile and relevant connections is thoroughly documenting your education and job experiences. LinkedIn allows you to include current and previous positions, skills you possess in your field, your education, and volunteer experiences.

- When completing each section, be as thorough as possible. The more relevant information you include under each section of your profile the better the network will be able to match you with companies and connections.

(continued on next page)

▌ While LinkedIn communicates information in a similar manner as traditional employment documents, the site is also live and interactive. After you complete your profile, LinkedIn will recommend connections, often within the companies and fields of employment you have added to your profile. Your connections are able to endorse you and suggest skills to be added to your profile.

▌ As you build a database of connections on your LinkedIn profile, you will notice the site enables you to track your profile views, gauge your ranking among other profiles from your companies, and observe trends in member traffic to your profile.

▌ For up-to-date maintenance of your profile and connections, the LinkedIn app can be downloaded to your devices such as a smart phone or tablet computer.

After you have completed your LinkedIn page, write a paragraph that explains the *ethos* you wanted to project in your page and how your content projects that *ethos*.

Compose

Activity 3.21 • **Write a Rhetorical Analysis**

In this assignment, you will make use of rhetorical vocabulary to analyze a text or combined text and images. A sample student essay in Chapter 6 (see p. 238) analyzes a speech archived on the *American Rhetoric* website (www.americanrhetoric.com), which features many presidential and other prominent speeches. Alternatively, you can write a rhetorical analysis of a Facebook page, a newspaper or magazine article, or website of your choice.

In your analysis, apply several of the rhetorical concepts you have studied this semester.

▌ Speaker or writer—Does the speaker's identity affect the text?

▌ Purpose—What was the speaker or writer trying to achieve?

▌ Audience—Who was the speech/text directed to? Are there multiple audiences?

▌ Rhetorical appeals—How does the speaker or writer use *ethos*, *pathos*, and *logos*?

▌ *Kairos*—What is special about the rhetorical moment of the text/speech in terms of place and time?

Activity 3.22 • **Reflect on Your Rhetorical Analysis**

Freewrite for five minutes about the writing of a rhetorical analysis. You can answer one or more of these questions or comment about something else related to the writing of the essay. What made you choose this particular essay to analyze? Was it easy or difficult to identify the rhetorical concepts? Why or why not? How did you choose to organize your essay? Did the writing of this essay further your understanding of rhetorical concepts?

If your instructor directs, revise your freewriting into a coherent paragraph with a topic sentence and points to support the thesis.

Activity 3.23 • **Write on Your Blog**

In your blog, do a freewrite exercise in which you argue for some type of policy change related to a topic you are interested in writing about. What is the *kairos* of your topic? Where can you use the three rhetorical appeals (*pathos*, *ethos*, and *logos*)?

Activity 3.24 • **Write in Your Commonplace Book**

Do a search on the Internet for *kairos*, *ethos*, *pathos*, and *logos*. Print out and paste a short section about each from the Internet. Then comment briefly about each section.

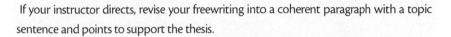

chapter 4
Inventing Rhetorically

My Invention Strategies

Jenelle Clausen
M.F.A., Creative Writing
Bowling Green State University

The key to writing based on research is to begin with an open mind. When I start thinking about topic ideas for a paper, I try not to solidify my opinion on a topic until I've researched the subject widely. The impulse I feel is often the exact opposite—I know enough about my topic that I know what angle I want to take, so now I just need sources to confirm that, right? Wrong! That kind of thinking limits topic options and inhibits learning. I want my writing to benefit me as well as my readers. If I want my readers to listen to me, I should listen to others who have already been part of the conversation concerning my topic.

I like to take time to explore a broad topic. If I start early on an assignment, then I have time to meander the Internet, search library databases, read books and talk to friends, librarians, and experts. I bookmark sources, physically and electronically, and keep a separate Word document with notes about sources, so I can later trace my way back to the information I need. Though I won't use all of my research as I narrow down my topic, it is helpful, since it immerses me in my subject and exposes me to diverse perspectives.

As I narrow down my topic, I also need to determine the audience for and purpose of my essay. When writing for class, the instructor is an audience, of course, because he or she wields the red grading pen. But it's important also to think outside the context of the classroom and consider whom I might want to reach in a larger or "real-world" context. What do I want to persuade this broader audience to think, feel, or do? How do I effectively communicate with this audience ("with" is important since a writer has to anticipate a reader's response(s), not just throw assertions at him or her)? And what is the answer to the looming question, "So what?" In other words, I need to clarify why others should also care about my topic. All of this will further guide my research and drafting.

Aristotle's Classification of Rhetoric

Aristotle, in *The Art of Rhetoric* (or *Rhetoric*), laid the groundwork for today's persuasive writing by being the first to write systemically about how to teach rhetoric. In contrast, his teacher, Plato, distrusted rhetoric. Plato deplored the way rhetoricians (or politicians) of his era skillfully manipulated the people of Athens, particularly the masses of up to 10,000 voters in the Assembly or 500 in the juries of the law courts. Aristotle, on the other hand, perceived great potential in rhetoric, when taught properly. Rhetoric, as he envisioned it, could be both persuasive and ethical, and in *The Art of Rhetoric* he laid out an organization and classification of rhetoric as he believed it should be taught.

Aristotle divided the process of writing and delivering a composition into five parts. The first of these was **invention**, during which the writer or speaker expanded a topic into ideas that were later arranged into a text or speech. According to the ancient Greeks, the rhetor *invented* these ideas, though they may have mirrored or adapted thoughts presented by previous rhetors. Today, we call this the **prewriting stage** of the writing process, an adaptation of Aristotle's invention stage.

The Five Canons of Rhetoric

Greek and Roman teachers of rhetoric divided rhetoric into five parts or canons. These canons corresponded to the order of activities in creating a speech, as they perceived the process: invention, arrangement, style, memory, and delivery. These five parts are described in many handbooks of rhetorical instruction, including the *Rhetorica ad Herennium*, which was composed by an unknown author between 86 and 82 CE:

> The speaker. . .should possess the faculties of Invention, Arrangement, Style, Memory, and Delivery. Invention is the devising of matter, true or plausible, that would make the case convincing. Arrangement is the ordering and distribution of the matter, making clear the place to which each thing is to be assigned. Style is the adaptation of suitable words and sentences to the matter devised. Memory is the firm retention in the mind of the matter, words, and arrangement. Delivery is the graceful regulation of voice, countenance, and gesture.

Today, classes in composition or writing studies still emphasize the necessity of **invention**, now interpreted as prewriting activities that enable writers to develop the logic and words needed for effective arguments. **Arrangement** involves organizing an argument into a logical format that leads the reader easily from the thesis to the conclusion. **Style** has to do with the author's voice and tone and the structure of sentences and paragraphs. **Memory** is used somewhat differently today, as students are no longer required to memorize compositions for oral presentation. Instead, memory is utilized in ways such as remembering how and where to retrieve information from the Internet, books, and other reference materials. Finally, **delivery**, which once involved gestures and tone of voice in an oral presentation, today has to do with document design, so that the final product is presented in a professional manner according to Modern Language Association (MLA) or American Psychological Association (APA) style. Delivery also involves grammatical accuracy because surface errors detract from the effective impact of a document. See Table 4.1 for a summary of the five parts of rhetoric.

Table 4.1 • The Five Parts (or Canons) of Rhetoric

English	Greek	Latin
invention	*heuresis*	*inventio*
arrangement	*taxis*	*dispositio*
style	*lexis*	*elocutio*
memory	*mneme*	*memoria*
delivery	*hypocrisis*	*actin*

The Modern Writing Process Overview

Prewriting (Inventing)

Writing is not only about putting the pen to paper. As did rhetors in ancient Greece and Rome, you have to think deeply and critically about a subject before you begin a composition. The "invention" step of the writer's process is designed to help you find a worthwhile topic and develop your ideas about that topic before you start to write a draft. It includes writing, discussion, and research, as well as informal writing to help you explore your thoughts and feelings about a subject. Whatever method you choose, keep a record of your thoughts and discoveries as you spend this time in close examination of your subject.

Drafting

It may seem odd that writing a draft should come in the middle of the writer's process. However, research has shown that students and professionals alike write more effective essays when they don't reach for the pen too quickly. If you have spent enough time in the invention stage, the actual drafting stage may go more quickly. After writing the first draft, in succeeding drafts you can add details, observations, illustrations, examples, expert testimony, and other support to help your essay entertain, illuminate, or convince your audience.

Revising

Today, we talk more about the revision stage of writing than did ancient rhetoricians. If you are a student who tends to write assigned essays at the last minute, you may have missed this step entirely, yet many writers claim this is the longest and most rewarding step in the writing process. To revise, you must, in a sense, learn to let go of your writing. Some students think their first drafts should stay exactly the way they are written because they are true to their feelings and experience. Many writers find, however, that first drafts assume too much about the reader's knowledge and reactions. Sometimes readers, reading a first draft essay, are left scratching their heads and wondering what it is the writer is trying to convey. Writers who revise try to read their writing as readers would, taking note of gaps in logic, the absence of clear examples, the need for reordering information, and so on. Then they can revise their content with the reader in mind.

Editing and Polishing

Once writers have clarified their messages and the methods by which they will present those messages, one more step must be taken. Particularly because their compositions are written, rather than presented orally, writers must go over their work again to check for correct spelling, grammar, and punctuation, as well as the use of Standard Written English. Some students finish with an essay, print it, and turn it in without ever examining the final copy. This is a critical mistake, because misspelled words and typographical and formatting errors can make an otherwise well-written essay lose its credibility. The five canons of rhetoric and the modern writing process are summarized in Table 4.2.

Table 4.2 • The Five Canons of Rhetoric and the Modern Writing Process

Five Canons of Rhetoric	Modern Writing Process
Invention—Devising the arguments that will make the case convincing, often basing them on models of famous speeches.	Prewriting—Determining the thesis, points of argument, counterargument, and rebuttal. Researching evidence to support the argument.
Arrangement—Ordering the argument into a logical format.	Drafting, revising, and editing—Putting ideas and prewriting into a useable form through a recursive process of drafting, revising, and editing.
Style—Finding suitable words and figures of speech. [Note: This may have been a recursive process, but the ancients did not consider that aspect important.]	
Memory—Retaining the argument in the mind, including its content and arrangement.	Knowing how and where to retrieve information from the Internet, books, and other reference materials.
Delivery—Effective use of voice and gestures to present argument.	Publication—Putting text, images, and other elements in a suitable format and releasing the document to an audience.

Activity 4.1 • Compare the Five Canons of Rhetoric and the Modern Writing Process

Collaborate

In your group, reread the discussions in this chapter on the five canons of rhetoric and the modern writing process and review the table above. What parts of the five canons correspond to the modern writing process? What step in the five canons is not included in the contemporary writing process? If the similarities and differences are not clear to you, consult the Internet. If you search for either "Five Canons of Rhetoric" or "Writing Process" you will find resources. What explanations can you offer for the differences? The similarities?

Stasis Theory

Stasis theory presents a series of four questions that were developed by Greek and Roman rhetoricians, primarily Aristotle, Quintilian, and Hermagoras. Answering these questions for an issue enabled rhetors to determine the critical (or stasis) point in a disagreement. This was a technique the ancients developed for the law courts to enable advocates to focus their arguments on the crux of the case. Quintilian, the great Roman teacher of rhetoric, explained in regard to a defendant:

> By far the strongest mode of defense is if the charge which is made can be denied; the next, if an act of the kind charged against the accused can be said not to have been done; the third, and most honorable, if what is done is proved to have been justly done. If we cannot command these methods, the last and only mode of defense is that of eluding an accusation, which can neither be denied nor combated, by the aid of some point of law, so as to make it appear that the action has not been brought in due legal form.

Marcus Fabius Quintilianus (Quintilian) was a Roman orator from Spain who taught stasis theory.

In other words, Quintilian is saying that in law cases, advocates have four choices in developing a focus for their arguments. You have probably watched a courtroom drama on television or film and can recall various defenses made on behalf of defendants. The strongest and most obvious defense is that the defendant is not guilty, that is, he or she did not do the deed in question. The same was true in Quintilian's day. However, sometimes an argument of innocence is not possible, perhaps because it seems obvious that the defendant did perform the deed in question. Thus, the advocate must develop a different strategy. For example, in defense of one accused of murder, the attorney may argue self-defense or mitigating circumstances (such as that the killing was an act of war). In rare cases, other defenses are offered; for example, if the supposed victim's body has not been found, the advocate can argue that the victim may still be alive. An attorney can discover these possible defenses by using stasis theory to analyze the situation.

Another great advantage of stasis theory is that, if pursued diligently, it prevents the rhetor from making the mistake of organizing an argument by simply forwarding reasons why he or she is correct and the opposition is wrong. That approach may please people who agree with the rhetor, but it will not likely gain any support from the opposition. Answering the stasis questions carefully forces the writer to consider aspects of the issue that may have been overlooked but are crucial to an effective argument.

The wording of the four questions has varied somewhat over time, but essentially they are questions of fact, definition, quality, and policy. The same questions can be applied to any issue, not only issues of law. The four stasis questions are as follows:

1. What are the facts? (conjecture)

2. What is the meaning or nature of the issue? (definition)

3. What is the seriousness of the issue? (quality)

4. What is the best plan of action or procedure? (policy)

Many writers prefer stasis theory to other prewriting techniques because answering the questions determines whether or not the different sides of an argument are at stasis. Being at **stasis** means that the opponents are in agreement about their disagreement—the stasis point—which can be identified by one of the four stasis questions. If the sides are at stasis, they have common ground to build upon, for they are arguing the same issue. There is, thus, a greater chance the sides can reach a workable consensus or compromise. If opponents are not at stasis, there is much more work to be done to reach consensus.

For example, in the argument about the teaching of evolution and/or intelligent design in schools, the two sides are not in agreement about how to discuss the issue. Those in favor of teaching evolution claim intelligent design should not be called science, which is an issue of definition. Those who propose teaching intelligent design along with (or instead of) evolution tend to focus on "proving" evidence, an issue of fact. Until the two sides can agree upon what is the stasis point, or crux of the issue, they cannot debate effectively. They are not presenting arguments about the same question.

The four stasis questions can be broken into the subquestions listed in Table 4.3 on the following page. If you want to find the stasis point, work through the list for your issue, answering all of the subquestions. However, for each question, you must identify not only how *you* would answer the question but also how the opposing side or sides would answer. For example, if you are considering the issue of climate change, people with different positions will not agree on the facts. Thus, you must identify the basic facts of climate change represented by your side, and then identify the facts that might be presented by the opposing side.

Table 4.3 • Stasis Questions

Fact
• Did something happen?
• What are the facts?
• Is there a problem/issue?
• How did it begin, and what are its causes?
• What changed to create the problem/issue?
• Can it be changed?
It also may be useful to ask the following critical questions of your own research and conclusions:
• Where did I obtain my data, and are these sources reliable?
• How do I know they're reliable?

Definition
• What is the nature of the problem/issue?
• What exactly is the problem/issue?
• What kind of a problem/issue is it?
• To what larger class of things or events does it belong?
• What are its parts, and how are they related?
It also may be useful to ask the following critical questions of your own research and conclusions:
• Who/what is influencing my definition of this problem/issue?
• How/why are these sources/beliefs influencing my definition of the issue?

Quality
• Is it a good thing or a bad thing?
• How serious is the problem/issue?
• Who might be affected by this problem/issue (stakeholders)?
• What happens if we don't do anything?
• What are the costs of solving the problem/issue?
It also may be useful to ask the following critical questions of your own research and conclusions:
• Who/what is influencing my determination of the seriousness of this problem/issue?
• How/why are these sources/beliefs influencing my determination of the issue's seriousness?

Policy
<ul><li>Should action be taken?</li><li>Who should be involved in helping to solve the problem/address the issue?</li><li>What should be done about this problem?</li><li>What needs to happen to solve this problem/address this issue?</li></ul> It also may be useful to ask the following critical questions of your own research and conclusions: <ul><li>Who/what is influencing my determination of what to do about this problem/issue?</li><li>How/why are these sources/beliefs influencing my determination of what to do about this issue?</li></ul>
Adapted from Brizee, Allen. "Stasis Theory." *OWL Purdue Online Writing Lab,* Purdue University, 1 Mar. 2013, owl.english.purdue.edu/owl/resource/736/1/.

Using Stasis Questions

To illustrate the use of stasis questions, a team of writers working together to compose a report on racism in America might use the stasis questions to talk through information they will later use in their report. In the following sample dialogue, team members disagree about what actions are racist.

"Flying the Confederate battle flag is racist."

"Flying the Confederate battle flag is *not* racist."

"Yes, it is, because it represents the Confederate states that supported slavery, and it's generally accepted that slavery in America was racist."

"Flying the Confederate battle flag is not racist, because it's a part of American history and Southern heritage."

"After the June 2015 shooting in the Charleston church, more people have come to see flying the Confederate flag as a racist act."

"Yes, but flying the flag is still protected by the First Amendment as free speech."

These two team members disagree about whether or not flying the Confederate battle flag is a racist act. This sort of disagreement might lead to a complete breakdown of group work if common ground cannot be found.

In this example, the team members go on to agree that some people still exhibit the Confederate battle flag (*fact*) on their vehicles and on their clothes, and that the flag is also displayed in museums (*fact*).

The group members agree that the issue is still very important to many people, since a number of American states have recently debated the flag in legislatures and assemblies. For example, the South Carolina Legislature voted in 2015 to remove the Confederate battle flag from the state capitol grounds, while some opposed to the change said the removal disrespected the state's Confederate history (*quality*).

Moreover, a number of legal suits have been filed for and against the display of the flag in public places. For example, the Supreme Court in 2015 decided that Texas's refusal to allow specialty license plates to bear the Confederate flag did not violate the First Amendment. However, those selling and displaying the flag have suggested that the flag does not represent an endorsement of slavery but, rather, regional pride (*quality*).

In this sense, the team members have achieved stasis on two of the four stases—*fact* (people still display the flag) and *quality* (it's a very important issue). Where the team members disagree, however, is in the stases of *definition* (is the display of the flag "racist"?) and *policy* (what should we do about this?).

Thinking about this disagreement using stasis theory allows people to build common ground so that parties who disagree can move toward resolution and action even if they can't agree on all levels. For example, team members who disagree about whether or not flying the Confederate battle flag is racist might still be able to agree on what to do about it.

> "Okay, we disagree about whether flying the flag is racist, but we can agree that flying the flag is probably protected under the First Amendment to the United States Constitution—that flying the flag is protected by our freedom of speech."
>
> "Yeah."
>
> "So, people are free to display the flag on their vehicles, on their clothes, and on their property, as well as in museums. But, state legislatures and assemblies, like the one in South Carolina, will have to debate and vote on whether or not the flag can be displayed on publicly funded property or in public symbols, such as state flags and seals. And it may be that the courts may some-

Figure 4.1 • Disallowed Texas License Plate

License plate that Texas refused to allow because of its incorporation of the Confederate flag.

times need to be involved, like in the case of the Supreme Court decision about license plates in Texas.

"That sounds pretty democratic. Sure."

Not every team situation is going to end this amicably; however, by using the stasis questions to help keep the dialogue going—on a reasonable course— team members can find common ground and work toward action that is acceptable to most, if not all, of the group members.[1]

Stasis Theory and Kairos

As you will remember from Chapter 3, the *kairos* of an argument is the context, opportune moment, or point in time in which the rhetor, the audience, the issue, and the current situation provide opportunities and constraints for an argument. If you keep *kairos* in mind as you analyze an issue, you take advantage of timeliness. For example, if you want to write an argument about the death penalty, you might consider that United States courts are increasingly questioning the validity of eyewitness testimony, evidence which has been the deciding factor in many death penalty cases.

As part of your use of stasis theory, consider the four questions in relation to *kairos*.

1. How do recent developments (new facts) or the local situation affect the issue? Will it change your audience's perception of the facts?

2. Does the current situation affect your audience's definition of the issue? Is it defined differently by an audience in this location than elsewhere?

---

1. Adapted from Brizee, Allen. "Stasis Theory for Teamwork." *OWL Purdue Online Writing Lab,* Purdue University, 17 Apr. 2010, owl.english.purdue.edu/owl/resource/736/03/.

3. Have recent events made the issue more or less important to your audience? Is it more or less important in your location than elsewhere?

4. Do recent events, locally or widely, affect the need or lack of need for action in your audience's perception?

As a rhetorician, it is important for you to be aware of the history of a controversy. But it is equally important to have an awareness of the *kairos* of the argument. Such an awareness enables you to adopt a "ready stance" and adjust your argument, so that it reflects an awareness of your audience's position and interests, as well as contemporary developments in the issue. Such a flexible stance may afford you an opportunity to be persuasive that you might otherwise miss.

Explore

Activity 4.2 • **Identify the Defense in a Television or Film Courtroom Drama**

As your instructor directs, watch a courtroom drama on television or film and decide what defense the defendant's attorney is offering. Report your conclusion to your small group or the class. Then, after you have discussed the stasis questions, identify which of the four questions the attorney in the drama is focusing upon as the crux of the defense. Discuss with your group or the class.

Explore

Activity 4.3 • **Use Stasis Theory to Explore Your Topic**

Choose an issue that interests you and answer all the stasis questions in Table 4.3 on pp. 128–29, both for your position and for the opposing argument. Elaborate with three or four sentences for each subquestion that is particularly relevant to your topic. Is your issue at stasis for any of the questions? Report to your group or to the class.

Compose

Activity 4.4 • **Evaluate a Public Debate**

Locate a public debate that has been reported recently in newspaper editorials, television programs, or other media that can be analyzed by using stasis theory. In a paper of 350 to 500 words, address these points.

- Describe the context (*kairos*).
- Identify the sides of the argument and their main points.
- Decide which stasis question each side is primarily addressing.
- Determine whether or not the issue is at stasis and explain your answer.
- Include a citation in MLA or APA format for your source or sources.

The $300 House Casebook

Situation: Professors Vijay Govindarajan and Christian Sarkar launched a competition on the *Harvard Business Network* blog for designs to build $300 houses for people in developing countries. Word of the competition spread quickly, and a wide variety of people began to write about the competition in editorials in *The New York Times, The Economist,* and in a companion blog, www.300house.com/blog.

Read the four articles written about the $300 house competition that appear on the following pages. Discuss them in class and in small groups. In particular, note that Matias Echanove and Rahul Srivastava write in their *New York Times* op-ed essay, "Hands Off Our Houses," that the idea of a $300 house is impractical and will fail in places such as Mumbai, India. In contrast, "A $300 Idea that Is Priceless," the editorial from *The Economist*, praises the design competition for initiating an "explosion of creativity." Yet, both articles agree on the point that new approaches need to be tried to improve the housing situation for the world's poor.

If you visit the website for the $300 house, www.300house.com, you can see that many things are happening to move the concept forward, though there is still no consensus about the best way to build houses for the poor.

Casebook Reading 1

The $300 House: A Hands-On Lab for Reverse Innovation?
by Vijay Govindarajan and Christian Sakar

The $300 house is the concept of a one-room shed built around a slum family's ecosystem.

Published in the *Harvard Business Review Online*.

David A. Smith, the founder of the Affordable Housing Institute (AHI) tells us that "markets alone will never satisfactorily house a nation's poorest citizens . . . whether people buy or rent, housing is typically affordable to only half of the population."

The result? Smith points to a "spontaneous community of self-built or informally built homes—the shanty towns, settlements, and ever-expanding slums that sprout like mushrooms on the outskirts of cities in the developing world."

We started discussing the issue, examining the subject through the lens of reverse innovation.

Here are five questions Christian and I asked ourselves:

How can organic, self-built slums be turned into livable housing?

What might a house-for-the-poor look like?

How can world-class engineering and design capabilities be utilized to solve the problem?

What reverse-innovation lessons might be learned by the participants in such a project?

How could the poor afford to buy this house?

Livable Housing. Our first thought was that self-built houses are usually built from materials that are available—cardboard, plastic, mud or clay, metal scraps and whatever else is nearby. Built on dirt floors, these structures are prone to collapse and catching fire. Solution: replace these unsafe structures with a mass-produced, standard, affordable, and sustainable solution. We want to create the $300-House-for-the-Poor.

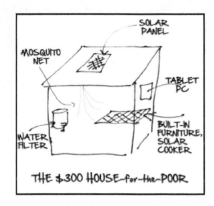

THE $300 HOUSE-for-the-POOR

Look and Feel. To designers, our sketch of this house might be a bit of a joke, but it's useful nonetheless to illustrate the concept, to get started. We wanted the house to be an eco-system of products and solutions designed around the real needs of the inhabitants. Of course it would have to be made out of sustainable, green materials, but more crucially, it would have to be durable enough to withstand torrential rains, earthquakes, and the stress of children playing. The house might be a single room structure with drop-down partitions for privacy. Furniture—sleeping hammocks and fold-down chairs would be built in. The roof would boast an inexpensive solar panel and battery to light the house and charge the mobile phone and tablet computer. An inexpensive water filter would be built in as well.

In effect, the house is really a one-room shed designed around the family ecosystem, a lego-like aggregation of useful products that "bring good things to life" for the poor.

World-Class Design. Our next question was: "Who will do this?" We decided that it would have to be a collaboration between global design and engineering companies and non-profits with experience solving problems for the poor. The usual suspects ran through our minds—IDEO, GE, TATA, Siemens, Habitat-for-Humanity, Partners In Health, the Solar Electric Light Fund, the Clinton Global Initiative, the Gates Foundation, Grameen. Governments may play an important part in setting the stage for these types of cross-country innovation projects.

The Reverse Innovation Payoff. Participating companies will reap two rewards. First, they will be able to serve the unserved, the 2.5 billion who make up the bottom of the pyramid. Second, they create new competencies which can help transform lives in rich countries by creating breakthrough innovations to solve several problems (scaled housing for hurricane victims, refugees, and even the armed forces).

A House of One's Own: Affordability. To move beyond charity, the poor must become owners of their homes, responsible for their care and upkeep. The model of social business introduced by Muhammad Yunus resonates strongly with us. Micro-finance must surely play a role in making the $300 House-for-the-Poor a viable and self-sustaining solution.

Of course, the idea we present here is an experiment. Nevertheless, we feel it deserves to be explored. From the one-room shacks in Haiti's Central Plateau to the jhuggi clusters in and around Delhi, to the favelas in São Paulo, the problem of housing-for-the-poor is truly global.

We ask CEOs, governments, NGOs, foundations: Are there any takers?

Govindarajan, Vijay, and Christian Sakar. "The $300 House: A Hands-On Lab for Reverse Innovation?" *Harvard Business Review Online,* Harvard Business Review, 26 Aug. 2010, hbr.org/2010/08/the-300-house-a-hands-on-lab-f.html.

Casebook Reading 2

Hands Off Our Houses

by Matias Echanove and Rahul Srivastava

Published in *The New York Times.*

Matias Echanove and Rahul Srivastava suggest that the $300 house will fail in places like Mumbai, India, because the concept ignores the reality of the slum's condition.

Mumbai, India

Last summer, a business professor and a marketing consultant wrote on *The Harvard Business Review*'s website about their idea for a $300 house. According to the writers, and the many people who have enthusiastically responded since, such a house could improve the lives of millions of urban poor around the world. And with a $424 billion market for cheap homes that is largely untapped, it could also make significant profits.

The writers created a competition, asking students, architects and businesses to compete to design the best prototype for a $300 house (their original sketch was of a one-room prefabricated shed, equipped with solar panels, water filters and a tablet computer). The winner will be announced this month. But one expert has been left out of the competition, even though her input would have saved much time and effort for those involved in conceiving the house: the person who is supposed to live in it.

We work in Dharavi, a neighborhood in Mumbai that has become a one-stop shop for anyone interested in "slums" (that catchall term for areas lived in by the urban poor). We recently showed around a group of Dartmouth students involved in the project who are hoping to get a better grasp of their market. They had imagined a ready-made constituency of slum-dwellers eager to buy a cheap house that would necessarily be better than the shacks they'd built themselves. But the students found that the reality here is far more complex than their business plan suggested.

To start with, space is scarce. There is almost no room for new construction or ready-made houses. Most residents are renters, paying $20 to $100 a month for small apartments.

Those who own houses have far more equity in them than $300—a typical home is worth at least $3,000. Many families have owned their houses for two or three generations, upgrading them as their incomes increase. With additions, these homes become what we call "tool houses," acting as workshops, manufacturing units, warehouses and shops. They facilitate trade and production, and allow homeowners to improve their living standards over time.

None of this would be possible with a $300 house, which would have to be as standardized as possible to keep costs low. No number of add-ons would be able to match the flexibility of need-based construction.

In addition, construction is an important industry in neighborhoods like Dharavi. Much of the economy consists of hardware shops, carpenters, plumbers, concrete makers, masons, even real-estate agents. Importing pre-fabricated homes would put many people out of business, undercutting the very population the $300 house is intended to help.

Worst of all, companies involved in producing the house may end up supporting the clearance and demolition of well-established neighborhoods to make room for it. The resulting resettlement colonies, which are multiplying at the edges of cities like Delhi and Bangalore, may at first glance look like ideal markets for the new houses, but the dislocation destroys businesses and communities.

The $300 house could potentially be a success story, if it was understood as a straightforward business proposal instead of a social solution. Places like refugee camps, where many people need shelter for short periods, could use such cheap, well-built units. A market for them could perhaps be created in rural-urban fringes that are less built up.

The $300 house responds to our misconceptions more than to real needs. Of course problems do exist in urban India. Many people live without toilets or running water. Hot and unhealthy asbestos-cement sheets cover millions of roofs. Makeshift homes often flood during monsoons. But replacing individual, incrementally built houses with a ready-made solution would do more harm than good.

A better approach would be to help residents build better, safer homes for themselves. The New Delhi–based Micro Homes Solutions, for example, provides architectural and engineering assistance to homeowners in low-income neighborhoods.

The $300 house will fail as a social initiative because the dynamic needs, interests and aspirations of the millions of people who live in places like Dharavi have been overlooked. This kind of mistake is all too common in the trendy field of social entrepreneurship. While businessmen and professors applaud the $300 house, the urban poor are silent, busy building a future for themselves.

Echanove, Matias, and Rahul Srivastava. "Hands Off Our Houses." *The New York Times,* 31 May 2011, www.nytimes.com/2011/06/01/opinion/01srivastava.html.

Sponsors of the $300 house competition respond to criticism.

The $300 House: A Hands-On Approach to a Wicked Problem

by Vijay Govindarajan with Christian Sarkar

Published in the *Harvard Business Review Online*.

When *The New York Times* printed "Hands Off Our Houses," an op-ed about our idea for a $300 House for the poor, we were both delighted and dismayed—delighted because the $300 House was being discussed, and dismayed because authors Matias Echanove and Rahul Srivastava, co-founders of the Institute of Urbanology, didn't seem to have read the series of blog posts about our idea.

Nearly every criticism the authors levy in their op-ed is answered in 12 blog posts, a magazine article from January/February 2011, a video interview, and a slideshow that integrated community and commentary, which were published between last October and this May.

In critiquing our vision, the authors cite Micro Homes Solutions as "a better approach." In fact, the leaders of that venture were invited several months ago to contribute a blog post to our series as a way of joining the discussion and helping us understand what they've seen on the ground there. They declined to be part of the conversation.

The authors also write that students who tried to write a business plan to serve the poor and who visited poor urban areas of India found "the reality here is far more complex than their business plan suggested."

Yet a fundamental tenet of our project and the blog series about it is that slums present complex challenges that can't be fixed with a clever shack alone. Rather than creating an echo chamber of rah-rah rhetoric, we told blog authors to focus on one of the many knotty issues that Echanove and Srivastava cite in their critique. From the start we asked: What are the complexities of financing these homes? How do you get energy and infrastructure into such dwellings? How do you get corporations to invest in a significant way? We acknowledged that we didn't have the answers. "Just because it is going to take longer than it should doesn't mean we should walk away," wrote Seth Godin in one of the posts. "It's going to take some time, but it's worth it."

The op-ed suggests that the $300 House doesn't acknowledge that "space is scarce" in urban poor areas. Yet, Sunil Suri wrote in a post on the urban challenge that "slums by their nature are located where land and space are limited." Suri proposed potential solutions, including innovative materials, new ways of thinking of the construction process, and building up.

The authors also say that "one expert has been left out of the challenge. . . the person who is supposed to live in it." But a post in the series on the co-creation challenge from Gaurav Bhalla addressed this squarely. "It will be unfortunate if the house were to be designed by those who will never live in it," wrote Bhalla. "Investments need to be made understanding the daily habits and practices of people for whom the house is being designed." Bhalla used the case study of the chulha stove, co-created by businesses, NGOs, and slum dwellers, to make his point. We are also bringing students to India and Haiti to do ethnographic research that will inform development of a $300 House, and when prototypes are developed, they will be deployed and tested with those who will live in them.

Echanove and Srivastava also state that a $300 House "would have to be as standardized as possible to keep costs low. No number of add-ons would be able to match the flexibility of need-based construction." While we agree that a one-size-fits-all approach will not work, we disagree that a $300 House would be inflexible. Core tenets from a blog post about the overall design challenge of creating a $300 House by Bill Gross include "give your customers options" and "make it aspirational." And David Smith's entry on the financial challenge shows that flexibility can be born out of financing options as well. A need-based approach alone also ignores the scale of the problem we are facing. "Triple the U.S. population by three. That's how many people around the world live on about a dollar a day," Godin writes. "Triple it again and now you have the number that lives on $2. About 40% of the world lives on $2 or less a day." In any situation where scale is required, so is some level of standardization.

The most puzzling critique in the op-ed was that "construction is an important industry in neighborhoods like Dharavi. Much of the economy consists of hardware shops, carpenters, plumbers, concrete makers, masons, even real-estate agents. Importing prefabricated homes would put many people out of business, undercutting the very population the $300 house is intended to help."

In fact, our contest's design briefing said these dwellings should be "self built and/or self-improvable." It also stated that the design should rely as much as possible on local materials, which of course would be harvested and crafted by local workers. Our goal is to increase demand for local trades, not drive them away. And the idea that jobs would disappear belies the fact that with progress comes new jobs; teachers for the kids who can now go to school; health care professionals for the families that can now afford check-ups; technology professionals who could service solar panels or internet access devices; farmers who could manage shared crop spaces in the neighborhoods. The $300 House project is a housing ecosystem project.

Finally, Echanove and Srivastava state that "The $300 house could potentially be a success story, if it was understood as a straightforward business proposal instead of a social solution."

We disagree completely. We do support other applications for low-cost housing—bringing these dwellings back to the industrialized world for hurricane relief, for example, would be a reverse innovation success story. However, trying to pigeonhole ideas as either "for good" or "for profit" is an outmoded way of thinking.

The authors have an implicit negative view on business. For them, profit seems to be a dirty word. For us, good business and social innovation are one and the same. The rising tide of New Capitalism, what Michael Porter calls "shared value" and what Umair Haque calls "thick value," is perhaps the most important reaction to the corruption and greed that spurred the most recent global economic crisis. The *Economist* was right when it suggested that this is a "can do" moment in history.

Our goal is neither to start yet another charity—one of our advisers, Paul Polak, tells us that "you can't donate your way out of poverty"—nor to start just another business. Rather we must encourage existing businesses to find ways to create new, scalable markets; to get NGOs to share their on-the-ground expertise; and to force governments to make it as simple as possible to work across the hybrid value chain in order to make such a project a reality and begin the process of instilling dignity in and creating options for individuals who now don't have either.

We are happy that Echanove and Srivastava share our passion for the problem of affordable housing, which is a wicked problem. We simply disagree with the idea that if it's a market, it can't also be a socially progressive solution. Trying to categorize the regeneration of slums as either a business problem or social problem is like trying to categorize a flame as either heat or light. It is both, always.

Govindarajan, Vijay, and Christian Sarkar. "The $300 House: A Hands-On Approach to a Wicked Problem." *Harvard Business Review Online,* Harvard Business Review, 7 June 2011, hbr.org/2011/06/when-the-new-york-times.html.

A $300 Idea that Is Priceless

from *Schumpeter*, a column in *The Economist*

Casebook Reading 4

Economist editorial praises the $300 House competition for initiating an "explosion of creativity."

Friedrich Engels said in "The Condition of the Working Class in England," in 1844, that the onward march of Manchester's slums meant that the city's Angel Meadow district might better be described as "Hell upon Earth." Today, similar earthly infernos can be found all over the emerging world: from Brazil's favelas to Africa's shanties. In 2010 the United Nations calculated that there were about 827m people living in slums—almost as many people as were living on the planet in Engels's time—and predicted that the number might double by 2030.

Last year Vijay Govindarajan, of Dartmouth College's Tuck School of Business, along with Christian Sarkar, a marketing expert, issued a challenge in a *Harvard Business Review* blog: why not apply the world's best business thinking to housing the poor? Why not replace the shacks that blight the lives of so many poor people, thrown together out of cardboard and mud, and prone to collapsing or catching fire, with more durable structures? They laid down a few simple guidelines. The houses should be built of mass-produced materials tough enough to protect their inhabitants from a hostile world. They should be equipped with the basics of civilized life, including water filters and solar panels. They should be "improvable," so that families can adapt them to their needs. And they should cost no more than $300.

Mr. Govindarajan admits that the $300 figure was partly an attention-grabbing device. But he also argues that it has a certain logic. Muhammad Yunus, the founder of Grameen Bank, has calculated that the average value of the houses of people who have just escaped from poverty is $370. Tata Motors has also demonstrated the value of having a fixed figure to aim at: the company would have found it more difficult to produce the Tata Nano if it had simply been trying to produce a "cheap" car rather than a "one lakh" car (about $2,200).

The attention-grabbing certainly worked. The blog was so inundated with positive responses that a dedicated website, 300house.com, was set up, which has attracted more than 900 enthusiasts and advisers from all over the world. On April 20th Mr. Govindarajan launched a competition inviting people to submit designs for a prototype of the house.

Why has a simple blog post led to such an explosion of creativity? The obvious reason is that "frugal innovation"—the art of radically reducing the cost of products while also delivering first-class value—is all the rage at the moment. General Electric has reduced the cost of an electrocardiogram machine from $2,000 to $400. Tata Chemicals has produced a $24 purifier that can provide a family with pure water for a year. Girish Bharadwaj, an engineer, has perfected a technique for producing cheap footbridges that are transforming life in rural India.

Another reason is that houses can be such effective anti-poverty tools. Poorly constructed ones contribute to a nexus of problems: the spread of disease (because they have no proper sanitation or ventilation), the perpetuation of poverty (because children have no proper lights to study by) and the general sense of insecurity (because they are so flimsy and flammable). Mr. Govindarajan's idea is so powerful because he treats houses as ecosystems that provide light, ventilation and sanitation.

Numerous innovators are also worrying away at this nexus of problems. Habitat for Humanity, an NGO, is building durable houses of bamboo in Nepal. Idealab, a consultancy, is on the verge of unveiling a $2,500 house that will be mass-produced in factories, sold in kits and feature breakthroughs in ventilation, lighting and sanitation. Philips has produced a cheap cooking stove, the Chulha, that cuts out the soot that kills 1.6m people a year worldwide. The Solar Electric Light Fund is demonstrating that you can provide poor families with solar power for roughly the same cost as old standbys such as kerosene and candles.

Profits and other problems

These thinkers, like the advocates of the $300 house, must solve three huge problems to succeed. They must persuade big companies that they can make money out of cheap homes, because only they can achieve the economies of scale needed to hit the target price. They need to ensure sufficient access to microloans: $300 is a huge investment for a family of squatters living on a couple of dollars a day. And they need to overcome the obstacle that most slum-dwellers have weak or non-existent property rights. There is no point in offering people the chance to buy a cleverly designed house if they have no title to the land they occupy. Solving these problems will in turn demand a high degree of co-operation between people who do not always get on: companies and NGOs, designers and emerging-world governments.

However, the exciting thing about the emerging world at the moment is a prevailing belief that even the toughest problems can be solved. And a similar can-do moment, in the late 1940s, offers a striking historical precedent for the application of mass-production techniques to housing: as American servicemen flooded home after the second world war to start families, Levitt & Sons built Levittowns at the rate of 30 houses a day by mass-producing the components in factories, delivering them on lorries and using teams of specialists to assemble them.

Some emerging-world governments are beginning to realize that providing security of tenure is the only way to deal with the problem of ever-proliferating slums. And big companies that face stagnant markets in the West are increasingly fascinated by the "fortune at the bottom of the pyramid." Bill Gross of Idealab reckons the market for cheap houses could be worth at least $424 billion. But in reality it is worth far more than that: preventing the Earth from becoming what Mike Davis, a particularly gloomy follower of Marx and Engels, has termed a "planet of slums."

"A $300 Idea That Is Priceless." *Schumpeter*, 28 Apr. 2011, *The Economist*, www.economist.com/node/18618271.

Activity 4.5 • Use Stasis Questions to Analyze the $300 House Casebook

Collaborate

In your small group, work through the stasis questions with one side of the controversy being those who support this design initiative. The other side will be those who foresee problems in applying this idealistic initiative in the real world; a viewpoint that is expressed in "Hands Off Our Houses." Identify a subquestion or subquestions in which the two sides are at stasis. Discuss why the two sides are at stasis on this point or points.

Use this analysis to help you write the essay specified in Activity 4.6.

Activity 4.6 • Persuasive Essay about the $300 House Casebook Utilizing Stasis Theory

Compose

After you have completed Activity 4.5, write a paper of approximately 750 words in which you:

- briefly present the idea of the design competition,
- summarize the arguments of those in favor of the initiative,
- explain the reservations expressed in "Hands Off Our Houses,"
- identify a stasis point, if one exists, and explain why you think the sides have common ground on that particular stasis question, and
- discuss whether the discovery of common ground might allow individuals involved in this debate to talk to one another and work toward solutions for the problem of substandard housing in slums worldwide.

As your instructor directs, cite your sources in APA or MLA style. After each of the three casebook readings is an MLA citation that you can import into your Works Cited. However, you will still need to write citations for your sources in the text.

Compose

Activity 4.7 • Comment on Your Essay about the $300 House

Freewrite for five minutes about your experience working through the stasis questions for the $300 House Casebook and writing an essay based on the information you collected by answering the stasis questions. Did you find the stasis questions useful in developing your argument for the essay? Why or why not? Is this a technique you would use again? Why or why not?

If your instructor directs, revise your freewriting into a paragraph to turn in.

Other Invention Strategies

Great myths have grown up around writers who can supposedly sit down, put pen to paper, and write a masterpiece. If these myths had developed about any other type of artist—a musician or a painter—we would scoff about them and ask about the years of study and practice those artists had spent before they created their masterpieces. Since all of us can write to some degree, perhaps it seems more feasible that great authors simply appear magically amongst us. Alas, it is not so; like all talented artists, good writers must learn their craft through consistent and continuous practice. Similar to how the ancient Greeks used **stasis questions** or *topoi* (a strategy or heuristic made up of questions about a topic which allows a rhetor to construe an argument) to generate raw material for their compositions, many writers today use the following invention strategies as prewriting activities.

Freewriting

One practice method developed in the 1970s and often attributed to Peter Elbow, author of *Writing without Teachers*, is called freewriting. This method is just what it sounds like—writing that is free of any content restrictions. You simply write what is on your mind. This method is freeform, but there is some structure—you must set a time limit before you begin, and once you begin, you must not stop. The time period is usually 10 to 20 minutes, and you must keep your pen or pencil moving on the page—no hesitations, no corrections, no rereading. Don't worry about spelling, or punctuation, or grammar—just download onto the paper whatever comes to mind. It will seem awkward at best; some have said it is downright painful. But after a few weeks of practice, you will realize it is effective and a wonderful individual method of getting at your thoughts on a subject.

Invisible Freewriting

If you just cannot stop paying attention to your spelling and grammar, or if you find yourself always stopping to read what you have written, you can freewrite invisibly. To do this, you will need carbon paper and a pen that is retracted or out of ink. You sandwich the carbon paper, carbon side down, between two sheets of paper and write on the top sheet with your empty pen. You cannot see what you are writing, but it will be recorded on the bottom sheet of paper. If you prefer to work on the computer, you can easily modify this technique by taping a blank sheet of paper over the monitor while you type.

Focused Freewriting

When freewriting, you are writing without sticking to any particular topic. You are exploring many ideas and your sentences may roam from your day at work, the letter you just got from your sister, or a story you read in the paper about a man who tracks the nighttime migrations of songbirds. With focused freewriting, you are trying to concentrate on one particular subject. You can write the name of that subject at the top of the page to remind you of your topic as you write. The rules are the same as the other types of freewriting, but you are focusing on one question or idea and exploring it in depth.

One drawback of focused freewriting is that students sometimes confuse it with a different step in the writing process: drafting. Remember that freewriting is "invention" work, intended only to help you explore ideas on paper. Drafting takes place only after you have explored, analyzed, and organized those ideas. Freewriting helps you think and write critically about a topic while drafting occurs once you have done the critical thinking necessary to come up with a unified, cohesive, and organized plan for an essay.

Listing/Brainstorming

This method of mapping is the least visual and the most straightforward. Unlike freewriting, where you write continuously, with listing you write down words and/or phrases that provide a shorthand for the ideas you might use in your essay, much as you would a grocery or "to-do" list. Brainstorming is a bit looser. Lists usually follow line after line on the page; brainstorming consists of words and phrases placed anywhere you want to write them on the page.

Example of Brainstorming about Climate Change

Global warming

Polar ice caps melting

Cities underwater as water rises

Natural process or human caused?

People will lose homes when in places where ocean will rise

UK built Thames barrier

How much will preventative measures cost, and who pays for them?

Clustering

When you think of a cluster, you think of several like things grouped together, often with something holding them together. Peanut clusters, a type of candy, are peanuts joined together with milk chocolate. Star clusters are groupings of stars, like the Pleiades or the Big Dipper, connected by their relative positions to each other in space. You can create clusters of like ideas by grouping your ideas around a central topic on a blank sheet of paper. Figure 4.2 shows a sample clustering exercise.

Figure 4.2 • Sample Clustering Exercise

Activity 4.8 • Try Different Prewriting Techniques

Compose

Choose a topic, and try each of the prewriting techniques listed below. Save your work. Then, in your group, discuss which technique or techniques you prefer.

▌ Freewriting

▌ Invisible Freewriting

▌ Focused Freewriting

▌ Listing

▌ Clustering

Activity 4.9 • Organize or Arrange Your Prewriting

Compose

The "invention" process is intended to get our ideas out of our heads and onto a piece of paper, but rarely do these ideas arrive in the most logical or effective order. Take some time to analyze the material that you produced when you completed the previous activity. Make a list, placing all the ideas in a logical order, and combine similar ideas.

Next, look for your most significant point, the most important thing you want to say about your subject. This may become your tentative thesis.

Then, identify which of the other items will help you communicate your thesis, and delete items that are irrelevant to it. Keep organizing and deleting until you are satisfied with your list of topics or main points.

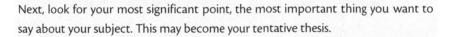

Reading 4.1

Take a Leap into Writing

by Craig Wynne

When I was working at Berkeley's College Academic Support Center, I often tutored second-language learners who struggled with sentences that had awkward constructions. Sometimes, I would say to a student, "What is it you're trying to

Craig Wynne is an Assistant Professor of English and Modern Foreign Languages at Hampton University who also consults professionals on overcoming writing anxiety. In this article, Wynne uses skydiving as both a figurative and literal representation of "jumping" into the writing process. As you read, think about the times in your academic career when you have had hesitations about writing and how that affected your writing process.

say here?" The student inevitably could state the point orally with accuracy and clarity. I would then say to the student, "Write down what you just said." The student would write it down with pen and paper. Then I'd say, "Okay, pretend you're the professor. Which do you think is the easier sentence to understand: what you wrote or what you typed?" The student would say, "What I wrote. Whenever I type, I'm always afraid of what the professor will say."

Craig Wynne says, "When jumping out of an airplane, you don't have time to think about consequences. You just have to do it. [. . .] The same principle applies to writing."

Photo Credit: Craig Wynne

Around that time, I read an article in *Writer* magazine entitled "Forget the Rules and Take a Leap," by an author named Deanna Roy. In this article, Roy had been suffering from writer's block, and she found that skydiving was a way for her to release her thoughts without fear of saying the "wrong thing." So I decided to put this idea into practice myself for the purposes of teaching my students about overcoming their inhibitions when it came to writing.

When jumping out of an airplane, you don't have time to think about consequences. You just have to do it. You can see from the photo, jumping wasn't an easy thing for me to do, but afterwards I was glad I had gone through with taking that leap.

The same principle applies to writing. You need to find a way to write without thinking about whether your words are spelled correctly or whether the professor won't like the idea. Those thoughts get in the way with your writing process. Some students can write with that kind of freedom on a computer, but others find that with the computer comes an uninvited editor who looks over their shoulder and criticizes. Yet, they can escape that editor by talking out their thoughts and then writing with pen and paper. Whatever works. This doesn't mean that writing is ever going to be easy. It's just easier if you can get your thoughts down on a piece of paper before that internal editor starts looking for errors.

A professor named Peter Elbow developed a process called freewriting, which helps writers take that leap from thoughts into words. To freewrite, you put your pen to paper and just write. You don't want to think about whether something is spelled incorrectly or whether the professor will like an idea. Freewriting is the chance for you to get your ideas down on paper (or on the computer). When you freewrite, you don't stop. You just write. Even if you have an idea you think sounds completely stupid or off-the-wall, just write it down. You never know. Sometimes, those "silly" ideas could contain something you might be able to use for your assignment. When I start a project, I begin by letting all my ideas out in words in a row, even if they don't sound quite right. Professor Elbow remarked that freewriting results in a lot of words that are garbage. That's true. However, eventually, I come to words that express an idea I like. In order to get to the point of liking my words, I have to take that leap onto the page. Eventually, I have to worry about grammar, structure, and the end product, but not while I'm freewriting.

Activity 4.10 • Consider "Take a Leap into Writing"

Collaborate

In your small group or on your own, consider and answer the following questions.

1. How do you write most easily? On a computer? With pen and paper? Share your experience getting words onto a page.

2. What do you think of Wynne's comparison of writing to skydiving? What do the two things have in common?

3. Do you have an internal editor that keeps you from writing freely? Can you describe your editor? What does it do?

Compose

Activity 4.11 • Focused Freewriting

Practice doing some focused freewriting by following these steps.

1. Write your topic at the top of a blank sheet of paper.

2. Write a list of at least 10 aspects or characteristics of your topic.

3. Choose two or three items from your list, and do a focused freewriting on each item for five to eight minutes.

4. Add more items to your list if you have discovered new ideas during your freewriting.

Artistic and Inartistic Proofs

In the previous chapter, we discussed the three appeals or means that a rhetor can use to persuade an audience: *ethos, pathos,* and *logos.* In *The Art of Rhetoric,* Aristotle divides these appeals or means of persuasion into two types of proofs: artistic and inartistic. Today, these proofs are still part of the writing process though we call them by different names.

Artistic proofs are logical arguments constructed by rhetors from ideas plucked from their minds. An individual then develops these thoughts into a line of reasoning and, in the process, explores and narrows the topic, creates a thesis, and determines the ideas that need to be conveyed to the audience. These proofs are the ones that Aristotle and other ancient rhetoricians believed were critically important, for they are the ones developed from the *rhetor's own mind* and, thus, *invented.* These ideas can be shaped into two types of arguments—deductive and inductive—which we will discuss in the next few pages.

Inartistic proofs are direct evidence that the speaker might use to support the argument, such as testimony, documents, and anything else that rhetors do not invent through their own thinking. Today, we would call these proofs research. They, also, are essential to writing, but they should *support* the writer's ideas, rather than lead them.

For Aristotle's students, the use of artistic and inartistic proofs might not have been a two-step process—first one and then the other, though the proofs are arranged that way in *The Art of Rhetoric,* as they are in this book. Rather, they might have developed both proofs in an alternating or recursive process. After developing basic ideas for a composition through invention, these students would then collect information from authorities (testimony). Then they would return to inventing artistic proofs about the project, followed by more references to inartistic proofs. Today, we have more resources for research than did the ancient Greeks, but this does not make artistic proofs any less important. The differences between artistic and inartistic proofs are summarized in Table 4.4.

Table 4.4 • Aristotle's Artistic and Inartistic Proofs

Artistic	Inartistic
Ideas from the rhetor's own mind, thus *invented*	Information gained from external sources
Personal knowledge	Authorities
Observation	Testimony
Patterns of reasoning	Documents

Activity 4.12 • **Begin with What You Know**

In your small group, make a list of controversial topics that you already have some knowledge about because of personal experience or course work. For example, one of you may be among the millions of Americans without health insurance or you may know someone else in this position. If so, you probably know about some of the failings of the American health care system. Alternatively, you may have lost a job during the Great Recession or been unable to find a job when you needed one. If so, you probably have some thoughts about the efforts of the federal government to deal with the economic crisis. These personal experiences give you knowledge which you can use as artistic proofs in an essay. Share your group's list with the class.

Collaborate

Develop Artistic Proofs through Observation

Close observation for descriptive detail can enhance almost any topic. If you are writing a paper on the effectiveness of recycling in your community, you might take a trip to your community's processing area for recycled glass. There you could gather information through observing the glass recycling process. Good observations become personal knowledge which makes them artistic proofs.

You may need to call to get permission to visit certain places. You'll need to identify yourself and your topic. Usually you can get permission to visit and observe. However, if you cannot get permission to visit an area, you can ask your contact if there is a similar area nearby. Again, look at your research questions before you visit to decide which questions might be answered by your observations. For example, if you have read about recycling centers in other communities, during your visit to the local center, you could observe the similarities and differences in their procedures. Good writers always gather more detail than they actually use so they have choices about what to include.

The key to successful observation is tuning the senses. Can you remember what your room smelled like when you woke up this morning, the first thing you saw when you opened your eyes, the way your sheets or blanket felt against your skin, the sounds in the room after you turned off your alarm, or the taste of the orange juice or coffee you had with breakfast? Our minds are trained to ignore seemingly unimportant information, so if you can't remember any sensory details from your morning, you're not alone. When conducting an observation, however, those sensory responses are an important part of your research. Sitting in the place you're observing, freewrite for at least five minutes on each of the senses: touch, taste, smell, sight, and sound. You might even freewrite on each of the senses from several different vantage points, depending on the size of the place or the event you're observing. Take notes on the responses given by those you speak with.

Within fifteen minutes of leaving the place you have been observing, take a few minutes to read over your notes and write a few overall impressions or add details you missed in your description. Look again at your research questions, and decide which ones have been answered by your visit.

Explore

Activity 4.13 • Observation Exercise to Develop Artistic Proofs

In this exercise, describe your classroom. Alternatively, go to another setting such as a museum, restaurant, or library and describe that space and the people in it.

- How large is the space, approximately? Describe the shape of the room, and the color and texture of the walls, the ceiling, and the floor.
- How is the space furnished? Describe the color, shape, and style of the furnishings.
- What about representing the other senses? Is the room silent or noisy? Does it have a characteristic smell? Describe.
- How many people are in the room? What are they doing? Describe their ages, general style of dress, and possessions such as computers, backpacks, or purses.
- Pick two or three people that stand out in some way from the other occupants and write a sentence or two about each, describing what it is about each person that caught your attention.

Porsche Macan S: Is This Compact Crossover Barbie's Dream Car?

By Dan Neil

Dan Neil, auto columnist for the Wall Street Journal, *reviewed the new Porsche Macan S in his weekly column "Rumble Seat." He calls the vehicle Barbie's dream car, meaning that Porsche has designed it with well-to-do, fashion-conscious women in mind. See if you think that stereotype fits the car.*

As you read the article, pay attention to how the author uses details from his personal knowledge of the auto world, as well as his close observation from driving and inspecting the Porsche, to enrich his writing. Notice, also, how some details—such as the $500 million Porsche spent to build an assembly line for the car in Leipzig, Germany—likely came from promotional materials or interviews with Porsche personnel.

You just knew when Porsche decided to build Barbie's Dream Car it was going to be awesome.

And it is. The 2015 Macan S ($49,900 MSRP) is Porsche's entry to the exploding luxury compact crossover segment, and it is a dram of excelsior, a proud, darling thing: quick off the line (5.0 seconds to 60 mph, with the optional launch control engaged) and nimble at the helm, with a steel-spring suspension (wishbone front and trapezoidal-link rear) that's as tight as a speed skater's buttocks. Actually, the Macan S drives shockingly well considering it weighs in around 4,500 pounds and is a foot taller than a 911. More on that later.

Curb appeal? Forget about it. Among the details to savor is the clamshell hood that extends to the front wheel arches, so that the hood shut lines go away. The Macan isn't dripping in aggression, design-wise, with soft,

Sexy Beast. The Porsche Macan S has a leg up in the luxury compact crossover market with soft contours and the best interior among its rivals.

Photo Credit: Porche Cars North America

rounded corners inherited from the 911 and an open, expressive face. It has nothing like the Range Rover Evoque's narrow, predatory stare. And yet the Macan is low, wide and stance-y, with staggered tires (a wider set in back) and heavy haunches. It's a Cayenne in short pants.

Porsche has made no secret of the desire to expand the brand to more women. Translating that desire into product design is a perilous business, especially for such a macho brand. But I think the Porsche design team, led by Michael Mauer, got exactly what it was looking for. The Macan hits a mall parking lot like a fishing lure hits the water, if smartly dressed women were largemouth bass.

The category, Alex, is premium/luxury compact crossovers and/or sport-utilities. The yard marks are wide, but you are going to shell out anywhere from about $40,000-$70,000—I recommend leasing such nonsense—and the competitive set includes the cream of the world auto-making crop: Acura RDX, Audi Q3, BMW X3, Land Rover Discovery Sport, Mercedes-Benz GLA, the Evoque and a few others.

In this category you are free to spend like you are on cocaine. There is such a thing as a Macan Turbo (with a 3.6-liter, 400-hp version of the V6) that starts at $72,300 and can top six figures when you start adding carbon-ceramic brakes ($8,150) and air suspension ($1,385).

Our Macan S test car—painted ermine-white with beige leather interior — came in at $72,620 and included 20-inch alloy wheels ($1,260), the active dampers ($1,360), the upgraded Bose stereo ($1,400) and infotainment package ($2,990) and the Premium Package Plus ($5,990). Oof!

The powertrain is a thing of beauty, starting with the all-aluminum, 90-degree, 3.0-liter direct-injection twin-turbo V6, producing a nicely focused 339 pound-feet, from 1,450 rpm all the way to 5,000 rpm, and peak horsepower from 5,500-6,500 rpm. Golly, what a sewing machine. When you switch to Sport + mode and add some throttle, the engine bawls, it purrs, it chuckles. Hot, guttural overrun sounds come courtesy of the active exhaust valve. But the symphony is turned way down in volume, a bit too far to seem threatening, just adorable. Growl, kitty, growl!

Downstream of the engine is Porsche's seven-speed dual-clutch PDK automatic transmission and the full-time all-wheel drive system, based around a digitally managed multi-plate center differential. The Macan's front diff is open and the rear is limited-slip, with the option of the Porsche Torque Vectoring Plus on the rear diff, slewing torque left or right as needed to help the car turn harder and accelerate sooner.

Romp it and all this actuates with greased flawlessness one might expect in a late-model Porsche, even to a fault. There isn't a sharp edge to be found is this car. Even in Sport + mode, the PDK acts like/drives like any other high-tech, torque-converter based automatic transmission, with upshift events that flutter among the ratios, never bang.

Honestly, Porsche. If the camera could zoom into the ghostly face of Ferdinand Porsche as he surveyed his legendary sports-car empire, now building glammy luxe crossovers for the recently divorced in West Palm Beach, would he have a single tear, like Iron Eyes Cody?

Oh, I've had it all explained to me: Porsche, now a holding of Volkswagen AG, has been fully entrained into the group's product slipstream. The Macan is a platform cousin to the Audi Q5, sharing VW's MLB platform, for light-duty vehicles with front-longitudinal engine orientation and all-wheel drive.

About a third of the Porsche's structure is common to the Audi, but Macan gets Porsche-proprietary engines and the PDK gearbox; exterior and interior; suspensions and dynamics software. Porsche AG also spent more than $550 million to construct the Macan assembly line in Leipzig, Germany—where car-building counts—with an annual capacity of 50,000 cars. So pedigree really isn't an issue.

And yet, I can't help thinking the Macan would have been a lot—what's the word?—lighter, had it not been born to share the girdle of the corporate platform.

If the Macan wins, it's to the credit of Porsche's interior-trim department. This is the best interior of any in the competitive set: clean and Nordic in design, wintry with polished alloy, rich with skins, with lots of very nice parts from the company's bins, including Porsche's new, three-spoke steering wheel, like the one in the 918 Spyder. The seats are terrific, and the fully upholstered rear cargo space large and useful (17.7 cubic feet). My kids had no problems riding in the back seat. The whole thing is surprisingly undiminished by the price point.

If the Macan stumbles, it might be because it feels a bit soft to enthusiasts. This truckette is well over two tons, and all the adaptive suspension, torque vectoring and sport tires only defray the costs of that mass. Yes, it has good road-holding in corners, considering, but the weight makes it feel antsy. Yes, the electric-assist steering is tactile and responsive, but it could be more of both. The short-stroke engine of the Macan S (69 mm stroke and 96 mm bore) spins like a bandit, but it's all so at a distance, so muted and isolated. The Macan's missing piece is driver involvement.

But maybe you don't feel like driving at the moment. In that case, switch on the Macan's optional Lane Keeping Assist, a ghost-in-the-machine system that will keep a car heading down a road with minimal input from the driver. Now you can smile. And don't forget to wave, Barbie.

Explore

Activity 4.14 • Find Artistic and Inartistic Proofs in a Reading

Much of the information for Dan Neil's column, "Porsche Macan S: Is This Compact Crossover Barbie's Dream Car?" comes from his own personal experience and observation. For example, his description of the car: "[I]t is a dram of excelsior, a proud, darling thing: quick off the line...with a steel-spring suspension (wishbone front and trapezoidal-link rear) that's as tight as a speed skater's buttocks," is his own evaluation or thought and, thus, an artistic proof. So is the sentence, "Porsche has made no secret of the desire to expand the brand to more women. Translating that desire into product design is a perilous business, especially for such a macho brand." That knowledge comes from his long experience with reviewing the automobile market.

However, the numbers Neil uses to describe the powertrain—"all-aluminum, 90-degree, 3.0-liter direct-injection twin-turbo V6, producing a nicely focused 339 pound-feet, from 1,450 rpm all the way to 5,000 rpm, and peak horsepower from 5,500-6,500 rpm"—may have come from the manufacturer's promotional literature or an interview, though the conclusion of "nicely focused" may be his own.

For this activity, go through the reading and highlight (or underline) the parts that you think come from Neil's own knowledge or observation. These are the artistic proofs. Information he has obtained from other sources (such as the car company) would be inartistic proofs.

If you aren't sure whether or not a sentence is Neil's own knowledge or observation, make a note of that in the margin. Discuss this as a class.

Activity 4.15 • Develop Criteria for Reviews

Explore

In your small group, discuss these questions in response to Neil's article about the Porsche Macan S.

1. What criteria did Dan Neil use in evaluating the Porsche Macan S? Share your answers with the class.

2. What reviews do you plan to write for Activity 4.16? Discuss in your group how each of you plans to develop criteria to evaluate your topics.

Individually, make a short list of criteria you will use to evaluate your topic for Activity 4.16.

Activity 4.16 • Write a Product Review

Compose

Choose a new product in a category you know well, such as a computer or a motorcycle, and write a review as if you were a columnist for a newspaper, magazine, or blog. Using the techniques explained in this chapter, such as freewriting or brainstorming, prewrite to elicit what you know about the product and the product category. Then, observe the product and try it out, so that you can review its positives and negatives. If you need specific information that you do not know, consult the product advertising, packaging, or instruction manual.

Like Dan Neil's auto product review, you can use vivid language and insider slang in order to provide an enjoyable experience for your reader. Remember, however, that this is an argument. You need to evaluate whether the product is a good or bad selection for its target audience and why.

Reading 4.3

Guardians of the Galaxy's Happy Satire of the Sad Origin Story

by Katie Kilkenny

Superhero origin stories, for the most part, aren't very original. They all to some extent involve a young child or particularly immature man falling prey to a terrible crime, accident, experiment, or, alternately, reluctantly getting chosen by higher powers. Then comes a period of

Katie Kilkenny's film review, published on theatlantic.com, makes use of the superhero origin story plot format to review Guardians of the Galaxy. *Superhero origin stories, according to Kilkenny, are not generally very original. However,* Guardians *adds a satire twist to the plot pattern because the deep trauma's of the film's heroes has not endowed them with any nobility, as it usually does in an origin story; rather, they are misfit sell-outs who are, nevertheless, called upon to save the galaxy.*

shock swiftly followed by a period of combat training—for, as all comic lovers understand, a true hero directs his mournful energies toward coordinating outfits, gadgets, and crime-fighting prowess around a theme. The takeaway: Superheroes are just like you and me until something genuinely terrible befalls them—then, an inhumanly noble hunger to fight crime takes over.

On the surface, *Guardians of the Galaxy,* Marvel's latest movie, is an origin story, too. Given the obscurity of the source comic, it has to be: Our heroes, a bunch of alien rogues, were introduced briefly in a 1969 issue of *Marvel Superheroes,* played benchwarmers to the likes of the Avengers for about 50 years, then were revived by writers Dan Abnett and Andy Lanning in 2008 to middling sales. To counteract the risk of the venture we follow recognizable white male Chris Pratt, newly buff and emotional, playing Peter Quill, a boy who was abducted by aliens and now calls himself "Star-Lord."

Sensibly, Peter's chosen alias is roundly mocked by his fellow Guardians in the film—as is his masculinity, wooing capabilities, general leadership, and other qualities that usually endorse newbie heroes in tights. Pratt is at the point in his career when critics would label him an "unlikely leading man"; here he actually plays one to his scrappy, squabbling intergalactic crew. As the title suggests, they're the real heroes of this kinda-sorta-superhero movie. If *Guardians of the Galaxy* is an origin story, it is also a satire of the origin story, one that emphasizes the power of the "We" over that of the "Chosen One."

Photo Credit: Everett Collection, Inc.

Every member of the Guardians has known deep trauma. Chris Pratt's lead Peter Quill lost his mom (cancer); Zoe Saldana's Gamora is practically dead to the last surviving member of her family Nebula (Karen Gillan); her previous colleague-in-crime Ronan (Lee Pace) slaughtered the family of Dave Bautista's Drax; and Rocket Raccoon (Bradley Cooper) doesn't even have a family since, as a human experiment in anthropomorphization gone wrong, he's basically a lab animal. As for his pet, the sentient tree Groot (Vin Diesel), who knows? He can only string together three words (the innocuous truth, "I am Groot"). Judging by the way he tortures his adversaries—pushing his roots into their nostrils, out other orifices—it's safe to assume the tree has issues, too.

But in contrast to the rest of the genre, these sob stories don't bestow nobility. No one's particular woes are more "super" than another's. In fact, any attempt at tragedy one-upmanship would counteract the movie's shaggy, communal comedy. The Guardians aren't superheroes so much as they are a heterogeneous mix of losers, bandits, and outlaws who know just how unexceptional they are. As Chris Pratt's character says to rally the troops, "I look around and I see losers. Like, people who have lost something."

The real reason they connect is because they're all lucky sellouts, not Chosen Ones. The point of their big entrée into superherodom is to scrape together some prize money by selling the mysterious Infinity Stone, this franchise's equivalent of the equally irrelevant MacGuffin in *The Avengers,* the Cosmic Cube. The film then becomes a series of encounters that all lead up to the faceoff with the slithery highest bidder. While *Guardians* welcomes comparisons to *Star Wars*, there's no Luke, paragon of high-minded heroic ideals—our heroes are all a bunch of opportunistic Hans, ineloquent Wookies, and cowardly C-3POs. Yes, they're a strong, sad bunch, but in total it's a managerial nightmare to corral a team around a single crime-fighting objective sans incessant arguments.

In fact, *Guardians of the Galaxy* makes the case that a hero's individual strength amounts to merely a culturally acceptable form of pigheadedness. Take the movie's portrayal of Drax, a conflicted vigilante with only one thing on his mind—avenging his murdered wife and child. It's a generic motivation, and another movie might try to use him to bring us to tears. But here he nearly dies in the attempt for revenge, thus endangering the greater mission, to make money. "We've all got dead people!" his compatriot Rocket Raccoon scoffs. And for one moment of wonderful lucidity a Marvel movie makes sport of Marvel's big, profitable trope: the prolonged mourning of buff guys in tights.

The lampooning is more playful than genuinely threatening to the Marvel universe, though. For however much Guardians critiques the usual fare, it's still bookended by Chris Pratt's tragic flashbacks, a technique reminiscent of Christopher Nolan's super-serious *Batman Begins*. The flashbacks are the movie's least convincing moments, either because they're too earnest for the self-conscious flick or the actor isn't as good at shedding tears as he is at acting a buffoon on *Parks and Recreation*.

The origin story isn't some morally fraught trope that needs toppling, either. In fact, psychologist Robin Rosenburg has noted that superhero origin stories teach us "how to be heroes, choosing altruism over the pursuit of wealth and power."

But if we're going to take them seriously as instructions for how to be altruistic super-individuals, origin stories could also teach teamwork. This is where *Guardians of the Galaxy,* at its most delightfully self-aware, has a new take. It doesn't pretend like its heroes are not all mortals with an interest in pursuing that plebeian concern, money. Even so, it does show that a group of flawed losers can take down a planetary dictator with an enchanted stone if, for one moment, they forget their own baggage and hack out a semblance of a plan first.

Collaborate

Activity 4.17 • **Discuss Review of *Guardians of the Galaxy***

Katie Kilkenny describes *Guardians of the Galaxy* as a superhero origin story. In your small group, discuss the following points and share your responses with the class.

1. Make a list of other superhero origin movies. In what ways do they fit the pattern Kilkenny lays out in her first paragraph? In what ways do they deviate from Kilkenny's pattern?

2. How does Kilkenny say *Guardians* fits the pattern, and in what ways does it not? What is the main strength of the movie, and how is it a new take on the superhero origin story?

3. Is Kilkenny's review effective? Why or why not?

Explore

Activity 4.18 • **Develop Criteria for Film Reviews**

In your small group, discuss the following points.

1. How does Katie Kilkenny employ the use of the superhero origin story movie plot pattern to create her criteria for reviewing *Guardians of the Galaxy*?

2. What film reviews do you plan to write for your next assignments? Is there a plot pattern such as a love story or buddy film that you can apply to your chosen movies? Perhaps there is an outstanding performance by an actor or an excellent rendering of a book into film. What other criteria might you employ? How would you evaluate a film based on your chosen criteria?

Individually, search the Internet for reviews of your chosen film to use as resources to back up you evaluation. Be sure to cite any quotes or paraphrases from other reviews you incorporate into your review. Then, write down the criteria you plan to use to review your film. Discuss these criteria with your group, and, if requested, turn in your writing to your instructor.

Activity 4.19 • **Write a Film Review**

Compose

In this assignment, you are a film critic. Write a review that could appear in a newspaper, magazine, or blog. Your style and tone will be dictated by your audience, so identify the publication just under the title of your review by saying something like this: "Written for Undergroundfilms.com." Be sure to read several reviews published in your chosen media outlet.

▌ Select a film you would like to review. Films that are social commentaries are particularly good for reviewing. It does not have to be a serious movie, but it should be one that makes you think about some social trend or historical event.

▌ After you decide on a film, learn about its context. Who is the director, producer, and primary actors? What films have these individuals worked on before? Have they won awards? Are they known for a certain style? Read and annotate other reviews of the film, marking sections that you might paraphrase or quote to support your opinions.

▌ Employ the criteria you developed in the previous activity to write a working thesis that makes an argument about your chosen film.

▌ Create a working thesis that makes an argument about the film. You can modify this thesis later, but it helps to identify early on what you want to argue.

▌ Use some of the invention strategies from this chapter to help you articulate what proofs you can use to support your argument.

▌ Near the beginning of your draft, briefly summarize enough of the film that your review will be interesting to those who have not seen it. However, don't be a "spoiler." Don't ruin the film for potential viewers by giving away the ending.

▌ Organize your essay into three main points that support your thesis and at least one counterargument that complicates or disagrees with your argument.

▌ Write a compelling introduction that uses one of the approaches discussed in Chapter 5, pp. 196-197. You want your reader to be interested in what you have to say. For example, you might begin with a startling quote from the film or a vivid description of a pivotal scene.

▌ Be sure to include specific examples and colorful details. These are essential to make your review interesting to the reader.

Activity 4.20 • **Reflect on Your Film Review**

Freewrite for five minutes about the movie review you just wrote. Answer one or more of the questions in the previous activity, or write about something else related to your product review. Why did you choose that particular film? What was it like combining your personal knowledge, observation, and information you obtained from the movie website or another review?

If your instructor requests, turn your freewriting into a polished paragraph with a thesis and supporting sentences.

Activity 4.21 • **Write on Your Blog**

Choose a controversial topic, and speculate in your blog whether or not that topic is at a stasis point for any of the stasis questions.

Activity 4.22 • **Write in Your Commonplace Book**

In your commonplace book, freewrite about how you do invention. What methods do you use to extract from your mind what you already know about a subject (what Aristotle would call artistic proofs)?

chapter 5
Writing Rhetorically

Praxis in Action

How I Write

Amy Brumfield
Instructor, Idaho State
University

Whether I have to write two pages or 200 pages, I break the writing process into steps so it never feels overwhelming. This is my personal approach to every assignment.

1. Make a mess. I read the assignment, and then grab a piece of paper. I write down every single thought I have about my topic until I have filled at least one whole page. I don't change or erase any idea, no matter how crazy, weird, or off topic it seems. In fact, I write until the ideas become really weird. My first thoughts are always boring, and boring essays are the hardest to write. At this point, I often do some basic background reading on my topic if I don't know the subject well.

2. Divide the ideas into basic categories, starting with the ideas that intrigue me most and which have the most avenues to explore.

3. Create a question about my topic that cannot possibly be answered with a simple yes or no. Ideally, it's a question that I can answer with a good guess but can't really explain from my current knowledge. I like the idea that the answer will teach me something or cause me to think differently by the time I finish researching the question.

4. Create a thesis that answers that question. I make sure the thesis has a topic, a viewpoint with an opposing side, and a reason for why it's right.

5. Reread the assignment to make sure that my thesis fits it.

6. Put the ideas into a logical order.

7. Write a pre-rough draft to make sure I have an argument of my own that isn't simply research material pasted together.

(continued on next page)

8. Start my main research by verifying the information I think I already know. I am often at least partly wrong about some of my conceptions.

9. Research wider. Because I have a thesis, I can classify each piece of evidence as "agrees with," "disagrees with," or "irrelevant to my argument." Because I have a basic draft, I can see where the evidence fits, and stick it in. Now I can revise and adjust until I have a real rough draft.

10. Reread the paper to see how my question and my thesis have changed. They always do.

11. Edit the paper with the new thesis in mind because I now know exactly what I want to argue.

12. Review and revise the introduction and the conclusion because they almost always can be improved.

13. Proofread, then have at least one other person give me feedback on my draft before I make final changes.

Enter the Conversation Through Writing

Cicero's famous work, *On the Ideal Orator*, is not a treatise or handbook about how to be an effective rhetorician. Instead, it is a dialogue, a conversation. The setting is a villa outside Rome belonging to Lucius Licinius Crassus, and the time is 91 CE, an era of dangerous unrest in the Roman Empire. Prominent and respected citizens gather with Crassus to escape, for a while, the political crisis developing in the city. Crassus and his guests settle at leisure under a wide, spreading plane tree, not only to enjoy its shade but also to pay homage to Plato's *Phaedrus*, which similarly took place under a plane tree, though in Greece. They take time this day to dialogue about the attributes of an ideal orator. The purpose of the arguments they present to each other is not to win out over the others but, conversing together, to come to knowledge. It is not a trivial pursuit. Cicero reveals what his characters do not know—soon they will all die horribly as part of the civil unrest in Rome, violence traceable to the failure of leaders to resolve their differences in nonviolent dialogue.

Throughout ancient times, dialogue appears alongside rhetoric. It was through dialogue that rhetoricians such as Aristotle, Isocrates, and Cicero taught their students rhetorical skills. Today, in the writing classroom, group discussion or pairs dialogue is also part of the teaching process. A rhetorical text, too, is a conversation with previous texts, responding to ideas they have presented. In addition, arguments include paraphrases and quotes from others' compositions, making them part of the conversation. Moreover, writers composing texts must anticipate their audiences' reactions—questions they might ask or objections they might raise—so responses to these questions and objections can be included in the argument. This process of responding to audiences in advance continues the conversation.

Respond to the Rhetorical Situation

When you are faced with a familiar situation that compels writing, it triggers a response that demonstrates you know the unspoken rules in play. For example, if a friend sends you a text asking you to meet after class for coffee, you know how to respond using the shorthand language of texting. If you are ill, instead of calling in sick, you may send an email to your supervisor. You know how to do that. Laura Klocinski writes in her *Digital Age* post, "Can Social Media Make Us Better Writers?", that participating in diverse social media such as Facebook, Twitter, Blogger, and more, each with its own format, helps us as writers because writers learn to use a different tone and style with each site. She says,

> You would not compose a blogger post in the same way you would write a short tweet. Facebook posts tend to be longer, with either personal or opinion topics. In contrast, LinkedIn is a professional network, which teaches you how to sell your work experience and skills. When switching from site to site, you are learning to communicate across different platforms. These changes in writing style help develop flexibility and rhetorical skills.

Though Klocinski does not use the term, she is talking about different rhetorical situations, a concept coined by Lloyd F. Bitzer. A rhetorical situation is the context in which speakers speak or writers write—a context created by the conversation that compels your response. The conversation may be immediate, as was your friend's text message asking you to meet for coffee, or it may be ongoing, as is your knowledge of how to tell your supervisor that you are taking the day off because you are ill. The conversation can be words, images, or actions, or some combination of the three.

If Twitter and Facebook had been around when Bitzer was writing in the 1960s, he would probably have used them as examples of different rhetorical situations. Rhetoric is pragmatic; we use it to perform tasks, not by physical action, but by words. A rhetor uses words to alter reality by engaging an audience and persuading the audience to change in some way. Sometimes the persuasive change is small, as when a friend's invitation causes you to meet for coffee. Other times rhetoric compels massive change, as when an enemy's surprise attack compels a declaration of war.

Bitzer and Klocinski would agree that, as critical thinkers, we innately search our brains for previous conversations that tell us the rules that are embedded in a rhetorical situation and guide us in how to respond. Bitzer writes,

> Cicero's speeches against Cataline were called forth by a specific union of persons, events, objects, and relations, and by an exigence which amounted to an imperative stimulus; the speeches in the Senate rotunda three days after the assassination of the President of the United States [John F. Kennedy] were actually required by the situation. So controlling is situation that we should consider it the very ground of rhetorical activity, whether that activity is primitive and productive of a simple utterance or artistic and productive of the Gettysburg Address.[1]

Usually, our responses to a rhetorical situation are appropriate, fluid, and effective. Other times, our understanding of the context is flawed; in those cases, our writing is likely to be less than successful in eliciting the desired response from our audiences. One of the purposes of this textbook is to enable you to become more aware of rhetorical situations, so, if you are not sure how to respond, you can seek out sources of information that will guide you in writing optimal responses.

This chapter presents you with several writing situations: a blog post about writing, an op-ed editorial, and an argumentative research paper. The discussions, writing prompts, and activities are designed to highlight the rhetorical situation in each. As you work your way through the chapter, keep the concept of rhetorical situation in mind.

Reading 5.1

Laura Klocinski, when she wrote this blog post, was a junior at Eastern Michigan University, majoring in Written Communication. "Can Social Media Make Us Better Writers?" was published on the blog My Campus.

Can Social Media Make Us Better Writers?
by Laura Klocinski

In the writing field, there is a natural hesitation about using social media as a tool. This is natural, considering that websites such as Twitter have contributed to the corruption of the English language, adding words such as "YOLO," "LOL" and "BRB" to our generation's vocabulary. However, I think it is often overlooked that our language is fluid,

---

1. Bitzer, Lloyd F. "The Rhetorical Situation." *Philosophy & Rhetoric,* vol. 1, no. 1, Jan. 1968, pp. 1-14. *JSTOR* www.jstor.org/stable/i40008864.

and new words are constantly being added. When social media was first introduced, its primary focus was non-professional interactions between friends. Many people believed that the social media trend would disappear just as quickly as it had miraculously appeared. However, social media sites have only grown, as have the uses. Now, social media is used professionally as well as privately. Advertising and Journalism, two fields that written communication majors often pursue, have become dependent on social media sharing. Even in reputable online newspapers such as the Washington Post and the New York Times, there are buttons enabling users to share articles on either Twitter or Facebook.

With so many social media sites available, including Facebook, Twitter, Tumblr, Blogger and more, it can be a challenge to keep track of them all. However, this plethora of sites may actually be helping us as writers. Each site has its own format, and you use a different tone when posting on each. You would not compose a blogger post in the same way you would write a short tweet. Facebook posts tend to be longer, with either personal or opinion topics. In contrast, LinkedIn is a professional network, which teaches you how to sell your work experience and skills. When switching from site to site, you are learning to communicate across different platforms. These changes in writing style help develop flexibility and rhetorical skills.

All writing projects and assignments have unique instructions, and many challenge you to adopt a new tone. While research papers need a factual and impartial perspective, we are encouraged to use a more personal and argumentative tone in persuasive writing. By using multiple platforms and becoming fluent in a number of styles, you will have an easier time switching gears for different writing assignments. I am not suggesting that we begin using "LOL" and hashtags in our academic and future professional work, but rather that we use our experience on a variety of platforms to become more flexible as writers, and use these platforms to explore new writing formats.

Activity 5.1 • Tailor Your Social Media Message

Collaborate

In your group, discuss tailoring a single message to post on different social media, as Laura Klocinski describes in "Can Social Media Make Us Better Writers?" First, decide what you want to say. Then revise, elaborate, and condense the words for at least three different social media such as Facebook, Twitter, Tumblr, and Blogger. Present your versions to the class.

Compose

Activity 5.2 • **Write a Blog Post about Writing**

Individually, write a blog post of about 300 words that would be appropriate for a blog like *My Campus* (mycampus.writingcommons.org) which publishes entries written by students about writing. For your topic, choose something you have learned this semester about writing.

Compose

Activity 5.3 • **Comment on Your Blog Post**

Freewrite for five minutes about the blog post you wrote for Activity 5.2. Answer one of the following questions, or write about something else related to your blog post.

1. How did you know how to write a blog post?

2. Did you read "Can Social Media Make Us Better Writers?" or other blog posts that talk about writing?

3. How did you know what tone and style to use?

If your instructor directs you to, convert your freewriting into a paragraph to turn in.

Reading 5.2

The op-ed "Laws Protecting Women From Up-skirt Photo Assaults Fall Short" was published in the Daily Beast. *Holly Kearl, a facilitator with the OpEd Project, leads workshops empowering women to write op-ed editorials. Sadly, the laws protecting women from such invasions still vary from state to state.*

Laws Protecting Women From Upskirt Photo Assaults Fall Short
by Holly Kearl

[In March 2014], the Massachusetts Supreme Judicial Court made an alarming decision.

In 2010, Michael Robertson was caught by Massachusetts Bay Transit Authority police taking cellphone photos and videos up female riders' skirts and dresses. His case went to the Massachusetts Supreme Judicial Court where the judges ruled on March 5 that the upskirt photos were legal. They reached this decision, they said, because the women were fully clothed at the time.

Legislators in Massachusetts immediately drafted a new law making it illegal for someone to take secret photographs and recordings, even when someone is fully clothed, and Governor Deval Patrick signed it into law on March 7.

If you were surprised by this ruling and the way the Massachusetts law had been written, then you will be even more surprised to learn that the law is not so unusual. If you live in states like Hawaii, New York, Virginia, or Washington, non-consensual upskirt photos in public places are illegal. But if you live in states like Alabama, Nebraska, or Oregon, these photos are legal, just like it was in Massachusetts.

Another surprising fact is that only 15 years ago, it was legal for people to plant a recording device in someone's home. The first law against "video voyeurism" passed in 1999 in Louisiana after Susan Wilson discovered her neighbor had installed a video camera in her house. When she reported it to the police, they said that someone watching her in her home through a secret video camera was not a crime. Fortunately, the video voyeurism law she advocated for in Louisiana was quickly adopted in several other states, including California, Michigan, and Ohio.

Fifteen years later, it is standard for states to have a law against non-consensual photos and recordings when people are in places where they have a reasonable expectation of privacy, like their home, a hotel room, or a public restroom. At the national level, the Video Voyeurism Prevention Act of 204 says it is illegal on federal property, such as a military base, national park, or prison, to capture an image of a private area of an individual without their consent, and to knowingly do so under circumstances in which the individual has a reasonable expectation of privacy. The narrow interpretation of the phrase "reasonable expectation of privacy" is why upskirt photos are still legal in so many places.

When I am waiting for a subway, in a store, or standing at a corner, waiting for the light to change, it seems reasonable to me, and probably to you, that I should expect privacy from this kind of violation. But many states do not interpret it this way. For example, in Nebraska, upskirt photos are legal because, as the law is written, lawmakers argue no one can have a reasonable expectation of privacy in a public place, including from someone photographing their intimate areas that are covered by clothing.

The concept of privacy in public spaces is much different today than even a few years ago when most of these laws were written. In 2013, 90 percent of American adults owned a cell phone and 58 percent owned a smartphone, according to the Pew Research Internet Project. This means that more people than ever have the ability to covertly take photos in public spaces, and social media and mobile phone apps mean it only takes a second to share them. The laws need to reflect this reality.

While having a law against upskirt photos doesn't mean an end to this problem, it can give more rights to victims who want to take action and it may act as a deterrent for would-be upskirt photographers. It is time for every state to update its law to make upskirt photos illegal.

Fortunately, just as in Massachusetts, a growing number of state legislators are working toward that goal. In Nebraska, Lincoln Senator Amanda McGill introduced a bill last month to outlaw the act of taking pictures of people's private areas in public places. In January, lawmakers in Oregon said they are working to update the Invasion of Personal Privacy law after a 17-year-old girl reported a man who tried taking upskirt photos of her at a Christmas Bazaar.

For other states that need to update their laws and want guidance on the best language to use, I recommend they look to the laws in Hawaii and Washington.

Hawaii's law, Violation of Privacy in the Second Degree, says it is illegal if a person intentionally "covertly records or broadcasts an image of another person's intimate area underneath clothing, by use of any device, and that image is taken while that person is in a public place and without that person's consent."

Washington's Voyeurism law specifically states it is illegal for someone to take photos or videotape of the intimate areas of a non-consenting person's body under circumstances where the person has a reasonable expectation of privacy, including public places.

No one should have to worry about someone taking violating photos of them in public spaces, but should that happen, everyone deserves the right to legal recourse, no matter where they reside.

Collaborate

Activity 5.4 • Discuss "Laws Protecting Women From Upskirt Photo Assaults Fall Short"

In your small group, discuss the following questions.

1. What is Holly Kearl arguing in "Laws Protecting Women From Upskirt Photo Assaults Fall Short"?

2. What evidence does Kearl give to support her argument?

3. What is the counterargument?

4. Kearl draws parallels to the laws making it illegal to plant a recording device in someone's home. Why does she do that?

5. Do you agree or disagree with Kearl's argument? Why?

Activity 5.5 • A Logical Fallacy in Upskirt Laws?

In your small group, look at the list of logical fallacies in Chapter 3, and decide if Nebraska's position regarding upskirt photos is a logical fallacy. Upskirt photos in Nebraska, according to Holly Kearl, "are legal because, as the law is written, lawmakers argue no one can have a reasonable expectation of privacy in a public place, including from someone photographing their intimate areas that are covered by clothing." Which logical fallacy might it be and why? Hint: a premise or step in the logic may be missing.

Collaborate

Activity 5.6 • What Is the Rhetorical Situation of an Op-Ed?

What is the rhetorical situation that Holly Kearl is responding to in "Laws Protecting Women from Upskirt Photo Assaults Fall Short"? Remember the discussion from the beginning of this chapter about the rhetorical situation being the place where writers write, a site created by factors such as audience and ongoing conversations that compel a response.

Explore

Activity 5.7 • Write an Op-Ed Argument

The OpEd Project (www.theopedproject.org) is an online initiative to "expand the range of voices" submitting op-ed essays to media outlets. According to its statistics, 80 to 90 percent of op-ed pieces are currently written by men, which is something it endeavors to change by helping women and members of other underrepresented groups develop the skills to get published in top media markets. Whether you are male or female, you may belong to an underrepresented group that is not having its voice heard as part of the national conversation about issues.

Collaborate

An op-ed is an opinion piece printed in a newspaper, magazine, blog, or other media outlet. The name derives from earlier times in print journalism when these opinion pieces would be printed on a page opposite the editorial page. Op-eds are written by individuals not affiliated with the publication, as opposed to editorials that are written by the publication's staff.

This assignment asks you to write an op-ed piece suitable for submission to a major newspaper or other media outlet. It does not require you to submit your text. That is up to you.

(continued on next page)

For this assignment, you need to do the following.

▌ Read op-eds that appear in the major regional newspaper or other media outlet for your city, such as the *Chicago Tribune,* the *Washington Post,* or the *Arizona Republic.* The OpEd Project provides a list of the top 100 U.S. media outlets on its website. Read several op-eds to get a sense of the topics and style of the articles that the newspaper or other media outlet prints.

▌ Notice that op-eds are not academic writing. They must be well-researched, but they also generally are written in a more casual and engaging style than traditional academic writing. You must first attract your audience's attention in order to present your case. Analyze how each op-ed you read captures the reader's interest.

▌ Choose a topic that is timely and of interest to the readers of the publication that you choose. Research that topic using some of the tools in Chapter 4 of this textbook.

▌ The length and structure of your op-ed should follow the pattern of pieces recently published in your publication.

▌ Keep your audience in mind—the readers of the publication.

▌ Follow the basic op-ed structure recommended by the OpEd Project, reprinted below.

▌ Read the "Tips for Op-Ed Writing from the OpEd Project," in the sidebar.

(continued on next page)

Tips for Op-Ed Writing from the OpEd Project

1. Own your expertise
Know what you are an expert in and why—but don't limit yourself. Consider the metaphors that your experience and knowledge suggest.

2. Stay current
Follow the news—both general and specific to your areas of specialty. If you write about Haiti, read the Haitian press. If you write about pop culture, read the media that cover it.

3. The perfect is the enemy of the good
In other words: write fast. You may have only a few hours to get your piece in before the moment is gone. But also . . .

4. Cultivate a flexible mind
Remember that a good idea may have more than one news hook; indeed, if the idea is important enough, it can have many. So keep an eye out for surprising connections and new news hooks—the opportunity may come around again.

5. Use plain language
Jargon serves a purpose, but it is rarely useful in public debate, and can obfuscate—sorry, I mean cloud—your argument. Speak to your reader in straight talk.

6. Respect your reader
Never underestimate your reader's intelligence or overestimate his or her level of information. Recognize that your average reader is not an expert in your topic and that the onus is on you to capture her attention—and make a compelling argument.

(*Note:* A lede (or lead) is a journalism term that means the beginning of your article that catches your reader's attention and establishes your topic.)

Basic Op-Ed Structure from the OpEd Project

(*Note:* This is not a rule—just one way of approaching it.)

Lede (around a news hook)

Thesis (statement of argument—either explicit or implied)

Argument (based on evidence, such as stats, news, reports from credible organizations, expert quotes, scholarship, history, and first-hand experience)

- 1st Point
  - Evidence
  - Evidence
  - Conclusion
- 2nd Point
  - Evidence
  - Evidence
  - Conclusion
- 3rd Point
  - Evidence
  - Evidence
  - Conclusion

Note: In a simple, declarative op-ed ("policy X is bad; here's why"), this may be straightforward. In a more complex commentary, the 3rd point may expand on the bigger picture (historical context, global/geographic picture, mythological underpinnings, etc.) or may offer an explanation for a mystery that underpins the argument (e.g., why a bad policy continues, in spite of its failures).

"To Be Sure" paragraph (in which you preempt your potential critics by acknowledging any flaws in your argument, and address any obvious counterarguments)

Conclusion (often circling back to your lede)

Compose

Activity 5.8 • **Freewrite about Your Op-Ed Essay**

Freewrite for five minutes about your writing of an Op-Ed essay. Answer one or more of these questions or write about something else related to the topic.

1.   Why did you choose your topic for an Op-Ed essay?

2.   What evidence did you offer to support your position?

3.   Did you have a counterargument?

As your instructor directs, revise your freewriting into a paragraph to turn in.

The Research-Based Argument Essay

A research-based argument draws upon the skills you have been developing all semester. You've written persuasive arguments, and you have also incorporated different kinds of research. Now you put those skills together in a somewhat longer and more carefully documented version. Being able to write a well-thought-out research paper is a skill required in numerous college courses. Each time you are asked to write a research-based argument essay, the instructor will define the rhetorical situation, so pay close attention to the wording of the assignment.

Also, your argument essay is a response to an ongoing conversation on your topic carried on by your research sources. Some sources will agree with each other, and others may disagree. By paraphrasing or quoting your sources' stances on the issue you write about, you are including them in your conversation. Also, the sources' stances and evidence that you cite provide a context for your own thesis about the issue.

The goal of a research-based argument paper is persuasion, and it should begin with an introduction in which you clearly state your position on an issue. For example, "Understanding the Effects of Mass Media's Portraits of Black Women and Adolescents on Self Image," the following research-based argument essay, takes the position that "Black-oriented media specifically tends to have a positive effect for Black women with strong ethnic identity, while Black women with weak ethnic identity were more at risk of the aversive effects of mainstream media."

Usually, an academic research-based argument relies upon *logos*—reasoning and evidence—as the primary appeal, though *pathos* and *ethos* have a place as well, if used appropriately. Cherish Green, the author of the essay offers evidence from articles published in academic journals including the *Annual*

Review of Psychology and *Psychology of Women Quarterly* to support her argument. Thus, she is participating in the ongoing conversation about how mass media portraits of Black women affect the self-image of Black women.

Student Research Paper, "Understanding the Effects of Mass Media's Portrayals of Black Women and Adolescents on Self-Image"
by Cherish Green

Reading 5.3

Undergraduate student Cherish Green won an award for outstanding research paper at Ohlone College for her research-based argument essay, "Understanding the Effects of Mass Media's Portrayals of Black Women and Adolescents on Self-Image."

Abstract

This paper explores the role mass media plays in the way in which Black women and adolescents see themselves. The articles used give insight into not only how Black women are directly affected by mass media, but how the effects can be indirect as well; in the sense that the stereotypes perpetuated shape how others see and treat Black women, and therefore shape how they see themselves. This paper examines research that suggests that ethnic media and ethnic identity may in fact play a larger role in determining self-image than mainstream media does for Black women. It also explores the ways in which the Black community rejects stereotypes of beauty and *blackness* presented by mainstream media by heightening the sense of group membership and providing their own standards of what it means to be beautiful and Black in America through Black-oriented programming.

* * *

Much research has been done on the role media plays in people's self-image. A majority of that research has focused on White women and White adolescent girls. When the research has included Black women and Black adolescents, the source of media has largely been mainstream, rather than Black-oriented. As a Black female, I was interested in how media has shaped my self-image as well as other Black women's. What I found was that media—Black-oriented media specifically—ends to have a positive effect for Black women with strong ethnic identity, while Black women with weak ethnic identity were more at risk of the aversive effects of mainstream media.

As it turns out, while media does affect how we view ourselves, ethnic identity plays a major role in how much we let media affect self-image. Ethnic identity is "a group-based identity formed and developed through a variety of socialization processes, including both personal experiences...and mediated experiences" (Allen, 1993, 2001; Berry & Mitchell-Kernan, 1982; Gecas, 1992, as cited in Fujioka, 2005, p. 451). For this reason, while certain images may be influential in self-image, just as many may be rejected because they do not resonate with those images that are prevalent in Black culture, specifically amongst members of one's social circle. Yuanyuan Zhang, Travis L. Dixon, and Kate Conrad's research actually suggests that media is not directly responsible for effects on Black women's self-image. They argued that women with stronger ethnic identity were less affected by media images than those with weaker ethnic identity (2009, p. 263). Black people's "significant" experiences, such as those with family and friends, are more effective than the more "generalized" experiences, like those presented by mainstream media (Gecas, 1992, as cited in Fujioka, 2005, p. 451). The Black community is likely to question whether or not an image truly reflects them or merely a stereotype of their community when the image is coming from mainstream media (Zhang, Dixon, Conrad, 2009, p. 264). Instead, the Black community looks to ethnic media for images that "foster and embrace Black ethnic socialization" (Allen, 2001, as cited in Fujioka, 2005, p. 452) and more typically look to other Black women as role models, and would therefore be more likely to reject a mainstream media ideal as a valid comparison (Schooler, Ward, Merriwether, Caruthers, 2004, p. 40).

For instance, where Michelle Obama has been criticized for not being what is seen as physically ideal by many in mainstream America, she is praised in the Black community as having "uniquely black beauty" (Quinlan, Bates, Webb, 2012, p. 123). Black beauty is typically defined as "light skin, straightened hair, and small facial features" (Brooks & Herbert, 2006, as cited in Quinlan et al., 2012, p. 122). Michelle Obama does not fit some of these stereotypically beautiful traits, but is still considered beautiful in her own right amongst the Black community.

One explanation for this inclusion of Michelle Obama as an example of Black beauty could be that Black women and adolescents do not measure beauty on a physical level alone. According to Lisa Duke's research in 2000, Black adolescent females questioned about beauty described it as largely based on attitude and character in addition to appearance (p. 378). Michelle Obama is generally seen as a positive role model in the Black community (Quinlan et al. 2012, p. 123). Despite her not outwardly fitting the stereotypes of Black beauty, she is acknowledged as having uniquely Black beauty due to the integrity of her character.

Another explanation for this behavior is that this negative portrayal of Black identity caused the Black community to express group loyalty by asserting a stronger group membership (Ellemers, Spears, Doosje, 2002, p. 178). The ideal standards of Black beauty were suspended to include Michelle Obama in response to mainstream media dismissing her beauty due to the fact that she doesn't fit their ideals.

Another way in which the Black community copes with mainstream media's threat to their ethnic identity is through programs that foster Black success, such as affirmative action (Fujioka, 2005, p. 453). Programs such as affirmative action contribute to group success and therefore increase the in-group status (Fujioka, 2005, p. 453).

Unfortunately, for Black women that loosely identify with their ethnic identity, the consequences of media's portrayal of them (both mainstream and Black media) can be dire. Black women who do not relate to Black ethnic identity tend to distance themselves from the Black community in response to aversive portrayals (Ellemers, et al., 2002, as cited in Fujioka, 2005, 453). These same women, usually in adolescence, are more at risk of developing body image disturbances that may lead to eating disorders such as anorexia and bulimia (Schooler et al., 2004, p. 39). During adolescence, Black girls are both developing a racial identity and learning what society's ideal of beauty is (Duke, 2002, p. 219). During this stage in their lives, many of them would rather be seen as a teen girl rather than a Black teen girl (Duke, 2002, p. 219). The messages they are receiving are often conflicting, as Black women tend to have a different body type than the White ideal, which is usually unachievable by many Black women. Even when viewing Black-oriented programming, such as rap music videos, these women tend to be more affected by media ideals (Ward, Hansbrough, Walker, as cited in Schooler et al., 2004, p. 45).

According to the social comparison theory (Festinger, 1954, as cited in Duke 2000, p. 379), people like to compare themselves to others that are similar to them. So it would make sense that Black women look to Black-oriented media to draw comparisons of ideal beauty, rather than mainstream media. Rap music videos, typically made by Blacks and featuring Black women, tend to portray the thin ideal (Zhang, et al., 2009, p. 263). For a Black woman with a strong ethnic identity, these images may not disturb her self-image, as Black culture does not emphasize thinness and appreciates larger body sizes (Streigel-Moore et al., as cited in Zhang et al., 2009, p. 265). However, a Black woman with low ethnic identity who tends to embrace mainstream culture is more susceptible to glamorizing thin ideals (Zhang et al., 2009, p. 272) seen in Black-oriented media as well. In Zhang's experiment, exposing women with high ethnic identity to thin images actually decreased body dissatisfaction; while as expected, women with low ethnic identity were more dissatisfied with their bodies (2009, p. 272). A possible explanation for high ethnic identity relating females feeling better about their bodies in response to the rap videos was that, having been a long stigmatized community, Blacks tend to see each other as allies rather than competition (Schooler et al., 2004, p. 44). Having any sort of media visibility is more important than the images necessarily being representative of the majority of the community.

But for many, self-image goes beyond physical appearances. According to Duke's research on Black adolescents that read mainstream magazines, such as *Seventeen*, these magazines lack not only a physical presence of Black women, but they fail to resonate with the experiences, perspectives, and needs of their large Black audiences (2002, p. 219)—giving the Black community all the more reason to dismiss mainstream ideals. Many of the girls in this study believed that rather than being part of a niche audience, more authentic Black images needed to be included in mainstream media. They felt underrepresented and invisible to the outside world.

While there is a small number of Black images regularly shown on television, the majority of these fictional characters aid in the perpetuation of Black stereotypes (Coleman, 1998, as cited in Quinlan et al., 2012, p. 120). Such stereotypes not only shape how others choose to deal with Black women, but indirectly, how Black women view themselves (Hudson, 1998, as cited in Quinlan et al., 2012, p. 120). These stereotypes can have detrimental consequences. Studies have suggested that the over-sexualized *Jezebel* Black female stereotype in the media has contributed to Black females becoming the emerging leading face of the AIDS epidemic (Townsend, Thomas, Neilands, Jackson, 2010, p. 273). This stereotype has transcended boundaries, crossing over into Black-oriented media. The modern Jezebel—a highly sexualized, materialistic, controlling, demanding woman—is especially present in rap music videos (Stephens and Phillips, 2003, as cited in Townsend et al., 2010, p. 274). Because of her strong prevalence in Black programming, those with both strong and weak ethnic identity may be exposed to such images and be affected by them. Many impoverished adolescent girls watch the rap music videos and see a message in which women relate to "their culture of poverty, yet have the economic means to procure middle-class goods" (Stephens and Phillips, 2003, as cited in Townsend et al., 2010, p. 274). They can relate to these Jezebels in the sense that they are from the same cultural background. They are part of a struggling minority group fighting to acquire what the predominantly White middle class has while preserving those values held ideal in the Black community. They aspire to be like these over-sexualized images in the same way White adolescent girls aspire to be like the models in *Seventeen* magazine. These aspirations put them at great sexual risk, in turn making them more likely to acquire sexually transmitted diseases such as the AIDS virus.

For Black women and adolescents, mainstream media is not a looking glass, but rather is a one way mirror into White America (Duke, 2000, p. 383). This allows them to repel many of the ideals that cause many White adolescent girls grief as they enter womanhood. Black women do not see a reflection of their culture, and values when consuming mainstream media, and are therefore largely unaffected by it. Strong ethnic identity allows for Black women to differentiate between what is ideal for their culture and what is supreme for the dominant culture, so that White standards of beauty become irrelevant to their lives and ideas of beauty. It also allows them to feel comforted by, rather than jealous of, the Black images presented in mainstream and Black-oriented media alike. However, ethnic identity does not grant Black women immunity to the effects of Black media portrayals completely. They are still faced with the task of mitigating these representations effectiveness to shape how others outside of the Black community feel about Black people in America and not letting them encroach on ideals already put in place in Black culture.

References

Duke, L. (2000). Black In A Blonde World: Race and Girls' Interpretations of the Feminine Ideal in Teen Magazines. *Journalism & Mass Communication Quarterly*, 77(2), 367–392.

Duke, L. (2002). Get Real!: Cultural Relevance and Resistance to the Mediated Feminine Ideal. *Psychology & Marketing*, 19(2), 211–233.

Ellemers, N., Spears, R., & Doosje, B. (2002). Self and Social Identity. *Annual Review of Psychology*, 53(1), 161.

Fujioka, Y. (2005). Black Media Images as a Perceived Threat to African American Ethnic Identity: Coping Responses, Received Public Perception, and Attitudes Towards Affirmative Action. *Journal Of Broadcasting & Electronic Media*, 49(4), 450-467. doi:10.1207/s15506878jobem4904_6

Schooler, D., Ward, L., Merriwether, A., & Caruthers, A. (2004). Who's That Girl: Television's Role In The Body Image Development Of Young White And Black Women. *Psychology of Women Quarterly*, 28(1), 38-47. doi:10.1111/j.1471-6402.2004.00121.x

Townsend, T. G., Thomas, A., Neilands T. B., & Jackson, T. R. (2010). I'm No Jezebel; I Am Young, Gifted, AND Black: Identity, Sexuality, and Black Girls. *Psychology of WomenQuarterly*, 34(3), 273-285. doi:10.1111/j.1471-6402.2010.01574.x

Quinlan, M. M., Bates, B. R., & Webb, J. B. (2012). Michelle Obama 'Got Back': (Re)Defining (Counter)Stereotypes of Black Females. *Women & Language*, 35(1), 119-126.

Zhang, Y., Dixon, T. L., & Conrad, K. (2009). Rap Music Videos and African American Women's Body Image: The Moderating Role of Ethnic Identity. *Journal of Communication*, 59(2), 262-278. doi:10.1111/j.1460-2466.2009.01415.x

Collaborate

Activity 5.9 • Discuss "Understanding the Effects of Mass Media's Portrayals of Black Women and Adolescents on Self-Image"

In your group, consider the following questions.

1. Who is the primary audience for "Understanding the Effects of Mass Media's Portrayals of Black Women and Adolescents on Self-Image"? Are there secondary audiences?

2. What evidence or assertions in the cited sources is Cherish Green, the author, responding to?

3. What is Cherish Green's contribution to the conversation about the effects of mass media's portrayals of black women?

The Sky Is Falling Casebook

What follows is a casebook of three readings about a single subject—a meteor that exploded over Russia. Reading these texts together will prepare you for developing arguments in response to Activities 5.10 through 5.13.

Situation: The meteor that exploded over Chelyabinsk, Russia, on Friday, February 15, 2013, injured hundreds of people and validated the claims of scientists and space enthusiasts who claim the Earth is in danger of collisions with asteroids. Efforts to obtain

A meteor exploded over Siberia, injuring hundreds and reigniting the debate over the need for enhanced methods to detect asteroids that could strike the Earth.

funding for telescopes that could better detect such events have previously been foiled by skeptics who claimed that believers in the danger from asteroids were mere "Chicken Littles," fearing that the sky is falling. See, for example, the *New York Times* article, "Vindication for Entrepreneurs Watching Sky: Yes, It Can Fall," in the following casebook.

The reality of injuries caused by the meteor's explosion increased the *ethos* or credibility of those who claim the danger from asteroids is real. However, how likely is it that a large asteroid could hit the Earth and cause massive damage? For different viewpoints on the danger, see the press release from the B612 Foundation and the Near Earth Object Program webpage reproduced in the casebook.

Should the U.S. government fund space telescopes for detecting asteroids that could strike Earth, causing massive damage? Or would it be a better use of public money to concentrate on "urgent problems on Earth"?

Casebook Reading 1

Vindication for Entrepreneurs Watching Sky: Yes, It Can Fall
by William J. Broad

A meteor exploding over Chelyabinsk, Russia, validated claims of those claiming earth is in danger from colliding asteroids.

Published in *The New York Times*.

For decades, scientists have been on the lookout for killer objects from outer space that could devastate the planet. But warnings that they lacked the tools to detect the most serious threats were largely ignored, even as skeptics mocked the worriers as Chicken Littles.

No more. The meteor that rattled Siberia on Friday, injuring hundreds of people and traumatizing thousands, has suddenly brought new life to efforts to deploy adequate detection tools, in particular a space telescope that would scan the solar system for dangers.

A group of young Silicon Valley entrepreneurs who helped build thriving companies like eBay, Google and Facebook has already put millions of dollars into the effort and saw Friday's shock wave as a turning point in raising hundreds of millions more.

"Wouldn't it be silly if we got wiped out because we weren't looking?" said Edward Lu, a former NASA astronaut and Google executive who leads the detection effort. "This is a wake-up call from space. We've got to pay attention to what's out there."

Astronomers know of no asteroids or comets that pose a major threat to the planet. But NASA estimates that fewer than 10 percent of the big dangers have been discovered.

Dr. Lu's group, called the B612 Foundation after the imaginary asteroid on which the Little Prince lived, is one team of several pursuing ways to ward off extraterrestrial threats. NASA is another, and other private groups are emerging, like Planetary Resources, which wants not only to identify asteroids near Earth but also to mine them.

"Our job is to be the first line of defense, and we take that very seriously," James Green, the director of planetary science at NASA headquarters, said in an interview Friday after the Russian strike. "No one living on this planet has ever before been hurt. That's historic."

Dr. Green added that the Russian episode was sure to energize the field and that an even analysis of the meteor's remains could help reveal clues about future threats.

"Our scientists are excited," he said. "Russian planetary scientists are already collecting meteorites from this event."

The slow awakening to the danger began long ago, as scientists found hundreds of rocky scars indicating that cosmic intruders had periodically reshaped the planet.

The discoveries included not just obvious features like Meteor Crater in Arizona, but wide zones of upheaval. A crater more than a hundred miles wide beneath the Yucatán Peninsula in Mexico suggested that, 65 million years ago, a speeding rock from outer space had raised enough planetary mayhem to end the reign of the dinosaurs.

Some people remain skeptical of the cosmic threat and are glad for taxpayer money to go toward urgent problems on Earth rather than outer space. But many scientists who have examined the issues have become convinced that better precautions are warranted in much the same way that homeowners buy insurance for unlikely events that can result in severe damage to life and property.

Starting in the 1980s and 1990s, astronomers turned their telescopes on the sky with increasing vigor to look for killer rocks. The rationale was statistical. They knew about a number of near misses and calculated that many other rocky threats whirling about the solar system had gone undetected.

In 1996, with little fanfare, the Air Force also began scanning the skies for speeding rocks, giving credibility to an activity once seen as reserved for doomsday enthusiasts. It was the world's first known government search.

The National Aeronautics and Space Administration took a lead role with what it called the Spaceguard Survey. In 2007, it issued a report estimating that 20,000 asteroids and comets orbited close enough to the planet to deliver blows that could destroy cities or even end all life. Today, with limited financing, NASA supports modest telescopes in the southwestern United States and in Hawaii that make more than 95 percent of the discoveries of the objects coming near the Earth.

Scientists lobbied hard for a space telescope that would get high above the distorting effects of the Earth's atmosphere. It would orbit the Sun, peering across the solar system, and would have a much better chance of finding large space rocks.

But with the nation immersed in two wars and other earthly priorities, the government financing never materialized. Last year, Dr. Lu, who left the NASA astronaut corps in 2007 to work for Google, joined with veterans of the space program and Silicon Valley entrepreneurs to accelerate the asteroid hunt.

The B612 Foundation refers to its planned telescope as the world's first private mission to deep space. Private groups, it says on its Web site, can carry out "audacious projects that previously only governments could accomplish—and at lower cost."

The plan is to launch a large telescope known as Sentinel that can find 90 percent of the asteroids larger than 460 feet in diameter that pass through the Earth's part of the solar system. They also want to discover smaller asteroids down to a diameter of 100 feet.

Such asteroids are much bigger than the meteor that hit the atmosphere over Russia, and the telescope would thus be blind to those kinds of smaller threats.

Last October, the B612 Foundation, based in Mountain View, Calif., signed a contract with Ball Aerospace to create prototype sensors for the Sentinel mission. The space telescope is to have a diameter of 20 inches. In theory, the system could be ready for launching by 2017 or 2018.

In an interview, Dr. Lu said the overall cost of the mission was now estimated at $450 million, including launching, insurance and operations. The group, far from that goal, has been soliciting money from citizens.

Friday's close approach to Earth of an asteroid named 2012 DA14, as well as the much smaller object whose shock wave broke windows and bones in Russia, prompted thousands of hits to the foundation's Web site and Twitter account, said Diane Murphy, a spokeswoman for the group.

"Everybody is calling," she said. "They see us as the solution. They're saying, 'When are you going to have the telescope up?' "

B612 is just one player. Last April, Planetary Resources unveiled plans to mine asteroids that zip close by Earth, both to provide supplies for future interplanetary travelers and to bring back metals like platinum.

The venture attracted some big-name investors, including Larry Page and Eric Schmidt of Google. The company also has plans to develop telescopes that would hunt for rocky intruders coming near the planet.

Dr. Green of NASA said the agency was preparing to launch a mission in 2016 that will fly to an asteroid and, in 2023, return a sample to Earth for detailed analyses. The insights are expected to help scientists learn more about the makeup of the threats whizzing through the cosmic shooting gallery.

"If you're going to protect the planet, you have to know your enemy," he said. "You have to get up close and personal."

Broad, William J. "Vindication for Entrepreneurs Watching Sky: Yes, It Can Fall." *The New York Times*, 16 Feb. 2013, *www.nytimes.com/2013/02/17/science/space/dismissed-as-doomsayers-advocates-for-meteor-detection-feel-vindicated.html.*

Casebook Reading 2

Astronauts introduced video illustrating frequency of asteroids hitting earth.

B612 Foundation Releases Video at Seattle Museum of Flight Earth Day Event Showing Evidence of 26 Multi-Kiloton Asteroid Impacts Since 2001

B612 Foundation Press Release

SEATTLE, WA (Earth Day, April 22, 2014)—At a press conference on Tuesday at the Seattle Museum of Flight, three prominent astronauts supporting the B612 Foundation presented a visualization of new data showing the surprising frequency at which the Earth is hit by asteroids. The astronauts were guests of the Seattle Museum for a special series of public events on Earth Day 2014.

Dr. Ed Lu, former US Shuttle and Soyuz Astronaut and co-founder and CEO of the B612 Foundation was joined by former NASA Astronaut Tom Jones,

President of the Association of Space Explorers and Apollo 8 Astronaut Bill Anders, first Chairman of the Nuclear Regulatory Commission and former Chairman and CEO of General Dynamics to discuss findings recently released from the Nuclear Test Ban Treaty Organization, which operates a network of sensors that monitors Earth around the clock listening for the infrasound signature of nuclear detonations.

Between 2000 and 2013, this network detected 26 explosions on Earth ranging in energy from 1-600 kilotons—all caused not by nuclear explosions, but rather by asteroid impacts. To put that in perspective, the atomic bomb that destroyed Hiroshima in 1945, exploded with an energy impact of 15 kilotons. While most of these asteroids exploded too high in the atmosphere to do serious damage on the ground, the evidence is important in estimating the frequency of a potential "city-killer-size" asteroid.

The Earth is continuously colliding with fragments of asteroids, the largest in recent times exploding over Tunguska, Siberia in 1908 with an energy impact of 5-15 megatons. More recently, we witnessed the 600-kiloton impact in Chelyabinsk, Russia in 2013, and asteroid impacts greater than 20 kilotons occurred in South Sulawesi, Indonesia in 2009, in the Southern Ocean in 2004, and in the Mediterranean Sea in 2002. Important to note as well is the fact that none of these asteroids were detected or tracked in advance by any existing space-based or terrestrial observatory.

The B612 Foundation released a new video visualization of these findings, showing the impact size range and location of all 26 explosions. The video is posted at https://b612foundation.org/portfolio/impact-video and can also be viewed on YouTube.com. The listing of all locations and size of impacts is also listed with additional FAQs at: https://b612foundation.org/impact-video-faq.

Hi res video can also be accessed on the ftp site: ftp://b612@spinefilms.com@spinefilms.com/Asteroid%20Impact%20Media; user: b612@spinefilms.com; password: asteroid.

Also attending the press conference in Seattle were students from Key Peninsula Middle School. In addition, Astronauts Ed Lu, Tom Jones, and Bill Anders joined Museum of Flight CEO Doug King to visit the Challenger Center at the Museum of Flight to discuss asteroids and space-related assets to detect and track asteroids and field questions from the students.

"While most large asteroids with the potential to destroy an entire country or continent have been detected, less than 10,000 of the more than a million dangerous asteroids with the potential to destroy an entire major metropolitan area have been found by all existing space or terrestrially-operated observatories," stated Lu. "Because we don't know where or when the next major impact will occur, the only thing preventing a catastrophe from a "city-killer" sized asteroid has been blind luck."

The B612 Foundation aims to change that by building the Sentinel Space Telescope Mission, an early warning infrared space telescope for tracking asteroids that would provide many years to deflect an asteroid when it is still millions of miles away. The B612 Sentinel Mission will be the world's first privately funded deep space mission that will create the first comprehensive dynamic map of our inner solar system, identifying the current and future locations and trajectories of Earth crossing asteroids. Sentinel will detect and track more than 200,000 asteroids in just the first year of operation, after a planned launch in 2018.

The B612 Foundation is named for the asteroid home of the "Little Prince" in the Antoine de Saint- Exupery classic novel. The Little Prince came to realize that what is essential in life, is often invisible to tthe human eye. Learn more at www.b612foundation.org; on Twitter @b612foundation.

B612 Foundation. *Video at Seattle Museum of Flight Earth Day Event Showing Evidence of 26 Multi-Kiloton Asteroid Impacts Since 2001.* Sentinel Mission, 17 Apr. 2014. B612 Foundation, archive.b612foundation.org/events/b612-earth-day-press-conference-at-the-seattle-museum-of-flight/.

Casebook Reading 3

NASA scientists say chance of sizable meteor striking earth is possible but not probable.

NASA Near Earth Object Program: Target Earth

On a daily basis, about one hundred tons of interplanetary material drifts down to the Earth's surface. Most of the smallest interplanetary particles that reach the Earth's surface are the tiny dust particles that are released by comets as their ices vaporize in the solar neighborhood. The vast majority of the larger interplanetary material that reaches the Earth's surface originates as the collision fragments of asteroids that have run into one another some eons ago.

With an average interval of about 10,000 years, rocky or iron asteroids larger than about 100 meters would be expected to reach the Earth's surface and cause local disasters or produce the tidal waves that can inundate low lying coastal areas. On an average of every several hundred thousand years or so, asteroids larger than a kilometer could cause global disasters. In this case, the impact debris would spread throughout the Earth's atmosphere so that plant life would suffer from acid rain, partial blocking of the sunlight, and from the firestorms resulting from heated impact debris raining back down upon the Earth's surface. Since their orbital paths often cross that of the Earth, collisions with near-Earth objects have occurred in the past and we should remain alert to the possibility of future close Earth approaches. It seems prudent to mount efforts to discover and study these objects, to characterize their sizes, compositions and structures and to keep an eye upon their future trajectories.

Because of the ongoing search efforts to find nearly all the large NEOs, objects will occasionally be found to be on very close Earth approaching trajectories. Great care must then be taken to verify any Earth collision predictions that are made. Given the extremely unlikely nature of such a collision, almost all of these predictions will turn out to be false alarms. However, if an object is verified to be on an Earth colliding trajectory, it seems likely that this collision possibility will be known several years prior to the actual event. Given several years warning time, existing technology could be used to deflect the threatening object away from Earth. The key point in this mitigation process is to find the threatening object years ahead of time so that an orderly international campaign can be mounted to send spacecraft to the threatening object. One of the techniques suggested for deflecting an asteroid includes nuclear fusion weapons set off above the surface to slightly change the asteroid's velocity without fracturing it. High speed neutrons from the explosion would irradiate a shell of material on the surface of the asteroid facing the explosion. The material in this surface shell would then expand and blow off, thus producing a recoil upon the asteroid itself. A very modest velocity change in the asteroid's motion (only a few millimeters per second), acting over several years, can cause the asteroid to miss the Earth entirely. However, the trick is to gently nudge the asteroid out of harm's way and not to blow it up. This latter option, though popular in the movies, only creates a bigger problem when all the pieces encounter the Earth. Another option that has been discussed includes the establishment of large solar sails on a small threatening object so that the pressure of sunlight could eventually redirect the object away from its predicted Earth collision.

No one should be overly concerned about an Earth impact of an asteroid or comet. The threat to any one person from auto accidents, disease, other natural disasters and a variety of other problems is much higher than the threat from NEOs. Over long periods of time, however, the chances of the Earth being impacted are not negligible so that some form of NEO insurance is warranted. At the moment, our best insurance rests with the NEO scientists and their efforts to first find these objects and then track their motions into the future. We need to first find them, then keep an eye on them.

"Near-Earth Object Program: Target Earth." *NASA*, NASA, 6 Jan. 2014, neo.jpl.nasa.gov/neo/target.html.

Compose

Activity 5.10 • Summarize Information from Casebook

Reread each of the three readings in The Sky is Falling Casebook, then summarize the information from each that is relevant to an argument you might write about this issue. Type the heading of each reading, and put the summary for each reading under the heading. Then, after each summary, write a paragraph critiquing or commenting on the reading. Thus, your assignment paper should look like this, if the dotted lines represent the text you write.

1. "Vindication for Entrepreneurs Watching Sky: Yes, It Can Fall"
Summary of information relevant to argument:

_____

My comment about "Vindication for Entrepreneurs Watching Sky: Yes, It Can Fall":

_____

2. "B612 Foundation Releases Video at Seattle Museum of Flight Earth Day Event Showing Evidence of 26 Multi-kiloton Asteroid Impacts since 2001"
Summary of information relevant to argument:

_____

My comment about "B612 Foundation Releases Video at Seattle Museum of Flight Earth Day Event Showing Evidence of 26 Multi-kiloton Asteroid Impacts since 2001":

_____

3. "NASA Near Earth Object Program: Target Earth"
Summary of information relevant to argument:

_____

My comment about "NASA Near Earth Object Program: Target Earth":

_____

Write an Argumentative Essay

In ancient times, orators began a speech by attracting the audience's attention in what was called the *exordium,* which we would call the opening or introduction. Next, they provided background information in a *narratio* (narration), followed by an *explication* in which they defined terms and enumerated the issues. During the *partition* they would express the thesis or main issue to be discussed, and in the *confirmation* they would provide evidence to support the thesis. Opposition arguments would be addressed in the *refutatio,* and the composition would be wrapped up with a *peroratio* or conclusion. The order of these different elements was not rigid in ancient times, nor is it today. Sometimes one or more sections were eliminated if they were not needed, but then, as now, an effective text included most of these elements. For example, if your audience is very familiar with a particular subject, you may not need to define terms, as you would with an audience who was unfamiliar with the material.

As did the ancient Greeks and Romans, when you write an argument, you begin with an introduction that gains your audience's attention and presents your thesis; likewise, you end with a conclusion that ties together what you have said or presents a call to action. However, you have a choice of several formats for what happens between that introduction and conclusion. Following are three prominent alternatives; your choice of which to use depends on your purpose and the type of evidence you have.

Toulmin Model

Created by Stephen Toulmin, the Toulmin model for persuasion grew out of the twentieth-century emphasis upon empirical evidence and is most effective for arguments that rely on evidence from scientific studies, surveys, or other data. His model requires six elements.

1. Claim: Rhetors present a claim or statement that they want the audience to accept.

2. Data: Data back up the claim, what Aristotle would have called inartistic proofs.

3. Warrant (or bridge): A warrant links data and facts to the claim, explaining why the data make the claim valid.

4. Backing (or foundation): Backing provides additional support for the argument.

5. Counterclaim: A counterclaim acknowledges any objections or weaknesses in the argument.

6. Rebuttal: The rebuttal responds to any counterclaims, removing possible objections to the argument.

Collaborate

Activity 5.11 • **Develop a Toulmin Argument for The Sky Is Falling Casebook**

Synthesizing information from the three readings in The Sky is Falling Casebook, outline the six steps of a Toulmin argument. Hint: Possible claims could be:

▊ The United States should fund space telescopes for detecting asteroids that could strike earth, causing massive damage.

or

▊ A better use of public money than building a space telescope is to concentrate on "urgent problems on Earth."

For your argument, give the following information.

1. Claim: Reword one of the two possible claims just mentioned or develop a third.

2. Data: Find statistics or authoritative quotes to support your claim.

3. Warrant: Explain how your statistics or authoritative quotes support the claim.

4. Backing: Give any additional explanations needed to support the argument.

5. Counterclaim: Reword the other side of the "Sky is Falling" argument.

6. Rebuttal: Refute the opposing argument with additional evidence or quotes.

Rogerian Argument

The Rogerian (or common ground) argument is named for psychologist Carl Rogers. It is most effective for arguments that attempt to establish common ground between opponents on an issue. Rogerian arguments exhibit these characteristics:

1. Includes an introduction: An introduction states the problem to be considered, explaining how it affects the people involved.

2. Presents common ground and common arguments: In a much different move than the Toulmin model, the rhetor voices the common ground between the two sides of the issue, as well as the arguments of the two sides, stated in neutral language.

3. Takes a position: The rhetor reveals his or her position, asking that the audience consider it but without saying it is better.

4. Ends with a positive: The Rogerian argument ends on a positive note, describing how the rhetor's position could, at least in some instances, benefit the opposition.

Activity 5.12 • Develop a Rogerian Argument for The Sky is Falling Casebook

Collaborate

Outline the steps in a Rogerian argument for The Sky is Falling Casebook. Hint: You could introduce the problem by explaining this: *A meteor exploded over Chelyabinsk, Russia, on Friday, Feb. 15, 2013, injuring hundreds of people. The potential exists for a major asteroid explosion that could destroy a city on Earth. Currently, only a fraction of asteroids that might strike the Earth are monitored, and additional funding would be required to better detect such events while there is still time to intervene.*

State your outline in this format.

1. Introduction: Paraphrase the statement above or write your own.

2. Common ground: Both sides value human life and want to spend public money efficiently. Common arguments: Should public money be spent on a space telescope or is the need greater for other problems on Earth? State both sides fairly.

3. Take a position: State your position on the issue and ask the audience to hear your evidence justifying that position.

4. End with a positive statement: Describe how your position on the issue, at least in some instances, benefits those with the opposing position.

General Modern Format

The general modern format for argument is one that will probably be familiar to you from previous English classes. It is a format that you can use when your argument does not fit neatly into either the Toulmin or Rogerian patterns. Moreover, you can adapt it to serve the needs of your argument. Organize your text similarly to the five-paragraph essay.

1. Introduction: State your thesis in an introductory section that provides background, an anecdote, quote, or other information that gets the attention of your audience and provides a context for your thesis.

2. Main points: Two or three sections each present a major point that supports your thesis.

3. Counterargument: The next section presents a counterargument, which anticipates audience questions or objections and is followed by a rebuttal of the counterargument.

4. Conclusion: A conclusion ties the argument together, perhaps by reflecting back to the introduction or issuing a call for action.

Collaborate

Activity 5.13 • Develop a General Modern Format Argument for The Sky is Falling Casebook

Develop an outline for an argument based on The Sky is Falling Casebook utilizing the General Modern Format. Hint: You might begin your argument with a startling statement similar to this one: *The meteor that exploded over Chelyabinsk, Russia, on Friday, Feb. 15, 2013, injured hundreds of people. It also validated the claims of scientists and space enthusiasts who warn that Earth is in danger from asteroid collisions.* Then state your thesis that either:

▊ The United States should fund space telescopes for detecting asteroids that could strike Earth, causing massive damage.

or

▊ A better use of public money is to concentrate on "urgent problems on Earth."

If you choose the first alternative, your major points would concentrate on the dangers of asteroids and the damage they could do if they struck Earth. If you choose the second alternative, your major points would concentrate on how remote the possibility is that a large asteroid would actually hit the Earth. Include statistics that support the idea that the money that could buy a space telescope would be better spent for something else. Do not forget to cite the opposing argument and refute it. Then write a conclusion that ties things together or calls for action.

Outline your General Modern Format argument essay using this format.

1. Introduction, including thesis.
2. Two or three main points that support your thesis.
3. A counterargument, followed by a rebuttal.
4. Conclusion.

Activity 5.14 • Write a Research-Based Essay Utilizing The Sky is Falling Casebook

Write a research-based essay utilizing the three readings in The Sky is Falling Casebook. Base your essay on one of the outlines you developed in Activities 5.11, 5.12, and 5.13. Choose the outline that you think best suits this topic.

Remember to cite your sources in MLA or APA Style. Following each casebook reading is an MLA citation that you can import into you Works Cited page. You will still need to write your own in-text citations, however.

If you need more information for your essay than is provided in the casebook, consult the B612 Foundation (b612foundation.org), NASA's Near Earth Object Program (neo.jpl.nasa.gov), or do an Internet search for keywords such as "Chelyabinsk meteor," and "asteroids hitting Earth."

Activity 5.15 • Freewrite about "The Sky is Falling" Essay

Freewrite for five minutes, answering one or more of these questions, or write about something else related to the writing of "The Sky is Falling" essay.

1. Did you choose to use the Toulmin Model, Rogerian Argument, or the General Modern Format?

2. Why did you make that choice?

3. What did you argue in your essay?

4. How did you support that argument?

5. What worked well and with what areas of the paper did you struggle?

If your instructor requests, turn your freewriting into a polished paragraph with a thesis and supporting sentences.

Write a Thesis Statement

A **thesis** may be a sentence or a series of sentences, or in a few cases it may be implied rather than stated explicitly, but a thesis is at the heart of any piece of writing. If a reader cannot identify your thesis, the meaning of your text is not clear. How do you develop a thesis? First, you determine your occasion for writing—who is your audience, what is your purpose, and what special circumstances are there (if any)? Then you write a

Table 5.1 • Argument Formats: A Comparison

Ancient Roman	General Modern Format
Standard pattern the ancients modified to suit the argument.	Good all-purpose format that can be adapted for the needs of the argument.
Introduction—*Exordium* Attracts the interest of the audience and identifies the argument.	Introduction Attracts the interest of the audience through its opening strategy and states the thesis.
Background or narration—*Narratio* Details the history or facts of the issue.	First main point Supports the thesis.
Definition—Explication Defines terms and outlines issues.	Second main point Supports the thesis.
Thesis—*Partitio* States the particular issue that is to be argued.	Third main point Supports the thesis.
Proof—*Confirmatio* Develops the thesis and provides supporting evidence.	Counterargument Acknowledges the opposing argument or arguments.
Refutation or opposition—*Refutatio* Addresses the arguments opposing the thesis.	Rebuttal of counterargument Refutes the opposing argument or arguments.
Conclusion—*Peroratio* Reiterates the thesis and may urge the audience to action.	Conclusion Ties together the elements of the composition and gives the reader closure. May summarize the essay and include a call to action.

Toulmin Model	Rogerian Argument
Good for an argument that relies on empirical evidence such as scientific studies or data collection.	Good when the object is consensus or compromise, so that opponents can work together while retaining their positions.
Claim Presents the overall thesis the writer will argue.	**Introduction** States the problem to be solved or the question to be answered. Often opponents will also agree there is a problem.
Data Supports the claim with evidence.	**Summary of opposing views** Describes the opposing side's arguments in a neutral and fair manner.
Warrant (also known as a bridge) Explains why or how the data support the claim. Connects the data to the claim.	**Statement of understanding** Concedes occasions when the opposing position might be valid.
Counterclaim Presents a claim that negates or disagrees with the thesis/claim.	**Statement of position** Avoids emotionally charged language, and identifies position.
Rebuttal Presents evidence that negates or disagrees with the counterclaim.	**Statement of contexts** Describes the specific contexts in which the rhetor's position applies/works well.
Conclusion Ties together the elements of the composition (if not included with the rebuttal).	**Statement of benefits** Presents benefits that may appeal to the self-interest of readers who may not yet agree with you; shows how your position benefits them. Ends on a positive note.
	Conclusion Ties together the elements of the composition (if not included in the statement of benefits).

working thesis that makes an assertion or claim about your topic, something that will be affected by your audience and purpose. For example, if you are writing a research paper about the advantages and disadvantages of biodiesel fuel, your claim may be stated differently depending on whether your audience is an English class or a chemistry class. In the latter, you might need to use technical language that would be unfamiliar to your English professor.

Working theses are statements that develop and change as essays are written; they are basic frameworks that provide a connection for the ideas you have decided to convey to your reader. Later, after you have completed a draft of your text, examine your working thesis. If needed, rewrite your thesis so that it states the main idea of your essay in a clear and engaging fashion. Consider the following examples of thesis statements.

Example: The United States should implement a guest worker program as a way of reforming the illegal immigration problem.

Example: Nuclear power should be considered as part of a program to reduce the United States's dependence on foreign oil.

Compose an Introduction

Experienced writers have different methods of creating a good introduction. One writer who tends to discover his paper as he goes along swears the best way to write an introduction is to write the entire paper and then move the conclusion to the beginning of the essay and rewrite it as the introduction. Another writer lets the paper sit around for a few days before she writes her introduction. A third always writes two or three different introductions and tries them out on friends before deciding which to use. However you choose to write the introduction, make sure it is interesting enough to make your reader want to read on.

The introduction to your essay is an invitation to your reader. If you invite readers to come along with you on a boring journey, they won't want to follow. In magazine and newspaper writing, the introduction is sometimes called a *hook* because it hooks the reader into reading the text. If a magazine writer does not capture the reader's attention right away, the reader is not likely to continue. After all, there are other and possibly more interesting articles in the magazine. Why should readers suffer through a boring introduction? Depending on the topic and pattern of your essay, you might employ different techniques to hook your readers and make them want to keep reading.

- An intriguing or provocative quotation

- A narrative or anecdote

- A question or series of questions

- A vivid sensory description

- A strongly stated opinion

Your introductory paragraph makes a commitment to your readers. This is where you identify the topic, state your thesis (implicitly or explicitly), and give your readers clues about the journey that will follow in the succeeding paragraphs. Be careful not to mislead the reader. Do not ask questions you will not answer in your paper (unless they are rhetorical questions). Do not introduce a topic in your introduction and then switch to another one in your paper.

Although the introduction is the first paragraph or so of the paper, it may not be the first paragraph the writer composes. If you have problems beginning your essay because you cannot immediately think of a good introduction, begin with the first point in your essay and come back to the introduction later.

Essay Starters

If, after you have done extensive invention (prewriting and research), you still find it intimidating to face the blank computer screen, try one of the essay starters below. These are phrases to get the words flowing. Then, later, after you have written a rough draft, go back and revise the beginning. Delete the essay starter and, in its place, write a real introduction. As you probably know, you do not need to say, "In my opinion," because what you write in your essay, unless you attribute it to someone else, is your opinion. See the section in this chapter on writing introductions.

In my opinion . . .

I agree . . .

I disagree . . .

Studies show . . .

Experts say . . .

My paper is about . . .

I am writing this essay because . . .

In the beginning . . .

Natalie Gorup suggests that introductions are worth special care and attention. She holds a M.A. in English and creative writing from the University of South Dakota.

"How I Write an Introduction"
by Natalie Gorup

First impressions matter. This is perhaps one of the reasons writing introductions can be so difficult—we feel the pressure of wanting to make a good first impression on our readers, just as we feel the pressure of wanting to "impress" our classmates or co-workers the first time we meet them. But because they matter so much, introductions are worth the care and attention we give to any first meeting.

When you "meet" your reader in your introduction, be kind. Be empathetic enough to realize that s/he has probably just spent a busy day doing many other things before reading your writing. Help to draw your reader in by both catching his or her attention and helping him or her to gently "wade in" to what you will be talking about. (Cannonballs might be exciting, but they are also sometimes unpleasantly shocking!) I like to think of the opening scenes of films, which often use a long shot, middle shot, close shot effect to situate their viewers and give them important information they might need for understanding the story that will follow. Janet Burroway suggests that creative writers use this technique as they help readers enter the world they have written, but the same technique can be applied to your critical writing.[1] Your readers will want to know where they are, why it is worth their time to be there, and where they might go with you during the course of your writing.

But then comes the challenge of fitting these concerns to scale. When I scale my introductions, I generally try to picture a funnel: the funnel's wide mouth is the top of the paragraph, while the funnel's narrowest point, its thesis, often appears at the end of the introduction. I have to arrive at this narrowest point before I can continue on with my argument, but I will need to decide how steep the slide from the mouth of the funnel to its narrowest point needs to be. If I start too broadly, I will set myself the task of covering a great distance in just one short paragraph; if I start too narrowly, I'll find myself repeating various versions of my thesis for a whole paragraph, but with no needed context! Finding the Goldilocks "funnel" is the ideal: make some wider connection to the reader-of-the-wider-world and then "zoom in" as you help that reader focus on what you have to say—because, after all, you are going to spend the rest of your essay illustrating just how important what you have to say might be.

When I chose to write on the striking absence of Lily Bart's private mental space in Edith Wharton's House of Mirth, for example, I didn't jump right into the depths of her psyche. I also didn't make sweeping statements about the mind in general. I began with the reader's experience of one character in one book: readers first know Lily as a character who has power in the physical spaces in which she moves, and so I write, "The arresting figure of Lily Bart captures Edith Wharton's readers from her first appearance in Grand Central Station nearly as much as Wharton's astute creation of the material world in which Lily moves does." Even by the end of this sentence, I begin to draw the comparison (after Judith Fryer)[2] between the arrangement of physical space and the arrangement of mental space, all to conclude with my main claim that Lily Bart's power is an empty one, because her power comes only from public spaces, with no private self to govern it. As a result of living on a theatrical social stage that makes the private public, Lily's private self became nonexistent. This complex thesis can be arrived at gently, by moving from Character→Character Trait→Claim about Cause of Character Trait.

Introducing complex ideas is challenging, but when you "teach" your points gently to your readers, with the gradual slide down the funnel, you can sometimes get it "just right."

Endnotes

1. Burroway, Janet. *Imaginative Writing: The Elements of Craft.* 2nd ed., Penguin Academics, 2007, pp. 136-9.
2. Fryer, Judith. *Felicitous Space: The Imaginative Structures of Edith Wharton and Willa Cather.* U of North Carolina P, 1986.

Reading 5.5

The Truth about Writer's Block
by Judith Johnson

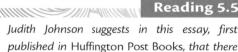

Judith Johnson suggests in this essay, first published in Huffington Post Books, *that there is no such thing as writer's block. She suggests what writers experience is the ebb and flow of the writing process.*

I don't choose to experience "writer's block" which I see as simply a matter of faulty perception. It is a mislabeling of a very natural part of the ebb and flow of the writing process. To say "I have writer's block" is to judge a temporary or permanent absence of writing momentum and productivity as wrong and therefore to see oneself as a failure in some way. The process of writing is an intricate interplay of conscious and unconscious dynamics and what actually lands on the page is a small part of it all. When we label and judge that process, we interfere with its natural flow and take a position of againstness with ourselves. It's all in how you look at it.

When a writer declares that he or she is experiencing writer's block, it is like grabbing hold of a fear (Fantasy Expectation Appearing Real) and fueling it with emotional distress. A way to reframe this is to simply trust that what appears to be a dry spell is a normal part of the process of being a writer and that either you need time to be away from the writing focus or that the process is largely unconscious at that time. Each writer has to make peace with this by finding their own particular rhythm and honoring that. For example, what works for me is not to have any rigid writing schedule, but rather to let the words come to me—and they always do—sooner or later. When working on a deadline, whether self-imposed or not, I never lose sight of the deadline, it is always there, but I don't beat myself up with it if time keeps passing and nothing is getting on paper. I'll notice that the topic is alive in me—turning this way and that finding its way to the paper. It takes a lot of trust to let this be. So far, it has never failed me.

I have lots of books and articles and projects on the back burner and no fear of running out of things to write about. I know that each piece of writing has a life of its own. For example, I have a poem that I started at the age of 16 that rumbles around in my head from time to time looking for its ending. I know it will end someday, but hasn't so far. That's not a problem to me—just a reality. I also keep what I call a "dump" file for each project and whether I am actively working on it or not, I capture ideas and information there.

In addition to building a strong bond of trust with yourself, here are some other keys to maintaining a good relationship with yourself as a writer:

Just Do It: There is a point at which every writer just has to sit down and write. Whether you write for five minutes or five hours straight doesn't matter, but if you are going to be a writer, you have to sit down and write.

Write with Freedom and Abandon, Then Edit Ruthlessly: It is important to give yourself permission to write whatever comes up without any judgment. Just focus on capturing your thoughts and ideas—forget about grammar, structure and eloquence. Just get a hold of whatever comes up. Then, just as

Michelangelo described the sculpting process as discovering a statue inside every block of stone, each writer must ruthlessly revise and refine a piece of work until pleased with it.

Get Out of Your Own Way: If you get into a pattern of negativity and beating up on yourself when writing, find a way to be more loving with yourself and do not feed the negativity.

Patience: Writing takes enormous patience. As with any other art form, you are constantly revising and refining your work. For an artist the equation is never time is money, but rather "do I feel complete with this piece? Is it my best effort given the time I have available?"

Flexibility, Cooperation and Balance: There is always some level of agitation just under the surface that propels a writer forward giving momentum to the working process. But there are always other forces at work and writing is only one of many activities in an individual's life. Finding your own rhythm and being willing to cooperate with the other elements of life that often seem to intrude on the writer's solitary endeavor are like moving between shooting the rapids and gliding along on calm waters, never quite knowing which is going to present itself and when. Experience teaches us all to go with the flow and somehow that seems to yield maximum inner peace and outward productivity.

Keeping a Sense of Humor and Humility: I've learned never to take myself too seriously as a writer. I do my best and need to laugh at myself from time to time when I give too much importance to what I write. If people get value from what I write, that's great and positive feedback is extremely gratifying. However, while writing is ultimately about communication, I find it very funny that I don't write to communicate, but rather because I simply need to write—I am compelled to do so. If the end product of my endeavors is of value to others, that's great, but the solitary process of engaging in the art form itself is entirely for me and I think that is pretty funny.

Letting Go of the Illusion of Control: A really good writer is never in control of the writing process. You may find that having a rigid schedule works well for you or you might be someone who writes when the spirit moves you to do so. Either way, a good writer taps into the wellspring of human consciousness and like love, you can't make that happen on demand.

Is writing challenging? Absolutely! However, it is a great way to learn some profound lessons in life and to be of service to others.

Explore

Activity 5.16 • Discuss "The Truth about Writer's Block"

In your small group, discuss the following questions.

1. How does Judith Johnson choose to reframe the concept of writer's block?

2. Johnson makes recommendations to deal with the "absence of writing momentum." Which of her suggestions makes the most sense to you? Which makes the least sense to you?

3. What do you think? Is there such a thing as "writer's block?"

Support Your Ideas with Source Materials

A research paper, by definition, makes use of source materials to make an argument. It is important to remember, however, that it is *your* paper, *not* what some professors may call a "research dump," meaning that it is constructed by stringing together research information with a few transitions. Rather, you, as the author of the paper, carry the argument in your own words and use quotes and paraphrases from source materials to support your argument.

▌ After you think you have completed enough research to construct a working thesis and begin writing your paper, collect all your materials in front of you (photocopies of articles, printouts of electronic sources, and books) and spend a few hours reading through the materials and making notes. Then, put all the notes and materials to the side and freewrite for a few minutes about what you can remember from your research that is important. Take this freewriting and make a rough outline of the main points you want to cover in your essay. Then you can go back to your notes and source materials to flesh out your outline.

▌ Use quotes for the following three reasons:

1. You want to "borrow" the *ethos* or credibility of the source. For example, if you are writing about stem cell research, you may want to quote from an authority such as Dr. James A. Thomson, whose groundbreaking research led to the first use of stem cells for research. Alternatively, if your source materials include the *New England Journal of Medicine* or another prestigious publication, it may be worth crediting a quote to that source.

2. The material is so beautifully or succinctly written that it would lose its effectiveness if you reworded the material in your own words.

3. You want to create a point of emphasis by quoting rather than paraphrasing. Otherwise, you probably want to paraphrase material from your sources, as quotes should be used sparingly. Often, writers quote source material in a first draft and then rewrite some of the quotes into paraphrases during the revision process.

▌ Introduce quotes. You should never have a sentence or sentences in quotation marks just sitting in the middle of a paragraph, as it would puzzle a reader. If you quote, you should always introduce the quote by saying something like this: According to Dr. James A. Thomson, "Stem cell research. . . . " Alternatively, you can make a short quote part of your sentence, as it is in this example: Dr. James A. Thomson found government regulations "restrictive and cumbersome."

▌ Avoid plagiarism by clearly indicating material that is quoted or paraphrased. See the appendix (at the end of the book) for more information about citing source material.

Support Your Thesis

After you have attracted the interest of your audience, established your thesis, and given any background information and definitions, you will next begin to give reasons for your position, which further develops your argument. These reasons are, in turn, supported by statistics, analogies, anecdotes, and quotes from authorities which you have discovered in your research or know from personal knowledge. Ideally, arrange your reasons so that the strongest ones come either at the beginning or at the end of this portion of the paper (points of emphasis), and the weaker ones fall in the middle.

Answer Opposing Arguments

If you are aware of a contradicting statistic or other possible objection to your argument, it may be tempting to ignore that complication, hoping your audience will not notice. However, that is exactly the worst thing you can do. It is much better to anticipate your audience's possible questions or objections and address them in your discussion. Doing so prevents you from losing credibility by either appearing to deceive your audience or being unaware of all the facts. Also, acknowledging possible refutations of your position actually strengthens your position by making you seem knowledgeable and fair-minded.

Vary Your Strategies or Patterns of Development

When composing your essay, you have many different strategies or **patterns of development** available to you. You may write entire essays whose sole strategy is argumentation or comparison and contrast, but more often, you will combine many of these different modes while writing a single essay. Consider the following strategies or patterns of development.

- **Analysis** entails a close examination of an issue, book, film, or other object, separating it into elements and examining each of the elements separately through other writing modes such as classification or comparison and contrast.

- **Argumentation** involves taking a strong stand on an issue supported by logical reasons and evidence intended to change a reader's mind on an issue or open a reader's eyes to a problem.

- **Cause and effect** is an explanation of the cause and subsequent effects or consequences of a specific action.

- **Classification** entails dividing and grouping things into logical categories.

- **Comparison and contrast** examines the similarities and differences between two or more things.

- **Definition** employs an explanation of the specific meaning of a word, phrase, or idea.

- **Description** uses vivid sensory details to present a picture or an image to the reader.

- **Exemplification** makes use of specific examples to explain, define, or analyze something.

- **Narration** uses a story or vignette to illustrate a specific point or examine an issue.

Include Effective Transitions

Transitions take readers by the hand and lead them from one part of your argument to the next. The best transitions have a light touch, not a hard grasp, so readers hardly realize they are being led. Phrases like "for example," "thus," "as a result," "therefore," and "moreover" are all transitions, and it is fine to employ them, but do not overuse them. In other words, do not have three sentences in a paragraph with the word "therefore."

The best paragraph transition begins the following paragraph where the previous one left off. In the following example from a student essay about obesity, the last sentence of one paragraph is this:

> Policy makers in America must hold the food industry accountable by creating stringent guidelines that create boundaries on the marketing of the food being advertised—not only to children, but to all Americans suffering from this disease; these policies may be what help in lowering the dangerous percentages of obesity threatening the lives of millions.

The next paragraph follows logically, giving more specifics about how obesity "threatens the lives of millions."

> Obesity is a major risk factor for non-communicable diseases, such as diabetes, cardiovascular diseases, and cancers.

Moreover, the repetition of the word "obesity" also serves as a transition.

Sometimes, you need to add a transition word or phrase to strengthen the link between one paragraph and the next (see Table 5.2). This list is not exhaustive. If you need additional transitions, try searching on the Internet for "writing transitions."

Don't worry too much about effective transitions in your first draft, but complete a revision pass through any text you write just to be sure your transitions are clear but not overworked.

Table 5.2 • Transition Words and Phrases

To emphasize	indeed, in fact, even, of course
To give an example	for example, namely, for instance, to illustrate, specifically
To prove	for, because, obviously, besides, in fact, in addition to
To show cause and effect	therefore, hence, accordingly, so
To provide additional support	additionally, again, as well, and, equally important

Write a Conclusion

After they have read the last paragraph of your essay, your readers should feel satisfied that you have covered everything you needed to, and you have shared an insight. You may have heard the basic rules: A conclusion cannot address any new issues, and it should summarize the main points of the essay. Although these are valid and reliable rules, a summary is not always the best way to end an essay. The prohibition against new ideas in the final paragraph also might limit certain effective closures like a call to action or a question for the reader to ponder.

One effective technique for writing a conclusion is to refer back to your introduction. If you began with a narrative anecdote, a sensory description, or a question, you can tie a mention of it to your ending point. Or, if you are composing an argumentative essay, you might choose to summarize by using an expert quote to restate your thesis, giving the reader a final firm sense of *ethos* or credibility. You might also end with a single-sentence summary followed by a suggestion or a call to action for the reader. Another effective way to end an argument can be a paragraph that suggests further research.

A conclusion doesn't have to be long. As a matter of fact, it does not even need to be a separate paragraph, especially if your essay is short. If your closing comments are related to the final paragraph of the essay, one or two sentences can easily be added to the final body paragraph of the essay.

Consider Elements of Page Design

Professors now take it for granted that you word-process your paper using a professional looking typeface such as Times New Roman. However, producing your text on a computer with Internet access gives you the option to do much more—including adding one or more images and other page design elements. Several of the assignments in this chapter offer you the opportunity to be creative with your project presentation. Even if you are required to submit your project in standard MLA or APA essay formats, however, you can still include one or more images, and it is important to consider where you place the images.

Some simple guidelines will help you design effective documents.

■   Use space as a design element. Do not overcrowd your pages. Place material so that important parts are emphasized by the space around them.

■ Rarely (if ever) use all capital letters. Words in all caps are hard to read, and on the Internet all caps is considered shouting.

■ Use headings to group your information and make your pages easy to skim. Readers often like to skim pages before deciding what to read. Indeed, many people will skim all the headlines, headings, and photo captions first, before reading the body text of any section.

■ Put important elements in the top left and lower right parts of the screen. English readers are trained to read from left to right, so our eyes naturally start at the upper left-hand corner of the screen. Our eyes, when skimming, don't flow line by line, but move in a Z pattern, as illustrated in the following diagram (see Figure 5.1).

Figure 5.1 • Eye Movement When Skimming a Page

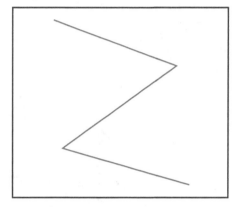

If you want to include a photo in your research paper, for example, you should put it either in the top left or the bottom right corner of the page, points of emphasis in the Z pattern. Today, with a sophisticated word processing program such as Microsoft Word, it is easy to import an image, size it, and move it to the desired place on a page. Once you have imported an image, you can click on it, hold your cursor at a corner, and enlarge or shrink the image by dragging the cursor. Also, by clicking on the image, you can activate the dialogue box that allows you to specify having the text run tightly around the image. Then you can easily move the image around on the page until you have placed it in a pleasing spot. Alternatively, Microsoft Word provides document templates that you can use for newsletters, brochures, and other types of projects.

If you look closely at Figure 5.2, you may notice that the text surrounding the image does not seem to make any sense (though it is actually Latin). That's because the text is Lorem ipsum text, sometimes called placeholder or dummy text, which designers use to create page layouts before they have the real text from writers. If you want to try using Lorem ipsum yourself, just do a search on the Internet for that name, and you will find sites that provide paragraphs of the nonsense words that you can utilize as placeholder text.

Figure 5.2 • Lorem Ipsum Text

Solupta ventemporios Obiscium

Pa que minullupta voles eaquibus, sa viduciur, sitae eum,Luptiaes

Lenis ut voloresed eum intias aruptatatur? Quia nempos et prae. Pel et denihita est explita denis sitem. Nam, optaturiore et adi dit, qui as et aut liquistia di reperest aspelicime non consequi dolorat voluptatium re, si untionse plitate maio doluptas enda ium arunt.

Met volor si consequi ut perferferum quodit ut quid ut explabore nonsequ aspedicto moluptae. Itati nemporitas atem rehentotae. Nem incim ellabore occuparum, nam que preprer uptur? Quiam etum fuga. Ut fugit que enis inumqui volorep udant, sequid quidem quis vendit volesse quodit ullenda secearum que velestrum, cus cor se adi ra voloreptat fuga. Ut incim fugitas quid mos voleni sam quatur restiorro molorem hilluptiae idelloribus.

Pariatur aut is dolorum quias volupta venimpo ribusciistem in rem

Sequundae senis mossunti vent ium

Ovide perciaspid qui vel millabo rerferio. Nam que volupic ietur? Optatuscit es dolorib erumquodit, samendebita doluptatia veligendunt, ut ex ex exeria pla nes estin num et digent, et porerovit, auda ipsam harume voluptius nullis elest, quam quis cus mi, es nem voluptatius net.

Offic torere doles eaturit aut laboreheni volorumquid mi, tetur, que con perro bearum aliciur, quos volore, accatur, optatem ra nos audam as eos aborposam ad ullatem eatias dust, consequi rendic tet que eumqui omnimolore estrum ipsanima denimagnatem excerspit litiumqui consedis ea ditiaec uptaest, ommod ut ende vella voluptae veles iunt aliquid que atet idus, vividicidem architiusae excepta ex estionet exceatiunt re essimol uptatqu asimost quatquiae dia ad magnihilla core voloro tempe nis

The image in this article has been effectively placed in the lower right corner, which is a point of emphasis.

Choose Evocative Photos to Illustrate Essays

The photo in Figure 5.3 of a demonstrator in Ferguson, Missouri, protesting the fatal police shooting of unarmed 18-year-old Michael Brown would be a good image to incorporate in an essay about police shootings of unarmed youths. The photo shows rhetorical gestures by both the protestor, with hands raised, and by the police in tactical gear, pointing their weapons toward the unarmed protestor. The photo was selected by both *Time* and *The New York Times* as one of the best photos of 2014.

Figure 5.3 • Evocative Photo Example

Photo Credit: Whitney Curtis/The New York Times/Redux

Reading 5.6

"How I Create a Multimedia Presentation"

by Jason Tham

Jason Tham says the first step in creating a multimedia presentation is to consider your deliverables. He is a Ph.D. student and instructor in rhetoric and scientific and technical communication at the University of Minnesota.

It is not uncommon for an instructor to require students to present their papers or arguments using a combination of texts, visuals, audios, and videos. A multimedia presentation, as I explain further below, is one that challenges you to consider communicating your ideas using more than one (hence "multi") form of composing technology. A typical multimedia presentation is the slideshow (like PowerPoint, Prezi, or Keynote) presentation, where you enhance your arguments using relevant images, sounds, and video clips in addition to text and your spoken words.

Moreover, a presentation can be interactive, requiring the audience to participate by making choices that affect the outcome of the experience. For example, audience members may choose between divergent endings to the experience or may contribute comments, images, or other content.

While multimedia or interactive presentation can be very effective for demonstrating ideas, I have seen how some presenters' insensitivity toward the rhetorical functions of different media results in boring presentations. Proper planning, however, increases the likelihood that a presentation will be both pleasant and persuasive.

So, whenever I am creating a multimedia presentation, my first step is to consider my deliverables, that is, what I wish to accomplish through this particular presentation. Sometimes my goal is to invoke urgency, other times I am more interested in creating a sense of community. First, I choose media that best serve my intentions. My intentions help determine the kind of media I employ. For example, when I intend to showcase an overview of content—instead of the details of this content—I make a collage of images on a PowerPoint slide to give my audience a bird's-eye view of my scope of presentation. This also simulates a family photo album or a yearbook viewing experience. However, when my intention is to "dive" deep into a certain topic, I use the Prezi canvas to create a sense of depth using the exciting zoom-in transition feature afforded by the slideware. While, if you intend to highlight synergy, collaborative editing apps like Google Slides and Zoho Show are great for demonstrating participatory effort.

Then, I proceed to evaluate my options. I usually look at what limits my options, i.e., time limit on the presentation, the physical environment in which I will deliver my presentation (e.g., classroom, lecture hall, roundtable, etc.), as well as my access to specific media (e.g., can I download an audio file for free, or do I need to purchase it?). These constraints are crucial as they inform my next step in exploring my media options—examining their rhetorical capabilities. For instance, a graph or statistical chart not only makes numbers more comprehensible but also conveys *logos* and tends to garner credibility for the presenter, or *ethos*. Photographs and videos are usually great for arousing emotions—*pathos*—because the audience can easily comprehend or make sense of their messages, which renders them rhetorically strong. The use of certain products and brand names as representations of a subject matter (e.g., using an Apple iPhone as a symbol for smartphone, or Facebook and Twitter as symbols of social media) is not uncommon in presentations as they carry the rhetorical capacity of referencing or reinforcing collectively assured characteristics—and, therefore build *ethos* and inspire *pathos*—especially when the representative object is a household name or item.

Colors are another important element that requires careful deliberation in creating a multimedia presentation. When choosing which color combination to employ, I always remind myself of the cultural meanings behind the colors and the rhetorical power they have over the audience (e.g., red tends to be an attention-getter, blue tends to suggest calmness or establishment, while green signifies nature and freshness). (By the way, red, blue, and green together would make a poor color combination according to color theory.)

Finally, when I consider my audience I think of much more than just its size. I try to find out as much as I can about my potential audience, such as their ages, socio-economic backgrounds, education levels, cultural affinities, professions, etc. Such sociographic information helps me to tailor the content of the presentation to be effective for my particular audience.

Following these steps, I am now able to select the most appropriate media, including images, text fonts, colors, videos and audio (if I choose to use them), animations, and transitions. Also important is the tone and manner of my presentation (e.g., humorous, authoritative, etc.). Of course, creating is just the beginning. After composing a presentation, I always polish it by practicing it and trying it out on colleagues to get a better feel for my presentation as well as feedback for revision. These steps have helped me to be a better presenter, not just someone who merely recites words on a PowerPoint slide without acknowledging the goals, options, and rhetoric of multimedia presentation.

Including Images in Your Projects: Copyright Implications

United States copyright law includes a provision called "fair use" that allows copyrighted images to be used for educational projects. However, copyright laws are complicated, and the implications of using digital images are still being determined in the courts. Clearly, if you take the photo yourself, you own the copyright. Many photographers post photos on websites such as Flikr.com and give permission for "fair use" of the images on the Internet, so long as their work is credited. Others, however, post their work for viewers to enjoy but do not allow it to be copied. Scanning a photo from a published work and using it once for a class project falls more clearly under the spirit of the "fair use" law than does putting such an image up on the Internet. If you are doing a web page or blog project that includes images, be sure to contact the copyright owner to obtain permission.

Compose

Activity 5.17 • Write a Research-Based Argument Paper

The Purpose of the Assignment

Writing a research paper gives you the opportunity to practice key academic writing skills, including locating and utilizing research materials, prewriting, drafting, and revision. It also requires you to take a position on a topic, create an argument, and support it with quotes and paraphrases from authoritative sources.

Purpose as a Writer

Your purpose as a writer is to convince readers to consider your argument carefully, and, if possible, to persuade them to agree with your point of view. To do this, include appropriate background material and definitions, as well as a consideration of opposing arguments.

Topic

Your topic should address a current issue about which you can take and support a position in the paper length your instructor specifies. Choose your topic carefully, as it should be one that engages your interest and enthusiasm.

Audience

Unless your instructor specifies otherwise, you can assume that your audience has general awareness of your issue but is unfamiliar with scholarly sources on the topic.

Sources

To do your research, you will need to utilize recent and credible sources that include a mix of recent books, scholarly articles, public speeches, and news articles. You may also use interviews, observation, and personal experience, if they are relevant to your topic. Sources will need to be cited in the text and in a works cited page or references page, according to MLA or APA style.

Information that you gather from your sources should support the argument you have created. A research paper is not an assignment in which you take information from sources and simply reorganize it into a paper. The expectation for this assignment is that you will use your sources to create an argument that is distinctly your own.

Thesis

Your essay should have a clear thesis that takes a position on an issue that can be supported within the word limitations of the assignment.

Rough Draft

As directed by your instructor, bring two copies of your rough draft essay to class for peer editing. The draft should have your sources credited in the text and should have a works cited or references page.

(continued on next page)

Final Draft

Submit your final draft in MLA or APA format in a folder with your rough draft and copies of all of your source materials with the location of quotes or paraphrased material highlighted. If you are using material from a book or books, copy enough of the text before and after your quotes or paraphrases so that your instructor can determine the context of the material being quoted.

Activity 5.18 • Freewrite about Your Research Paper

Freewrite for five minutes, answering one or more of these questions, or write about something else related to the writing of your research paper.

1. Why did you choose that particular topic?

2. What was it like combining personal knowledge or background information with paraphrases or quotes from your sources?

3. What worked well, and with what areas of the paper did you struggle?

If your instructor requests, turn your freewriting into a polished paragraph with a thesis and supporting sentences.

Activity 5.19 • Write on Your Blog

Write an informal review of a film you have seen recently. What did you like, and what did you dislike? Would you recommend the film to a friend?

Activity 5.20 • Write in Your Commonplace Book

Find a piece from the Opinion/Editorial section of your local newspaper that interests you. If you were going to write a letter to the editor in response, what might you say?

chapter 6
Revising Rhetorically

How I Revise

Sarah Gray, Ph.D. Candidate and Instructor at Middle Tennessee State University in Nineteenth-Century American and Gothic Literature

I don't think it's possible to overemphasize the importance of revision in the writing process. For me, this process begins with a hard copy of the project on which I'm working. I find that reading my work away from my computer screen allows me to see new angles or incomplete thoughts more clearly than rereading on the computer. By retreating from the computer to a comfortable chair or couch, colorful pen in hand (as long as it's not red!), I allow myself a new perspective that I wouldn't otherwise find.

While changing the mode in which I read my work is important, allowing myself enough time to gain some critical distance from my argument is imperative. Ideally, I allow my paper at least a few days to "rest" while I complete other tasks or work on other projects. This way, the construct I've created for the paper has a chance to fall away, so I don't read my paper already knowing what it's supposed to say. This approach allows me to pay attention to things like organization and clarity; plus, I can see more clearly if my argument is fully supported.

Once I've achieved this critical distance, and I've retreated to an alternate location with my previously mentioned colorful pen, I proceed to annotate my text. I'll ask myself questions in the margins, strike out sentences that no longer seem to fit, draw arrows to rearrange my paragraphs, and rewrite or add information in the margins. I always print these pages one-sided, so I have enough space on the back to do more in-depth revisions, explore new ideas, and take notes for additional research. I often also use this blank space to record questions I may have for my professors.

Allowing enough time for revision also means that I'll have time to reach out to my peers for feedback. I regularly make use of my university's writing center where I've received invaluable advice on everything from brainstorming topics to focusing my argument. Also, a reader who's unfamiliar with my topic or argument is much more likely than me to notice if something isn't explained well enough. After all, an argument is only as good as a writer's ability to make others hear it.

Revision Is Part of the Writing Process

In ancient times, the focus of the rhetor was upon the presentation of oral arguments in the form of speeches, and students trained to perform in pressured situations before a law court or assembly. Though a speaker might spend time in preparation, most speeches were one-time opportunities. If the words were not well-chosen and well-spoken the first time, there was no second chance to influence an audience.

With modern written documents, a composition does not have to be perfect when the words first appear on the page. A document is not truly finished until it is transmitted to an audience, and, even then, important documents are often circulated in draft stages to colleagues for comments before they are presented to an audience.

Many writers claim that revising is the most rewarding step in writing, the time when they have words on a page to work with and can manipulate them to create a composition that communicates effectively. Yet, many students feel that their first drafts should stay exactly the way they've written them because these writings are truest to their feelings and experience. They are sure they have made their point clearly. In reality, a first draft often leaves the reader scratching his or her head and wondering what it was the writer meant to say. To communicate effectively, a writer must learn to interact with readers to ensure he or she communicates a message clearly.

Begin Revision by Rereading

The first step of revising is rereading. This step can be simple, if you are reading something written by someone else. When it is your own writing, it becomes infinitely more difficult. After all, you know what you meant to say—you know the research behind the writing and why you chose certain words or phrases. You even know how every sentence is supposed to read—even though you may have left out a word or two or three—and your mind can trick you into seeing the missing words right where they belong. Unfortunately, the reader does not have your understanding, so communication can break down. You need to learn to read your own work critically, as if it were written by a stranger. One of the first aids in this process is to read your work aloud. You can often hear stumbling blocks quicker than you can see them.

You can also learn to read your own work more objectively by reading and commenting on other writers' work. Look at the structure of essays, at the way the writers use transitions and topic sentences, and at the sentence structure and choice of words. As you learn to see how good writers put ideas and words together, you will begin to think about the readings in a more thorough manner—thinking of alternative, perhaps even better, ways to express the message of each essay. You will also learn to read your own work with a more critical eye.

Reading 6.1

Shitty First Drafts

by Anne Lamott

Anne Lamott, in the essay from her popular book about writing, Bird By Bird *(1994), lets the reader in on a secret. Beautiful words do not flow naturally onto the page for even the best-known and most popular writers. Almost all write shitty first drafts. Lamott explains how the process works for her—letting the words pour out without worrying how good they are.*

Now, practically even better news than that of short assignments is the idea of shitty first drafts. All good writers write them. This is how they end up with good second drafts and terrific third drafts. People tend to look at successful writers, writers who are getting their books published and maybe even doing well financially, and think that they sit down at their desks every morning feeling like a million dollars, feeling great about who they are and how much talent they have and what a great story they have to tell; that they take in a few deep breaths, push back their sleeves, roll their necks a few times to get all the cricks out, and dive in, typing fully formed passages as fast as a court reporter. But this is just the fantasy of the uninitiated. I know some very great writers, writers you love who write beautifully and have made a great deal of money, and not one of them sits down routinely feeling wildly enthusiastic and confident. Not one of them writes elegant first drafts. All right, one of them does, but we do not like her very much. We do not think that she has a rich inner life or that God likes her or can even stand her. (Although when I mentioned this to my priest friend Tom, he said you can safely assume you've created God in your own image when it turns out that God hates all the same people you do.)

Very few writers really know what they are doing until they've done it. Nor do they go about their business feeling dewy and thrilled. They do not type a few stiff warm-up sentences and then find themselves bounding along like huskies across the snow. One writer I know tells me that he sits down every morning and says to himself nicely, "It's not like you don't have a choice, because you do—you can either type or kill yourself." We all often feel like we are pulling teeth, even those writers whose prose ends up being the most natural and fluid. The right words and sentences just do not come pouring out like ticker tape most of the time. Now, Muriel Spark is said to have felt that she was taking dictation from God every morning—sitting there, one supposes, plugged into a Dictaphone, typing away, humming. But this is a very hostile and aggressive position. One might hope for bad things to rain down on a person like this.

For me and most of the other writers I know, writing is not rapturous. In fact, the only way I can get anything written at all is to write really, really shitty first drafts.

The first draft is the child's draft, where you let it all pour out and then let it romp all over the place, knowing that no one is going to see it and that you can shape it later. You just let this childlike part of you channel whatever voices and visions come through and onto the page. If one of the characters wants to say, "Well, so what, Mr. Poopy Pants?," you let her. No one is going to see it. If the kid wants to get into really sentimental, weepy, emotional territory, you let him. Just get it all down on paper, because there may be something great in those six crazy pages that you would never have gotten to by more rational, grown-up means. There may be something in the very last line of the very last paragraph on page six that you just love, that is so beautiful or wild that you now know what you're supposed to be writing about, more or less, or in what direction you might go—but there was no way to get to this without first getting through the first five and a half pages.

I used to write food reviews for *California Magazine* before it folded. (My writing food reviews had nothing to do with the magazine folding, although every single review did cause a couple of canceled subscriptions. Some readers took umbrage at my comparing mounds of vegetable puree with various ex-presidents' brains.) These reviews always took two days to write. First I'd go to a restaurant several times with a few opinionated, articulate friends in tow. I'd sit there writing down everything anyone said that was at all interesting or funny. Then on the following Monday I'd sit down at my desk with my notes, and try to write the review. Even after I'd been doing this for years, panic would set in. I'd try to write a lead, but instead I'd write a couple of dreadful sentences, xx them out, try again, xx everything out, and then feel despair and worry settle on my chest like an x-ray apron. It's over, I'd think, calmly. I'm not going to be able to get the magic to work this time. I'm ruined. I'm through. I'm toast. Maybe, I'd think, I can get my old job back as a clerk-typist. But probably not. I'd get up and study my teeth in the mirror for a while. Then I'd stop, remember to breathe, make a few phone calls, hit the kitchen and chow down. Eventually I'd go back and sit down at my desk, and sigh for the next ten minutes.

Finally I would pick up my one-inch picture frame, stare into it as if for the answer, and every time the answer would come: all I had to do was to write a really shitty first draft of, say, the opening paragraph. And no one was going to see it. So I'd start writing without reining myself in. It was almost just typing, just making my fingers move. And the writing would be terrible. I'd write a lead paragraph that was a whole page, even though the entire review could only be three pages long, and then I'd start writing up descriptions of the food, one dish at a time, bird by bird, and the critics would be sitting on my shoulders, commenting like cartoon characters. They'd be pretending to snore, or rolling their eyes at my overwrought descriptions, no matter how hard I tried to tone those descriptions down, no matter how conscious I was of what a friend said to me gently in my early days of restaurant reviewing. "Annie," she said, "it is just a piece of chicken. It is just a bit of cake."

But because by then I had been writing for so long, I would eventually let myself trust the process—sort of, more or less. I'd write a first draft that was maybe twice as long as it should be, with a self-indulgent and boring beginning, stupefying descriptions of the meal, lots of quotes from my black-humored friends that made them sound more like the Manson girls than food lovers, and no ending to speak of. The whole thing would be so long and incoherent and hideous that for the rest of the day I'd obsess about getting creamed by a car before I could write a decent second draft. I'd worry that people would read what I'd written and believe that the accident had really been a suicide, that I had panicked because my talent was waning and my mind was shot.

The next day, though, I'd sit down, go through it all with a colored pen, take out everything I possibly could, find a new lead somewhere on the second page, figure out a kicky place to end it, and then write a second draft. It always turned out fine, sometimes even funny and weird and helpful. I'd go over it one more time and mail it in. Then, a month later, when it was time for another review, the whole process would start again, complete with the fears that people would find my first draft before I could rewrite it.

Almost all good writing begins with terrible first efforts. You need to start somewhere. Start by getting something—anything—down on paper. A friend of mine says that the first draft is the down draft—you just get it down. The second draft is the up draft—you fix it up. You try to say what you have to say more accurately. And the third draft is the dental draft, where you check every tooth, to see if it's loose or cramped or decayed, or even, God help us, healthy.

Collaborate

Activity 6.1 • Discussing "Shitty First Drafts"

In your small group, consider these questions in your discussion about "Shitty First Drafts."

1. Anne Lamott says that the image of a writer's process that most people have is "the fantasy of the uninitiated." What does she claim most people think about how professional writer's write?

2. What is the reality of a writer's first draft process, as Lamott describes it? What does she mean by saying that she starts "writing without reining myself in"?

3. Do you agree with Lamott about the process of writing a first draft? Why or why not?

Qualities of Effective Writing

Reading the work of some professional writers, you may have developed the idea that the best writing is writing that is difficult to understand, writing that sends the reader to the dictionary with every sentence, or writing that uses many technical or specialized terms. Often, we think something difficult to read must be well written. Although it is sometimes difficult to read about topics that are new to us because we're learning new vocabulary and struggling with complex ideas, it simply is not true that the best writing is hard to read. Indeed, the most effective writing, the kind of writing you want to produce in your classes, is simple, concise, and direct.

Keep It Simple

Simple means "unadorned" or "not ornate." *Writing simply* means saying something in common, concrete language without too much complication in the sentence structure. Writing simply doesn't mean you have to use only short or easy words. It doesn't mean that all your sentences will be simple sentences. It doesn't mean that you can't use figures of speech or intricate details. Simple writing means that you try to get your point across in a direct and interesting way. You aren't trying to hide your ideas. Instead, you are trying to amplify those ideas and begin an intelligible conversation with your reader.

For example, Greg McKeown, in an article about something Bill Gates and Warren Buffett have in common—focus—uses this analogy about how our eyes focus:

> Imagine if the moment you woke up this morning your eyes focused one time and then never adjusted again. You would be out of focus all day. Our eyes produce clarity through a perpetual process of adjustment.[1]

Using simple sentences, McKeown creates a sophisticated image of how the eyes work.

Simple writing means that you try to get your point across in a direct and interesting way. You aren't trying to hide your ideas. Instead, you are trying to amplify those ideas and begin an intelligible conversation with your reader.

Rely on Everyday Words

When writing about computers or other technical subjects, it's tempting to use **jargon** or specialized words you might use when talking to others with the same knowledge, interest, and background. When writing for a limited audience whose members are familiar with technical terms, a bit of jargon might be acceptable. However, most of the writing you will do in college and later in the workplace will address a larger audience. You will want to avoid the use of highly technical terms, acronyms, and abbreviations.

If it seems that the writers in this text use many big words or technical terms, stop for a minute to consider the original audience for each of the essays. Consider how your vocabulary grows each year as you read, discuss, and consider new ideas. The everyday words of a tenth grade student will probably be fewer in number than the everyday words of a junior in college. Similarly, the everyday words of a college freshman will be different from the everyday words of a computer professional with three years of work experience. Use words that

---

1. McKeown, Greg. "The One-Word Answer to Why Bill Gates and Warren Buffett Have Been So Successful." *LinkedIn Pulse.* LinkedIn Corp., 7 July 2014. Web. 17 Oct. 2015.

are comfortable and familiar to you and your readers when you write, and you will write clear, effective essays.

Use Precise Words

We sometimes assume that the reader will know what we mean when we use adjectives like "beautiful," "quiet," or "slow." However, the reader has only his or her own ideas of those adjectives. You can make your writing more interesting and effective by adding concrete details to give the reader an image that uses at least two of the five senses.

You can use details from all of the senses to make your writing even more concrete and precise. What are some of the sensual qualities of the experience or thing? Can you compare it to another thing that your readers may be familiar with to help them understand it better? Can you compare it to something totally unlike it? Can you compare it to a different sense to surprise readers and help them understand the image you are trying to create?

A good way to practice your ability to write original concrete images is to expand on a cliché. A **cliché** is an overused saying or expression. Often, clichés begin as similes that help make images more concrete. They become clichéd or overused because they lose their originality, or they don't contain enough detail to give us the entire picture. Choose a cliché and write a sentence that expands the cliché and uses the senses to create a clear picture of the thing described. You might try some of the following clichés:

> She is as pretty as a picture.
>
> It smelled heavenly.
>
> It was as soft as a baby's bottom.
>
> His heart is as hard as stone.
>
> It tastes as sour as a pickle.
>
> We stared at the roaring campfire.
>
> We listened to the babbling brook.

Precise details allow us to experience the world of the writer. We leave our own views and perceptions and learn how someone else sees the world. We learn what "quiet" is like for one writer and what "beautiful" means to another. Fill in the gaps between your words and ideas with vivid images and your writing will become more interesting and more effective.

Be Concise

Rid your writing of excess words and leave only that which makes your meaning clear and concrete. Becoming aware of several common problems can help you make your writing more concise. When you begin a sentence with either "it is" or "there is," you transfer all the meaning of the sentence to the end of the sentence. This is known as a **delayed construction**. You have delayed the meaning. The reader must read on to find out what "it" or "there" refer to. They don't get anything important from the beginning of the sentence.

Examine the following sentences:

It is important to change the oil in older gasoline engines.

There is an apple on the table.

There isn't anything we need to fear except our own fear.

We can rewrite these sentences, making them more concise, by deleting the "there is" or the "it is" and restructuring the sentence.

Changing the oil in older gasoline engines is important.

An apple is on the table.

We have nothing to fear but fear itself.

Notice that the second group of sentences is shorter and the important information is no longer buried in the middle. Revising this type of sentence can make your writing more concise and get information to the reader more effectively.

If you think you may be guilty of using "it is" and "there is" (or "it's" and "there's") too often, you can use most word processing programs to seek these constructions out. Use the "search" or "find and replace" tool that's found in the Edit portion of your pull-down menu. Type "it is" and ask your computer to find every place you use this construction in your document. When you find a sentence that begins with "it is," revise the sentence to make it more concise. Do the same with "there is," "it's," and "there's." After you become more aware of these errors by correcting them, you'll find that you notice the errors before or as you make them. You will begin to write more concisely, and you'll have fewer delayed constructions to revise.

You can also make your writing more concise by avoiding common wordy expressions. Sometimes when we're nervous about writing or insecure about our knowledge of a topic, we try to hide that insecurity behind a wall of meaning-less words, such as in the following sentence:

> At this point in time, you may not have the ability to create a web page due to the fact that you've avoided using computers for any-thing other than playing Solitaire.

This sentence is full of deadwood phrases that add no meaning to the sen-tence. If we take out the unneeded words, we have this sentence:

> You may not be able to create a web page because you've only used your computer to play Solitaire.

Your computer may have a grammar checker that will identify some commonly used wordy expressions. If your computer doesn't have a grammar checker, or if your instructor has asked you not to use the grammar checker on your computer, you can still learn to revise the wordiness out of your paragraphs. Use the computer to separate a paragraph of your writing into sentences. As you scroll through the paragraph, hit the hard return or "Enter" key on your keyboard twice every time you find a period. Once you have separated the sentences, look at each sentence. What is the important idea in the sentence? What words are used to convey that idea? What words don't add any mean-ing to the sentence? Delete words that don't convey meaning, and revise the sentence to make it more concise.

Use Action Verbs

Action verbs are words that convey the action of a sentence. They carry much of our language's nuance and meaning. Many inexperienced writers use only "to be" verbs: *am, is, are, was, were, be, been,* and *being.* If you use too many of these verbs, you risk losing much of the power of language. If I say someone is coming through the door, I've created a picture of a body and a doorway. If I say someone marches or slinks through the door, I've added information not only about movement but also about the quality of that movement. I've given my subject the attitude of a soldier or a cat. For example, consider this sentence written by Howard Rheingold:

> Thirty thousand years ago, outside a deceptively small hole in a limestone formation in the area now known as southern France, several adolescents shivered in the dark, awaiting initiation into the cult of toolmakers.

By using the verb "shivered," especially when accompanied by the words "in the dark," Rheingold paints a word picture much more vivid than he would have conveyed with the use of a "to be" verb. Using interesting verbs can enliven your writing.

If you want to focus upon using more action verbs, skim through your essay and circle all the "to be" verbs. Read the sentences with circled "to be" verbs more closely, and choose several to rewrite using active verbs in place of the "to be" verbs. You won't be able to do this for every sentence, but replace them where you can and your writing will become more lively, more concise, and more effective.

Fill in the Gaps

When we write, we sometimes forget that we are writing to an audience other than ourselves. We expect that our readers are people just like us, with our experiences, memories, and tastes. Because we have assumed they're so much like us, we expect our readers to be able to read more than what we've written on the page. We expect them to read our minds. We may leave large gaps in our essays, hoping the reader will fill in exactly the information we would have included.

If I'm writing an essay about my childhood in the South, and I say it was always so hot in the summer that I hated to go outside, I might think my reader knows what I mean by hot. However, there are many different ways to be "hot." In east Texas where I grew up, the hot was a sticky hot. Eighty degrees made me long for a big glass of sweetened iced tea with lots of ice. The heat made my clothes cling. Sweating didn't help because the sweat didn't dry. I spent the day feeling as if I'd never dried off after my morning shower. In New Mexico, I never really felt hot unless the temperature got above 110 degrees. At that point, the heat would rush at me, making it difficult to breathe. I would open the door to leave the house, and it felt as if I had opened the oven door to check on a cake. If I say I was hot in the summer without describing how heat felt to me, my reader may not get the message I'm trying to convey. Don't expect your reader to know what you mean by "hot" or by any other general description. Instead, take a minute to add details that will fill in the gaps for the reader.

Speak Directly

To *speak directly* is to say, up front, who is doing what. Sometimes we don't tell the reader who is completing the action or we tell him or her too late. Let's look at a few sentences.

The steak was stolen from the grill.

The decisive battle was fought between the Confederate and the Union armies in Vicksburg, Mississippi.

The red truck has been driven into the side of the green car.

Although we might be able to guess who the actors are in each of the sentences, the first and last sentences don't tell us directly. Even if the reader can guess that it was a dog who stole the steak from the grill or my neighbor who drove the red truck into the side of the green car, the reader has to stop and figure out who is doing what before he or she can read on. This slows the reader down and diminishes the effectiveness of your writing.

Language professionals call this **passive voice**. The action comes before the actor. Note that sometimes, as in the first and last sentences above, the writer doesn't mention the actor at all. To identify passive verbs in your writing, look for verbs coupled with another action word that ends in "-ed" or "-en" such as "was stolen" or "was forgotten."

Find the action and the actor in the sentence to make sure that they are in the most effective order. The most effective sentence order is actor first, then action. If the sentence does not specify the actor but leaves it implied, chances are that it is a passive sentence. For example, read this sentence: "The red truck was driven into the green car." It does not say who the driver was, and thus it is a passive sentence.

Rewriting some of your sentences to eliminate use of the passive voice will make your writing stronger and more interesting.

Strengthen Your Voice

The activities in this book ask you to take positions on controversial issues and make your opinion clear to your audience. You are required to draw upon a range of sources to support your claims in argumentative texts. In effect, your voice joins other voices in a written conversation about your topic, as you use quotes, paraphrases, and summaries from sources combined with your own words.

Beware of over-use of secondary sources, which can cause a paragraph to read like a string of quotations. That may work for a rough draft, but as you revise, include your voice by interpreting what the sources are saying. Table 6.1 is an example of an original, unrevised paragraph on the left that is primarily source material strung together. The column on the right, highlighted in red, shows the student's comments about the source material.

Table 6.1 • Integrating Evidence

Original Paragraph—Poorly integrated evidence	Revised Paragraph—Well integrated evidence
Gabrenya, Latane & Wang (1981) and Albanese & Van Fleet (1985) note that as group sizes increase there is a tendency for the effort put in by the group to be less than the average effort put in by individuals engaged on the same task separately. Albanese & Van Fleet (1985) report on the 'free-rider problem', where the collective nature of the 'contract' obscures the fact of one member failing to honour their part of the contract. Gabrenya, Latane & Wang (1981, p180) discuss the phenomenon of 'social loafing' and typically define it as "one where everyone puts in a little less".	One phenomenon that can greatly impact the effectiveness of groups is that as group sizes increase there is a tendency for the effort put in by the group to be less than the average effort put in by individuals engaged on the same task separately (Gabrenya, Latane & Wang 1981; Albanese & Van Fleet 1985). The phenomenon has been described using various terms. Writers influenced by industrial economics describe it as the 'free-rider problem', where the collective nature of the 'contract' obscures the fact of one member failing to honour their part of the contract (Albanese & Van Fleet 1985, p230). Writers who are organizational psychologists tend to label the phenomenon as 'social loafing' and typically define it as "one where everyone puts in a little less" (Gabrenya, Latane & Wang 1981, p120). Whatever the terminology used to describe this phenomenon, it is one that is problematic for groups.

Source: "Expressing Your Voice in Academic Writing." *UniLearning*, 2000, unilearning.uow.edu.au/academic/4bi.html.

In the highlighted version, the student's voice begins and ends the paragraph. Notice particularly that the last student comment ties together what the sources are saying.

Explore

Activity 6.2 • **Apply Qualities of Effective Writing**

With a draft of your writing project in front of you, either on a computer screen or in printed form, review the list of Qualities of Effective Writing described in this chapter and listed below. Read the explanation about each quality, and then read your draft, looking for places you can revise to improve your draft.

- Keep it simple.

- Rely on everyday words.

- Use precise words.

- Be concise.

- Use action verbs.

- Fill in the gaps.

- Speak directly.

- Strengthen your voice.

Explore

Activity 6.3 • **Share Your Own Grammar Cartoon**

Find a cartoon that illustrates a point about grammar, print it, and share it with your small group. To locate such cartoons, you could try doing a key-word search in your browser for "grammar cartoons." Have your group choose the cartoons you like best, and share them with the class.

Copyright © 2013 Dan Piraro.

Activity 6.4 • When You Reeeaaallly Want to Describe Something

Explore

This activity requires a thesaurus or access to the *Visual Thesaurus* website (www.visualthesaurus.com).

▮ Strunk and White's *The Elements of Style,* in an entry on "Misused Words and Expressions," says,

"*Very.* Use this word sparingly. Where emphasis is necessary, use words strong in themselves."

With a partner, paraphrase and discuss this Strunk and White writing tip. For example, instead of "very red," you could write "crimson" or "burgundy."

▮ To demonstrate Strunk and White's advice in (1) above, revise the following sentence, getting rid of the adverb "very."

Julie is very pretty.

No, don't say, "Julie is beautiful." Make a list of more precise and vivid words that could be used instead. Refer to a thesaurus (or the *Visual Thesaurus* website) to find words such as "stunning" and so on.

▮ As a class, brainstorm other intensifying adverbs such as "awfully" or "extremely" that you tend to use as words of emphasis (in writing or in everyday speech), and list those words on the board.

▮ In pairs again, compose a short paragraph of two or three sentences about a subject or event (e.g., a tornado, a celebrity sighting, a sports event, a news event, a concert, etc.), and intentionally use as many common or trite intensifying words as possible.

▮ Exchange the short paragraph you composed in (4) above with another pair of classmates. Revise the other partnership's dialogue with the use of a thesaurus. The revised dialogue should not contain any "intensifiers" or trite words of emphasis. Replace such words and phrases with more powerful and concise language. For example, "I was really happy to see the Hornets win. They totally beat the Giants," could be revised to read (with the help of more concise and powerful words): "I was thrilled to see the Hornets thrash the Giants."

▮ Read your "before" and "after" dialogues to the class. Afterward, discuss which words were eliminated and how the words that replaced those intensifiers changed the tone and/or meaning of the dialogue.

Source: Adapted from a lesson plan at "When You Reeeaaallly Want to Say Something." *Lesson Plans,* 3 July 2008. *Thinkmap Visual Thesaurus,* www.visualthesaurus.com/cm/lessons/when-you-reeeaaallly-want-to-say-something/.

Remember to Proofread

It is understandably difficult to find the errors in an essay you have been working on for days. A few tricks used by professional writers might help you see errors in your essay more clearly.

1. With pencil in hand, read the essay aloud, slowly—and preferably to an audience. When you are reading aloud, it is more difficult to add or change words, so you tend to catch errors you would not see reading silently to yourself. Plus the reactions of your audience may point out areas where future readers may become confused or lose interest.

2. Another trick is to read the essay backwards, sentence by sentence. This forces you to look at sentence structure and not at the overall content of the essay. If you are working on a computer, another way to accomplish this is to create a final edit file in which you hit the hard return twice at the end of every question or statement. You might even go so far as to number the sentences so they look more like grammar exercises. Then look at each sentence individually.

Reading 6.2

In this blog entry, Mignon Fogarty offers her top-ten list of grammar mistakes and misunderstandings. Notice that Fogarty disagrees with Safire, saying it is okay to split infinitives. Fogarty is writing more recently than Safire and probably has a less formal audience in mind.

Grammar Girl's Top Ten Grammar Myths
by Mignon Fogarty

10. A run-on sentence is a really long sentence. Wrong! They can actually be quite short. In a run-on sentence, independent clauses are squished together without the help of punctuation or a conjunction. If you write "I am short he is tall," as one sentence without a semicolon, colon, or dash between the two independent clauses, it's a run-on sentence even though it only has six words.

9. You shouldn't start a sentence with the word "however." Wrong! It's fine to start a sentence with "however" so long as you use a comma after it when it means "nevertheless."

8. "Irregardless" is not a word. Wrong! "Irregardless" is a bad word and a word you shouldn't use, but it is a word. "Floogetyflop" isn't a word—I just made it up and you have no idea what it means. "Irregardless," on

the other hand, is in almost every dictionary labeled as nonstandard. You shouldn't use it if you want to be taken seriously, but it has gained wide enough use to qualify as a word.

7.   There is only one way to write the possessive form of a word that ends in "s." Wrong! It's a style choice. For example, in the phrase "Kansas's statute," you can put just an apostrophe at the end of "Kansas" or you can put an apostrophe "s" at the end of "Kansas." Both ways are acceptable.

6.   Passive voice is always wrong. Wrong! Passive voice is when you don't name the person who's responsible for the action. An example is the sentence "Mistakes were made," because it doesn't say who made the mistakes. If you don't know who is responsible for an action, passive voice can be the best choice.

5.   "i.e." and "e.g." mean the same thing. Wrong! "e.g." means "for example," and "i.e." means roughly "in other words." You use "e.g." to provide a list of incomplete examples, and you use "i.e." to provide a complete clarifying list or statement.

4.   You use "a" before words that start with consonants and "an" before words that start with vowels. Wrong! You use "a" before words that start with consonant sounds and "an" before words that start with vowel sounds. So, you'd write that someone has an MBA instead of a MBA, because even though "MBA" starts with "m," which is a consonant, it starts with the sound of the vowel "e"—MBA.

3.   It's incorrect to answer the question "How are you?" with the statement "I'm good." Wrong! "Am" is a linking verb and linking verbs should be modified by adjectives such as "good." Because "well" can also act as an adjective, it's also fine to answer "I'm well," but some grammarians believe "I'm well" should be used to talk about your health and not your general disposition.

2.   You shouldn't split infinitives. Wrong! Nearly all grammarians want to boldly tell you it's OK to split infinitives. An infinitive is a two-word form of a verb. An example is "to tell." In a split infinitive, another word separates the two parts of the verb. "To boldly tell" is a split infinitive because "boldly" separates "to" from "tell."

1.   You shouldn't end a sentence with a preposition. Wrong! You shouldn't end a sentence with a preposition when the sentence would mean

the same thing if you left off the preposition. That means "Where are you at?" is wrong because "Where are you?" means the same thing. But there are many sentences where the final preposition is part of a phrasal verb or is necessary to keep from making stuffy, stilted sentences: "I'm going to throw up," "Let's kiss and make up," and "What are you waiting for" are just a few examples.

© *Huffington Post*

Stationary means "fixed in place, unable to move;" *stationery* is letterhead or other special writing paper. (Hint: *Station**e**ry* with an *e* comes with an <u>e</u>nvelope.) Examples: Evan worked out on his *stationary* bike. The duke's initials and crest appeared atop his personal *stationery*.

© *Huffington Post*

Eminent means "distinguished or superior;" *imminent* means "impending, sure to happen." Also, *eminent* domain is the right of a government to take over private property for public use. Examples: The rain was *imminent*; it would arrive soon, soaking the *eminent* dignitaries on the stage. (Think of *imminent* and *impending*, which both begin with the same letters.)

Top Ten Distractions for Writers, or Any Job Really
by Sam Scham

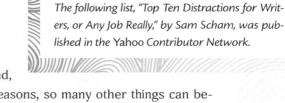

Reading 6.3

The following list, "Top Ten Distractions for Writers, or Any Job Really," by Sam Scham, was published in the Yahoo Contributor Network.

When you have a set goal in mind, whether it is for personal or work reasons, so many other things can become easy distractions. For writers in particular, life seems to get in the way. There are other pressing matters that we have to worry about.

1. The Internet
The Internet is a very huge distraction these days. For writers who do research online for their great idea, it is easy to stumble upon different links and steer away from the main point in focus. If you find yourself doing this, try to limit the time you do research therefore getting off the Internet earlier and allow more time for writing.

2. The Radio
Music can help a writer generate ideas and feelings. Listening to the radio can be a distraction if you leave it on for too long. If you are like me, you are able to write the best in silence. You need to be able to hear yourself think. If you are listening to the radio and it is hard to turn away from it, listen to it in segments. Listen to some music and when a commercial comes on, mute the radio and start writing. Maybe, before you know it, you will forget that you were ever listening to the radio.

3. The Television
The television and the radio are similar in many ways. For one, it is hard to turn off, especially if you are in the middle of a show that you want to finish. But then, you see a commercial for what is coming up next and you are intrigued to watch it. At the end of the current show, turn off the TV and get writing. Soon, you will not notice the absence of the picture box.

4. Own Procrastination
You want to sit down and write, but at the same time you don't, you have no motivation. The solution is to take a day off, do not think of it at all. Work on any other pressing matters like home chores or calling up an old friend that you've been meaning to catch up with. On the next day, wake up and get writing. Just jump right into it and it will be like you never took a break.

5. Other People

Especially if you live with family or friends other people always being around can be a huge distraction. In order to solve this, find out when everyone will be out and fit in time to write while they are gone. If that just doesn't work with your everyday schedule, find a nice place outside or at the local library where you can work in peace without other people bugging you.

6. Other Responsibilities

Work, chores, walking the dog; these everyday responsibilities are tiring and at the end of the day you just cannot get the energy to write. Try writing in the morning, even if it is just for a few minutes. Get the best out of what you got and do not get discouraged.

7. Telephones

With cell phones these days, you can be getting texts at every minute either from friends or social networks. When you are writing, the best way to refrain from your cell phone is by turning it completely off and leaving it somewhere out of sight so that you are not tempted to check it.

8. Outdoor Activities

Especially on a really nice day, you may want to forget the writing and spend some time outdoors. That is completely fine. Enjoy life to the fullest. If you end up not writing for the day, remember that there is always tomorrow. But be careful not to put it off for too long and too often. If you really want to spend time outside, take the writing with you and kill two birds with one stone.

9. Everyday Needs

You need to eat sometime and when you work and do everything else, cooking can really tire you out and make you not want to write. On those days, try to make simple meals if you absolutely do not want to order out. There is nothing wrong with having a bowl of cereal for dinner.

10. Being Bored

We all get bored sometimes, even of our own writing. Take a break. Do not work on writing your big project, but work on something else. A day or two later go back to that big project and start working on writing it again and if you are still bored, put it to the side again. At least you cannot say that you did not try.

Activity 6.5 • Write a List of Your Writing Habits

Compose

As you write an essay assigned by your instructor, keep notes about your writing process. What distracts or keeps you from writing? What works well when you write? What kind of prewriting do you do? What are the best (or worst) conditions for you when you write?

Organize your notes about your writing process into a theme such as "Best Places to Write" or "Ways to Avoid Procrastinating." As Sam Scham does, write two or three sentences about each of your writing habits.

Gain Feedback by Peer Editing

Your instructor may schedule class periods for peer workshops. These workshops are opportunities for you to get responses from your readers. Often, you will be divided into groups of three or four students, and you will be given a list of questions to answer about your peers' essays. Your peers will get copies of your essay, and they will give you comments as well. The first peer workshop can be a difficult experience. It is never easy to take criticism, constructive or not. Taking criticism in a small group is even more difficult. There are several things you can do to make your peer groups more productive.

When Your Essay Is Being Reviewed

1. Write down everything the reviewers say. You think you will remember it later, but often you will forget just that piece of advice you need. More importantly, writing while the reviewers speak is an effective way to keep the channels of communication open. It is hard to come up with a defense for your paper if you are busy writing.

2. Save your comments until all the reviewers are done. If you have specific questions, write them in the margins of your notes. If they ask you questions, make a note to answer them when everyone is done. If you allow yourself to speak, you will be tempted to start defending your essay. Once you start defending your essay, two things happen. First, you stop listening to the comments. Second, you offend your reviewers, making it less likely that they will give you honest criticism in the future.

3. The first comment you should make to your reviewers is "Thank you." The second comment can be anything but a defense. Your readers are

only telling you how they have interpreted your essay. They are giving you their opinions; you do not have to make the changes they suggest.

4. Save all the comments you get on your essay. Set them aside for a day or so. Then make the changes that you think will make your essay better.

When You Are the Reviewer

1. Read an essay through, at least one time, just to browse the content of the essay. Appreciate the essay for what it does well. Try to ignore any problems for now. You will get back to them the second time you read and begin your comments in the margins. Every essay will have at least one thing about it that is good.

2. Always begin your comments with a sincere discussion of what you like about the essay.

3. Be specific in your comments. Your peers will probably understand you better if you say, "The topic sentence in paragraph four really sets the reader up for what the essay accomplishes in paragraph four. But I can't really find a topic sentence for paragraph six, and the topic sentences in paragraphs two and three could be improved." Note how this statement gives a positive response and then identifies specific places where the author can improve the essay. This works much better than a generalized statement like, "Topic sentences need work."

4. Be descriptive in your comments. It is often helpful for students to hear how you are reading their essays. "Paragraph five seems to be telling me . . . " or "I got the feeling the essay's overall message is . . . " are good ways to start descriptive sentences.

5. Realize that you are analyzing a paper and not a person. Directing your comments toward the essay, "Paragraph nine doesn't really have anything new to add, does the paper need it?" sounds better to the listener than "You repeat yourself in paragraph nine. Do you really need it?"

Independent Reviewing

If your instructor does not require peer editing, you can ask someone to review your essay. Choose someone you trust to give you an honest opinion. It might not be effective to ask a parent, spouse, or girlfriend/boyfriend to give you a critique if you know they are going to like anything you write, just because you wrote it. It might be better to ask another student who has recently had an English class or one of your current classmates. In exchange, you might offer to look over their work. Remember, you learn to read your own essays better by reading other peoples' essays more critically.

Sample Questions for Peer Review

When you have revised your paper several times, have a peer answer these questions regarding its overall content, paragraph development, and word choice and sentence structure.

Overall Content

1. What is the thesis or main point of the essay? Where does the writer state this main point? If the main point is implied rather than stated, express it in a sentence. Does the main point give a subject and an opinion about the subject? How might the writer improve his/her thesis?

2. What is the purpose of this essay? What are the characteristics of the audience the writer seems to be addressing (formal, fun-loving, serious, cynical, laid-back, etc.)?

Paragraph Development

1. Do each of the paragraphs in the essay work to support the main point of the essay? Which paragraphs seem to wander from that main point? What other information needs to be added to develop the main point?

2. List two places in the essay where the writer uses vivid sensory details. How effective are those details? Are they used to support the thesis of the essay? Identify two places in the essay where the writer needs more effective details. What kind of details might he or she include?

3. What grade would you give the introduction? How does it draw the reader into the essay? What specific things can the writer do to make the introduction more inviting?

4. Which paragraph do you like the best? Why? Which paragraph in the essay do you like the least? Why? What can the writer do to improve his/her paragraphs?

5. What grade would you give the conclusion? How does it provide closure for the essay? What specific things can the writer do to make the conclusion more effective?

Word Choice and Sentence Structure

1. Are adequate transitions used between the paragraphs? Find an effective paragraph transition and identify it. Why does it work? Find two places between paragraphs that need more or better transitions. What can the writer do to improve these transitions?

2. Are a variety of sentences used? Where might the writer vary the sentence structure for better effect? What two sentences in the essay did you find most effective? Why?

3. Are there any words that seem misused or out of place? What positive or negative trigger words are used? Do they enhance the message of the essay or detract from it?

Compose

Activity 6.6 • Peer Editing

As your instructor directs, exchange your paper draft with another student, or work in groups. Then, review the essay you are given, answering the questions about overall content, paragraph development, and word choice and sentence structure that you find in the section "Sample Questions for Peer Review."

Examples of Peer Reviewed Student Essays

Sample Student Essay
Rhetorical Analysis Assignment

Rhetorical Analysis of President Reagan's
"Challenger Speech"

FIVE, FOUR, THREE, TWO, ONE, WE HAVE LIFT OFF! THE SPACE SHUTTLE CHALLENGER HAS CLEARED THE LAUNCH PAD. This was supposed to be a glorious day in American history, a mile stone in the United States Space Program. Instead this day quickly turned into one of the most horrific scenes witnessed live by the American

> This is an effective attention-getting beginning to your essay.

public, which included thousands of school children, who watched from the comfort and safety of their classrooms.

On January 28, 1986, the space shuttle Challenger was scheduled for launch in Florida. It would mark the second flight by the United States Space program and it was the first educational launch program. On this particular flight there was to be a teacher on board, she was the first teacher on a space shuttle as a result of a special program from NASA. Although there were some clear concerns regarding whether the shuttle should launch, NASA officials gave the green light and the mission moved forward. Within seconds of lift off, the space shuttle Challenger burst into flames and disintegrated in mid flight, instantly killing all seven passengers aboard. The nation was shocked, especially thousands of young children who eagerly watched the live coverage on television. Within hours of the explosion President Ronald Reagan went on live television and addressed the nation from the White House. President Reagan was scheduled to address the nation on that particular day to report on the state of the Union, instead he went on television and paid tribute to the Challenger Seven. President Reagan delivered one of the most inspirational, and motivational speeches of his tenure as the President of the United States. It is a speech, like all great speeches, that would out live his presidency, and be regarded as one of the great speeches of our time.

> Background information provides context for the speech.

> The thesis is that Reagan's speech was inspirational.

The nation stood still, not knowing what to make of the days events. In such times of sorrow people tend to need support, guidance, and reassurance. The American people needed someone to follow, a shoulder to lean on, a vision of the future, a leader. President Reagan went on live television and paid tribute to the "Challenger Seven" in a speech from the White House. President Reagan sat alone behind a large desk surrounded in the background by family pictures. President Reagan used his *ethos* as a credible individual; he was the leader of the free Nation. He gave the speech from the White House, which is clearly recognized by the American public as a symbol of power and security. The

> Discusses elements that increased Reagan's *ethos,* such as giving the speech from his desk at the White House, surrounded by family photos. These elements showed him to be a powerful leader who is still a husband and father.

image of him sitting behind a great desk flanked by pictures of family and loved ones borrowing once again from their *ethos*. This was a not only the President of the United States delivering this speech, this was a husband, a father, and a son too.

The occasion for the speech was obvious: The Nation had just witnessed seven brave individuals perish before their very eyes. These brave souls were, husbands, sons, daughters, fathers, and they had paid the ultimate sacrifice for mankind. President Reagan portrayed all of these different roles played by each of the "Challenger Seven" from behind that desk. As the speech proceeded, President Reagan was careful to not down play the Challenger incident, but he appealed to *logos*, or logic, by saying "But we have never lost an astronaut in flight. We've never had a tragedy like this one." Here he used *pathos* to emphasize the severity of the incident while at the same time letting the nation know that there have been other brave astronauts who have also paid the ultimate price for the visions and progress of mankind. President Reagan throughout his speech used his words very carefully and with great insight. His words and the double meaning or relation to the events of the day made a huge impact on the delivery and acceptance of his speech by the American public. As he stated "Your loved ones were daring and brave, and they had that special grace, that spirit that says, Give me a challenge, and I'll meet it with joy." As one can see, President Reagan is using the word challenge here, this is a direct reference to the space shuttle Challenger.

> Identifies the *kairos* of the situation.

> Reagan appeals to *logos* or logic as he points out that the United States had never before lost an astronaut in flight.

> Appeal to *pathos* here is not as strong as the one in the next paragraph.

President Reagan goes on to address the thousands of children who also witnessed the event, addressing the emotion or *pathos* of the occasion. He states, "And I want to say something to the schoolchildren of America who were watching the live coverage of the shuttle's take-off. I know it's hard to understand, but sometimes painful things like this happen. It's all part of the process of exploration and discovery. It is all part of taking a chance and expanding man's horizons. The future doesn't belong to the fainthearted; it belongs to the brave. The Challenger crew was

> Significant appeal to *pathos*, as Reagan addresses school children directly. Millions had been watching the takeoff, as a teacher was aboard.

pulling us into the future, and we'll continue to follow them." Here President Reagan's audience is the children, who in turn are the future of the nation. By saying that the Challenger was taking them towards the future, he is saying what everybody already knows. The children are the future of the nation and he is telling them that they must continue to move forward, for one day they will be the leaders of the country.

President Reagan's message is very clear: This was a tragedy, yet we as a nation must continue to move forward in order to honor the memory of the "Challenger Seven." President Reagan, utilizing *logos*, then mentions the NASA employees in his speech. Here he does not blame or degrade the space program or its employees. Instead he praises there hard work and dedication to the American people and the space program. He does not speculate on the cause of the explosion nor does he address any issues related to who is to blame. He completely omits any negative or accusatory comments in his speech. This was a very tactful and extremely intelligent move by Reagan. He knew the American public had many questions regarding the explosion. He also knew that those questions needed to be answered and that it was his responsibility to provide those answers to the nation. Yet on this day, and in this speech, it was not the right time to do so.

> Your voice comes through as you praise Reagan for not raising questions or making negative remarks during this particular speech.

President Reagan in closing his speech borrows from the *ethos* of the past when he stated "There's a coincidence today. On this day three hundred and ninety years ago, the great explorer Sir Francis Drake died aboard ship off the coast of Panama... a historian later said, He lived by the sea, died on it, and was buried in it. Well, today, we can say of the Challenger crew: their dedication was, like Drake's complete."

President Reagan's speech on the space shuttle Challenger served several purposes. First, it paid tribute to the seven astronauts who lost their lives in the explosion. Second, it provided the nation with a much needed reassurance that everything was going to be all right. And although this was terrible accident

> Discussion of Reagan's purposes makes a good conclusion.

and set back for our country, he also left no doubt that the Nations commitment to NASA and the space program would not only survive, but continue to advance forward into the future.

Sample Student Essay: Short Op-Ed Argument

What Marriage Means to Me

I came out to my parents as a lesbian when I was seventeen years old. My parents cried and I thought I'd never want to live another day. It seems silly to say, but I met the love of my life while I was in high school. I had never felt more accepted or loved before in my life till I met her. As a member of the LGBT community, I was wary of the life ahead of me. I experienced bullying, denial from my parents, and homophobic comments and harassment. I believe adamantly in the protests and movements promoting gay marriage and by extension human rights. From not only a logical consideration of the facts but also a personal experience of being a lesbian member in society, I believe the United States should refute DOMA nationally and allow the LGBT community to have access to civil marriage to reflect their equality and discourage otherness in their population.

> Certainly a dramatic opening, which would catch your reader's attention.

> Clear thesis, though you might clarify somewhere in the essay what you mean by "otherness."

Civil marriage is so much more than a recognized partnership. Civil marriage provides access to many legal benefits in taxes, estate planning, government, employment, medical, death, family, housing, consumer, and others. Denial of these legal benefits, along with others, reflects multiple human rights violations. Implicitly, a lot of these benefits reflect at the core of the pursuit of happiness, one of the most basic human rights in the United States. The inability to have the rights that come with marriage means that LGBT is a marginalized population.

> Good that you mention the legal benefits being denied, including taxes, estate planning, medical, etc.

The battle for same sex marriage making national news has happened in my own hometown, El Paso, Texas. In 2009, our mayor John Cook passed a law approving benefits for domestic partners, including same sex couples. A local pastor launched a recall motion and managed to revoke the law in 2012. I remember the movement quite well. John Cook released comments to the *Huffington Post* that resonated strongly with 16-year old me and continue to do so today: "Where do I stop? Do I all of a sudden say ... when you call 911 when you're divorced, committing adultery, you ain't going to get no ambulance or fire truck? And don't expect me to pick your trash up, because that would be condoning sin?" Where does it stop? At what point is civil marriage recognized as a legal institution, a completely different institution from that of religions?

> Excellent use of a quote. Calls attention to this example from your own hometown.

Civil marriage is not an affront to any religion, but a set of rights and benefits that should be given to everybody. In the separation of church and state, there was a born recognition that in the diversity of religion and opinions, the government was to be held responsible for a certain set of laws that would be extended to everybody. The denial of these rights to the LGBT community reflects negatively on our government's ability to be genuine in its delivery of human rights.

> Yes, many opponents of gay marriage make this claim. Good that you address counterargument, You could say a little more about it.

Nationally recognized civil marriage means more than legal benefits. It is a reflection of the stance the government and American society takes on the LGBT community. This stance as of today is troubling. The LGBT community has had instances of extreme hate crimes that go as far as rape and homicide. The denial of civil marriage only promotes and condones a violation of LGBT members.

> This sentence somewhat repeats what you say in paragraph two.

According to *Time,* 75% of Americans believe there are federal laws prohibiting discrimination based on sexual orientation. They're wrong. There's actually no law stopping this behavior, and this reflects all too much in the reported violence against LGBT members. A 2013 report from the National Coalition of Anti-Violence Programs (NCAVP) revealed a worrying increase in police misconduct against LGBT members. From the survivors of police violence, 48% reported police misconduct and 26.8% reported hostility in police attitudes.

> Interesting statistic.

Violence and discrimination against the LGBT community happens from a very young age. According to the Centers for Disease Control and prevention (CDC), LGBT children are twice as likely as their heterosexual peers to attempt suicide. In a 2009 survey conducted by the CDC, eight of ten students had been verbally harassed at school, four of ten had been physically harassed at school, six of ten felt

> Good that you are using reputable sources such as the CDC.

unsafe at school, and one of five had been the victim of a physical assault at school. Matthew Shepard is only one face of many to experience the horrors of violence against the LGBT community. At the age of 21, he was brutally tortured and left to die in an act of hate crime.

The government has a lot to do with the issue of LGBT individual's safety and legal defenses. Equality in all respects fights against the social stigma held for the LGBT community. A government that provides equal human rights to all, denies discrimination on the basis of sexual orientation and gender identity, and promotes social wellness for all its population is one that makes that population feel undivided and safe. The current social dialogue on civil marriage for same-sex partners reflects a long history of LGBT struggles and a pivotal point in our government's stand in their rights.

The key argument against civil marriage for the LGBT community is driven by the ideal that marriage is a religious institution and threatens the religion along with their idea of family life. This argument is incredibly invalid on multiple levels but ties back to the previously mentioned quote of John Cook. It is unethical on part of the government to deny rights based on religious beliefs or traditions.

> You mention the religion issue earlier. Might be good to edit, so that you do not repeat points.

As a modern country, our government should be able to uphold equality and human rights to all its citizens. Civil marriage is a stepping-stone for equality and human rights for the LGBT community.

Wanting to marry and have children is not just a heterosexual American dream. It is mine and it is that of many individuals from the LGBT community. It should not only be a dream, but a right to be able to pursue this dream. I adamantly feel that I shouldn't be discriminated based on my sexual orientation. Speaking as both the sixteen year old feeling hurt and conflicted as the pastor spoke hateful words against the LGBT community and the young woman

> Strong conclusion that, like the introduction, connects you personally to the issue.

in love today, I hope that our government is capable of making the right call in my and many other's rights and equalities in the United States. This is an issue that strikes not only in the hearts of adult LGBT individuals but children and generations to come and how they are going to live their lives as equal members or stigmatized populations. Civil marriage for the LGBT community means a step closer to equality.

Sample Student Essay: Short Research Paper in MLA Style

Student last name 1

Name of Student

Name of Professor

Name of Course

Date

Emerging Mobile Phone Technology Empowers

Mobile phone technology is a late 20th century invention, but it is an emerging technology because it continues to evolve and innovate. The earliest phones were huge, affectionately referred to as bricks. They were not cool. Only rich people had them, and they look ridiculous in old photographs with the clunky phones, poised like they think they look cool. As with most technology, when it became more affordable, more people began to use them. Now it is expected that an individual have a mobile phone. In the rare case where someone does not have a mobile phone, it is often seen as a revolutionary choice, a form of protest about the desire to not be connected all of the time. Mobile phones of today are more and more becoming smart phones, essentially handheld computers that do more than computers of the 20th century could do. They are extensions of one's self. They are not just for voice anymore. The newest mobile phones boast about the megapixels of the camera, the quality of the speakers, the processor and the amount of storage it has. Mobile phone technology is revolutionizing the way people use technology, most interestingly in how they are used in developing countries.

> Your voice comes through as you describe the old, clunky phones that people at the time thought were cool. Also, later in the paragraph when you discuss that not having a mobile phone is a form of protest.

> Your thesis prepares the reader for a discussion of mobile phone technology, including its use in developing countries.

Mobile phones are used in restaurants to process credit card transactions. They have apps to process fingerprints at crime scenes. Many of the smartest mobile phones have photo editing and sharing capacity. There are apps to edit music. It is truly a democratization of technology that was previously too expensive for an individual to own. Mobile phones are (usually) less expensive than a

> This paragraph makes good use of your background knowledge.

Student last name 2

computer, but give the same kind of access to information previously only available to those who could afford a computer. Mobile phone technology has revolutionized many industries, including business and even public health. During the Arab Spring and any other form of civic protest around the world, mobile phones were essential for organizing and communication. Mobile phone technology is empowering for women and girls in ways we could not even imagine 10 years ago.

Another advantage to mobile phone technology is that mobile phones, even smart phones with lots of apps, are small and easy to hide. This makes it possible for women and girls to keep the ownership of mobile phones private if they are concerned that their husbands or fathers do not want them to have mobile phones. According to "Connecting to Opportunity: A Survey of Afghan Women's Access to Mobile Technology," conducted by the U.S. Agency for International Development, 48% of the women and girls who report not have a mobile phone cite their husbands or fathers not wanting them to have them as the primary reason they do not have mobile phones. This is an unfortunate cultural issue that needs to be dealt with via education campaigns and may improve as younger generations age ("Connecting to Opportunity"). If Afghan men come to see mobile phones as a way for improving their economic situation, perhaps attitudes toward female online access will shift, and there will be less of this kind of resistance to women and girls having mobile phones.

> Good that you provide a context for the coming paraphrase from a source.

> Here your comment follows up on the point from the USAID article.

Most Americans cannot imagine life without computers and the Internet. The two are so ingrained in the culture that it is often expected for high school students to own laptops they are able to bring to school. Children can navigate touch screen tablets before they attend Pre-K school. More than a million people own iPhones, using them for all sorts of things from communication to entertainment to business. Paypal offers a device its customers can use to process credit and debit card payments on an iPhone or iPad. No longer do businesses have to have landlines to process credit cards. Now the farmer who brings her crops to the

> It is a little jarring to have a paragraph about American use of technology in between two paragraphs about mobile phones in developing countries. You might consider reordering your paragraphs.

farmers' market can accept Visa or Mastercard in addition to cash. Mobile technology has revolutionized the way small business is done in the United States, in addition to developing countries around the world.

Mobile phones used to be too expensive for those in developing nations. "Between 2004 and 2009, approximately 80 percent of new mobile subscribers worldwide came from Africa, the Middle East, Asia and Eastern Europe" ("Connecting to Opportunity"). These countries lack infrastructure resources for landline phones for dialup or DSL and the thought of owning a computer is seen as more of a fantasy. Mobile phones have become less expensive to produce and voice and data plans have come down in price.

According to "Empowering Women through Mobile Technology" a fact sheet published by the United States Department of State, mobile phones and mobile technology are essential to improving the lives of women around the world. Mobile phones create an independence that women have never experienced before. Women farmers are given real time access to information about crops and weather to help handle their crops better. They are able to find out prices for produce and handmade goods in other areas so that they can negotiate a better price in real-time, which improves the economic status of the farmer. Women report feeling safer with a mobile phone. Texting or SMS messaging on mobile phones has lead to literacy campaigns so that women can better communicate using mobile phones. Women also use mobile phones for public action, organizing and civic engagement ("Empowering Women through").

> You might consider occasionally having a quote from one of your sources. A quote would add emphasis.

The Mobil Technology Programme is a response to data published by the GSMA Developing Fund which showed that more than 300 million women in developing countries did not have regular access to mobile technology. The Cherie Blair Foundation for Women, the organization that put together the Mobile Technology Programme, argues that access to mobile technology empowers women by providing access to financial programs and banking that help women to become entrepreneurs ("Mobile Technology Programme").

> Your paper is beginning to focus more on mobile phones empowering women in third world countries. You could have rewritten your thesis to include this aspect.

Student last name 4

Afghanistan is a prime example of the power of mobile technology in a developing country. According to Connecting to Opportunity: A Survey of Afghan Women's Access to Mobile Technology, conducted by the U.S. Agency for International Development, Afghanistan was isolated from mobile technology until 2002. Since the first mobile phone contract in 2002, over 20 million people residing in Afghanistan have mobile phones. This is even more impressive when one knows that the total population of Afghanistan is 30 million. Roughly two out of three people have mobile phones in Afghanistan. According to this survey, approximately 80% of Afghan women have access to a mobile phone in some capacity, either owning outright or have the ability to borrow one. Also, according to the survey, young women are one of the largest mobile phone user groups in Afghanistan. In rural areas of Afghanistan, women often engage in mobile phone sharing. Like other developing countries, the use of mobile phones is for banking, farming, and health care. The Afghanistan literacy rate for women is about 18%, according to the survey, which argues that while literacy programs are important, it is also important that mobile phone apps provide a voice option for those whose reading ability is limited. Adding voice commands to mobile phones is an emerging technology that nongovernment organizations are pushing for as a way to empower the population of Afghanistan, especially women and girls ("Connecting to Opportunity").

> An amazing statistic.

ExxonMobil Foundation funded an initiative to increase economic opportunity for women. As part of the initiative, ExxonMobil surveyed of mobile phone adoption and use in three developing countries, Egypt, Nigeria, and Indonesia. The results of the survey showed that the "rapid adoption" of mobile technology is a primer for empowering women entrepreneurs. The ExxonMobil report led the Cherie Blair Foundation to develop a pilot program to develop apps tailored for women entrepreneurs in developing countries ("Mobile Technology Can").

The GSMA mWomen Programme is the initiative that was born from ExxonMobil research and Cherie Blair foundation. The focus of the program is to close the

> Interesting that the program addresses reasons why women might not have mobile phones of their own.

Student last name 5

gender gap in mobile phone ownership in developing countries. The idea is that if women own mobile phones then they will be empowered in business, healthcare and civic engagement. The program addresses the reasons why women might not own a mobile phone of her own. Barriers to mobile phone ownership is cost, technology literacy and family or cultural reasons such as the husband not wanting the wife to have a mobile phone of her own ("Gsma Mwomen Programme").

In addition to empowering women economically, mobile phone technology can improve the health of women and their families. In May of 2013, PBS reported a story of a first time mother in Africa who received text messages from an organization called Mobile Alliance for Maternal Action, often referred to by MAMA. The mother receives text messages several times a week with medical and health information helpful to her as her baby grows (Cheers).

There have also been technology innovations to improve the sexual health of women with mobile technology. Prototypes of STD testing that can be done with

> You have cited quite a range of information about mobile technology.

a mobile phone are in development. Testing like this is useful in more than one situation. It makes testing more available for those who are too embarrassed to go to the doctor or have circumstances that prohibit them from accessing a doctor. The technology is also useful for sex workers because the plan is for them to be able to test clients before providing services. It is one more way for women to protect themselves. Thus, mobile phone technology is revolutionizing public health as well (Smith).

In conclusion, mobile technology can only continue to improve the lives of people in developing countries, particularly empowering women. The more young women who start using mobile technologies, the more open to new technologies they will be. The first step, which is in the process of being accomplished, is to put mobile phones into the hands of as many women and girls in developing countries. Giving them access is revolutionary. The next step is to develop apps tailored to their needs such as farming apps, banking apps, health apps. Making sure these apps work with voice for those who cannot read is imperative and still the revision stage, as they

Student last name 6

do not always work as well as tech developers would like. Literacy programs are needed to teach women and girls how to read, so they can use the apps and communicate via texting or SMS messaging. And, of course, technology like this needs to be subsidized until it is affordable enough for anyone to go in and purchase a mobile phone. Electricity and running water were not considered human rights until the early 20th century. Mobile technology— access to information in real-time—is part of the new frontier of human rights. Women and girls—all people—have a right to technology that can improve their lives. Attitudes need to change. Mobile phones are not a luxury anymore; they are a necessity to participate in the 21st century marketplace.

> Well said that mobile technology is a new frontier of human rights.

Student last name 7

Works Cited

Cheers, Imani M. "In South Africa, Using Mobile Technology to Improve Maternal Health Access." *The Rundown: A Blog of News and Insight,* PBS, 5 May 2013, www.pbs.org/newshour/rundown/in-south-africa-using-mobile-technology-to-improve-maternal-health-access/. *PBS Newshour,* PBS, www.pbs.org/newshour.

"Connecting to Opportunity: A Survey of Afghan Women's Access to Mobile Technology." *USAID,* USAID, 21 May 2013, www.usaid.gov/where-we-work/afghanistan-and-pakistan/afghanistan/survey-afghan-women-technology.

"Empowering Women Through Mobile Technology." *U.S. Department of State,* U.S. Department of State, 10 July 2010, www.state.gov/documents/organization/149807.pdf.

"GSMA mWomen Programme." *Katerva,* 23 Apr. 2011, katerva.org/nominees/empowering-women-with-mobile-phones/.

"Mobile Technology Can Help Women Entrepreneurs, Report Finds." *Philanthropy News Digest (PND),* 15 May 2012, philanthropynewsdigest.org/news/mobile-technology-can-help-women-entrepreneurs-report-finds.

"Mobile Technology Programme." *Cherie Blair Foundation for Women RSS,* www.cherieblairfoundation.org/programmes/mobile/.

Smith, Catharine. "Mobile 'App' To Diagnose Sexually Transmitted Diseases." *The Huffington Post,* 9 Nov. 2010, 9:04 a.m., updated 25 May 2011, www.huffingtonpost.com/2010/11/09/mobile-app-to-diagnose-std_n_780847.html.

Sample Student Essay: Research Paper in APA Style

Running Head: OBESITY IN AMERICA　　　　　　　　　　　　　　1

Understanding the Negative Impact Food Industry Advertising

Has on Obesity in America

Name of Student

Student's University

OBESITY IN AMERICA　　　　　　　　　　　　　　　　　　　2

Abstract

This paper examines the negative impact food industry advertising has had on the crisis of obesity in America. The articles explored in this paper provide an in depth look at how obesity has multiplied over the years to become an epidemic threatening the lives of millions. These articles also discuss America's public opinion about obesity, as well as the government's role in addressing this challenging national problem. This paper considers the policies that have been implemented to help fight one of the nation's biggest downfalls, as well as what is yet to be done.

Keywords: obesity, food industry, health

Understanding the Negative Impact Food Industry Advertising
Has on Obesity in America

In 2004, the U.S. Centers for Disease and Control and Prevention (CDC) ranked obesity as the number one health risk facing America ("Obesity In America"). Ten years later, obesity is not just considered a health risk, but an *epidemic* endangering the lives of millions of Americans. Staggering numbers reveal that the rates of obesity in the United States continue to skyrocket. Countless reports and studies have sought to find answers to the obesity puzzle that plagues America's future, and while useful information has been discovered, we are far from extinguishing the problem. Americans continue on their journey to combat obesity, (which is identified in an individual when their body mass index is 30 or higher), by dieting, exercising, and trying the latest fads in weight loss.

> Good to begin paper with this startling statistic. Then, your next sentence says that the situation is even worse. Very effective.

But despite the efforts to eliminate obesity, studies now suggest that if obesity rates continue to rise, 42% of Americans will be obese by the year 2030 ("Adult Obesity," 2012). Unfortunately there are significant elements working against the millions of people fighting for their lives. The food industry is spending more money than ever before on marketing ads in the United States. Without any strict regulations and policies that limit what these money giants can do, the food industry continues to cater to America's addiction to sugars and fat by marketing unhealthy foods constantly. Policy makers in America must hold the food industry accountable by creating stringent guidelines that create boundaries on the marketing of the food being advertised—not only to children, but to all Americans suffering from this disease; these policies may be what help in lowering the dangerous percentages of obesity threatening the lives of millions.

> Good thesis. This is something you can argue.

Obesity is a major risk factor for non-communicable diseases, such as diabetes, cardiovascular diseases, and cancers (Rodrigo, 2013, pg. 22).

OBESITY IN AMERICA   4

With more than two-thirds of U.S. adults being overweight or obese (Ogden et al., 2014), it is no wonder why obesity is considered America's health crisis. Sadly, obesity in the U.S. is not just affecting adults, but children as well. About 30 percent of low-income preschoolers are also overweight or obese (Centers for Disease Control and Prevention, 2011). Obesity has no specific demographic. It is affecting millions, from the rich to the poor, and the young to the old; the American diet is being equally destructive in terms of the wrath it sheds on its victims. Because obesity is associated with a number of serious physiological ailments, it should be of no surprise that obesity has serious economic consequences, and as a nation, we are paying the price for the extra pounds.

> Your information from sources in this paragraph helps to establish the problem.

"The annual medical costs alone have been estimated as high as $190 billion dollars—21 percent of all medical spending" in the country (Cawley & Meyerhoefer, 2011, pg. 22). Whether you are suffering from obesity or not, we must recognize that obesity is affecting all of us, in one-way or another. There are many factors that contribute to obesity. Some blame obesity on genes, while others think watching too much television and having little physical activity are the main culprits. While these are all valid justifications for America's excess weight, and while many consider obesity to be a simple case of bad personal choices, little has been done to identify the outside sources that might be contributing to this wide spreading disease.

> Here you establish that the problem affects everyone, not just the obese.

> This sentence prepares the reader for the next paragraph.

In the 2005 article "Junk-Food Nation" by Gary Ruskin and Juliet Schor, the authors explain the negative influence that the food industry has on the war against obesity in the United States. "Big food's strategy is to deny that the problem (obesity) is caused by the product (junk food). Instead lack of exercise is the culprit" (Ruskin & Schor, 2005, pg.17). In 2001, the Bush administration continuously took sides with the "big food" industry, facilitating their efforts to weaken the World Health Organizations' global anti-obesity strategy. The White House went as far as questioning the scientific basis for the linking of fruit and vegetable consumption to decrease the risk of obesity and diabetes (Ruskin & Schor, 2005 pg.17). More troubling is that

OBESITY IN AMERICA   5

these actions happened behind the scenes, where corporate interests took

precedents before public health and public opinion. As it turns out, "not

a lot of subtlety is required to understand what was driving

President Bush's administration policy" (Ruskin & Schor, 2005,   Yes, it is troubling

pg. 17) in regards to the obesity crisis in America. Many food   that corporate
                                                                        interests are put
industry giants such as Coca-Cola, Pepsi, Kraft, were all lead-   before public
                                                                        health.
ing contributors during the 2000 presidential campaign.

   With the food industry buying its way into everything, including the

obesity strategy in America, it is no coincidence that this epidemic is ex-

ploding as rapidly as it is. The food industry spends a whopping $4.2 billion

dollars per year on marketing ads in the United States. Energy dense and

nutrient poor foods are marketed everywhere, from billboards, to television

commercials, and now even social media websites like Facebook. "The food

industry spends billions of dollars each year to develop products, packag-

Good use of quote   ing, advertising and marketing techniques that entice us to buy
to draw attention
to this point   more food because selling more food means making more profits.
about the billions
spent by the   And businesses exist to make profits" (Cohen 2007). While pro-
food industry on
advertising.   fessional food marketers argue that they are only offering Ameri-

                         cans what they want, they dodge the fact that the consumer is

largely manipulated by portion size, variety, and cheap prices--all

factors strategically created by the marketers themselves. Coca Cola and

General Mills make millions of dollars every year by using researched meth-

ods of advertising similar to those used by McDonald's and Burger King

(Stanish, J.R., 2010). With slogans like "Bet You Can't Eat Just One", the food

industry is really giving America a taste of it's lethal feeding. When the pri-

mary purpose of food production is profit, and not nutrition, the public re-

ally suffers. But catchy slogans and selling points are not the only tools food

industry advertising is using to manipulate the public. Food manufacturers

are notoriously known for making false or misleading claims about their

products, many trying to create a smokescreen that promotes health and

nutrition. The truth is that the "Advertising of fruits and vegetables is almost

non-existent," says Frances M. Berg in his book *Underage and Overweight*

(as cited in Burg 97). Various studies have shown that out of thousands

OBESITY IN AMERICA   6

of ads with regular television advertising exposure, little to no advertisements promote fruits and vegetables. With food marketing being a largely self-regulated process, the food industry has been able to take advantage and has not been held accountable for the negative role it plays in America's battle with obesity. If the Federal Trade Commission (FTC) and Federal Communications Commission (FCC) played a larger role in the marketing food process, stronger regulations could be implemented. We must not allow food companies and their billions of dollars to dig deeper graves for Americans fighting obesity.

> You made this point in a quote earlier in the paragraph. Better to edit, so you don't repeat yourself.

It is imperative that America understands that the transformation of a nation does not happen with drugs, weight-loss surgery, or other extreme forms of dieting; even all the exercise in the world will not save us. True change stems from a nation's conscious decision to address issues through policy.

The law has proven an integral part of many major public health victories over the past century. Bans on smoking in public buildings, the removal of lead from paint and gasoline, and the requirement of school vaccinations are all the result of legislation and legal efforts. Today, many experts consider obesity to be the next frontier of public health law ("Law, Nutrition" 2013).

> Interesting point that this strategy worked with bans on smoking and lead paint.

It is unclear whether Americans truly comprehend the severity and the negative role the food advertisement industry has on obesity affecting the nation, but there is a clear understanding that obesity is threatening. In a recent study conducted by the Associated Press-NORC Center for Public Affairs Research, significant findings showed that the American public considers obesity as the most serious health issue, second only to cancer. While the data showed that there is a strong public support for government policies that add more physical activities for children at schools, there is little public support for policies that constrain consumer choices, such as the taxation of unhealthy food and drinks like soda (Associated Press, 2013).

> Yes, effective that you mention resistance to policies that restrict consumer choices.

Clearly there are Americans who oppose obesity in the country, but are also against the government telling them what they can and cannot eat; yet others feel that the government has both the power and the duty to regulate private behavior in order to promote public health (Goston, L.O., 2007). In either case, it is obvious that obesity is making waves in the headlines and is catching many people's attention. The past few years have brought about a decent amount of legislative initiatives to combat obesity in the country, and we are heading in the right direction. First Lady, Michelle Obama has persistently continued to fight against childhood obesity in the United States. Her "Let's Move!" initiative has helped raise awareness about child obesity all throughout the country. "Let's Move!" has been able to promote the implementation of healthier foods in schools and is focused on raising a healthier generation of kids in America.

> Good that you mention successful programs.

New advertisement regulations have also been enforced to limit the number of ads that target children 18 and younger. Restaurants are now providing calorie counts and nutritional contents in their menus. All steps in the right direction, it is simply not enough.

Additional regulations are needed to regulate the commercial activities of the food industry. Federal responsibility for the regulation of advertising lies mainly with the Federal Trade Commission (FTC). By agreement with the Food and Drug Administration (FDA), the FTC has primary authority over food advertising, whereas the FDA regulates food labeling ("Enforcement policy," 1994). Currently the FTC is taking action only in cases where the agency finds that food advertisement is being deceptive. The agency favors requiring more information over banning information, and avoids broad restrictions limiting both deceptive and non-deceptive speech (FTC, 2002)." The idea that consumers, young and old, should have the freedom to choose what they eat from a broad marketplace continues to be the status quo. Critics have suggested that with food industry lobbyists continuing to buy into the pockets of politicians, no real change will happen any time soon, costing the lives of many. With 150 million Americans that are obese or overweight, Physician Deborah Cohen agrees:

> I don't find this source in your references.

Too many will die before their time due to heart disease, diabetes and other ailments. While the nation remains focused on waging war on terrorism, which has claimed thousands of lives, millions are dying prematurely because they aren't getting the government protection they need from the Sirens of the food industry (Cohen, 2007).

> This well-written quote draws attention to your conclusion.

With more and more research being conducted to identify the correlation between food advertisement and obesity and America, it is possible that if future studies provide compelling evidence, the federal government will be forced to address this issue more firmly. While there are many variables that contribute to a person being overweight and obese, regulations on advertisement and provisions and guidelines to hold the food industry accountable can only help the cause and could very well save the lives of many. We must not allow large food corporations to control the future of America; no amount of profit is worth the lives of millions of people.

References

Adult obesity rates could exceed 60 percent in 13 states by 2030, according to new study (2012, September 18). Retrieved http://www.rwjf.org/en/library/articles-and-news/2012/09/adult-obesity-rates-could-exceed-60-percent-in-13-states-by-2030.html

Cawley, J., & Meyerhoefer, C. (2012). The medical care costs of obesity: An instrumental variables approach. *Journal of Health Economics,* 31(1), 219-230.

Cohen, D. (2007, February 20). A desired epidemic: Obesity and the food industry. *Washington Post.* Retrieved from http://www.washingtonpost.com/wpdyn/content/article/2007/02/20/AR200702200133

Law, nutrition & obesity. (2013). Retrieved from http://www.yaleruddcenter.org/what_we_do.aspx?id=7

Gostin, L. O. (2007). Theory and definition of public health law. *Journal of Health Care Law & Policy,* 10, 1.

Obesity in America: Understanding obesity. (n.d.). Retrieved from http://obesityinamerica.org/understanding-obesity

Obesity in the United States: Public perceptions. (2014). Retrieved http://www.apnorc.org/projects/Pages/Obesity-in-the-United-States.aspx

Ogden C. L., Carroll, M. D., Kit, B.K., & Flegal K. M. (2014). Prevalence of childhood and adult obesity in the United States, 2011-2012. *Journal of the American Medical Association, 311*(8), 806-814.

Rodrigo, C. P. (2013). *Current mapping of obesity.* Nutricion Hospitalaria, 28, 21-31. Retrieved from http://www.nutricionhospitalaria.com/pdf/6915.pdf

Ruskin, G., & Schor, J. (2005). Junk food nation. *Nation, 281*(6), 15 17. Retrieved from EBSCO.

Stanish, J. (2010, January 1). The Obesity epidemic in America and the responsibility of big food manufacturers. Student Pulse, 2(11). Retrieved from http://www.studentpulse.com/articles/320/the-obesity-epidemic-in-america-and-the-responsibility-of-big-food-manufacturers

United States, Federal Trade Commission. (1994, May 13). Enforcement policy statement on food advertising. Retrieved from http://www.ftc.gov/public- statements/1994/05/enforcement-policy-statement-food-advertising

Additional Sample Student Paper: Research Paper in APA Style

Runnning Head:

CHANGES IN BEHAVIOR CAN AFFECT SPECIES INVASION SUCCESS   1

Changes in Behavior Can Affect Species Invasion Success

Name of Student

Student's University

CHANGES IN BEHAVIOR CAN AFFECT SPECIES INVASION SUCCESS   2

Abstract

This paper explores invader species, including birds, mammals, and insects and the likelihood that a particular species will succeed in a new environment. Once a species has been introduced to a new setting, several factors affect a species' ability to reproduce and adapt. New species must compete with any preexisting species that occupy the same resource niche, so aggressive species are more likely to succeed. Alternatively, if a species can change its behavior or alter the habitat, it increases its chances of survival over time.

Keywords: invader species, species adaptability

Your abstract could briefly mention the research that supports your argument, even mentioning the names of well-known scientists that you cite in your paper.

CHANGES IN BEHAVIOR CAN AFFECT SPECIES INVASION SUCCESS   3

Changes in Behavior Can Affect Species Invasion Success

Introduction

Invasive species, including birds, mammals, and insects are rapidly changing ecosystems worldwide. Some species make more effective invaders than others. However, the reasons that make some species successful invaders are not clearly understood. Important drivers that affect if a species can invade include

> Interesting that the reasons are not well understood. I'm glad that you elaborate later about why this is.

ability to move into a new habitat, invadability of the new environment, and niche availability of the new environment. The behavior a species displays can play an important role in the ability to invade. However, some species have behaviors that change, which make them even more likely to be successful invaders.

Some environments are more likely to be invaded than others. Environments are more likely to be invaded if they have resources that can be exploited. In a source-sink environment, organisms will follow increased resources. The amount of biodiversity may also play a role. A large amount of biodiversity and a very small amount of resources do not lend themselves to invasion (Tilman, 1997). Table 1 summarizes some of the factors that may make it possible for inva-

> Your paper is relatively free from jargon, but you might explain the meaning of source-sink, depending upon whether your audience would recognize the term.

> Good that you include tables. However, it would be helpful to tell your audience more specifically what the table shows, as many will read the text before looking at tables and graphs.

sion to occur. All of these factors are important to consider when analyzing whether a change in behavior will affect susceptibility of an ecosystem to invasive pressure.

In order for an invasion to occur, the species must be propagated to a novel environment. This in itself can be a challenge and many species do not make it. Once introduced into the new environment, the species must colonize. Many species will die off after a few generations. If a species can colonize the new environment and perpetuate itself, then there is a chance that the invasion will be successful and establish itself (Duncan, 2003). Once established, if the species continually moves to new environments, it is an invader.

Many of the examples used in this paper are from birds. Birds provide excellent examples for invasion success because they have been frequently introduced into novel ecosystems by humans. The frequency of introduction allows for more successful invasions than in other species. Figure 1 demonstrates the process of a successful invasion when pertaining specifically to birds that have been introduced by humans.

> Excellent that you walk the audience through your argument, explaining any points that the reader might question.

There are many challenges to overcome to move to a new ecosystem. In many cases, there is a preexisting species already occupying the niche the new species could occupy. This may create competition that the invading and native species had not encountered before. A species that is or becomes more aggressive may have a better chance to succeed. As the habitat is different, so are the resources. Species that have the ability to exploit new resources, such as food, have a better chance at thriving in the new environment.

There are two main ways that a species can changes its behavior to become a more successful invader. The first is behavioral flexibility and the ability to adapt to a new environment. This means that the species already has behavioral plasticity in its native range, though it may not necessarily be expressed there. The species will try new behaviors to see if they are successful in the new habitat. If the innovation is successful, then the species fitness is increased. This allows for a species to be more successful in a new environment.

The second way is for a species to adapt to a new environment over time. Through generations, a species will become accustomed to the novel ecosystem. This can happen through changes to the native habitat or other selective pressures. This allows for new behaviors to be expressed and propagate to new environments. The new beneficial behaviors that are successful in the new environment may not have been beneficial in the previous environment. These behaviors could increase fitness and be propagated in the novel habitat. It is also possible for this to occur through a founder's effect. If an invading species is cut off from its previous habitat, it is possible for genetic bottlenecking to occur. This could change the behaviors expressed.

Behavioral Flexibility

Behavioral flexibility in a species is comprised of two main components. First, the species must be able to respond to novel stimuli. This allows for a more rapid response to new conditions, which could potentially aid in colonization. Second, individuals have the ability to identify and consume unfamiliar food and respond to novel stimuli (Martin, 2005). This ability provides a good measure for behavioral flexibility (Sol, 2002). The more a species uses new feeding behaviors, the more flexible they are. The more likely an individual is to consume novel foods the more likely a species will fare better in a new environment. Some species already possess this flexibility in their native range. This may allow these species to be better invaders.

> Effective use of topic sentence and transitions in this paragraph.

Another measure of behavioral flexibility is brain size. Larger brain size, relative to body size is directly related to cognitive ability (Sol, 2008). This translates to the ability for innovations or behavioral flexibility. Brain size has also been correlated with feeding innovation (Sol, 2002). Species with larger brain size has been shown to increase success for coping with novel habitats. This has been shown extensively in birds and more recently in mammals.

In birds, feeding innovation and larger brains had a higher probability of introduction success (Sol 2002). This is numerically displayed in Table 1. Sol (2002) controlled for other variables that have been shown to affect successful invasions in birds. There are three other main factors that affect invasion success in birds. Dichromatic birds are more efficacious invaders than monochromatic. Birds that are display human commensalism also have more advantages. Nest location also plays a large role. Ground nesters do better than other nesting sites (Sol, 2002).

Mammals have the largest body size to brain size ratio of any other animals. If brain size does have an impact on the ability to respond well to novel habitats, than mammals should be able to succeed in the new habitats. Sol (2008) compared mammal invasion success and several different factors: habitat generalism, diet, annual fecundity, mating system, native geographic range, and whether the introduction was on an island or a mainland. After taking into account all of these factors, relative brain size was a significant predictor of establishment success. The number of individuals originally released and habitat generalism also increased success.

> Interesting point about brain size.

Some species, such as the house sparrow (Passer domesticus), display more flexibility as an invader than as a resident. This is demonstrated with, once again, flexibility in feeding. As Figure 3 displays, invaders are more likely to approach and consume novel foods. This example reveals that feeding innovation does not necessarily need to be expressed in a native habitat for a species to possess a capacity for it. This would make prediction for invasion success based on expressed feeding innovation difficult.

Adaptive Behaviors

Behaviors can change due to selective pressures, causing a species to diverge a different way. Over time, this could possibly lead to speciation or just a shift in behavior for the entire species. Selective pressures that could cause this change could include habitat destruction or climate change. As a result of these pressures, animals may need to move to new habitats. The selective pressures could shift the behavior of the species to adapt to the novel environment.

Western bluebirds (Sialia mexicana) lost much of their natural habitat in the early 20th century due to logging and agriculture. As nest box programs were implemented, the populations of western bluebirds were reestablished. This repopulation brought them closer to the mountain bluebirds (Sialia currucoides) territory. Female western bluebirds usually disperse away from their natal population to breed and the males would either stay or disperse. More aggressive males are more likely to disperse away from their natal populations, venturing into

> Interesting that human intervention initiates species invasion.

CHANGES IN BEHAVIOR CAN AFFECT SPECIES INVASION SUCCESS   7

novel environments. The more aggressive males are more likely to out com-pete the less aggressive males for breeding territories of both western and mountain bluebirds. This aggression is therefore an adaptive trait that makes these birds a more successful invader (Duckworth, 2007).

The bullfinches in Europe are an example of a species that may lead to an adaptive behavior that could lead to an invasion. Newton et al. found that observers in Western Europe heard calls from bullfinches that were previ-ously not heard in that region. After an investigation, it was found that the northern bullfinch (Pyrrhula p. pyrrhula) was migrating further west than previously. This example is not a complete invasion, however. This species had previously migrated to this area but not in the numbers recorded in 2004 (Newton, 2006). This could lead to a changed migratory route over generations. The possible selective pressures that elicited this change is a food shortage causing the birds to migrate further is search of more food.

Differentiating between mechanisms of a behavioral change can sometimes be difficult. There are some examples of invasive species that have not been studied enough to determine the cause of the change in behavior. For instance, a species of fire ant (Solenopsis invicta) has in-vaded southeastern United States from its native range in Ar-gentina. S. invicta has two social forms polygyne and monogyne. Monogyne means to have only one queen, while polygyne forms have multiple queens. In Argentina, the queens in the polygyne social form are closely related while in the invaded ranges the queens are more distantly related. Another difference in the so-cial make-up of S. invicta is that in the U.S. the colonies are more densely populated. In the polygyne colonies, the ants have reduced nest mate recognition allowing for reduced intraspecific aggression. This in turn al-low for a reduction in territoriality which leads to a further increase in colony density. This increase in population density allows the ants to be a better competitor against the native ants (Holway 1999). After a genetic study was completed on these ants and a decrease in genetic diversity was found in comparison to the native populations, it was hypothesized that

> Here you discuss clearly why it is difficult to identify the factor that causes success or failure for invading species.

CHANGES IN BEHAVIOR CAN AFFECT SPECIES INVASION SUCCESS   8

the invasion to the United States actually caused a founder effect. This could be the reason that the behavior altered from one location to another (Chapman, 2001). On the other hand, it is possible that without disease or natural predators this type of behavior was more adaptive.

Another Argentine ant (Linepithema humile) is an excellent example of a behavior change that increases its invasion success. In Argentina, L. humile commonly displays intense intraspecific aggression. However, in its introduced ranges in California and Chile these ants show very little intraspecific aggression. This, once again, leads to increased population density, as well as a lack of natural predators. The high densities of L. humile allow it to fight off native ants more easily and collect food more quickly (Holway 1999, Holway 2001).

Conclusion

The affect that behavior changes have on invasion could be studied more. It seems to add another aspect to the invasion issue. However, there are some problems that make this issue difficult to study. Firstly, observation of a species colonizing a novel environment is rare. To catch a species while undergoing the change necessary to invade is not always possible. This can leave questions as to the mechanism of the behavioral change. This is the main reason why birds are so frequently used in this type of study. Birds have been introduced repeatedly by humans providing a large number of successful and unsuccessful invasions to compare. Secondly, it seems that a behavioral change is not always necessary for a species to invade successfully. Many species can invade keeping the same set of behaviors that are displayed in their native habitat. They find niche availability in other habitats without having to adapt.

Behavior change in a species just adds one more dimension to an already complex issue. Although there are trends of what makes a successful invader, it is still difficult to predict whether an individual species will thrive in a new environment. With a better understanding of the mechanisms that cause the change in behavior, a prediction of the type of animal that would take advantage of this type of change could be made. Adding this dimension just gives a fuller understanding of the topic and should be explored further.

You make a good case why species invasion should be studied further.

Table 1. (Lonsdale, 1999) This table describes some of the reasons that habitats are susceptible to invasion.

Term in invasion ecology	Conventional definition
Disturbance	removal of competing vegetation (Hobbs 1991)
Native species resistance to invasion	competitive ability of native species
Resistance to disturbance	ability of native ecosystems or species to recover from disturbance
Ecosystem resistance to invasion	intrinsic resistance of native ecosystem to invasion through community structure (Williamson 1996: 193-196)
Invasibility	overall susceptibility of sites to invasion (Williamson 1996: 55)
Invasion potential	intrinsic ability of species to invade (di Castri 1989)
Propagule pressure	number of propagules arriving at a site (Williamson 1996: 45)

Figure 1. (Duncan, 2002) This figure shows the how birds introduced by humans fail or succeed to become invaders.

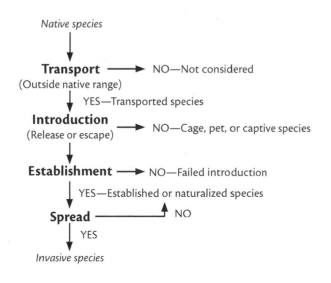

CHANGES IN BEHAVIOR CAN AFFECT SPECIES INVASION SUCCESS 11

Figure 2. (Chapman, 2001) This figure describes the way that unicoloniality can be achieved in eusocial insects.

a.
Introduction ⇒ Ecological release ⇒ Habitat saturation ⇒ Unicoloniality

b.
Introduction ⇒ Loss of genetic variation ⇒ Increase in matched matings and diploid male production ⇒ Reduced success of solitary colony foundation ⇒ Unicoloniality

c.
Introduction ⇒ Evolution of 'green beard' allele ⇒ Unicoloniality

d.
Introduction ⇒ Loss of genetic variation ⇒ Loss of nestmate recognition ⇒ Unicoloniality

CHANGES IN BEHAVIOR CAN AFFECT SPECIES INVASION SUCCESS 12

References

Chapman, Roselle E. & Bourke, Andrew F. G. 2001. The influence of sociality on the conservation biology of social insects. *Ecology Letters,* 4, 650-662.

Duckworth, Renee A. & Badyaev, Alexander V. 2007. Coupling of dispersal and aggression facilitates the rapid range expansion of a passerine bird. *PNAS,* 104, 15017-15022.

Duncan, Richard P., Blackburn, Tim & Sol, Daniel. 2003. The ecology of bird introductions. *Annu. Rev. Ecol. Evol. Syst.,* 34, 71-98.

Holway, David A. & Case, Ted J. 2001. Effects of colony-level variation on competitive ability in the invasive Argentine ant. *Animal Behaviour,* 61, 1181-1192.

Holway, David A. & Suarez, Andrew V. 1999. Animal behavior: an essential component of invasion biology. *Tree,* 14, 328-330.

Ingram, Krista K. 2002. Flexibility in nest density and social structure in invasive populations of the Argentine ant, *Linepithema humile. Oecologia,* 133, 492-500.

Lonsdale, W. M. 1999. Global patterns of plant invasions and the concept of invisibility. *Ecology,* 80, 1522-1536.

CHANGES IN BEHAVIOR CAN AFFECT SPECIES INVASION SUCCESS   13

Mack, Richard N., Simberloff, Daniel, Lonsdale, W. Mark, Evans, Harry, Clout, Michael & Bazzaz, Fakhri. 2000. Biotic invasions: causes, epidemiology, global consequences and control. *Issues in Ecology,* 5, 1-22.

Martin II, Lynn B. & Fitzgerald, Lisa. 2005. A taste for novelty in invading house sparrows, Passer domesticus. *Behavioral Ecology,* 16, 702-707.

Newton, Ian, Hobson, Keith A., Fox, Anthony D. & Marquiss, Mick. 2006. An investigation into the provenance of northern bullfinches Pyrrhula p. pyrrhula found in winter in Scotland and Denmark. *Journal of Avian Biology,* 37, 431- 435.

Sol, Daniel, Bacher, Sven, Reader, Simon M. & Lefebvre, Louis. 2008. Brain size predicts the success of mammal species introduced into novel environments. *The American Naturalist,* 172, 63-71.

Sol, D. & Lefebvre, L. 2000. Behavioral flexibility predicts invasion success in birds introduced to New Zealand. *Oidos,* 90, 599-605.

Sol, Daniel, Timmermans, Sarah & Lefebvre, Louis. 2002. Behavioral flexibility and invasion success in birds. *Animal Behaviour,* 63, 495-502.

Sol, Daniel & Price, Trevor D. 2008. Brain size and the diversification of body size in birds. *The American Naturalist,* 172, 170-177.

Tilman, David. 1997. Community invisibility, recruitment limitation, and grassland biodiversity. *Ecology,* 78, 81-92.

Activity 6.7 • Write on Your Blog

Compose

Choose one of your previous blog postings, and revise it using the suggestions provided in this chapter.

Activity 6.8 • Write in Your Commonplace Book

Compose

Choose one of the readings in this chapter that you think could be improved, and write in your commonplace book about how it could be changed. Give specific examples.

chapter 7
Researching Rhetorically

How I Research

Rosalie Krenger
M.A. Student, Emporia State University
Assistant to the Director of Creative Writing and Teaching Associate

When I research, I always try to be open, unbiased, and prompt. I start off with a good, open-ended research question. I like questions that provide me with direction in my research but are open enough that I might find information I hadn't considered or be led to other questions I could investigate. I also make sure I look at issues from as many sides as possible. Knowing multiple sides of an issue allows me to make a convincing argument by giving me the opportunity to rebut or concede argument points where appropriate, which adds to my *ethos* as a writer. Thus, I resist the urge to only search for sources that support my thesis.

Actually, doing the research can sometimes be frustrating for me because it doesn't immediately produce tangible results, i.e. words on a page. So it's often tempting to put it off until a deadline draws near. However, starting my research as soon as I learn of an assignment makes for an easier writing process and a better paper in the end. It gives me not only enough time to thoroughly investigate my topic but also to change my thesis if need be. Moreover, I have time to submit an interlibrary loan request if I discover an important book on my topic that my college library doesn't have.

In addition to books in the library, I like to use databases like *JSTOR* and the *MLA International Bibliography* that are accessible through the library's webpage. I start with keywords or phrases and begin weeding out sources that aren't appropriate to my research, aren't credible, or weren't published recently. Also, I check the reference pages of my selected journal articles, as they often lead me to other relevant books or articles. I make sure to save as many of the sources as possible on my computer, so I can revisit them as I write. I also create my works cited page as I go, which saves a lot of time later.

Approaching research in this way strengthens my writing, lends to my *ethos*, and makes the process much smoother because I feel confident that I know my subject.

Research Provides Inartistic Proofs

As discussed in Chapter 4, ancient Greeks began the writing process with invention, a stage in which they searched their memories for data related to the topic at hand. This information constituted artistic proofs, knowledge that rhetors invented from their own minds, emotions, and observation. However, rhetors also supplemented their invented proofs with information that was gleaned from other sources such as the testimony of witnesses, evidence given under torture, and written contracts. Yes, evidence given under torture was considered a legitimate proof. None of these inartistic proofs were generated from the rhetor's mind or "invented." As such, the Greeks considered these sources of information to be inartistic proofs.

Today, the range of inartistic proofs available to writers and speakers is vastly expanded—scientific studies, opinions from authorities, videotapes of events, government documents, and so on. You can locate these in the traditional way—library books and print periodicals—but more likely you will begin your search with the Internet, a resource the ancients could not have imagined. However, as in ancient times, it is still the task of today's rhetor to locate available resources, sift through them to locate those that are relevant, evaluate their reliability and validity, and incorporate them into a text to support an argument.

Researching rhetorically, the title of this chapter, refers to making use of your *ethos* or credibility as a writer by incorporating your expert knowledge gained from everyday experiences and the subjects you have studied. You may decide, like Shanna Farrell, author of Reading 7.2, "What Does It Mean to Drink Like a Woman?", to write about a topic that has immediate relevance to your own life. Farrell uses her own experience to challenge the conventional wisdom that women like "girlie" drinks that use fruity flavors to disguise the flavor of alcohol.

Researching rhetorically also involves maximizing as well as "borrowing" the credibility of source materials you quote or paraphrase in your text. When you quote or paraphrase an expert, your paper gains authority that it would not otherwise have. For example, if you are the parent of a child with attention deficit hyperactivity disorder (ADHD), your experiences caring for that child and interacting with the health care and educational systems, as well as the reading you have done to seek out effective treatment, qualifies you to speak with authority about what it is like to raise such a child. If you are writing a paper about educational options for children with ADHD, you can cite some of your own experiences, but you will also want to quote or paraphrase opinions of authorities about the best ways to provide a quality educational environment for these children. These expert opinions can be found in books, periodicals, and possibly government documents, and including them will increase your power to convince an audience.

You Do Research Every Day

Although the words "research paper" sound imposing to many students, research is really a natural part of your experience. You do research every day, often without being aware of the process, whether it is determining the calorie count of a serving of sugar-free ice cream or calculating the dollar amount you will spend on gasoline for a weekend trip.

Ideally, a research paper grows out of questions you have about the way the world works—issues or things that you have thought about that intersect your own life. For example, you may worry about how your student loan debt will affect you after you graduate, and you know that many other college students face the same issue. A research paper about the effects of student loan debt would be a more formal response to a question that already interests you. Because of your personal connection, you find the topic interesting enough to consider researching the issue to find out real answers to your questions about that topic.

The information gathering you do for a research paper builds on the informal research skills you already have by adding additional places to look for information and additional tools to use in that search.

How do you go about finding the best reference sources to support your general knowledge? A key factor to keep in mind is the credibility of each of the sources you choose. Citing information from a source written in the last three years is generally more credible than a source published ten years ago because the information is obviously more current. Peer-reviewed journals and books published by reputable publishers are probably the most credible sources. Information from a news magazine such as *Time* has more credence than material found in popular magazines such as *Glamour* or *People,* which are designed for entertainment rather than covering the news. Indeed, many instructors will forbid the use of *Wikipedia* as a source, not because all the information is inaccurate (because it is not), but because the reader has no way of evaluating whether information is correct or not since the entries were written by volunteers and the content has not been vetted by a reputable publisher or other authoritative organization.

Don't be reluctant to ask for help. Your instructor may be willing to suggest resources on your topic, as will librarians. Some instructors may refer you to specific books or authors. Others may demonstrate a journal search for you, in the process finding you valuable sources. Librarians can be valuable allies in your search, as their job is to serve your needs as a library patron. If you ask for help, a librarian will often run a search for you in the online catalog or may even walk with you into the stacks to find appropriate source materials.

Primary and Secondary Research

If you've ever purchased a major consumer product, say a computer, chances are you already knew quite a bit about what was available before you took out your charge card. For example, many of your friends probably have computers as well as definite opinions about what brands and models are preferable, and they have shared those opinions with you. Perhaps you already own a computer and like it so much that you want to upgrade to the next model, or maybe you have complaints about its performance. Still, before you made your purchase, you probably did some research on the Internet, reading product specifications and reviews. Maybe you tried out a computer or two at the local Apple Store or another retailer. If you went through this sort of process before buying a computer or another consumer product, you already know the basics of primary and secondary research.

Primary research involves personal interaction with your subject. Interviews with people on the scene of an event and questionnaires are all primary sources. Novels, poems, diaries, and fictional films are also primary sources because they stand alone and are not interpreting anything else. To return to the computer purchase analogy, when you visited the Apple Store or other retailers to examine computers, you were doing primary research. When you looked at product reviews in magazines, you were doing secondary research. Similarly, when you read a *Time* magazine article that analyzes climate change and quotes prominent experts in the field, you are conducting secondary research.

A little later in this chapter, an activity asks you to interview someone who has had an unusual life experience and write a profile of that person. You may be able to gather all the information you need for this assignment by doing an interview, though it might be a good idea to revisit the observation exercise (Activity 4.13) in Chapter 4. If you know the person personally, you can also utilize that prior knowledge.

Secondary research sources analyze, collate, or synthesize existing primary research. An author doing secondary research collects primary sources and interprets what the primary research means.

The majority of your sources in a research paper may be secondary research. You should choose your sources carefully because the credibility of information from secondary research depends on the validity of the primary research being discussed, the qualifications of the writer, and the reputation of the publisher. Your writing will be stronger if it also includes discussion of primary research, when that is possible, along with the findings from secondary research.

Many writing assignments ask you to combine your own experience or primary research with information gained from secondary research in books or periodicals. For example, you might be asked to write an essay about recycling. You can include your own experience with recycling or visit a recycling center in your community and report what you see. You can also support this primary research with secondary research in books or periodicals in which authorities offer facts and opinions about the effectiveness of recycling. In addition, you can interview an authority on recycling, perhaps a professor or chairperson of a community committee, as an additional secondary source.

You may notice that many magazine articles or books refer to other books, statistical studies, or additional evidence but do not document sources in the text or give a bibliography. In this course, however, your instructor will probably ask you to document outside references following the Modern Language Association (MLA) or American Psychological Association (APA) format. The purpose is to train you in academic writing, which differs from journalism or popular writing in that all sources are credited both in the text and in a works cited page. Documentation also benefits those who read your essays and might want to use the same sources for additional research of their own. It is, therefore, not a check against plagiarism but an important tool for other researchers.

Reading 7.1

In this article, Alexander L. Ames argues that primary sources add depth and help bring a research topic to life. Ames is a Ph.D. student in the history of American civilization at the University of Delaware.

Bringing History to Life with Primary Sources
by Alexander L. Ames

History sometimes bores because of the way it is taught. Often, educators merely present students with information they are supposed to remember, rather than encourage students to explore historic documents and draw conclusions. As a Museum Studies intern at Mystic Seaport, a maritime history museum in Mystic, Connecticut, I worked with other interns to create his-

tory education programs targeted at high school audiences. We presented students with primary sources and asked them to think critically about the documents, to develop their own ideas about history.

My favorite program we developed related to the Temperance Movement, a mid-nineteenth century social reform movement that aimed to put an end to alcohol consumption. Members of the Greenman family, prominent shipbuilders and storeowners who lived in Mystic, became involved in Temperance as the movement gained national momentum. We traced the development of their beliefs through historic documents relating to their business and civic activities. For example, we showed students pages from the 1840s account books of the family-owned Greenman General Store that had frequent references to the sale of alcohol. By the 1850s, those references had vanished. Also, we gave students newspaper articles from the 1870s in which the Greenmans publicly stated their support of Temperance, indicating the passion with which the Greenmans advocated against alcohol. The text of the education program encouraged students to discover the Greenmans apparently stopped selling alcohol, a decision that affected the company's profits, *before* their public announcement of their change in attitude toward alcohol.

Students going through the educational program realized they would not know this fascinating detail, which hints the Greenmans were willing to lose company revenue in support of their beliefs, if they had not scrutinized account books from the nineteenth century. Moreover, we asked students to think about whether they could cite negative evidence—that is, the *absence* of liquor sales in the 1850s account books—as sufficient grounds for assuming the Greenmans changed their business practices by that decade? What other evidence would help support this conclusion—an open ended question students can answer in a variety of ways.

Focusing on historical evidence allows us to ask deeper questions about our conclusions. The questions we encouraged the students at Mystic Seaport to think about show the debatable nature of historical conclusions based on primary sources. While applied here to a museum activity, this strategy of poring over primary sources can be used in almost any research context. Original documents get us as close as possible to whatever subject we are studying. They also add depth to our interpretations by encouraging critical analysis of sources.

What Does It Mean to Drink Like a Woman?

by Shanna Farrell

I am a woman who likes whiskey. I order Manhattans. I drink Old Fashioneds. And nearly every time I announce this request to a bartender, I get the knowing nod—the unvoiced approval and the respect that comes along with defying the expectations of what a woman usually drinks.

And usually this approving bartender is a male. By nature of its history, bartending is a male-dominated industry, one in which women tend to work a little harder to earn the same credibility bestowed upon our dark-spirits willing counterparts.

Reading 7.2

One of the familiar ways to begin an essay or article is to tell an anecdote that illustrates the topic being discussed in the text. In "What Does It Mean to Drink Like a Woman?" Shanna Farrell tells an anecdote, but it is about her own experience, not someone she has interviewed. A writer's decision to include herself in the text only works well when the writer is an authority on the subject. In this case, the essay is about what women drink, and the writer uses her own experience to challenge the conventional wisdom that women like "girlie" drinks that use fruity flavors to disguise the flavor of alcohol. Though she does not have a graduate degree or other scholarly qualification, she is, for this topic, an authority.

"What It Means to Drink Like a Woman?" was first published at Punch, an online magazine that publishes narrative journalism about wine, spirits, and cocktails.

"It's kind of a thrill when a woman orders whiskey," says Toby Cecchini, a longtime bartender and the owner of New York's Long Island Bar. "You serve three hundred white wines to women and when a female comes in and asks for a single malt, it blows my mind. Red carpet for you, ladies." As a woman, ordering a Manhattan or an Old Fashioned affords more attention from the bartender and, admittedly, I find it empowering.

But why? Why do I get more attention for ordering a spirit-forward drink, and why do I—why does any woman—find this empowering? In a sense, by ordering whiskey with confidence, I'm challenging the stereotype that women have dainty palates while disproving the assumption that I'm not interested in spirits—a stereotype that, in part, stems from historic mores that are deeply woven into the cultural fabric that dictates gender roles.

While there have long been behavioral codes, Emily Post was the first to formalize them in 1922 with her highly influential book *Etiquette*. The book gave explicit instructions for the conduct of women, which proclaimed that she be passive and not draw attention to herself, take a man's arm after dark because she might trip, not allow a drunk man into her house and—my personal favorite— "never pay a party call on a gentleman."

These rules enabled stereotypes about the fragility of women, which translated into drink trends assuming woman prefer cocktails that disguise the taste of alcohol, because, well, alcohol can be aggressive. In the 1950s the Pink Lady became popular, which, according to The Bartender's Book, was considered a both inoffensive and visually appealing choice for "that nice little girl who works in files." Gender stereotypes were further perpetuated by the Lemon Drop, which was first introduced in the 1970s, likely at Henry's Africa in San Francisco. Henry's Africa was a classic singles bar where the Lemon Drop—a sweet drink that masked the taste of alcohol—was marketed to women to lure them inside. In 1988, Cecchini created the Cosmopolitan specifically for women. "I literally invented the Cosmo for waitresses who were on my staff," he says. "I understood a bit about how women drank." Some women do genuinely prefer lighter drinks to more spirituous cocktails. But so do some men. However, it became widely accepted that all women cleave to innocuous concoctions.

Before I earned a reputation as a whiskey drinker, there were numerous occasions when people—mostly men—would presume that I wanted something juicy or sweet. I'd sit down at a bar and be recommended anything but a spirit-forward cocktail. I'd go to a friend's place for a party and immediately be told that there were mixers—like juice or soda—for the array of spirits residing on the kitchen table while the host swirled Scotch around in his rocks glass. I'd be at a celebration and handed a shot, wherein I would ask what I was holding and be told, "It's pink; you'll like it."

The ways in which certain cocktails have been perceived, discussed and used as marketing tools reify the ideas about how women drink. They've since been embedded in our collective cultural consciousness along with ideas about women in the profession of bartending.

Prior to the women's movement in the 1970s, females struggled to be treated as equal in many professions, but the best example in bartending dates back to World War II. When men went overseas, women dominated bars as part of their patriotic duty to hold down the home front. But when men returned after the war they lobbied for ways to get their bartending jobs back and ensure that they kept them. Both Michigan and California passed laws that made it illegal for a woman to tend bar unless she was the daughter or wife of the bar owner.

Valentine Goesaert, a bar owner in Michigan, challenged this law in court but lost after the state argued that tending bar could lead to "moral and social problems" for women; this hypocrisy is highlighted by the fact that the susceptibility of men to "moral and social problems" was never mentioned. The law—which dictated, quite literally, that bartending was a male profession—stayed on the books until the early 1970s when a similar law in California was challenged and finally overturned in the federal Supreme Court.

Dale DeGroff remembers the issue lasting well after the laws had changed: "You did not see women behind the bar in the 1970s and '80s in big cities. You just didn't. It was considered a man's world." When DeGroff opened the Rainbow Room in 1986, he hired four women to tend bar. "That's probably four more women than anyone else around had hired," he says. However, management tried to put these ladies in the front of the house—where they were easier to see—causing several of them to leave.

More than 30 years later, things are finally changing. Along with updated ideas about etiquette brought to us by the women's movement, the internet is one of the primary reasons for this shift. There is an abundance of information available on spirits, which is helping to generate interest among women and allow them to challenge stereotypes. While whiskey experienced a 50% drop in sales from 1970 to 2000, it is making a comeback due, in large part, to an increase in female whiskey enthusiasts. A 2008 Nielsen survey revealed that women account for the fastest-growing segment of worldwide whiskey consumers. This is reflected in the rise of female memberships in several whiskey clubs, like the UK's Scotch Malt Whiskey Society, whose female membership doubled from 2008 to 2009, and at Seven Grand's Whiskey Society in L.A., where nearly half of its members are women.

Cecchini has noticed this shift, which is reflected in the way people order in a general sense. "In the five years since my last bar closed, things have changed," he says. "I've never made so many Manhattans and Old Fashioneds than I have in the past four months since Long Island Bar opened."

There are also more female bartenders than ever before. Reiner and Audrey Saunders—now two of the most influential figures in the cocktail world— paved the way for a new generation of female bartenders, a growing population. Reiner and Saunders were doing innovative things—like featuring gin over vodka—when they came up in the New York cocktail scene in the 1990s. This garnered attention from people like DeGroff and earned them much-deserved respect by their predecessors. In fact, they trained many of the most notable male bartenders working today. Ivy Mix, one of Reiner's bartenders, co-founded Speed Rack—a female bartending competition conceived to help women establish credibility and celebrate their contributions to the cocktail world.

This sea change has served as the impetus for gender-related discussions, which is now a hot topic in the cocktail world. "It seems like every writer that is calling me wants to talk about women in bartending," says Reiner. Hopefully, these conversations will serve to further challenge gender biases and allow us to cultivate a deeper understanding of where they are rooted.

While I find the attention that I receive when I order whiskey empowering because it validates my interest in spirits, there are more ways for a female to demonstrate her knowledge about cocktails than by ordering a spirit-forward drink. I'm ordering what I like, which just so happens to be a Manhattan or an Old Fashioned. But maybe tomorrow I'll be interested in trying a new gin or vodka, regardless of what its flavor profile insinuates or what kind of reaction I get from the bartender.

Collaborate

Activity 7.1 • Analyze "What Does It Mean to Drink Like a Woman?"

1. First, annotate the essay by identifying paragraphs that come from primary sources, including the author's experience and observation and information that comes from the interview of a bartender. Second, locate information that the author found in secondary sources. Do this by making a copy of the essay and making notations in the margins. Then, in your group, consider how Shanna Farrell combines her own knowledge with secondary sources.

2. Shanna Farrell writes that she is challenging certain assumptions. What are they? What is the primary argument of the essay?

3. Farrell could have begun her essay by telling the story of another woman who ordered spirits at bars, but she chose to make the opening anecdote about herself. What do you think of that choice? Does it make her essay stronger or weaker?

4. If Farrell had wanted to expand her essay by incorporating more academic-type sources, what resource would you suggest that she consult? Notice that she does mention a Nielson survey. Try searching for a Gallup poll (gallup.com) and/or do a *Google Scholar* search (scholar.google.com). If you locate a journal article on your topic in *Google Scholar*, you can likely find the same scholarly journal in one of your college's databases for free. Discuss what you find.

5. What topics might individuals in your group write about while using themselves as a source of information, as Farrell did, as well as incorporating research? Identify and discuss them.

Interviews

Depending on your topic, your community probably has some excellent sources sitting behind desks at the nearest college, city hall, or federal office building. If you are looking into the environment, you could contact the Environmental Protection Agency, an attorney who specializes in environmental law, a professional employee of the park system or the Bureau of Land Management, a college professor who works in the natural sciences, or a group in your area dedicated to beautification and restoration efforts. If you don't know anyone connected with these organizations, a look at several organization or local government websites should give you the information you need.

When you contact the person you'd like to interview, identify yourself and your reason for wanting to speak with him or her. Most people are happy to assist college students in their research, and almost everyone is flattered by the attention. If your first choice refuses, ask him or her if they know anyone who might be knowledgeable about your topic and available for an interview. When you get a positive response, arrange an hour and a location convenient for both of you. If the interview is scheduled more than a week from the initial contact, you can write a letter confirming your appointment, or you can call the day before the scheduled interview to confirm the time and location.

Once you've scheduled the interview, make a list of questions you will ask your interview subject. There are two types of questions you can ask your subject: open and closed. **Open questions** leave room for extended discussion because they don't have a yes, no, or specific answer:

■   What is the most positive experience you've had with [topic]?

■   When did you decide to study [topic]?

■   What's the most negative experience you've had with [topic]?

Questions like these allow for extended discussions. Even if it seems your subject has finished his or her response to the question, let a few moments of silence pass before you ask another question. Silence can be uncomfortable for some people, and he or she might feel compelled to expand on the response to your question in interesting ways.

Closed questions are useful for gathering specific information. Questions such as "When did you graduate?" and "How long have you been involved in [topic]?" are closed questions. Although closed questions are important to an interview, be sure they're balanced by questions that allow your subject room to talk and expand on his or her ideas.

Before the interview, confirm the exact location of your appointment. If you are unfamiliar with the planned meeting place, go by the day before to make sure you can find it. Take several pens or pencils with you to the interview in addition to a writing tablet with a stiff back. If possible, use a recorder to record the interview, but be sure to ask your subject if it is okay. Most people will allow recording, if you assure them that the recording is only for your use in collecting information for your research paper. If you are using a recorder, test its operation before you get to the interview location so you won't have any surprises when you're with your subject or discover later that the machine was not working.

Although you've prepared a list of questions to follow, don't be afraid to ask a question that isn't on your list. If your subject mentions briefly an experience that seems relevant to your topic, you might want to ask him or her more about that experience, even though it isn't on your list of questions. Indeed, the best way to interview may be to read over your questions just before you meet your subject, then not refer to them during the interview. Before you leave, however, look over your list to see if you have missed any questions of importance.

Remember to let lulls in the conversation work for you by drawing your interview subject into further explanations or illustrations of previous comments. If you interview a talkative person who strays from the topic, try to steer him or her back to the questions you've prepared, but if you can't, don't worry. You'll probably get useful information anyway. Be courteous and attentive. Even if you're recording the interview, take notes. It makes both the subject and the interviewer feel more comfortable and serves as a backup, should your recording not work.

Within 15 minutes after leaving the interview, jot down some notes about your subject's appearance; the sights, sounds, and smells of the place where you conducted the interview; and any overall impressions of the meeting. Make sure you have the date and location of the interview in your notes because you will need it for documentation on your works cited page.

Activity 7.2 • Reconstruct Interview Questions for "What Does It Mean to Drink Like a Woman?"

Explore

Read through "What Does It Mean to Drink Like a Woman?" and make note of the people Shanna Farrell interviewed to write the essay. Then reconstruct what interview questions she may have asked to obtain the information and quotes attributed to these individuals. For example, Farrell may have asked this question of Toby Cecchini: "What is your reaction when a woman orders whiskey?"

You can use this technique of reconstructing interview questions for other texts, which may help you in developing your own interview questions relevant to your research.

Compose

Activity 7.3 • **Write Interview Questions**

After you define your research project, you may decide to interview an individual who is knowledgeable about your topic. Before you go to your interview, it is a good idea to write down the major questions you want to ask your interview subject, even if you plan to record the session. At the interview, you will not necessarily ask your questions in the order you write them here, but doing this activity will help you keep the areas of inquiry in mind. Before you leave the interview, you might want to glance over the questions again, to be sure you have not missed any crucial topic.

1. Write five questions you intend to ask your interview subject.
2. After the interview, make some notes about the appearance of your subject and the setting where the interview took place.

Compose

Activity 7.4 • **Summarize Your Interview**

After reading through your notes from your interview and possibly listening to the recording, if you made one, summarize what your interview subject said about your topic. Remember, a summary is a distillation of the information. You are not arguing here with your subject, just trying to record his or her information as accurately as possible. Include actual quotations, properly punctuated, if you think you may want to use them in your research report. Make note of other sources or individuals that your subject may have suggested you consult.

Compose

Activity 7.5 • **Write a Profile of a Person**

Apply your interview and observation skills by writing a profile of a person who is unusual in some way. Your profile should include description, quotes, and whatever background explanations are needed to provide a context, so the story flows logically from one element to another. The length should be approximately 750 to 1,000 words. Answering the following questions will help you elicit information you need to write your profile.

1. History—What is the history of the person? Does the history affect the present?
2. Qualities—What qualities make this person worth writing about? Can you give examples that *show* the qualities?
3. Values and standards—What does the subject believe in most strongly? How does that shape his/her actions? Can you give specific examples?
4. Impact—How does the subject affect those around him or her? This may include both positives and negatives. Give examples.
5. Description—Write a physical description of the person, including any unusual aspects that make the person stand out in a crowd. Describe the setting where you interviewed the person or where the person works or lives.

Surveys

Comprehensive surveys that involve large populations such as the Gallup polls are conducted by many people and require large investments in time and money. A small survey involving fellow students, friends, or colleagues, can illuminate local issues or localize topics of national or international impact. For example, if you are writing using the sources in the Research Casebook in this chapter to write an essay about Americans' attitudes toward climate change, you can do a small survey to see if local people share the attitudes measured by the Gallup organization. However, you need to mention in your essay that your survey was indicative but unscientific because your sample size was small and the subject pool was not scientifically selected.

Activity 7.6 • Conduct a Survey

Compose

Conduct a survey by following these steps:

1. Use an online survey tool to deliver your questionnaire to your subjects, such as SurveyMonkey, Zoho Survey, or Survey Gizmo; or you can print out paper questionnaires, which you will hand out to subjects at a specific time and place.

2. Introduce your survey to your subjects by making a leveling statement that provides a context for your questions. For example, if your survey is to measure attitudes about climate change, your statement could be something like this: The United Nations' Intergovernmental Panel on Climate Change (IPCC) recently reported, "Global emissions of greenhouse gases have risen to unprecedented levels despite a growing number of policies to reduce climate change." A leveling statement makes sure your subjects have similar knowledge about your topic, but it should not influence their answers on the questionnaire.

3. Decide what information you need from your subjects, and design several closed-ended multiple choice or true/false questions (perhaps five). Also develop a small number of open-ended questions (perhaps one or two), such as "What do you think about climate change?" Open-ended questions allow participants to input more detailed responses but are more time consuming to analyze because you must code or group the responses.

4. Before you utilize your questionnaire, ask a few fellow students or friends to test it, and discuss their answers with them afterward to see if any of the survey questions were confusing or biased.

5. Use the online survey tool to analyze your mulitple choice and true/false questions. If you created open-ended questions, you can group the answers and/or use quotes from the responses.

Secondary Research Sources Expected by Professors

You have been assigned a research paper or project. What does your professor expect? First of all, you need to understand the assignment. What specifically does your professor want you to research? Do you have instructions about what kinds of sources your professor wants? Are restrictions placed on what Internet or database sources you can use? Possibly, your instructor has specified that you need to use books, journals, major magazines and newspapers, and certain web-based information. This means that you are to use reputable sources to obtain a balanced, impartial viewpoint about your topic. So, how do you find these sources?

Neither you nor your professor should be surprised that you can find enough material for your research paper through the Internet, even if your professor says you can use only print sources. Your library has full-text databases such as *JSTOR* and *Academic Search Complete* (*EBSCO*) that will provide you with PDF images of actual journal pages, not web pages. Moreover, *Google* and other online libraries have the full-text versions of many book chapters or entire books.

However, in many cases the latest books in a field are not online, so you need to venture into the actual library building to find some of the best sources for your research. This is also true of primary sources such as letters and maps. Moreover, librarians can aid you in finding the research materials you need.

Consider the following secondary research sources.

> Books: In these days of easy-to-find resources on the Internet, students may wonder why they should bother with books at all. However, scholarly books treat academic topics with in-depth discussion and careful documentation of evidence. College libraries collect scholarly books that are carefully researched and reviewed by authorities in the book's field. Look for recently published books rather than older books, even if they are on your topic. Academic books or well-researched popular books often have bibliographies or lists of additional references at the end of the book. These lists are useful for two reasons. First, if such lists of books are present, it is a good clue this is a well-researched book, and, second, it gives you a ready list of other possible resources you can consult for your research project.

Scholarly journals: Just having the word "journal" in the title does not mean it is a journal. *Ladies Home Journal,* or *The Wall Street Journal,* for example, are not journals. Your instructor means peer-reviewed journals in which the authors have documented their sources. Peer-reviewed means that articles have been reviewed by experts in the field for reliability and relevance before being published. Your library should have print indexes to journals in which you can look up your topic. You may also be able to find journal articles—sometimes in full text—through the online databases offered by your college library.

Major magazines and newspapers: These publications report the news based on the actual observation of events and interviews with experts and also present informed editorial opinions. Examples are magazines such as *Time* and *Fortune* and newspapers such as *The New York Times,* the *Boston Globe, The Wall Street Journal,* and the *Washington Post.* You can locate full-text articles directly from the online versions of major print magazines and newspapers. Often, these publications charge a fee for articles not published recently. However, you can often find the same articles free through one of your library databases.

Special interest publications: These are periodicals that focus on a specific topic but are written for a wider audience than scholarly journals. Authors of articles base their articles on interviews with experts, recent scholarly books and journals, and other reputable sources. Examples include *Psychology Today* and *Scientific American.*

Government documents: Government documents present a wealth of information for many contemporary events and issues. Your library may be a federal depository, which means that users can locate many federal documents onsite. If so, you can look up government sources in the online library catalog. Government documents are also available through online databases.

Encyclopedias: Encyclopedias can be useful to browse when you are looking for topics. They are also helpful for providing background information such as dates when events occurred. However, most instructors prefer that you do not use encyclopedias as sources in your paper. This is particularly true for *Wikipedia,* the online encyclopedia that is assembled by volunteers who have specialized knowledge on topics and, thus, has no systematic vetting of the contents. However, *Wikipedia* entries often include bibliographies which can be useful in pointing you to books, articles, or other websites that can be used as references.

Web pages: The problem with web-based information is that anyone with some knowledge of computers can put up a website on the Internet. Thus, information from websites must be carefully evaluated as to author, publishing organization, etc. You can follow the website review guidelines later in this chapter to determine the credibility of a site. Another option, however, is to find sources through one of the websites that screen sites and organize them by topic. Two of these that are discussed later are the *Internet Public Library,* (ipl.org), and the *Open Directory,* (dmoz.org).

As you use the categories above to find secondary sources for your paper or project, realize that your topic influences your choice of reference materials. If you are writing about a literary topic such as Shakespeare's *Othello,* you will find a number of relevant books and journal articles. If your topic is more contemporary, such as the current status of the country's housing market, you may be able to find some books or journal articles for background information, but you will need to use recent magazine and newspaper articles to find the latest information.

As you examine your sources, remember that gathering the information should help you discover what you think about your topic, not just what others think. This will enable you to create a paper based on *your* ideas and opinions, with source materials supporting your position.

Employ Computerized Library Catalogs

Public Access Catalogs (PACs) or computerized catalogs, accessed through the Internet, have replaced card catalogs. A library computerized catalog provides bibliographical information about the library's collection, including thousands of books, photos, videos, journals, and other items. Generally, catalogs can be accessed by any of the following methods: keyword, subject, author, title, or call number. You may also find books that are available in digital form through the catalog. In addition, on the library home page, you will find links to other information and services such as database searches, interlibrary loans, and course reserves.

Types of Computerized Searches

Conducting a computerized search involves accessing the library's catalog using one of the following search methods.

- **Keyword**—Unless you know the author or title of a book, keyword is the best type of search because it finds the search word or words anywhere in the bibliographical citation.

    Example: water quality

- **Title**—Type the exact order of words in the title.

    Example: History of the United Kingdom

- **Author**—Type the author's name, putting the last name first. You don't need to include a comma.

    Example: Miller Henry J.

- **Subject**—Type the exact Library of Congress subject heading.

    Example: Spanish language—Grammar, Historical

- **Call Number**—Type the exact call number.

    Example: B851.P49 2004

If you have a general topic, you probably want to use the keyword search, for subject search actually refers to the exact Library of Congress subject-search designations, and, unless you use the precise search terms specified by that classification system, you may not get the results you want. The use of keywords, however, will lead you to hits on your topic. Then, once you have found one book that is in your topic area, you can examine the screen for Library of Congress subject headings and click on those to browse for more books.

An invaluable resource of any library is the Interlibrary Loan department. Here you can request books your library does not own, as well as journal articles from periodicals not in the library's collection or obtainable through the library's databases. Books and articles are obtained for you by the staff on a minimal or no-fee basis. This is extremely helpful because you can request books you find in bibliographies. However, it generally takes seven to 10 days to obtain books through an interlibrary loan, so you need to plan well in advance. To request an item, you simply go to the Interlibrary Loan depart-ment in your library or fill out a form on the library's website.

Explore

Activity 7.7 • **Locate Books on Your Topic**

Using the online card catalog at the library, locate three books about your topic. Write down the titles, authors, publishers, dates of publication, and catalog num-bers. Now, go to the stacks and find the books. While you are there, find two other books nearby on the same topic. Check the table of contents and index to see if they contain information you can use.

Utilize Electronic Library Resources

College and university libraries increasingly rely on databases to provide digi-tal versions of articles published in journals, magazines, newspapers, and gov-ernment documents, as well as other publications and materials. Generally, the databases are available to students and faculty through the Internet via the library home page, though a library card and a password may be required for off-campus access.

Library databases make use of online forms similar to those of a library com-puterized catalog. Searches are by subject, title, author, and name of publi-cation. Advanced search features are available. Some databases provide the full-text versions of articles published in newspapers, journals, and magazines. Others give publication information only, such as title, author, publication, date of publication, and an abstract of the article. Popular databases include *Lexis-Nexis, Academic Search Complete* (see Figure 7.1), *Periodical Archive Online (ProQuest), Project Muse,* and *JSTOR.*

Explore

Activity 7.8 • **Locate Newspaper and Magazine Articles**

Go to your library's online databases, and choose one that relates to your topic. Then access it and type in your topic. Try using various key words. Jot down titles, authors, and publication information concerning any articles that look interesting. If full-text versions are available, save them to your computer or disk drive or email them to yourself. If not, find out if your library has a hard copy version or microfilm of the articles.

Figure 7.1 • Academic Search Complete

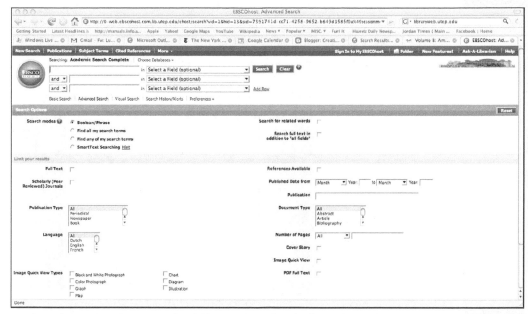

Academic Search Complete is one of *EBSCO*'s popular online databases that can be accessed by students through their library's website. The database indexes full-text articles on a wide variety of topics.

Find Internet Information

The World Wide Web is an incredible resource for research. Through it, you can find full texts of pending legislation, searchable online editions of Shakespeare's plays, environmental impact statements, stock quotes, and much, much more. Finding credible research sources is not always easy. Anyone with an Internet connection and a little knowledge can put up a web page and claim to be an expert on a chosen topic. Therefore, information from the Internet must be scrutinized with even more diligence than print sources. For example, if you enter the word "environment" in one of the keyword search engines, you may receive thousands of "hits," or sites that relate to that topic from all over the world. How do you sift through all of that feedback in order to find information relevant to your topic? It is a problem that has not been completely solved on the Internet.

To maximize your chances of finding the information you want by using Internet search engines, choose one of the major engines such as *Google, Yahoo,* or *Bing.* The big search engines browse all publically available sites and return "hits" based on your key words; these should be chosen carefully so that they are neither too broad nor too narrow. Some engines may also offer suggestions that narrow your search, such as scholarly articles, news, and related searches. Alternatively, you can do a keyword search for "best search engines" to try more specialized engines that are currently popular.

Browse through your "hits," selecting sites that look promising, going several pages deep into the search, as search engines rank "hits" based on popularity, and what you are looking for might not be on the first page. Try alternative key words for your topic, also, such as "climate change," rather than "global warming." If you are using Internet sites as part of your research portfolio, read carefully the Evaluate Sources section later in the chapter.

Indexing Projects

One of the best ways to find Internet resources is through indexing projects such as *Internet Public Library,* www.ipl.org (Figure 7.2), and *DMOZ* or *Open Directory,* www.dmoz.org (Figure 7.3). In both cases, librarians or volunteer researchers have personally reviewed and selected websites that are of value to academic researchers. These indexing websites are organized by subject areas but also have keyword search engines. Thus, you might quickly locate the most authoritative websites without having to wade through masses of search engine hits.

Figure 7.2 • Internet Public Library

The *Internet Public Library*'s "Resources by Subject" page, ipl.org/div/subject, offers access to authoritative Internet websites by subject or keyword search.

Figure 7.3 • DMOZ

DMOZ (the Open Directory) claims to be the largest and most comprehensive human-edited directory of the Web. Volunteer researchers review and index websites of interest to academics and students.

Google Books

Google Books, books.google.com, offers full-text versions of books and magazines that are provided free by publishers and authors, as well as books that are out of copyright. In addition, it gives bibliographic information and snippets of text for copyrighted books that can be purchased through bookstores or found in libraries. It is an easy source for discovering books on your topic that might not be available at your college library. You can read them online, if full-text is available, even doing keyword searches inside the books. If full-text is not available, you can request books through interlibrary loan or purchase them through a bookstore. In many cases, the *Google Books*' page also offers a purchase link.

Scholarly Journal Articles

Google Scholar, scholar.google.com, allows you to keyword search a multitude of scholarly journals. If it does not provide full text for an article, it will give bibliographic information, including the database where the article is available, such as *JSTOR* or *Academic Search Complete.* You can learn publication information for interesting articles through *Google Scholar*; then you can utilize one of your library's online databases to locate full-text of the articles.

Another resource for journal articles is the *Directory of Online Open Access Journals,* doaj.org, which allows you to search peer-reviewed online journals that offer free access. You can search either by journal or keywords.

Government Documents

Government documents and information about government services, everything from census reports to presidential speeches, can easily be found through the Internet and are indexed at a variety of sites, including these:

▌ Gateway to government information and websites, fedworld.ntis.gov

▌ State and national government services and agencies, usa.gov

▌ United States Congress elected officials and legislation, congress.gov

▌ U.S. Government consumer publications, publications.usa.gov

Explore

Activity 7.9 • Find a Journal Article in *Google Scholar*

Go to *Google Scholar* either through google.com or directly at scholar.google.com and search for a journal article on your chosen topic. If the *Google* link does not offer you full text, then go to the index of electronic journals on your college library website and search for the journal. Likely, your library will offer a database that provides full text for the article. Note: The advantage of this method of finding journal articles is that *Google Scholar* indexes articles from journals available in many different databases.

Compose

Activity 7.10 • Compare and Contrast Media

Your instructor will select an article on a topic or event that is currently in the news. Find another article on the same subject either from the same news outlet or another major news source (*The New York Times, The Wall Street Journal, CNN, Time,* etc.). Compare and contrast how the reporting of the event is similar or different in the two texts. Note: You are not to write a report on the content of the articles themselves; instead, identify the author's perspective in each text and how it influences how the news is portrayed to readers.

Look for opinions, adjectives with positive or negative connotations, facts or evidence presented, the tone of the headline, and the text itself. Also consider the target audience.

Organize your observations in a one- to two-page report with a clear thesis that presents your evaluation of the two texts.

Make a Research Plan

Research is not something you tack on after you have completed your argument. Rather, it should be part of the writing process close to the beginning, once you have decided on a general topic. In the Internet age, the problem is deciding where to start and how to sort through the information glut to find sources applicable for an academic paper.

1. Begin with the assignment. Your instructor may ask you to compare two subjects or perhaps it is to analyze cause and effect. The topic may already be defined for you within certain parameters. Pay close attention to what you are asked to do.

2. You probably already know some things about your topic. You may even have an opinion you think you want to argue. However, to make an effective argument, you need to research the topic with an open mind and learn what experts think and studies show about the issue. First, you want to get an overview of the topic or issue, and where you start depends somewhat on the topic you choose.

    a. Current events? Recent developments in an ongoing issue? A major Internet-accessible newspaper such as *The New York Times* may start you on the right track. In addition to perusing the latest edition or doing a key word search in the search box, you can look at the site index at the bottom of the page for a link to *Times Topics*, a page that leads you to collections of articles on major current topics. The *Times* charges for access after the first few articles, but you can search for free and then access articles through one of your library's databases, if necessary.

    b. What do people think about an issue? Try a polling organization such as Gallup, Inc. (www.gallup.com) or the Pew Research Center, (www.pewresearch.org).

    c. Commercial products? Companies? Look for products' and corporations' websites. Remember that you are seeing only what the companies want you to see, so be prepared to look for sources for the other side of the story.

    d. *Google* it? If you just want some background information, a quick key-word search may give you what you need. Then you can do a more careful search later.

    e. *Wikipedia* it? You may have heard that your instructor does not want you to use *Wikipedia* as a source, but you can read a *Wikipedia* article and follow links to sources the *Wikipedia* authors used. Often these sources are authoritative, and *Wikipedia* can help you get to them quickly.

3.   Focus on academic sources. The previous quick and dirty approaches will give you a general perception of your topic and may have turned up newspaper articles, book references, or journal articles that you can put on your working bibliography. However, once you have a general idea of the topic or issue, you need to begin thinking about moving on to the more sophisticated research required of an academic paper.

  a.   Check *Google Scholar* (scholar.google.com). *Google Scholar* indexes across databases and disciplines, giving you access to journal articles, publically accessible books, and case law. Once you have a citation, you may have to locate it in one of your library's databases to obtain an article for free, but many books and other sources are freely available through *Google Scholar.*

  b.   Go to the college library, either online or in person. Search the library databases by discipline and the computerized catalog for books.

4.   Follow the research trail. Once you locate a few good books or articles, search their bibliographies for other references.

5.   Consider the dates of your sources. Unless you are using a landmark case, book, or article, your sources should be recent—preferably no more than five years old.

6.   Utilize stasis theory or one of the other prewriting techniques in Chapter 4, Inventing Rhetorically, to develop your argument by discovering the critical points in an issue.

7.   Develop a working thesis. Reread the section in Chapter 5 about composing a thesis. A working thesis must be debatable. If you cannot state arguments on both sides, then it probably is not an arguable thesis.

8.   Start outlining your argument. Revisit the three essay formats discussed in Chapter 5: the Toulmin model, Rogerian argument, and the general modern format. Decide which works best for your argument and draft major points.

9.   Take a look at the sources you have and consider looking for additional ones if they are needed. Focus on developing your argument, rather than accumulating information. Look for at least two good sources for each of your major points. You can use a source for more than one major point, but aim for variety in your sources. Incorporate books, journal articles,

surveys, and government reports. Consider interviewing an expert or observing your issue in action, if feasible.

10. Look for a counterargument. Allow your sources to disagree with each other, with you as the referee. It is much better for you to voice any objections to your argument and then answer them than to leave your readers to discover weaknesses in your argument.

11. Do not be overpowered by your sources. Remember that you carry the argument, and your source materials are there to support your major points. At the same time, be sure your sources are all credible academic sources. If you use information from a biased source, such as a political website, be sure it is clearly labeled as such.

Evaluate Sources

Many people tend to believe what they see in print. They may think that if information is in a book or a news magazine, it must be true. If you read critically, however, you know that all sources must be evaluated. With the Internet, perhaps even more than with print texts, it is important to evaluate your sources. Here are some guidelines to consider when evaluating sources.

▌ **Who is the author?** This question is equally important, whether the source in question is a book, a magazine, or a website. If you have the dust jacket of the book, the back flap will quickly provide you with essential information to screen the author. In the short biographical sketch, usually included along with a photo, you can learn the author's academic credentials and university affiliation, what previous books the author has published, and other qualifications that the publisher thinks qualify the author to write this particular book. If there is no dust jacket (as is often true with library books), you can try to find information about the author through an Internet search engine or a reference text such as *Contemporary Authors*. A magazine or journal will often provide brief biographical information at the end of the article or on a separate authors' page. If the text is on a website, determining the authorship is more complex, as authors often are not named. In that case, you are forced to rely on the credibility of the entity publishing the website. Many websites have a link called something like "About Us" or "Mission Statement," and that page will give you some idea about the motivations of the entity sponsoring the site. Is it selling something? Is it part of an organization that has a political agenda? These are things to keep in mind when considering the bias of the site's content.

■ **For what audience is the text written?** Determining this may require some detective work. In the case of a book, the preface or introduction may give you some clues. With magazines and journals, consider the demographics of the readership. With a website, a little clicking around in the site and a look at the kind of texts, graphics, and advertising used (if any) should tell you what readers the site is designed for.

■ **What sources does the author rely upon?** If you are working with an academic text, the sources should be clearly cited in the text by author and page number, footnotes, or endnotes. If it is a more popular book or article, sources are acknowledged less formally; however, a credible author will still make an effort to credit sources. For example, an article might say, "According to the March issue of the *New England Journal of Medicine. . . .*"

■ **Does the text have an obvious bias?** Ask yourself if the argument is logical and if sources are mentioned for any statistics or other evidence. Are any opposing viewpoints discussed fairly? Does the author engage in name calling (a clear sign of bias)? Are there obvious holes or contradictions in the argument? For most purposes, you are looking for texts which do not appear to have been written with a biased agenda. However, in some cases, the opposite is true. If you are looking for a political candidate's position on a certain issue, then reading the candidate's book or going to the candidate's website will provide you with a biased viewpoint but one which you can analyze for the purposes of your paper. When dealing with information from sources with an obvious agenda, though, you must be careful not to represent the material as unbiased in your text.

■ **What do others think of the text?** You can find reviews of books, movies, television shows, speeches, and other media by typing the word "review" along with the title in *Google* or another search engine. For a book, you can also look for a review in *Book Review Digest* or *Book Review Index*, two publications you can find in the reference section of the library. Also, *The New York Times* and other newspapers review prominent popular books. Most magazines and newspapers print letters to the editor, which may offer comments on controversial articles. *The Scout Report,* which can be found at the *Scout Project*, scout.wisc.edu/report, reviews selected websites. If you locate a review of your text, you can cite the review in your research paper to provide additional evidence of the text's credibility.

Activity 7.11 • Locate and Evaluate a Source

Explore

Locate one source (book, magazine or newspaper article, or website page) that you think would be a credible source for a research paper. For that source, answer the questions in the Evaluate Sources section.

Activity 7.12 • Evaluate a Website

Explore

Go to the Internet and look up a website related to a topic you are researching. Answer these questions as fully as you can.

1. Who is the author of this source? Is the author credible on this topic? Why or why not?

2. What does the text focus on? Is it thoughtful and balanced, or does it seem one-sided? What gives you that impression?

3. When was the website last updated?

4. What is the purpose of this site? Is it to provide information? Or is it trying to persuade readers to accept a particular point of view?

5. How professional is the tone, and how well-designed is the site? How carefully has it been edited and proofread? Are there any grammatical and spelling errors that compromise its credibility?

6. What kinds of links does the site provide? Do they add to the website's credibility or detract from it?

Activity 7.13 • Prepare an Annotated Bibliography

Compose

An annotated bibliography is a list of bibliographical citations with a few sentences or a paragraph for each entry that offers explanatory information or critical commentary about the source. Many instructors request an annotated bibliography as a step in writing a research paper because it is an indication of the scope and direction of your research. Create an annotated bibliography by following these steps.

1. Select 10 quality sources about your topic. These should be, as your instructor directs, a mix of books, scholarly journal and magazine articles, government documents, and selected texts from websites.

2. Skim the text of each source and read portions more closely that seem relevant to your topic.

3. Write a bibliographical citation for each source in MLA or APA style. (See the appendix that follows this chapter for MLA and APA style samples.)

4. Write a few sentences for each source in which you

    (a) summarize the content and purpose of the source, and

    (b) explain how you might use the source in your research paper.

Sample Annotated Bibliography in MLA Style
Topic: Double Humor in Double Consciousness

Adichie, Chimamanda Ngozi. *Americanah*. Trans. Carlos Soler. New York: Random House, 2014.

> This novel addresses and critiques a Nigerian national who experiences being a member of a minority in America. Adichie critiques Africans in America who do not want to be identified as black because blacks are treated worse than other minorities. Part of Adichie's main character's argument is that immigrants from Africa lose the ability to define themselves by their home country when they come to the United States. They become black and resistance is futile.

> Adichie writes from the perspective of a Nigerian living in America. She is aware of the struggle to define one's self instead of letting society do it for her. Adichie uses humor to make her point, which will provide examples for my paper.

Burciaga, José Antonio. *Drink Cultura: Chicanismo*. Santa Barbara: Joshua Odell Editions, Capra, 1993.

> This collection of stories touches on the experiences of living on the US-Mexico border. Like Adichie, Burciaga uses humor to talk about the complexities of being a member of a minority in America. Being from Mexico and living on the U.S.-Mexico Border, Burciaga's experience as a minority is different from Adichie's main character.

> Burciaga wrote from the perspective of a Chicano living on the US-Mexico Border. He was born in El Paso. His essays are a product of his experiences growing up in that border city. His humor, which I will discuss in my paper, is also from a minority, but it distinct from the African humor in Adichie's book.

Du Bois, W.E.B. "The Humor of Negroes." *Mark Twain Quarterly* 5.3 (1942): 12. *JSTOR*. Web. 2 June 2015.

> In this essay, nearly 40 years after the Soul of Black Folk, Du Bois writes humorously about humor and race. Drawing attention to minorities often being laughed at, Du Bois defines what is and is not funny when it comes to race.

Du Bois's landmark discussion of humor and race provides a context for discussion and examples for both Adichie's and Burciaga's humor.

---. *The Souls of Black Folk. The Project Gutenberg Ebook,* n.d. Web. 12 Oct. 2015.

In the forward to this book, a collection of essays about race, Du Bois identifies the concept of double consciousness and "the problem of color line." Writing in 1906, Du Bois deftly addresses the tender topic of race in the United States at the beginning of the twentieth century. Part of Du Bois' goal was to start a conversation about what it was like to be a minority in the United States and the social issues associated with it.

Du Bois was the first African American to earn a doctorate and one of the founders of the NAACP. Du Bois's *ethos* comes from both his education and personal experience. His discussion of double consciousness will be the cornerstone of my paper.

Sample Annotated Bibliography in APA Style
Topic: Federal Aviation Administration User Fees

Horne, T. A. (2007, February). User fee debate. *AOPA Pilot Magazine, 50,* 27.

The author of this article is an experienced, commercial rated pilot that has flown for over 30 years. He also sits on the Aircraft Owners and Pilots Association (AOPA) board. This article explains what the Federal Aviation Administration (FAA) has proposed and what it means to pilots. Congress is cutting the budget for the FAA and in turn wants to impose fees for anyone who flies into a controlled airspace. This would have a very tragic effect on general aviation. This is huge because if anyone is flying anywhere around a decent-sized city, they are going to fly through these airspaces. Also, the FAA wants to charge for approaches into airports and landing on airport runways. This is bad because all of these charges would add up to more than $200. This would discourage people from flying, making them sell their aircraft. This would slowly dissolve the general aviation industry. I can use this article to explain what is going on and why the government wants to charge these fees.

Boyer, P. (Director) (2007, October 6). AOPA's Reasonable analysis of user fee issues at AOPA expo. *AOPA expo 2007*. Lecture conducted from AOPA, Hartford, CT.

This lecture was given by the president of AOPA, Phil Boyer. He spoke of the fees that the FAA is trying to impose and what they would mean for general aviation pilots. He explains that the fees that the FAA wants are directed toward general aviation and not toward the airlines. He also gave some examples of what would be better for everyone, if the FAA really is in a crisis. This source is important because it provides an explanation and breakdown of these user fees and gives some examples of what could be put in place of these proposed fees.

Hedges, S. (2015, February 4). No user fees in president's budget plan. Retrieved from http://www.aopa.org/News-and-Video/All-News/2015/February/04/NO-USER-FEES-IN-PRESIDENTS-BUDGET-PLAN

After three budgets including user fees, the Obama administration finally bowed to pressure from Congress and the Aircraft Owners and Pilots Association and did not include a provision for user fees for general aviation in the budget for 2016. AOPA's President Mark Baker described the omission of the user fees as a "big victory for the future of general aviation." Thus, this article indicates a reversal of the Obama administration's position on user fees.

Network, A. (2009, October 12). Aero-tv: airventure meet the boss—Randy Babbitt tackles user fees. Retrieved from http://www.youtube.com/watch?v=J14ut3O_j3M

This video is from AirVenture, which is a fly-in expo. Randy Babbitt is one of the head officials for the FAA and he explains that the FAA needs money to meet the needs of the industry. He says that the planes now are more efficient, making them use less fuel which means that the fuel tax in effect now is less effective. He goes on to explain that the FAA needs to make up this deficit, but it does not know exactly where it is going to come from. This is important because it is a government official who is explaining the situation the FAA is in and what he thinks will happen.

Tennyson, E. A. (2014, March 4). White House budget contains user fee
despite opposition. Retrieved from http://www.aopa.org/News-
and-Video/All-News/2014/March/04/White-House-budget-
contains-user-fee-despite-opposition

The Obama White House's year 2015 spending plan includes a
provision of a $100-per-flight user fee to underwrite air traffic
control. The Aircraft Owners and Pilots Association continues
to oppose such a surcharge. In addition, the House aviation sub-
committee sent a letter to the president, indicating bipartisan opposition of the user fee. "Your continued support for any proposal
to implement a per-flight-fee on commercial and general aviation
would only serve to undermine the strength of our aviation transportation system and the jobs that rely on this important segment
of our nation's economy," the letter warned. This article indicates
the Obama administration's continued support of user fees in the
face of substantial opposition.

Research Casebook on Climate Change

The following three readings provide enough information for you to write a
short essay about American attitudes toward climate change. You can supplement them, if your instructor wishes, with other Gallup polls (www.gallup.
com), the two articles mentioned in *The New York Times* reading, and other
texts you may find by searching your library's online databases or the Internet.

Situation: The same week in April 2014 that the United Nations' Intergovernmental Panel on Climate Change released a report warning of the potentially
severe adverse future effects of climate change, a Gallup research survey
showed most Americans having low levels of concern about the issue. Only
"a little more than a third [of Americans] say they worry 'a great deal' about
climate change or about global warming, putting these concerns at the bottom
of a list of eight environmental issues." Environmental factors scoring higher
levels on Gallup's worry list included water pollution, toxic waste, soil and water contamination, air pollution, extinction of plant and animal species, and
destruction of tropical rain forests.

Interestingly, according to the Gallup survey, education doesn't impact Americans' attitudes toward climate change, with postgraduates no more worried
than high school graduates about its effects. Rather, politics and age are the

defining factors. More than half of Democrats say they "worry about it a great deal," compared with 29% of independents and 16% of Republicans. Historically, Gallup polls indicate that Republicans are much more likely than Democrats or Independents to say "that concerns about global warming are exaggerated and that warming's effects will not affect them personally in their lifetimes." Young Americans aged 18 to 29 are "more worried about global warming than older adults, particularly those 50 and older."

Casebook Reading 1

Nearly 40% are "Concerned Believers" in global warming; others are mixed.

One in Four in U.S. Are Solidly Skeptical of Global Warming
by Lydia Saad

Published by Gallup, April 22, 2014

PRINCETON, NJ -- Over the past decade, Americans have clustered into three broad groups on global warming. The largest, currently describing 39% of U.S. adults, are what can be termed "Concerned Believers"—those who attribute global warming to human actions and are worried about it. This is followed by the "Mixed Middle," at 36%. And one in four Americans— the "Cool Skeptics"—are not worried about global warming much or at all.

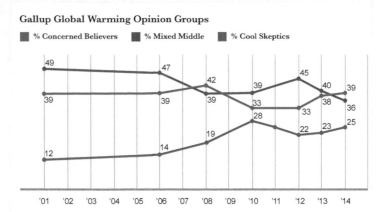

Gallup Global Warming Opinion Groups

■ % Concerned Believers   ■ % Mixed Middle   ■ % Cool Skeptics

The rate of Concerned Believers has varied some over the past decade and half, but is currently identical to the earliest estimate, from 2001. Over the same period of time, the ranks of Cool Skeptics have swelled, while the Mixed Middle—once the largest group—has declined modestly.

These groupings stem from a special "cluster" analysis of four questions that measure Americans' belief and concerns about human-induced global warming, all of which have been asked together on Gallup's annual Environment survey seven times since 2001. The latest results are from the March 6-9, 2014, Environment poll. However, the groupings derive from analysis of seven years of combined data.

Gallup has recently reported on a number of the individual trends included in the cluster analysis as part of its Climate Change series. This analysis provides a unique way of summarizing Americans' overall stance on global warming.

Perceived Cause of Global Warming Is Major Discriminator

Concerned Believers and Cool Skeptics are of entirely different mindsets when it comes to how much they worry about global warming. Concerned Believers say they worry "a great deal" or "fair amount" about the issue, while Cool Skeptics worry only "a little" or "not at all." Additionally, Concerned Believers think media reports about the issue are either correct or underestimated, while Cool Skeptics think they are exaggerated. And, most starkly, 100% of Concerned Believers say the rise in the Earth's temperature over the last century is due to the effects of pollution, while 100% of Cool Skeptics say it is due to natural changes in the environment. Finally, two-thirds of Concerned Believers believe global warming will pose a serious threat to their own way of life in the future, while 100% of Cool Skeptics disagree.

Americans in the Mixed Middle are individuals who hold a combination of views. For instance, some believe humans are the cause of the Earth's warming, but aren't worried about it. Others say global warming is a natural phenomenon, but that it will pose a serious risk in their lifetime. In one way or another, those in the Mixed Middle fail to line up with the orthodoxy on either side of the climate science issue.

Global Warming Clusters Differ by Gender, Age, and Politics

Concerned Believers are more likely to be women than men, 60% vs. 40%. Cool Skeptics skew even more strongly male—34% female vs. 66% male— while the Mixed Middle is just slightly more female than the overall U.S. adult population.

Global warming groups are also highly differentiated by age and politics. The majority of Concerned Believers are younger than 50, and identify as or lean toward the Democratic Party, whereas the majority of Cool Skeptics are 50 years or older and are more likely to identify as or lean Republican. Similarly, the plurality of believers are self-described liberals, while two-thirds of skeptics call themselves conservative.

Notably, education is not a strong discriminator for the polarized groups, as a little over one-third of each group has no college experience, roughly 30% has some, and about one-third has a college degree or some advanced education. On the other hand, lack of college education is a distinguishing characteristic of the Mixed Middle, with nearly half this group reporting no more than a high school diploma, and less than one-quarter finishing college.

Gallup Global Warming Opinion Groups—Detail of 2014 Attitudes March 6–9, 2014

	Concerned Believers %	Mixed Middle %	Cool Skeptics %
How much personally worry about global warming?			
A great deal	67	24	
A fair amount	33	26	
Only a little		31	31
Not at all		19	69
No opinion		1	
Seriousness of global warming in the news:			
Underestimated	58	30	
Correct	42	19	
Exaggerated		46	100
No opinion		5	
Cause of the rise in Earth's temperatures:			
Effects of pollution from human activities	100	51	
Natural changes in environment		41	100
No opinion		8	
Will global warming pose a serious threat to your way of life in your lifetime?			
Yes	65	30	
No	35	68	100
No opinion		2	

Bottom Line

Gallup's "cluster analysis" of Americans' views on four key global warming questions finds the public naturally breaking into three groups. The two at the extremes are near polar opposites of each other, disagreeing about the cause of global warming and how it's presented in the news, as well as having sharply different personal reactions to the issue.

Gallup Global Warming Opinion Groups—Demographic Profile
March 6–9, 2014

	Concerned Believers %	Mixed Middle %	Cool Skeptics %
Men	40	45	66
Women	60	55	34
18 to 29	23	27	10
30 to 49	39	29	34
50 to 64	25	21	33
65 and older	14	23	23
High school or less	37	48	35
Some college	29	28	30
College graduate	14	12	17
Postgraduate	19	10	18
Republicans/Lean Republican	18	42	80
Democrates/Lean Democratic	76	44	11
Conservative	18	33	65
Moderate	38	42	24
Liberal	42	23	9

The ranks of skeptics expanded between 2008 and 2010 due to the decline in concern about global warming as documented in Gallup's original trends. In particular, the percentage of Americans believing that global warming is caused by pollution from human activities dropped sharply in 2010. The same pattern has been seen with personal worry about global warming and the perception that the seriousness of the issue is exaggerated in the news. All of these findings are likely linked to the high profile «Climategate" controversy that emerged in late 2009, raising questions about the objectivity of some leading climate science researchers, as well as the legitimacy of some of their findings.

The broader, and perhaps more important, point is that even while skepticism rose—causing a corresponding increase in the percentage of Americans who can be categorized as "Cool Skeptics"—the percentage of "Concerned

Believers" has recovered to pre-Climategate levels, while the Mixed Middle has dwindled. As with many issues in the past decade, Americans' views have grown more polarized.

Survey Methods

Results for this Gallup poll are based on telephone interviews conducted March 6-9, 2014, on with a random sample of 1,048 adults, aged 18 and older, living in all 50 U.S. states and the District of Columbia.

For results based on the total sample of national adults, the margin of sampling error is ±4 percentage points at the 95% confidence level.

Interviews are conducted with respondents on landline telephones and cellular phones, with interviews conducted in Spanish for respondents who are primarily Spanish-speaking. Each sample of national adults includes a minimum quota of 50% cellphone respondents and 50% landline respondents, with additional minimum quotas by time zone within region. Landline and cellular telephone numbers are selected using random-digit-dial methods. Landline respondents are chosen at random within each household on the basis of which member had the most recent birthday.

Samples are weighted to correct for unequal selection probability, nonresponse, and double coverage of landline and cell users in the two sampling frames. They are also weighted to match the national demographics of gender, age, race, Hispanic ethnicity, education, region, population density, and phone status (cellphone only/landline only/both, and cellphone mostly). Demographic weighting targets are based on the most recent Current Population Survey figures for the aged 18 and older U.S. population. Phone status targets are based on the most recent National Health Interview Survey. Population density targets are based on the most recent U.S. census. All reported margins of sampling error include the computed design effects for weighting.

In addition to sampling error, question wording and practical difficulties in conducting surveys can introduce error or bias into the findings of public opinion polls.

Saad, Lydia. "One in Four in U.S. Are Solidly Skeptical of Global Warming." *Gallup,* 22 Apr. 2014, www.gallup.com/poll/168620/one-four-solidly-skeptical-global-warming.aspx.

IPCC: Greenhouse Gas Emissions Accelerate Despite Reduction Efforts

Many pathways to substantial emissions reductions are available, according to this second casebook reading.

Press Release by IPCC, April 13, 2014

BERLIN, 13 April 2014—A new report by the Intergovernmental Panel on Climate Change (IPCC) shows that global emissions of greenhouse gases have risen to unprecedented levels despite a growing number of policies to reduce climate change. Emissions grew more quickly between 2000 and 2010 than in each of the three previous decades.

According to the Working Group III contribution to the IPCC's Fifth Assessment Report, it would be possible, using a wide array of technological measures and changes in behaviour, to limit the increase in global mean temperature to two degrees Celsius above pre-industrial levels. However, only major institutional and technological change will give a better than even chance that global warming will not exceed this threshold.

The report, entitled Climate Change 2014: Mitigation of Climate Change, is the third of three Working Group reports, which, along with a Synthesis Report due in October 2014, constitute the IPCC's Fifth Assessment Report on climate change. Working Group III is led by three Co-Chairs: Ottmar Edenhofer from Germany, Ramón Pichs-Madruga from Cuba, and Youba Sokona from Mali.

"Climate policies in line with the two degrees Celsius goal need to aim for substantial emission reductions," Edenhofer said. "There is a clear message from science: To avoid dangerous interference with the climate system, we need to move away from business as usual."

Scenarios show that to have a likely chance of limiting the increase in global mean temperature to two degrees Celsius, means lowering global greenhouse gas emissions by 40 to 70 percent compared with 2010 by mid-century, and to near-zero by the end of this century. Ambitious mitigation may even require removing carbon dioxide from the atmosphere.

Scientific literature confirms that even less ambitious temperature goals would still require similar emissions reductions.

For the report, about 1200 scenarios from scientific literature have been analyzed. These scenarios were generated by 31 modelling teams around the world to explore the economic, technological and institutional prerequisites and implications of mitigation pathways with different degrees of ambition.

"Many different pathways lead to a future within the boundaries set by the two degrees Celsius goal," Edenhofer said. "All of these require substantial investments. Avoiding further delays in mitigation and making use of a broad variety of technologies can limit the associated costs."

Estimates of the economic costs of mitigation vary widely. In business-as-usual scenarios, consumption grows by 1.6 to 3 percent per year. Ambitious mitigation would reduce this growth by around 0.06 percentage points a year. However, the underlying estimates do not take into account economic benefits of reduced climate change.

Since the last IPCC assessment report, published in 2007, a wealth of new knowledge about climate change mitigation has emerged. The authors of the new, fifth Working Group III report have included about 10,000 references to scientific literature in 16 chapters.

Stabilizing greenhouse gas concentrations in the atmosphere requires emissions reductions from energy production and use, transport, buildings, industry, land use, and human settlements. Mitigation efforts in one sector determine the needs in others.

Cutting emissions from electricity production to near zero is a common feature of ambitious mitigation scenarios. But using energy efficiently is also important.

"Reducing energy use would give us more flexibility in the choice of low-carbon energy technologies, now and in the future. It can also increase the cost-effectiveness of mitigation measures," Pichs-Madruga said. Since publication of the Fourth Assessment Report there has been a focus on climate policies designed to increase co-benefits and reduce adverse side-effects.

Land is another key component for the 2°C goal. Slowing deforestation and planting forests have stopped or even reversed the increase in emissions from land use.

Through afforestation, land could be used to draw carbon dioxide from the atmosphere. This could also be achieved by combining electricity production from biomass and carbon dioxide capture and storage. However, as of today this combination is not available at scale, permanent underground carbon dioxide storage faces challenges and the risks of increased competition for land need to be managed.

"The core task of climate change mitigation is decoupling greenhouse gas emissions from the growth of economies and population," Sokona said. "Through providing energy access and reducing local air pollution, many mitigation measures can contribute to sustainable development."

"Climate change is a global commons problem," said Edenhofer. "International cooperation is key for achieving mitigation goals. Putting in place the international institutions needed for cooperation is a challenge in itself."

The Working Group III report consists of the Summary for Policymakers released today, a more detailed Technical Summary, the underlying 16 chapters, and three annexes. Working Group III chapter teams were formed by 235 authors and 38 review editors from 57 countries, and 180 experts provided additional input as contributing authors. More than 800 experts reviewed drafts of the report and submitted comments.

"The IPCC has been able to recruit from a diverse and immensely accomplished team of authors who are the leading experts in their respective fields," said Rajendra Pachauri, Chairman of the IPCC.

"I am grateful to the many contributors who have provided their time and talent for the preparation of this report. Their work has enabled the IPCC to cover a broad perspective while assessing climate change mitigation on a comprehensive basis," he said. "The Working Group III report is a valuable input to the Synthesis Report, which is to be completed in October 2014. I am also certain that the contents of the report will be used productively in the negotiations under the UNFCCC."

The Working Group III Summary for Policymakers, full report and further information are available at www.mitigation2014.org and www.ipcc.ch. The full report will be posted on these websites on Tuesday 15 April.

Notes for editors

The Intergovernmental Panel on Climate Change is the international body for assessing the science related to climate change. It was set up in 1988 by the World Meteorological Organization and the United Nations Environment Programme to provide policymakers with regular assessments of the scientific basis of climate change, its impacts and future risks, and options for adaptation and mitigation.

Working Group III, which assesses options for the mitigation of climate change, is co-chaired by Ottmar Edenhofer, Potsdam Institute for Climate Impact Research, Ramón Pichs-Madruga, Centre for World Economy Studies, and Youba Sokona, South Centre. The Technical Support Unit of Working Group III is hosted by the Potsdam Institute for Climate Impact Research and funded by the government of Germany.

At the 28th Session of the IPCC held in April 2008, the members of the IPCC decided to prepare a Fifth Assessment Report (AR5). A Scoping Meeting was convened in July 2009 to develop the scope and outline of the AR5. The resulting outlines for the three Working Group contributions to the AR5 were approved at the 31st Session of the IPCC in October 2009.

The Working Group III (WGIII) contribution to the Fifth Assessment Report of the IPCC, titled Climate Change 2014: Mitigation of Climate Change, assesses the options for mitigating climate change and their underlying technological, economic and institutional requirements. It transparently lays out risks, uncertainty and ethical foundations of climate change mitigation policies on the global, national and sub-national level, investigates mitigation measures for all major sectors and assesses investment and finance issues.

Working Group I of the IPCC released the Summary for Policymakers of its report, on the physical science basis of climate change, in September 2013, and published the full report in January 2014. Working Group II released its report, on impacts, adaptation and vulnerability, on 31 March 2014. The Fifth Assessment Report will be completed by a Synthesis Report to be finalized in October.

IPCC: Greenhouse Gas Emissions Accelerate Despite Reduction Efforts. IPCC Intergovernmental Panel on Climate Change, 13 Apr. 2014, www.ipcc.ch/pdf/ar5/pr_wg3/20140413_pr_pc_wg3_en.pdf.

Casebook Reading 3

This scientific perspective suggests catastrophic global climate change begins with ice sheet collapse in Antarctica.

Scientists Warn of Rising Oceans as Antarctic Ice Melts

by Justin Gillis and Kenneth Chang

Published in *The New York Times,* May 12, 2014

The collapse of large parts of the ice sheet in West Antarctica appears to have begun and is almost certainly unstoppable, with global warming accelerating the pace of the disintegration, two groups of scientists reported Monday.

The finding, which had been feared by some scientists for decades, means that a rise in global sea level of at least 10 feet may now be inevitable. The rise may continue to be relatively slow for at least the next century or so, the scientists said, but sometime after that it will probably speed up so sharply as to become a crisis.

"This is really happening," said Thomas P. Wagner, who runs NASA's programs on polar ice and helped oversee some of the research. "There's nothing to stop it now. But you are still limited by the physics of how fast the ice can flow."

Two papers scheduled for publication this week, in the journals *Science* and *Geophysical Research Letters,* attempt to make sense of an accelerated flow of glaciers seen in parts of West Antarctica in recent decades.

Both papers conclude that warm water upwelling from the ocean depths has most likely triggered an inherent instability that makes the West Antarctic ice sheet vulnerable to a slow-motion collapse. And one paper concludes that factors some scientists had hoped might counteract such a collapse will not do so.

The new finding appears to be the fulfillment of a prediction made in 1978 by an eminent glaciologist, John H. Mercer of the Ohio State University. He outlined the uniquely vulnerable nature of the West Antarctic ice sheet and warned that the rapid human release of greenhouse gases posed "a threat of disaster." He was assailed at the time, but in recent years scientists have been watching with growing concern as events have unfolded in much the way Dr. Mercer predicted. (He died in 1987.)

Scientists said the ice sheet was not melting because of warmer air temperatures, but rather because of the relatively warm water, which is naturally occurring, from the ocean depths. That water is being pulled upward and toward the ice sheet by intensification of the winds around Antarctica.

Most scientists in the field see a connection between the stronger winds and human-caused global warming, but they say other factors are likely at work, too. Natural variability of climate may be one of them. Another may be the ozone hole over Antarctica, caused by an entirely different environmental problem, the human release of ozone-destroying gases.

Whatever the mix of causes, they appear to have triggered a retreat of the ice sheet that can no longer be stopped, even if the factors drawing in the warmer water were to reverse suddenly, the scientists said. At this point, a decrease in the melt rate back to earlier levels would be "too little, too late to stabilize the ice sheet," said Ian Joughin, a glaciologist at the University of Washington and lead author of the new paper in Science. "There's no stabilization mechanism."

The basic problem is that much of the West Antarctic ice sheet sits below sea level in a kind of bowl-shaped depression [in] the earth. As Dr. Mercer outlined in 1978, once the part of the ice sheet sitting on the rim of the bowl melts and the ice retreats into deeper water, it becomes unstable and highly vulnerable to further melting.

Richard B. Alley, a climate scientist at Pennsylvania State University who was not involved in the new research but has studied the polar ice sheets for decades, said he found the new papers compelling. Though he has long feared the possibility of ice-sheet collapse, when he learned of the new findings, "it shook me a little bit," Dr. Alley said.

He added that while a large rise of the sea may now be inevitable from West Antarctica, continued release of greenhouse gases will almost certainly make the situation worse. The heat-trapping gases could destabilize other parts of Antarctica as well as the Greenland ice sheet, causing enough sea-level rise that many of the world's coastal cities would eventually have to be abandoned.

Gillis, Justin, and Kenneth Chang. "Scientists Warn of Rising Oceans From Polar Melt." *The New York Times,* 12 May 2014, www.nytimes.com/2014/05/13/science/earth/collapse-of-parts-of-west-antarctica-ice-sheet-has-begun-scientists-say.html.

Synthesizing Casebook Sources

How can Americans ignore the effects of global trends that have led to melting of the polar ice caps and rising oceans, as well as fluctuations in regional temperatures and precipitation? Perhaps it is because the issue is complex and interrelated with other factors. *The New York Times* article in the casebook, "Scientists Warn of Rising Oceans as Antarctic Ice Melts," points out that the melting of the West Antarctic ice sheet is not happening because of warmer air temperatures but because of naturally occurring warmer water rising from the ocean depths. While scientists think there is a connection between global warming due to human-caused greenhouse gases and the increasing winds that pull the warm water upward, most do not attribute the dramatic slow-motion collapse of the Antarctic ice sheet totally to human causes.

The three articles in the research casebook provide you with an opportunity to develop an argument that is more sophisticated than taking an extreme view, such as "Global warming will lead to widespread calamities due to rising water" or "There is no such thing as global warming." Your audience is more likely to listen to what you have to say if you look for common ground and acknowledge the complexities of the issue.

The three readings give you an opportunity to synthesize what scientists are saying about the factors causing the West Antarctic ice sheet to melt with the Gallup poll about American attitudes toward global warming and the IPCC press release about accelerating greenhouse gas emissions. The key to a more sophisticated working thesis, in this case, may be noticing that Americans' low score on worrying about climate change (about one-third of the population, according to the Gallup poll) is more understandable when you keep in mind what the *Times'* article asserts about the complexity of the issue.

Activity 7.14 • Discuss the Casebook on Climate Change

Use stasis theory or one of the other prewriting techniques in Chapter 4, Inventing Rhetorically, to discover the critical points in the argument over climate change in a discussion with your small group.

Activity 7.15 • Develop a Working Thesis on Climate Change

In your group, develop a working thesis for a short essay on climate change based on the three casebook readings. Refer to the section in Chapter 5 about composing a thesis.

Explore

Activity 7.16 • **Collect More Information about Climate Change**

▪ Outline what additional information you could possibly collect from primary and secondary research for a short essay about climate change. You would not necessarily use all of these avenues of research. Rather, give some thought to options and decide if they would be useful.

▪ Work through the section in this chapter, Make a Research Plan, to identify academic sources on climate change.

▪ Could you interview a local meteorologist or researcher on climate change? What could you learn about the impact on local weather that would strengthen your essay?

▪ What about doing a short survey of your classmates and friends to determine their attitudes toward the issue? What would that add to your research collection?

Compose

Activity 7.17 • **Write a Short Essay about Climate Change**

As directed by your instructor, write a short essay (750 words to 1200 words) about climate change. Cite your sources using APA or MLA style, whichever your instructor prefers. If you decide to use the Casebook readings, you can import the MLA citation at the end of each reading into your Works Cited.

Avoid Plagiarism

Plagiarism is defined as follows by the Writing Program Administrators (WPA), a group of English professors who direct college composition programs: "In an instructional setting, plagiarism occurs when a writer deliberately uses someone else's language, ideas, or other original (not common-knowledge) material without acknowledging its source." A keyword here is "deliberately." Instructors, however, may have difficulty distinguishing between accidental and deliberate plagiarism. The burden is upon you as the writer to give credit where credit is due. Review these examples of plagiarism.

▪ Turning in a paper that was written by someone else as your own. This includes obtaining a paper from an Internet term paper mill.

▪ Copying a paper or any part of a paper from a source without acknowledging the source in the proper format.

▪ Paraphrasing materials from a source without documentation.

▪ Copying materials from a text but treating it as your own, leaving out quotation marks and acknowledgement.

The guidelines provided in Table 7.1 can help you identify when it is appropriate to give credit to others in your writing.

Table 7.1 • Choosing When to Give Credit

Need to Document	No Need to Document
• When you are using or referring to somebody else's words or ideas from a magazine, book, newspaper, song, TV program, movie, web page, computer program, letter, advertisement, or any other medium. • When you use information gained through interviewing another person. • When you copy the exact words or a "unique phrase" from somewhere. • When you reprint any diagrams, illustrations, charts, and/or pictures. • When you use ideas given to you by others, whether in conversation or through email.	• When you are writing your own experiences, your own observations, your own insights, your own thoughts, or your own conclusions about a subject. • When you are using "common knowledge"—folklore, common-sense observations, or shared information within your field of study or cultural group. • When you are compiling generally accepted facts. • When you are writing up your own experimental results.

The Online Writing Lab (*OWL*) at Purdue University provides an excellent handout on avoiding plagiarism, including the information about when to give credit to sources in the table above. See owl.english.purdue.edu.

Reading 7.3

Anatomy of a Fake Quotation
by Megan McArdle

In this article, originally published in The Atlantic, *Megan McArdle tells the story of how a fake Martin Luther King, Jr. quote was created and posted on the Internet.*

Yesterday, I saw a quote from Martin Luther King Jr. fly across my Twitter feed: "I mourn the loss of thousands of precious lives, but I will not rejoice in the death of one, not even an enemy."—Martin Luther King, Jr. I was about to retweet it, but I hesitated. It didn't sound right. After some Googling, I determined that it was probably fake, which I blogged about last night.

Here's the story of how that quote was created.

It turns out I was far too uncharitable in my search for a motive behind the fake quote. I assumed that someone had made it up on purpose. I was wrong.

Had I seen the quote on Facebook, rather than Twitter, I might have guessed at the truth. On the other hand, had I seen it on Facebook, I might not have realized it was fake, because it was appended to a long string of genuine speech from MLK Jr. Here's the quote as most people on Facebook saw it:

> I will mourn the loss of thousands of precious lives, but I will not rejoice in the death of one, not even an enemy. Returning hate for hate multiplies hate, adding deeper darkness to a night already devoid of stars. Darkness cannot drive out darkness; only light can do that. Hate cannot drive out hate, only love can do that.

Everything except the first sentence is found in King's book, *Strength to Love*, and seems to have been said originally in a 1957 sermon he gave on loving your enemies. Unlike the first quotation, it does sound like King, and it was easy to assume that the whole thing came from him.

So how did they get mixed together?

Thanks to Jessica Dovey, a Facebook user, that's how. And contrary to my initial assumption, it wasn't malicious. Ms. Dovey, a 24-year-old Penn State graduate who now teaches English to middle schoolers in Kobe, Japan, posted a very timely and moving thought on her Facebook status, and then followed it up with the Martin Luther King, Jr., quote.

> I will mourn the loss of thousands of precious lives, but I will not rejoice in the death of one, not even an enemy. "Returning hate for hate multiplies hate, adding deeper darkness to a night already devoid of stars. Darkness cannot drive out darkness; only light can do that. Hate cannot drive out hate, only love can do that." MLK Jr.

At some point, someone cut and pasted the quote, and—for reasons that I, appropriately chastened, will not speculate on—stripped out the quotation marks. Eventually, the mangled quotation somehow came to the attention of Penn Jillette, of Penn and Teller fame. He tweeted it to his 1.6 million Facebook followers, and the rest was Internet history. Twenty-four hours later, the quote brought back over 9,000 hits on Google.

The quote also went viral on Twitter, and since the 140-character limit precluded quoting the whole thing, people stripped it down to the most timely and appropriate part: the fake quote. That's where I saw it.

The speed of dissemination is breathtaking: mangled to meme in less than two days. Also remarkable is how defensive people got about the quote—though admirably, not Penn Jillette, who posted an update as soon as it was called to his attention. The thread for my post now has over 600 comments, and by my rough estimate, at least a third of them are people posting that I need to print a retraction, because of the nonfake part of the quotation. But I didn't quote that part; I was only interested in the too-timely bit I'd seen twittered.

Even more bizarrely, several of these readers, who clearly hadn't read too closely, started claiming that I had retroactively edited the post to make them look like idiots, even going so far as to scrub all the versions in RSS readers so that they, too, showed that I was talking about the truncated version. Even if you think I am the sort of low scoundrel who would do such a thing, this seems like a lot of work for not much reward. I'm not sure whether it's even possible to completely scrub an RSS feed, but even if it were, I'd have had to notify my bosses, who tend to frown on retroactive editing.

Meanwhile, several other people began confabulating a provenance for it. *Obviously*, he was talking about Vietnam, and what sort of moral midget couldn't understand that? This even though the latest citation for the true part of the quote was a book published in 1967, which would have been written earlier than that, when U.S. casualties in Vietnam were still relatively low. Moreover, the ambiguity with which the antiwar movement viewed the North Vietnamese makes "enemy" a hard fit.

It is, of course, not strange that people might look for possible confirming facts. What's strange is that they were sure enough of themselves to make fun of anyone who disagreed. Yet several other people on the comment thread had linked to a version of the quotation from 1957. I am second to no one in my admiration for Dr. King. But I do not think that he prefigured Vietnam by seven years.

Which only illustrates why fake quotes are so widely dispersed. Though one commenter accused me of trying to make people feel stupid for having propagated the quote, that was hardly my intention—we've all probably repeated more fake quotations than real ones. Fake quotations are pithier, more dramatic, more on point, than the things people usually say in real life. It's not surprising that they are often the survivors of the evolutionary battle for mindshare. One person actually posted a passage which integrated the fake quotation into the larger section of the book from which the original MLK words were drawn.

We become invested in these quotes because they say something important about us—and they let us feel that those emotions were shared by great figures in history. We naturally search for reasons that they could have said it—that they could have felt like us—rather than looking for reasons to disbelieve. If we'd put the same moving words in Hitler's mouth, everyone would have been a lot more skeptical. But while this might be a lesson about the need to be skeptical, I don't think there's anything stupid about wanting to be more like Dr. King.

Ms. Dovey's status now reads: "has apparently gone back in time and put her words into one of MLK's sermons. I'm somewhere between nervous and embarrassed and honored . . . I really hope I haven't said anything he wouldn't agree with . . . Only what I feel in my heart."

A lot of us were feeling the same thing—and I think it's clear from his writings that MLK would have too. There's no reason to be embarrassed about that.

Activity 7.18 • Discuss "Anatomy of a Fake Quotation"

In your small group, discuss the following questions.

1. How was the fake quotation created? How did it spread on the Internet?

2. Note the speed and the reach of the fake quote. What does Megan McArdle suggest the story of the fake quote says about why fake quotes can become so widely disbursed?

3. What is your reaction to this story of the fake quotation?

Activity 7.19 • Write on Your Blog

In your blog, write a summary and a response to a source you might use to research your topic. Is it useful for your research? Why or why not?

Activity 7.20 • Write in Your Commonplace Book

Copy a quote from a source that you think makes a critical point about the argument paper you are writing. Then comment about the quote—what does it mean and why is it important?

appendix
Citing Sources

EasyBib is one of the citation generators available on the Internet through a keyword search. Most offer a free version, with upgraded features for a subscription fee. Note that *EasyBib* encourages users to double-check their entries both for content and form. Citation generators assist with documentation format, but they cannot eliminate errors.

Evolving Formats of Document Citation

The widespread use of the Internet for research is changing the way sources are cited in documents. This is certainly true of electronic sources because of the ephemeral nature of web pages. Although documents may look like print sources (often with title, author, and publication information), they also share a characteristic of live performances in that you can access them after they have occurred only if you can find a recorded version. Once web pages are removed from a website, you cannot view them unless they have been archived. Also, web pages can be updated or changed, while retaining the same appearance, which makes systematic documentation difficult.

In the past, Modern Language Association (MLA) style recommended excluding the URL (web address) of web page documents in the works-cited list because URLs are so prone to change. However, more recently MLA has taken the position that including that information adds value because even outdated URLs can be useful in tracking down information on the web. Therefore, MLA's eighth edition recommends that students include URLs in the works-cited list unless the instructor prefers they do not. When providing the URL for a web page in your list, omit "http://" or "https//" and then type the web address followed by a period. For example, the web page for *The New York Times* would be nytimes.com.

Due to the ever-changing nature of the web, some web publications include stable URLs (sometimes called permalinks), while others sometimes include digital object identifiers (DOIs). Permalinks, as the name suggests, do not change, and DOIs remain attached to a source regardless of changes made to their respective URLs. So, whenever possible, it is preferrable to include either a permalink or DOI instead of a URL when citing a web source. While a permalink will be formatted the same way as a URL, an entry that includes a DOI would appear thus:

Chan, Evans. "Postmodernism and Hong Kong Cinema." *Postmodern Culture,*
     vol. 10, no. 3, May 2000. *Project Muse,* doi:10.1353/pmc.2000.0021.

American Psychological Association (APA) style suggests including the elements of a citation in the same order as you would for a print source, adding information about electronic retrieval after the standard information. Like MLA, APA suggests giving the DOI whenever possible and the permalink or the URL of the item being cited if the DOI is not available.

Interestingly, the prevalence of Internet sources is changing the way all sources are cited. MLA style previously recommended adding the word "print" after print-based source citation information and "web" after the citation of a source accessed on the Internet; however, that is no longer the case. In the eighth edition of their style guide, MLA has streamlined the citation process to shift the focus from publication medium to citing simple elements common to most sources.

When You Have a Choice of Electronic Source Format, Choose a PDF

When searching for articles in online databases or web pages, you may be offered a choice of formats: HTML or PDF. If you have that choice, select the PDF because it will have page numbers. Essentially, a PDF document reproduces print documents exactly, so that reading one is just like reading the original article except that it is not surrounded by the other content of the original publication.

If you are utilizing electronic documents as sources and they are not PDFs, you may be missing several of the usual elements of document citation, such as author name, publisher or sponsoring organization, page numbers, and even a title. In this case, give as much information about these traditional elements of citation as you can, and review the examples that follow for help with formatting. As an easy rule of thumb, though, keep this in mind: The more of the traditional elements used to classify and place a document within the scholarly world that are missing, the less likely the text is to be credible and reliable. If readers cannot tell where the information originated, how are they to trust it?

MLA Style

For MLA style, you may refer to the *MLA Handbook for Writers of Research Papers,* eighth edition and the MLA website, www.mla.org. *The Purdue Owl,* owl.purdue.english.edu, is also an excellent reference.

A research paper written in MLA style should be double-spaced, with margins set at one inch on all sides. Choose a standard typeface such as Times New Roman in 12 pt. type.

Beginning on the first page, insert page numbers on the upper right-hand side of the page preceded by your last name. For example, if your last name is Smith, then "Smith 1" will appear in the upper right corner of the first page.

Do not create a cover page unless your instructor specifies doing so. Instead, on the upper left-hand side of the first page, give your name, your instructor's name, the course, and the date. These items should all be flush left, double-spaced, and set on separate lines.

Double-space again and center the title. Follow the title with another double-space and indent the first line of text. Indent each paragraph. Note that you should not add any extra spaces between any of any of the elements described here. Your entire document should be uniformly double spaced with no extra spaces between any of the elements or paragraphs. This includes the works-cited list.

Bibliographic Documentation

In MLA style, bibliographic information appears either on the works-cited page or in an Annotated Bibliography. The title, either "Works Cited" or Annotated Bibliography, should appear centered on the top margin of the last page of a researched essay. The "Works Cited" page should be double-spaced with no extra line spacing between entries. The first line of each entry begins at the left margin, and all subsequent lines of a particular entry are indented 1/2 inch from the left margin. All entries should be in alphabetical order. The Annotated Bibliography is formatted like the "Works Cited" page with the addition of an annotation or description of the source in a paragraph following the citation.

Key Changes in MLA's Eighth Edition

Citation formatting is standard and no longer depends on source type.
Previously, MLA citation format was based on the type of source being cited. Newspaper citations were formatted differently than book chapters, and both were formatted differently if accessed via the web rather than in print. As previously mentioned, the fluid nature of information availability and access fueled by the web makes individual citation formats unfeasible, so now there is one universal format for all source types.

Citations now include "containers."
Just like it sounds, "containers" are what "hold" the source. For example, if you read a short story in an anthology, the anthology is the container. Likewise, if you watch a television show on Hulu, Hulu is the container. In each instance, you should include the title of the source (the short story or television show) and its container (the anthology title or Hulu) in the citation.

The abbreviations, "vol." and "no." have been added to magazine and journal article citations to refer to volume and issue numbers.

As previously discussed, MLA now recommends inclusion of URLs in citations.

What has not changed?
The overall principles of citing and plagiarism remain unchanged as do the use and format of in-text citations.

The Core Elements

MLA's eighth edition constructs works-cited entries based on a set of simple core elements found in most source types, both digital and print. If a given element is not relevant to the type of source you're citing (e.g. page numbers on a web page) it should be omitted from your "Works Cited" page. Each element is followed by the punctuation mark shown below, and the last element should be followed by a period.

(1)Author. (2)Title of Source. (3)Title of Container, (4)Other Contributors, (5)Version, (6)Number, (7)Publisher, (8)Publication Date, (9)Location.

Author

The term "author" spans a range of possibilities in MLA 8. It refers to the person or group primarily responsible for producing the work or the aspect of the work you focus on in your research. The individual who fits the author role for your Works Cited entry, then, may actually be an editor, translator, performer, creator, adapter, director, illustrator, or narrator. The key question to consider when determining who to list as your author is: "Who or what aspect in this work am I focusing on in my discussion?"

When a work has one author, begin the entry with the author's last name, followed by a comma and the rest of the name, followed by a period. When an entry has two authors, list the primary author first following the single author format, then add the second author's name with the first name first followed by "and":

Greengard, Samuel. *The Internet of Things*. MITP, 2015.

Baron, Naomi S. "Redefining Reading: The Impact of Digital Communication Media." *PMLA,* vol. 128, no. 1 Jan. 2013, pp. 193-200.

Selby, Jan, and Clemens Hoffman. *Divided Environments: Rethinking Water Security, Climate Change and Conflict*. Tauris, 2014.

If your source has three or more authors, include only the first name that appears followed by a comma and "et al.":

Burdick, Anne, et al. *Digital_Humanities*. MIT P, 2012.

Two or More Selections from the Same Collection or Anthology

> **Note**: To avoid repetition on the list of Works Cited, cite an anthology or reader as a separate entry. Then cross-reference entries to the anthology as in the example:

Burns, Gary. "Marilyn Manson and the Apt Pupils of Littleton." Petracca and Sorapure, pp. 284-90.

Fox, Roy. "Salespeak." Petracca and Sorapure, pp. 56-72.

Petracca, Michael and Madeleine Sorapure, editors. *Common Culture: Reading and Writing About American Popular Culture*. 5th ed., Pearson, 2007.

Note: Alphabetize each entry among other entries on the works-cited page. Do not group the entries from the anthology together unless they fall next to one another alphabetically. Also, remember that you will have no parenthetical citation referencing the editors Petracca and Sorapure. You should cite Burns and Fox in the parenthetical citations in your paper.

Other Authors

As mentioned above, the contributor who fits the author role may not be the one responsible for writing the source content. For example, if you're discussing the choices made by a team of editors regarding what to include in an anthology, collection, or reader, you would list the editors in the author position, as in this example:

Mennuti, Rosemary B., et al., editors. *Cognitive-Behavioral Interventions: A Handbook for Practice*. Routledge, 2006.

Similarly, when discussing works in translation, the author will depend on whether you're discussing the translation itself (in which case you would list the translator in the author position as in the first example following) or the actual work (in which case the translators appear as "Other Contributors" as outlined in the second example):

Pevear, Richard, and Larissa Volokhonsky, translators. *Crime and Punishment*. By Feodor Dostoevsky, Vintage eBooks, 1993.

Dostoevsky, Feodor. Crime and Punishment. Translated by Richard Pevear and Larissa Volokhonsky, Vintage eBooks, 1993.

Media productions such as film and television will also require creative consideration of the author element. Again, the person or people you choose to list in the author position will depend on the aspect of media on which you focus in your research. If you're discussing Sarah Michelle Gellar's performance as Buffy in *Buffy the Vampire Slayer,* your entry would appear thus:

Gellar, Sarah Michelle, performer. *Buffy the Vampire Slayer.* Mutant Enemy, 1997-2003.

However, if you're discussing the same television show as part of Joss Whedon's body of creative work, you would cite it thus:

Whedon, Joss, creator. *Buffy the Vampire Slayer.* Mutant Enemy, 1997-2003.

Lastly, if you're writing about the series in general without focusing on its creator or a particular actor, you would exclude the author element and begin your entry with the title of the work as follows:

Buffy the Vampire Slayer. Created by Joss Whedon, performance by Sarah Michelle Gellar, Mutant Enemy, 1997-2003.

Pseudonyms and online usernames or "handles" also fill the "author" element as in the following examples:

@persiankiwi. "We have report of large street battles in east & west of Tehran now - #Iranelection." *Twitter,* 23 June 2009, 11:15 a.m., twitter.com/ persiankiwi/status/2298106072.

Stendhal. *The Red and the Black.* Translated by Roger Gard, Penguin Books, 2002.

Tribble, Ivan. "Bloggers Need Not Apply." *The Chronicle of Higher Education,* 8 July 2005, chronicle.com/article/Bloggers-Need-Not-Apply/45022.

The term, "author," does not have to refer to a person. A source may be created by a corporate author such as a government agency, or other kind of organization. In such cases, your works-cited entry would appear thus:

United Nations. *Consequences of Rapid Population Growth in Developing Countries.* Taylor and Francis, 1991.

If a source does not include or refer to an author, simply skip the author element. Do not list the author as "Anonymous."

Beowulf. Translated by Alan Sullivan and Timothy Murphy, edited by Sarah Anderson, Pearson, 2004.

Title of Source

The next element of your works-cited entry is the title of your source. Include the full source title and any subtitles exactly as they appear in the work. The only exception to this is in regards to capitalization and the colon between the main title and subtitle, which are standardized. A title of a part of a longer work, such as a book chapter or web page should be placed in quotation marks.

Thompson, Jason. "Magic for a People Trained in Pragmatism: Kenneth Burke, and the Early 9/11 Oratory of George W. Bush." *Rhetoric Review,* vol. 30, no. 4, 2011, pp. 350-71.

Titles of longer, or "self contained," works such as whole books or web sites should be italicized. Likewise, titles of "container" works such as journals, magazines, and anthologies should be italicized.

Macfie, A. L. *Orientalism: A Reader.* New York UP, 2000. *Google Books*, books. google.com/books?id=0FrJAwAAQBAJ.

Variant Title Forms

Untitled Sources. If your source is untitled, provide a description, neither italicized nor in quotation marks, to fill the title element. Use sentence rather than title capitalization as in the example below:

Mackintosh, Charles Rennie. Chair of stained oak. 1897-1900, Victoria and Albert Museum, London.

Your description might contain the title of another work if it's commenting on or responding to that work. This will be the case if you wish to use comments on a blog post or other such interactions as sources as in these examples:

Jeane. Comment on "The Reading Brain: Differences between Digital and Print." *So Many Books,* 25 Apr. 2013, 10:30 p.m., somanybooksblog. com/2013/04/25/the-reading-brain-differences-between-digital-and-print/#comment-83030.

Mackin, Joseph. Review of *The Pleasures of Reading in an Age of Distraction,* by Alan Jacobs. *New York Journal of Books,* 2 June 2011, www. nyjournalofbooks.com/book-review/pleasures-reading-age-distraction.

Short untitled messages, such as Tweets, are cited by typing the full text of the message, without any changes, in the title element, enclosed in quotation marks.

@persiankiwi. "We have report of large street battles in east & west of Tehran now - #Iranelection." *Twitter,* 23 June 2009, 11:15 a.m., twitter.com/persionkiwi/status/2298106072.

To document an email, use the subject line as the title, and enclose it in quotation marks.

Boyle, Anthony T. "Re: Utopia." Received by Daniel J. Cahill, 21 June 1997.

Title of Container

If your source forms only a part of a larger whole, then that larger whole is considered the "container" that holds the source. The container title is usually italicized and it may be a book that is part of a larger collection, a periodical like a journal or magazine, a television series, or a web site, among other things.

Arabian, Soheila, and Vida Rahiminezhad. Review of *Americanah*, "Journey and Return: Visiting Unbelonging and Otherness in Adichie's Americanah." *Journal of UMP Social Sciences and Technology Management*, vol. 3, no. 3, 2015, pp. 536-41.

"Nested" Containers

Sources often have more than one container, each smaller container "nested" within a larger one. This is often the case especially with online sources. Perhaps you located your journal article through JSTOR, read a book of short stories on Google Books, or watched a television show through Netflix. Each of these instances is an example of a source being held in multiple containers. In your works-cited page, you should attempt to account for all the containers enclosing your source. To do this, you will simply add the core elements 3-9 (Title of Container through Location), omitting irrelevant or unavailable elements, to the end of the entry until all additional containers are accounted for. Remember that whatever element is last in each container should be followed by a period.

Pavienko, Sonia, and Christina Bojan. "Exercising Democracy in Universities: The Gap between Words and Actions." *AUDEM: The International Journal of Higher Education and Democracy*, vol. 4, 2013, pp. 26-37. *Project Muse*, muse.jhu.edu/article/557647.

In the above example, the first container is the journal, *AUDEM*, and the second is the journal database, Project Muse. Since the location is the last element in the first container, it is followed by a period. You'll note that, especially in the second container, many of the core elements are missing. Indeed, we only have the title and location for the second container, and this is fine. As noted above, simply omit those elements that are irrelevant to the container you're working with.

Other Contributors

Like the author element, other contributors encompass a wide range of possible roles. These are some of the most common descriptions you will use for this element:

adapted by	introduction by
directed by	narrated by
edited by	performance by
illustrated by	translated by

Chartier, Roger. *The Order of Books: Readers, Authors, and Libraries in Europe between the Fourteenth and Eighteenth Centuries.* Translated by Lydia G. Cochrane, Stanford UP, 1994.

If your contributor can't be described by one of the above phrases, you can express the role as a noun or noun phrase, followed by a comma. For example: general editor, or guest editor.

If a source has multiple contributors, as will often be the case with films and television shows, include the ones most relevant to your research. For example, if you're focusing on a particular episode of a television show as well as the performance of a key actor, you would cite your source as follows:

"Hush." *Buffy the Vampire Slayer,* created by Joss Whedon, performance by Sarah Michelle Gellar, season 4, episode 10, Mutant Enemy, 1999.

Version

If your source indicates that it's one version of a work released in multiple forms, include reference to that version in your citation. Book editions will likely be the most common versions you'll find:

The Bible. Authorized King James Version, Oxford UP, 1998.

Miller, Casey, and Kate Swift. *Words and Women.* Updated ed., HarperCollins Publishers, 1991.

Works in other media may also offer versions:

Scott, Ridley, director. *Blade Runner.* 1982. Performance by Harrison Ford, director's cut, Warner Bros., 1992.

Number

If your source is part of a numbered sequence, like a volume of a collection of books, or a journal, indicate the volume number:

Gustafsson, Amanda. "Beware the Invisible." *Papers from the Institute of Archaeology,* vol. 20, 2010, www.pia-journal.co.uk/articles/10.5334/pia.343/.

Often in the case of journals and some other periodicals, issues are not only in volumes but also in numbers:

Baron, Naomi S. "Redefining Reading: The Impact of Digital Communication Media." *PMLA,* vol. 128, no. 1, Jan. 2013, pp. 193-200.

Television series are also typically numbered by season and episode:

"Hush." *Buffy the Vampire Slayer,* created by Joss Whedon, performance by
Sarah Michelle Gellar, season 4, episode 10, Mutant Enemy, 1999.

Publisher

Publishers are the organizations primarily responsible for making a work avail-able to the public. If your source lists more than one publisher, and they seem to be given equal importance, list them both, separated by a forward slash (/).

Films and television series are often produced by multiple companies, so you should cite the organization primarily responsible for producing it. Web sites, also, are often associated with multiple companies or organizations, but the key publisher's name can often be found at the bottom of the home page or on the "About" page if one is available on the site. Below are a few examples of the different types of publishers you might cite in your works-cited list.

Jacobs, Alan. *The Pleasures of Reading in an Age of Distraction.* Oxford UP, 2011.

Gogh, Vincent van. *Cypresses.* 1889. *European Paintings,* The Metropolitan
Museum of Art, New York, www.metmuseum.org/art/collection/
search/437980.

Note the date, 1889, in the citation above for van Gogh's painting. This is an optional element in MLA 8, which is used to inform the reader of the year in which the piece was created. This element is useful when consulting works of art as well as literary works originally published in the early twentieth century or before. This element is always placed immediately following the title of the work and is, itself, followed by a period.

Publication Date

Sources may be associated with more than one publication date, especially those published online. When you have multiple dates associated with your source, cite the one that is most meaningful or relevant to your research. If you consult a work online that is also available in print, the only date you should concern your-self with is the online publication date, since you did not consult the print source. For the most part, the amount of information you provide for your date should depend on the amount given in your source. If your source lists month, day, year, and time, you should include all of these elements in your citation.

Wheaton, Wil. "Hello, World." *WIL WHEATON Dot NET.* 30 Sept. 2015,
wilwheaton.net/2015/09/hello-world/.

As with all other elements in MLA 8, the key to determining what date you include in your citation is the aspect of the source you're exploring as well as the version you consult. Especially in the case of film and television, you will need to use the date most closely associated with the version you consult and the research you're conducting. For example, if you consult an episode of a television series via the DVD set, your entry would look like this:

"Hush." *Buffy the Vampire Slayer: The Complete Fourth Season,* created by
Joss Whedon, performance by Sarah Michelle Gellar, episode 10, WB
Television Network, 2003, disc 3.

> **Note:** Notice in the above examples how the version of the television show being consulted also affects the title of the container and the publisher in comparison to how this source is cited in earlier examples.

Location

How you specify your source's location depends on the medium of publication. Some sources will have page numbers, some will not. Some sources will have web addresses, some will have Digital Object Identifiers (DOIs), and some will not. Additionally, physical objects, such as a piece of art viewed in a museum, will have actual, physical locations which you will need to specify in your Works Cited list.

In a print source or a PDF that offers page numbers, use "p." to indicate a single page and "pp." to indicate a range of pages. Provide URLs, permalinks, or DOIs for web sources unless your instructor prefers you leave these out. If you're citing a DVD or CD set, indicate the disc number in the location. If you're viewing a physical object, such as a piece of art, indicate the physical location of the piece (i.e. Museum of Modern Art, New York) for the location. Below are examples of each of these types of locations.

Adichie, Chimamanda Ngozi. "On Monday of Last Week." *The Thing around
Your Neck,* Alfred A. Knopf, 2009, pp. 74-94.

Visualizing Emancipation. Directed by Scott Nesbit and Edward L. Ayers, dsl.
richmond.edu/emancipation/.

"Hush." *Buffy the Vampire Slayer: The Complete Fourth Season,* created by
Joss Whedon, performance by Sarah Michelle Gellar, episode 10, WB
Television Network, 2003, disc 3.

Bearden, Romare. *The Train.* 1975, Museum of Modern Art, New York.

MLA Parenthetical (In-Text) Documentation

Parenthetical documentation refers to the process of citing sources within the text. Citing sources within the text is necessary for students to indicate when they are using words, thoughts, or ideas that are not their own but borrowed from an outside source. Whether students use a direct quote, a paraphrase, or a summary of the information, they must properly provide credit to the original author(s) of that source. Using appropriate sources for support and documenting these sources accurately adds to the credibility and value of a student's essay. The following examples provide guidelines for proper parenthetical documentation.

Direct Quote (three lines or less)

"Scientists estimate that the rangewide population of the San Joaquin kit fox prior to 1930 was 8,000 . . . " (Conover 44).

Direct Quote (more than three lines)

Conover's 2001 study of the San Joaquin kit fox found the following:

> For the most part, in the "real" world, kit foxes escape their predators and the high temperatures of their desert environment by spending the day underground in a den. In Bakersfield, they follow suit. Kit foxes move every couple of weeks to a new den. Moving to different dens may be one reason why they have persisted; the constantly changing abodes provided new places to hide. (199)

> **Note:** For a direct quote that is more than three lines, the passage should be indented 10 spaces and set as a block, as shown here.

Direct Quote When the Author Is Named in the Text

Hildebrand states that "generals of Alexander the Great brought news to Europe of vegetable wool which grew in tufts of trees in India" (144).

Information from Printed Source (but not a direct quote)

It is common to see an Osprey make its nest on an electric power pole (Askew 34).

Electronic Sources

Many electronic sources are not numbered with pages unless they are presented in a PDF file. If paragraphs are numbered, use numbers following the abbreviation, par. Most often the source will not have page, paragraph, section, or screen numbers. In this case, include no numbers in the parentheses. Instead, include the words that come first in the source's title.

(Lukasik, "Adding Control")

APA Style

For APA style, you will want to refer to the *Publication Manual of the American Psychological Association* and the website provided by the American Psychological Association, www.apastyle.org, which offers free tutorials for APA style. *The Purdue Owl* also offers excellent information at owl.english.purdue.edu.

APA specifies that your essay should be typed in 12 pt. Times New Roman type and double-spaced, with one-inch margins. In addition, APA style specifies the following general rules for formatting a paper or essay:

- Running heads—Create running heads for your page numbers, flush left, beginning on the title page. Also, on the title page, you should have a running head that reads like this:

  Running head: TITLE OF YOUR PAPER

  On succeeding pages, the flush left header should include only the title of your paper, not the words "Running Head."

- Title page—In addition to the running heads, your title page will contain the title of the paper (one- or two-line title), followed by your name on the second or third line, and then the name of your college on the next line, all centered.

- Unless your instructor specifies otherwise, the second page of your paper is a 150- to 200-word abstract that summarizes the major aspects of your paper.

- Begin your essay on the third page, after the running head, which is the title of your paper and the centered title. Indent each paragraph and double-space.

- At the end of your paper, include your References, which lists your sources according to APA citation style.

Bibliographic Documentation

In APA style, bibliographic documentation appears either in the References or the Annotated Bibliography. The title, either References or Annotated Bibliography, should appear centered on the top margin of the last page of a researched essay. The References or Annotated Bibliography page should be double-spaced with no extra line spacing between entries. The first line of each entry begins at the margin, and all subsequent lines of a particular entry are indented on the left margin five spaces for a References Page. All entries should be in alphabetical order. The Annotated Bibliography is formatted like the References page with the addition of an annotation or description of the source in a paragraph following each citation.

> **Note**: APA suggests that when you are citing a source from the web or an online database you should give the DOI (Digital Object Identifier) of the source in the References List. If the DOI is not available, you can give the URL (web address) for the text. APA does not require that you give the date you access a source on the Internet unless you have reason to believe that the text may change or disappear from the Internet. Also note that if you cite an entire website, simply include the website address in parentheses in the text with no entry in the References page. The following entries are typical citations for APA style. Examples are offered for both print, online, and database versions, when applicable.

Book

Greengard, S. (2015). *The internet of things* (The MIT Press Essential Knowledge Series). Boston, MA: MIT.

Book with Two Authors

Selby, J., & Hoffman, C. (2014). *Divided environments: Rethinking water security, climate change and conflict.* London, ENG: Tauris.

Book with Multiple Editors

Mennuti, R.B., Freeman, A., & Christner, R.W. (Eds.). (2006). *Cognitive-behavioral interventions in educational settings: A handbook for practice.* New York, NY: Routledge.

Online Edition of Book

Macfie, A. L. (2000). *Orientalism: A reader.* New York, NY: New York University Press. Retrieved from http://books.google.com

Scholarly Article in Print Journal

Thompson, J. (2011). Magic for a people trained in pragmatism: Kenneth
      Burke, and the early 9/11 Oratory of George W. Bush. *Rhetoric*
      Review, 30 (4), 350-371.

Scholarly Article Found in Online Database

Pavienko, S., & Bojan, C. (2013). Exercising democracy in universities: The
      gap between words and actions. *AUDEM: The International Journal*
      of Higher Education and Democracy, 4, 26-37.

      Note: APA does not suggest that you include the database
      name, as essays may be found in more than one database.

Scholarly Article with DOI from Journal Published Online

Gustafsson, A. (2010). Beware the invisible. *Papers from the Institute of*
      Archaeology, 20. http://doi.org/10.5334/pia343

      Note: This citation includes a DOI (digital object identifier),
      which provides a permanent way to locate an article, even if
      databases or websites change.

Book Review

Arabian, S., & Rahiminezhad, V. (2015). Journey and return: Visiting
      unbelonging and otherness in Adichie's *Americanah* [Review of
      Americanah, by Ngozi Adichie]. *Journal UMP Social Sciences and*
      Technology Management, 3(3), 536-541.

Book Review Published Online

Garner, D. (2011, September 27). An unearthed treasure that changed
      things [Review of *The Swerve: How the world became modern,* by
      Stephen Greenblatt]. *The New York Times.* Retrieved from http://
      www.nytimes.com/2011/09/28/books/the-swerve-how-the-world-
      became-modern-by-stephen-greenblatt-review.html

An Editorial

Wolfe, G. (2011). The operation of grace [Editorial]. *Image: A Journal of the*
      Arts and Religion, 70, 3-4.

An Editorial Published Online

Milwaukee verdict a wake-up call for gun dealers [Editorial]. (2015, October
20). *Los Angeles Times* Retrieved from http://www.latimes.com/
opinion/editorials/la-ed-adv-gun-shop-liability-20151019-story.html

Magazine Article

Perry, A. (2011, September 26). Epidemic on the run. *Time, 178*, 46-49.

Magazine Article from Online Database

Neuwirth, R. (2011, September). Global bazaar: Shantytowns, favelas and
jhopadpattis turn out to be places of surprising innovation. *Scientific
American, 305*, 56-63.

Note: APA does not require you to cite the database where you
obtained the article unless you think the article would be difficult to find.

Online Magazine Article

Williams, M. E. (2015, October 20). "Star Wars" lets Princess Leia age
realistically: Is this an alternate Hollywood universe? *Salon.* Retrieved
from http://www.salon.com/2015/10/20/star_wars_lets_princess_
leia_age_realistically_is_this_an_alternate_hollywood_universe

Interview

Wald, P. M. An interview with Patricia M. Wald, Judge, ICTY (1999-2001), for
the Ad Hoc Tribunals Oral History Project [Interview by S. Briand
& D. P. Briand]. (2014). In *Ad Hoc Tribunals Oral History Project.*
Retrieved from http://hdl.handle.net/10192/30832

Online Speech

King, M. L., Jr. (1963, August 28). *I have a dream* [audio file]. Speech
presented at March on Washington for Jobs and Freedom at the
Lincoln Memorial, Washington, D.C. Retrieved from http://www.
americanrhetoric.com/speeches/mlkihaveadream.htm

Page on a Website

Lukasik, A. (n.d.). Adding control with an Arduino for a Robot Arm. Retrieved
from http://makezine.com/projects/building-robot-arm-part-4-
adding-control-ardu

Image from a Website

Van Gogh, V. (1889). *Cypresses* [Painting]. Retrieved from
> http://www.metmuseum.org/toah/works-of-art/49.30.

Blog Post

Wheaton, W. (2015, September 30). Hello, world. [Blog comment] Retrieved
> from http://wilwheaton.net/2015/09/hello-world

Government Document

United States. Senate Hearing. (1964) *El Chamizal dispute: Compliance with
> convention of the Chamizal.* Cleofas Calleros Papers. University of
> Texas at El Paso Library Special Collections (#33-9).

Government Document Online

Travis, W. B. (2005). *Letter from the Alamo, 1836.* Texas State Library &
> Archives Commission, Retrieved from http//www.tslstate.tx.us/
> treasures/republic/Alamo/travis01.gov

A Film or DVD

Simien, J. (Director). (2014). *Dear white people* [Motion picture on DVD].
> United States: Lionsgate Roadside Attractions.

Television Program

Tyson, N. D. (Writer), & Druyan, A., & Soter, S. (Directors). (2014, March 9).
> Standing up in the Milky Way [Television series episode]. In L. Hanich
> & S. Holtzman (Producers), *Cosmos: A spacetime odyssey.* National
> Geographic Channel.

APA Parenthetical (In-text) Documentation

Direct Quote (three lines or less)

"Scientists estimate that the rangewide population of the San Joaquin kit fox
> prior to 1930 was 8,000 . . . " (Conover, 2001, p. 44).

Direct Quote (more than three lines)

Conover's 2001 study of the San Joaquin kit fox found the following:

> For the most part, in the "real" world kit foxes escape their preda-
> tors and the high temperatures of their desert environment by

> spending the day underground in a den. In Bakersfield, they follow suit. Kit foxes move every couple of weeks to a new den. Moving to different dens may be one reason why they have persisted; the constantly changing abodes provided new places to hide. (p. 199)

Note: For a direct quote that exceeds three lines, indent the passage 5 spaces and set as a block, as shown here.

Direct Quote When the Author Is Named in the Text

Hildebrand (2004) stated that "generals of Alexander the Great brought news to Europe of vegetable wool which grew in tufts of trees in India" (p. 144).

Information from Printed Source (but not a direct quote)

It is common to see an Osprey make its nest on an electric power pole (Askew, 2015, p. 34).

Naming the Author of a Reference in Your Text, but Not Using a Direct Quote

Thompson (2002) maintained that . . .

In 2002, Thompson discovered . . .

Electronic or Other Sources Missing Author, Date, or Page Numbers

If your source provides section notations or paragraph numbers, indicate those. Use the paragraph ¶ symbol or the abbreviation para. and number.

(Bussell, 2000, ¶ 9) or (Bussell, 2000, para. 9)

If you include a quote from a text that has neither page numbers nor paragraph or section numbers, then simply give the author and the date:

(Bussell, 2000)

If there is no author, as in an editorial, then give part of the name of the text and the date:

("Respect your audience," 2009)

If there is no date, then use n.d. If you have no date, no page number, and no author, your in-text citation will look as follows:

("The future of space," n.d.)

Acknowledgments

"A $300 Idea that is Priceless." From *The Economist*, Apr. 28, 2011. Reprinted with permission. All rights reserved.

Adams, Scott. Dilbert © 2008 Scott Adams. Used by permission of Universal Uclick. All rights reserved.

Ames, Alexander. "Bringing History to Life with Primary Sources." Student essay reprinted with permission.

Broad, William J. "Vindication for Entrepreneurs Watching Sky: Yes, It Can Fall." From *The New York Times,* Feb. 16, 2013. Reprinted with permission. All rights reserved.

Cohen, Arna. "Do You Know Where Your Mascara is Made?" Reprinted from *All Animals,* Mar/April 2014.

Echanove, Matias and Rahul Srivastava. "Hands Off Our Houses." From *The New York Times,* May 31, 2011. Reprinted with permission. All rights reserved.

Fogarty, Mignon. *Grammar Girl: Quick and Dirty Tips for Better Writing.* Copyright © 2008 by Mignon Fogarty. Reprinted with permission of St. Martin's Press. All rights reserved.

Gorup, Natalie. "How I Write an Introduction." Student essay reprinted with permission.

Govindarajan, Vijay. "The $300 House: A Hands-On Lab for Reverse Innovation?" From *HBR. org*, Aug. 26, 2010. Reprinted with permission of Harvard Business Publishing. All rights reserved.

Govindarajan, Vijay and Christian Sarkar. "The $300 House: A Hands-On Approach to a Wicked Problem." From *HBR.org*, June 7, 2011. Reprinted with permission of Harvard Business Publishing. All rights reserved.

Green, Cherish. "Understanding the Effects of Mass Media's Portrayals of Black Women and Adolescents on Self-Image." Student essay reprinted with permission.

Hamblin, James. "The Point When Science Becomes Publicity." From *The Atlantic*, Dec. 12, 2014. Reprinted with permission. All rights reserved.

Jayawardhana, Ray. "Alien Life, Coming Slowly into View." From *The New York Times,* March 27, 2011. Reprinted with permission. All rights reserved.

Johnson, Judith. "The Truth About Writer's Block." From *The Huffington Post,* July 25, 2011. Reprinted with permission. All rights reserved.

Kearl, Holly. "Laws Protecting Women From Upskirt Photo Assaults Fall Short." From *The Daily Beast,* Mar. 12, 2014. Reprinted with permission. All rights reserved.

Kilkenny, Katie. "Guardians of the Galaxy's Happy Satire of the Sad Origin Story." From *Theatlantic.com*, Aug. 4, 2014. Reprinted with permission. All rights reserved.

Klocinsky, Laura. "Can Social Media Make Us Better Writers?" From mycampus.writingcommons.org, Mar. 12, 2014.

King, Jr., Martin Luther. "I Have a Dream" speech given at the Lincoln Memorial, Aug. 28, 1963.

Knowles-Carter, Beyoncé Giselle, Chimamanda Ngozi Adichie, Terius Nash, Chauncey Hollis, Raymond DeAndre Martin. Lyrics from *Flawless*. Produced by Columbia Music Group. Copyright © 2013 by Columbia Music Group.

Lamott, Ann. "Shitty First Drafts." Reprinted from *Bird by Bird*. Copyright © by Ann Lamott. Reprinted with permission of Random House. All rights reserved.

Lewis, Jeff. Photo of the Shout, Color, Throw event at Dodger Stadium. Copyright © 2014 by AP Images. Reprinted with permission. All rights reserved.

Lincoln, Abraham. Gettysburg Address, Soldiers' National Cemetery, Gettysburg, PA, Nov. 19, 1863.

Mayo, Virginia. Photo of flash mob in Brussels, Belgium. Copyright © 2012 by AP Images. Reprinted with permission. All rights reserved.

McArdle, Megan. "Anatomy of a Fake Quotation." From *The Atlantic*, May 2, 2011.

Meyers, Justin. "How to Make a Kindle Cover from a Hollowed Out Hardback Book." Reprinted from *Wonder How To*, March, 2011.

Piraro, Dan. Bizarro Cartoon. Copyright © Dan Piraro. Reprinted with permission. All rights reserved.

Roose, Kevin. "Miscrosoft Just Laid Off Thousands of Employees with a Hilariously Bad Memo." From *New York Magazine*. Reprinted with permission. All rights reserved.

Rosen, Jeffrey. "The Web Means the End of Forgetting." From *The New York Times,* July 25, 2010. Reprinted with permission. All rights reserved.

Saad, Lydia. "One in Four in U.S. Are Solidly Skeptical of Global Warming." From *Gallup.com,* Apr. 22, 2014. Reprinted with permission. All rights reserved.

Salinas, Brenda. "'Columbusing': The Art of Discovering Something that is Not New." From *NPR. org,* July 6, 2014. Reprinted with permission of National Public Radio. All rights reserved.

Schalet, Amy. "The Sleepover Question." From *The New York Times*. Reprinted with Permission. All rights reserved.

Scham, Sam. "Top Ten Distractions for Writers, or Any Job Really." From *Yahoo.com,* Aug. 12, 2008. Reprinted with permission. All rights reserved.

Shemtob, Zachary, and David Lat. "Executions Should Be Televised." From *The New York Times,* July 21, 2011. Reprinted with permission. All rights reserved.

Singh, Rajesh Kumar. Photo of Holi celebration in India. Copyright © 2012 by AP Images. Reprinted with permission. All rights reserved.

Skinner, E. Benjamin. "People for Sale." From *Foreign Policy,* March/April 2008. Reprinted with permission. All rights reserved.

Tham, Jason. "How I Create a Multimedia Presentation." Student essay reprinted with permission.

Wade, Lisa. "Why Has Godzilla Grown?" Reprinted from *Sociological Images*. Copyright © 2014 by Lisa Wade. Reprinted with permission. All rights reserved.

Wynne, Craig. "Take a Leap Into Writing." Reprinted with permission of Craig Wynne.

STUDENT FORMS
AND WORKSHEETS

STUDENT ACKNOWLEDGEMENT OF PLAGIARISM POLICY

PLAGIARISM AND ACADEMIC DISHONESTY STATEMENT

Academic honesty is highly valued at UNR. Plagiarism (copying all or part of someone else's work and passing it off as your own) is a serious form of academic misconduct and will not be tolerated. The following definitions and possible courses of action are taken from the Academic Standards section of the university catalog:

Academic dishonesty is defined as: cheating, plagiarism or otherwise obtaining grades under false pretenses. Plagiarism is defined as submitting the language, ideas, thoughts or work of another as one's own; or assisting in the act of plagiarism by allowing one's work to be used in this fashion.

Disciplinary procedures for incidents of academic dishonesty may involve both academic action and administrative action for behavior against the campus regulations of student conduct....Academic action may include: (1) canceling the student's enrollment in the class without a grade; (2) filing a final grade of "F"; (3) awarding a failing mark on the test or paper in question; (4) requiring the student to retake the test or resubmit the paper.

Please note that "the work of another" does not just mean whole papers or articles copied from another source. It includes any information, ideas, sentences, or phrases that came from somewhere other than your own head (i.e. books, articles, internet sites, videos, documents, lecture notes or handouts from other courses, and any other sources). Whether you are quoting directly or paraphrasing, sources must be properly acknowledged by providing references and an MLA-formatted Works Cited page (or other formal citation style approved by your instructor). Citations should also be given for little-known facts and statistics. Finally, you are not allowed to submit papers you have written for other classes at UNR or elsewhere. If you have questions as to what constitutes plagiarism, please talk to your instructor, or see the UNR webpage "Academic Standards" at the following URL: http://www.unr.edu/student-conduct/policies/university-policies-and-guidelines/academic-standards/policy.

I _____ (student's name) acknowledge that I have read and understand the University of Nevada, Reno's Plagiarism and Academic Dishonesty Policy.

_____   _____

Signature of student   Date

CALL FOR CORE WRITING STUDENT ESSAYS

SUBMISSION LINK

https://corewriting.forms-db.com/view.php?id=14229

INSTRUCTIONS

Complete the Online Permission Form to Use Student Writing.

FIRST DEADLINE

Monday, December 31, 2018

SECOND DEADLINE

Friday, May 31, 2019

- ◆ Complete the relevant fields and check boxes.
- ◆ Draw your name in the Signature Box.
- ◆ Ask a Witness to draw their name in the Witness Signature Box.
- ◆ Upload files.
- ◆ Fill in today's date.
- ◆ Click Submit.

Core Writing Program (CWP) | University of Nevada Reno (UNR) | Department of English | Permission Form

CONTACT

Citlalin Xochime, Ph.D., CWP Assistant Director | cxochime@unr.edu | Frandsen Humanities 135

Best of the Core Writing Contest
2018–2019 CORE WRITING CONTEST FOR UNDERGRADUATE STUDENTS

The Core Writing Program is holding a contest for students who have completed or are currently enrolled in the following Core Writing classes during the 2018–2019 academic year:

ENG 098, 100J, 101, 102, 102H, 113, and 114

The Core Writing Program will recognize up to three excellent essays in each of the following categories:

◆ Narrative Essay
◆ Textual Analysis
◆ Researched Argument

Authors will be awarded a **$50 gift certificate to the ASUN Wolf Shop.** Instructors will be recognized, and essay contest winners **will be published in the next editions of the English Department's student essay readers:** *Composition Currents* or *Research Currents*.

To enter, please complete the online submission form at:
https://corewriting.forms-db.com/view.php?id=13623

ONLINE INSTRUCTIONS:

◆ Complete the relevant fields and check boxes.
◆ Upload files.
◆ Fill in today's date.
◆ Click Submit.

PRE- & POST-CONFERENCE WORKSHEET

You should use this worksheet to prepare for conferences with your writing instructor and to reflect on your conferences. Be sure to bring this worksheet with you to your conference and to keep all completed worksheets for your records.

Conference #: _____ Date: _____

Instructor: _____

PRE-CONFERENCE

I am meeting for a conference in order to (discuss, ask, about, explain. . .):

After this conference, I hope to (know, better understand, feel. . .):

Based on comments and feedback I've received so far, I'd like to (talk about, focus on. . .):

POST-CONFERENCE

After this conference, I feel:

As a result of our conversation, I'm going to work on:

I still have some questions about:

PRE- & POST-CONFERENCE WORKSHEET

You should use this worksheet to prepare for conferences with your writing instructor and to reflect on your conferences. Be sure to bring this worksheet with you to your conference and to keep all completed worksheets for your records.

Conference #: _____ Date: _____

Instructor: _____

PRE-CONFERENCE

I am meeting for a conference in order to (discuss, ask, about, explain. . .):

After this conference, I hope to (know, better understand, feel. . .):

Based on comments and feedback I've received so far, I'd like to (talk about, focus on. . .):

POST-CONFERENCE

After this conference, I feel:

As a result of our conversation, I'm going to work on:

I still have some questions about:

WRITING CENTER PLANNING & REFLECTION FORM

You should use this worksheet to prepare for writing center consultations and to reflect on the feedback you receive during your consultation. Be sure to bring this worksheet with you to your writing center consultation and to keep all completed worksheets for your records.

Conference #: _____ Date: _____

Writing Center Consultant: _____

PRE-WRITING CENTER CONSULTATION

At the writing center consultation, I hope to (know, better understand, feel, work on. . .):

Three specific questions I have for my writing center consultant are:

1. _____

2. _____

3. _____

POST-WRITING CENTER CONSULTATION REFLECTION

After this writing center consultation, I feel:

As a result of my conversation with the writing center consultant, I'm going to work on:

I still have some questions about:

WRITING CENTER PLANNING & REFLECTION FORM

You should use this worksheet to prepare for writing center consultations and to reflect on the feedback you receive during your consultation. Be sure to bring this worksheet with you to your writing center consultation and to keep all completed worksheets for your records.

Conference #: _____ Date: _____

Writing Center Consultant: _____

PRE-WRITING CENTER CONSULTATION

At the writing center consultation, I hope to (know, better understand, feel, work on. . .):

Three specific questions I have for my writing center consultant are:

1. _____

2. _____

3. _____

POST-WRITING CENTER CONSULTATION REFLECTION

After this writing center consultation, I feel:

As a result of my conversation with the writing center consultant, I'm going to work on:

I still have some questions about:

WRITING CENTER PLANNING & REFLECTION FORM

You should use this worksheet to prepare for writing center consultations and to reflect on the feedback you receive during your consultation. Be sure to bring this worksheet with you to your writing center consultation and to keep all completed worksheets for your records.

Conference #: _____ Date: _____

Writing Center Consultant: _____

PRE-WRITING CENTER CONSULTATION

At the writing center consultation, I hope to (know, better understand, feel, work on. . .):

Three specific questions I have for my writing center consultant are:

1. _____
2. _____
3. _____

POST-WRITING CENTER CONSULTATION REFLECTION

After this writing center consultation, I feel:

As a result of my conversation with the writing center consultant, I'm going to work on:

I still have some questions about:

PEER REVIEW WORKSHEET A

You can use the following worksheet to receive peer feedback or to analyze your own writing. This worksheet guides you to create a final draft that meets the minimum requirements of the assignment. (See PEER REVIEW WORKSHEET B for organization, mechanics, and style review questions.)

Assignment: _____ Date:_____

Peer: _____

1. Review the assignment prompt and identify what this writing project should accomplish:

2. Identify what kinds of formatting features this document should evidence:

3. Where does this draft succeed in meeting the requirements?

4. Where does this draft still need more development to meet the minimum requirements?

5. Where does this draft succeed with formatting?

6. Where does this draft lack consistency with formatting?

7. Explain in a paragraph or two your revision suggestions—keep in mind that revision suggestions are not just how to fix something but also how to develop ideas further, how to refine ideas, where examples can clarify concepts, etc.

PEER REVIEW WORKSHEET A

You can use the following worksheet to receive peer feedback or to analyze your own writing. This worksheet guides you to create a final draft that meets the minimum requirements of the assignment. (See PEER REVIEW WORKSHEET B for organization, mechanics, and style review questions.)

Assignment: _____ Date:_____

Peer: _____

1. Review the assignment prompt and identify what this writing project should accomplish:

2. Identify what kinds of formatting features this document should evidence:

3. Where does this draft succeed in meeting the requirements?

4. Where does this draft still need more development to meet the minimum requirements?

5. Where does this draft succeed with formatting?

6. Where does this draft lack consistency with formatting?

7. Explain in a paragraph or two your revision suggestions—keep in mind that revision suggestions are not just how to fix something but also how to develop ideas further, how to refine ideas, where examples can clarify concepts, etc.

PEER REVIEW WORKSHEET A

You can use the following worksheet to receive peer feedback or to analyze your own writing. This worksheet guides you to create a final draft that meets the minimum requirements of the assignment. (See PEER REVIEW WORKSHEET B for organization, mechanics, and style review questions.)

Assignment: _____ Date:_____

Peer: _____

1. Review the assignment prompt and identify what this writing project should accomplish:

2. Identify what kinds of formatting features this document should evidence:

3. Where does this draft succeed in meeting the requirements?

4. Where does this draft still need more development to meet the minimum requirements?

5. Where does this draft succeed with formatting?

6. Where does this draft lack consistency with formatting?

7. Explain in a paragraph or two your revision suggestions—keep in mind that revision suggestions are not just how to fix something but also how to develop ideas further, how to refine ideas, where examples can clarify concepts, etc.

PEER REVIEW WORKSHEET B

You can use the following worksheet to receive peer feedback or to analyze your own writing. This worksheet guides you to create a final draft that effectively communicates your purpose by focusing on organizational, developmental, and stylistic considerations. (See PEER REVIEW WORKSHEET A for minimum requirement review questions.)

Assignment: _____ Date:_____

Peer: _____

1. Identify the intended audience for the document and describe in which ways the document considers this audience's needs and expectations:

2. Identify the document's purpose and which conventions it employs to accomplish this purpose:

3. Describe two effective stylistic choices in the document. Make sure that you provide a detailed explanation of how they are effective.

4. Explain in a paragraph or two your revision suggestions—keep in mind that revision suggestions are not just how to fix something but also how to develop ideas further, how to refine ideas, where examples can clarify concepts, etc.

PEER REVIEW WORKSHEET B

You can use the following worksheet to receive peer feedback or to analyze your own writing. This worksheet guides you to create a final draft that effectively communicates your purpose by focusing on organizational, developmental, and stylistic considerations. (See PEER REVIEW WORKSHEET A for minimum requirement review questions.)

Assignment: _____ Date:_____

Peer: _____

1. Identify the intended audience for the document and describe in which ways the document considers this audience's needs and expectations:

2. Identify the document's purpose and which conventions it employs to accomplish this purpose:

3. Describe two effective stylistic choices in the document. Make sure that you provide a detailed explanation of how they are effective.

4. Explain in a paragraph or two your revision suggestions—keep in mind that revision suggestions are not just how to fix something but also how to develop ideas further, how to refine ideas, where examples can clarify concepts, etc.

PEER REVIEW WORKSHEET B

You can use the following worksheet to receive peer feedback or to analyze your own writing. This worksheet guides you to create a final draft that effectively communicates your purpose by focusing on organizational, developmental, and stylistic considerations. (See PEER REVIEW WORKSHEET A for minimum requirement review questions.)

Assignment: _____ Date:_____

Peer: _____

1. Identify the intended audience for the document and describe in which ways the document considers this audience's needs and expectations:

2. Identify the document's purpose and which conventions it employs to accomplish this purpose:

3. Describe two effective stylistic choices in the document. Make sure that you provide a detailed explanation of how they are effective.

4. Explain in a paragraph or two your revision suggestions—keep in mind that revision suggestions are not just how to fix something but also how to develop ideas further, how to refine ideas, where examples can clarify concepts, etc.

University Libraries

Mathewson-IGT Knowledge Center (KC), DeLaMare (DLM), Savitt Medical,
Learning Resource Center (LRC) & Basque

Q: How do I locate information about the University Libraries?

A: Google it! Yes, Google "UNR libraries" OR "UNR Knowledge Center" OR "DeLa-Mare", etc.

Q: How may I get help with my research?

A: From the library homepage you may email, call, chat and schedule individual consultations with a librarian from your major or with a Core Writing librarian. Drop-in research help is also available during most library hours at the Service Desk on the second floor of the Knowledge Center. **Peer Research Consultants** are available at the Service Desk in the afternoons and evenings.

Q: How do I find and access sources?

A: The following library tools can be used *on or off* campus, and all are accessible from the library homepage:

- OneSearch—use UNR's Google-like search engine to locate over 80 different content types (books, articles, images, reports, etc.)

- The Library Catalog—use this to search for digital/print books and multimedia

- A-Z databases—use these to locate news, magazine, trade, and scholarly articles

- Subject and Course Guides—use these discipline-specific guides to begin your research

- Quick How To Guides - use these do-it-yourself guides to get help with your research

Q: What other services do you offer?

A: Printing, borrowing items from other libraries, course reserves, group study rooms, anatomy models, laptops, chargers, video equipment checkout, high-end software, and MORE!

Q: Where can I go to get help WRITING my paper?

A: The University Writing Center in the Pennington Student Achievement Center. For current hours visit their website at www.unr.edu/writing-center.

UNR ENGLISH WORKS

LET ENGLISH WORK FOR YOU!

"I love English majors. I love how smart they are. I love their intellectual curiosity..... Most of all, I love to hire them."

—Steve Strauss, Small Business Columnist, 2013

"The awesome part about [the English] major is its flexibility...The skills you learn can be applied to a ton of different industries—from business, education, government, and research, to publishing, entertainment, media, and communication."

—Inside Jobs, 2013

WHY STUDY ENGLISH AT UNR?

Marketable Skills. An English major or minor can help you stand out from the crowd on the job market. Gain the kind of skills employers want in critical reading, research, editing, oral presentation, writing, and language use.

Flexibility. We offer four major and minor specializations, from writing to TESOL.

Award-Winning Faculty. Learn from faculty who have won teaching and/or research awards!

Internship Program. Get hands-on experience at local presses, nonprofits, and other groups before you even graduate.

...and much, much more!

WANT TO LEARN MORE?

Please contact the Director of Undergraduate Studies at keniston@unr.edu to learn more about how to add English into your course of study. Or you can schedule an appointment by calling our office at (775) 784-6689 or emailing roxiet@unr.edu.

http://www.unr.edu/liberal-arts/degrees/english

Useful Phone Numbers

Admissions and Records

(775) 784-4700 x2

Fitzgerald Student Service Bldg., 2nd floor

Disability Resource Center

(775) 784-6000, TTY: 327-5131

English Placement

(775) 784-6709

Core Writing Program, Frandsen Humanities, Room 131

Foreign Language Placement (credit by exam)

(775) 784-6055

Edmund J. Cain Hall, Room 241

Math Center (085)

1664 N. Virginia Street

Reno, NV 89557

mathcenter@unr.edu

Phone (775) 784-4433

Pennington Student Achievement Center, Room: 300 | Admin: 303/304

Student Financial Aid & Scholarships

(775) 784-4666

Fitzgerald Student Service Bldg., 3rd floor

Tutoring Center

1664 N. Virginia Street

Reno, NV 89557

urban@unr.edu

Phone (775) 784-6801

Pennington Student Achievement Center, Suite 320

Writing Center

1664 N. Virginia Street
Reno, NV 89557
writing_center@unr.edu
Phone (775) 784-6030
Pennington Student Achievement Center, Suite 350

Campus Escort (775) 742-6808

Campus Police (775) 784-4013

National Suicide Prevention Lifeline: 1 (800) 273-8255

Hope Line Network: 1 (800) 784-2433

University after-hours crisis cell phone: (775) 297-8315

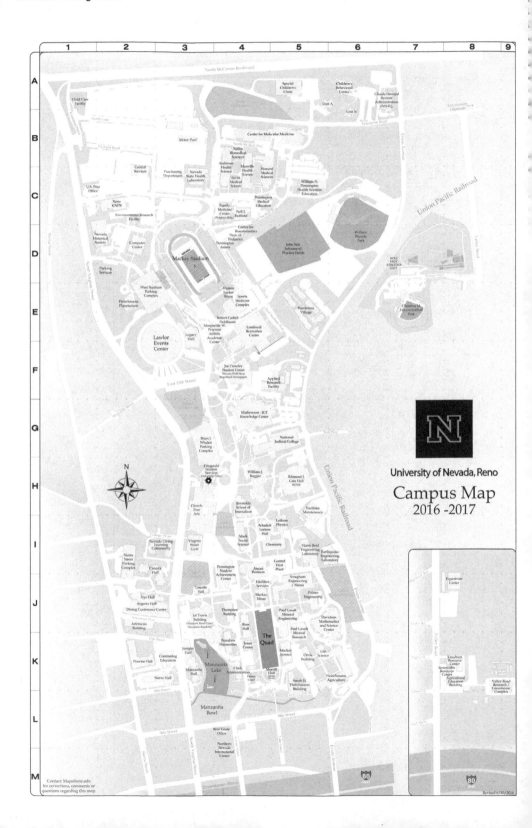

University of Nevada, Reno

Campus Map
2016 -2017

Index

Page numbers in bold indicate activities. Page numbers followed by *t* indicate tables, and those followed by *fig* indicate figures.

abstracts, 328
academic conversations, 17, 23–25, **25**, 26, 174
action verbs, 224–225
ad hominem arguments, 99–100, **103**
ad populum arguments, 100, 101*t*
ad vericundiam arguments, 100, 102*t*
Adichie, Chimamanda Ngozi, 69, **70**
advertisements, 71–72, **72–73**
aesthetic reading, 48–49, **81**
Agrippa, Heinrich Cornelius, 4
Aimes, Alexander A., 274–275
Alien Life Coming Slowly into View, 110–113, **113**
All-Star Rockers Salute Buddy Holly, 75-76
American Psychological Association (APA), 123, 273, 299–301, 321, 327–337
analysis, 204
Anatomy of a Fake Quotation, 315–318, **318**
ancient Roman format, 194*t*
annotated bibliography, **297**, 298–301, 322–328, 330–334
annotations, 35, 59–60, 61, 65*fig*, **91**
appeals, Aristotle's, 92-93, 150
argument
    artistic proofs, 150–152
    cogent, 99
    elements of, 49–50, **58**
    formats for, 194–195*t*
    kairos and, 84–86, **91**, **118-119**
    logos and, 93, **96**
    opposing, 49, 50
    rhetorical, 11–13
    role of, 27
    types of, 12–13
    valid, 98
argumentation, 204
argumentative essay, 189–193, 194–195*t*, 196, 196–197, 206, **212–213**
Aristotle, 1,2,3, 4, 13, 14, 93, 97, 98, 103, 109–110, **114**, 122, 126, 150, 151*t*, **162**
arrangement, 122–123, 123*t*, 125*t*
Art of Rhetoric, The (*On Rhetoric*; Aristotle), 6, 122, 150
artistic proofs, 150–152, 151*t*, **151**, **152**, **156**, 270
Athens, 5–6
audience, 49, 50, **58**, 61, 66–69, 83-86, **91**, **92**, 98, 118, 296
Augustine of Hippo, 4
author
    close reading and, 58, 61
    evaluating, 295–296
author searches, 287

B612 Foundation Releases Video, 184–186
backing, 190, **190**
begging the question arguments, 100, 102*t*, **103**
beliefs, personal, 59, 61
Beyoncé, 69, **70**
bias, 296
bibliographic documentation
    for APA, 328–333
    for MLA, 322–327
bibliography, annotated, **297**, 298–301, 322–327, 328–333
Bitzer, Lloyd F., 165–166
blogs, **33**, **80**, **119**, **162**, **168**, **213**, **267**, **318**, 325, 331
Book Review Digest, 296

Book Review Index, 296
book reviews, 296, 324, 330
books, 284, **288**, 291, 322–324, 329
Booth, Wayne C., 93
brainstorming, 145–146
Bringing History to Life with Primary Sources, 274–275
Broad, William J., 181–184
Brumfield, Amy, 163–164
Burke, Kenneth, 4, 25
Burkean Parlor, 25

call numbers, 287
call to action, 49, 50, 189, 194, 206
Can Social Media Make Us Better Writers? 165, 166–167, **167**
capitalization, 207
cause and effect
    confusing, 100–101, 102*t*, **103**
    as strategy, 204
Chang, Kenneth, 310–312
Changes in Behavior Can Affect Species Invasion Success, 258–267
Cicero, 4, 164, 166
claim statement, 50, **58** 189
Clark, Amber Lea, 83
classification, 204
Clausen, Jenelle, 121
cliché, 222
climate change casebook, 301–313, **313–314**
close reading of text, 58–61, 65*fig*, **66**
closed questions, 280
clustering, 146, 146*fig*, **147**
cogent argument, 99, **99**
Cohen, Arna, 37–47
collaborative groups, 26
"'Columbusing': The Art of Discovering Something that is Not New" (Salinas), 8–11, **11**, 12
common ground argument, 190–191
common ground, finding, 12–13, 67
commonplace books, **31–32, 81, 119, 162,** **213, 267, 318**
comparison and contrast, 204
computerized library catalogs, 286–288, **288**
computerized searches, 287–288
conciseness, 223–224
conclusion, 49, 50, **58**, 97–100, 189, 192, 206
confirmation, 189
content, overall, 237, **238**
conversations, academic, 23–25, **25**, 26, 174-175
copyright, 211
counterargument, **170, 174**, 192, 194*t* 295
    see also opposing arguments, answering
counterclaim, 190, **190**, 195*t*

credibility, 47, 67, **76**, 93, 109–110, **113**, 114 181, 202-203, 206, 270–272, 273, 295-296, **297**
    see also ethos
critical reading, **48**
critical thinking, 36, **37**, 49
cultural differences, 6–7

data, 189, **190**, 195*t*,
databases, 284-285, 287, 288, **288**, 289*fig*, 293, 294, 325–326, 328, 331–333
debatable issue, 49, 50, **58**
deductive argument, 150
deductive fallacy, 99
deductive reasoning, 97–98, **98**
definition, 127, 128*t*, 130, 131, *194t* 204
delayed constructions, 223
delivery, 122–123, 123*t*, 125*t*
democracy, 5
description, 204
design, elements of, 206–208
development, patterns of, 204
dialogue, 164–165
directness, 225–226
Directory of Online Open Access Journals, 292
distractions, 233–234
"Do You Know How Your Mascara is Made?," 37–47, **47–48**, 49
documentation, 273, 281, 314–315, 315*t*, 322–323
DOI (Digital Object Identifier), 321, 328,329, 330
drafting, 124, 125*t*
dummy text, 208
DVDs, 326, 332

Echanove, Matias, 133, 135–137
editing, 124, 125*t*
editorials, 324, 330, 333
effective writing, qualities of, 220–227, **228**
efferent reading, 48, 49
either/or arguments, 100, 102*t*
Elbow, Peter, 144
Elliott, Meaghan, 1
Emerging Mobile Phone Technology Empowers, 245–250
emotion, 93, 103–104, **116**
encyclopedias, 285–286
enthymeme, 97–98
essay starters, 197
ethos, 1, 13, 14*fig*, 27, 83, 85, 93, 109–110, 113–114, **113, 114, 115, 116–118,** **119**, 174, 181, 202, 206
    see also credibility
everyday words, 221–222, **228**
evidence, 49, 50, 150

Executions Should Be Televised, 12, 94–96, **96**
exemplification, 204
exordium, 189, 194*t*
explication, 189, 194*t*
eye movement, 207*fig*

fact, 127-128, 128*t*, 130, 131
"fair use" provision, 211
false dichotomy arguments, 100
Farrell, Shanna, 270, 275–278, **279**, **281**
feedback from peer editing, 235–236
film reviews, 23–25, 157–160, **160–162**
films, 326, 332
five-paragraph essay, 191–192
"Flawless," 69, **70**
focused freewriting, 145, **147**, **150**
Fogarty, Mignon, 230–232
formal fallacy, 99
foundation, 190
freewriting, 37, 60–61, **66**, **119**, **144**–145,
    147, **150**, **162**, **168**, **174**, **193**, **202**, **213**

gaps, filling, 222, 225, **228**
general modern format, 191–192, **192**, 194*t*
Gettysburg Address, 28–29, **29**, 85, 166
Gillis, Justin, 310–312
Ginsburg, Ruth Bader, 30–31
Google Books, 291
Google Scholar, **279**, 291–292, **292**, 294
government documents, 270-271, 285, 292,
    325–326, 333
Govindarajan, Vijay, 133–135, 138–142
grammar cartoons, **228**
Grammar Girl's Top Ten Grammar Myths,
    230–232
grammar myths, 230–232
Gray, Sarah, 215
Greek culture, 5–6
Green, Cherish, 174–180, **180**
Gorup, Natalie, 198–199
Guardians of the Galaxy review, 157–160,
    160

Hamblin, James, 62–65
Hands Off Our Houses, 13, 133, 135–137
Hauser, Gerard A., 4
headings, 207
Hermagoras, 126
hook, 172, 173, 196–197
How I Create a Multimedia Presentation,
    209–211
How I Write an Introduction, 198–199
How to Make a Kindle Cover from a Hollowed
    Out Hardback Book, 77–79
Hudson, Hoyt, 4

"I Have a Dream" speech, 85–90, **91–92**, 104,
    110
images
    choosing, 208–209
    copyright and, 211
    documentation for, 325, 331
    interaction between text and, 76–79, **76**, **80**
    page design and, 206-207
inartistic proofs, 150–151, 151*t*, **156**,
    270–271
indexing projects, 290, 291*fig*
inductive argument, 150
inductive fallacy, 99
inductive reasoning, 98–99, **99**
informal fallacy, 99
informal groups, 26
Interlibrary Loan department, 287–288
Internet, research and, 284, 286, 286–288,
    289–292, **297**
Internet Public Library, 286, 290, 290*fig*
intertextuality, 70
interviews, 272, 279–281, **281–282**, 315*t*,
    325, 331
in-text documentation, 326–327, 333-333
introduction, 189, 190, 192, 194*t*, 195*t*,
    196–197
invention, 122–123, 123*t*, 125*t*, 144–147,
    147, **161-162**, 270
invisible freewriting, 145
IPCC: Greenhouse Gas Emissions Accelerate
    Despite Reduction Efforts, 307–310
Isocrates, 36
"it is" constructions, 223

jargon, 221–222, 259
Jayawardhana, Ray, 110–113, **113**
Jefferson, Thomas, 110
Johnson, Judith, 199–201, **202**
Joseph, Sister Miriam, 4
journals, scholarly, 285, 291–292, **292**, 323–
    324, 329–330

kairos, 14, 14*fig*, 84–86, **91**, **92**, 118, **119**,
    131–132, **132**
Kearl, Holly, 168–170, **170–171**
Kennedy, John F., 166
keyword searches, 287, 289–290
Kilkenny, Katie, 157–160, **160**
King, Martin Luther, Jr., 85–90, **91–92**, 104,
    110
Klocinski, Laura, 165–167, **167**
knowledge, personal, 59, 61
Krenger, Rosalie, 269

Lamott, Anne, 217–220, **220**
Lat, David, 94–96, **96**

Laws Protecting Women From Upskirt
    Photo Assaults Fall Short, 168–170,
    170–171
Leith, Sam, 2
library catalogs, 286–288, **288**
Library of Congress, 287
Lincoln, Abraham, 28–29, 85, 104
listing, 145
logical fallacies, 99–102, 101–102*t*, **103**, **171**
logos, 1, 13–14, 14*fig*, 83, 93, **96**, 113–114,
    114, **115**, **118**, **119**, 174
Lorem Ipsum text, 208

magazines, 285, **288**, 291, 324–325, 330–331
main points, 192
major premise, 97–98
McArdle, Megan, 315–318, **318**
McKeown, Greg, 221
memory, 122–123, 123*t*, 125*t*
Meyers, Justin, 77–79, **80**
Microsoft Just Laid Off Thousands of
    Employees With a Hilariously Bad
    Memo, 15–19, **20**
minor premise, 97–98
*MLA Handbook for Writers of Research
    Papers*, 321
Modern Language Association (MLA), 123,
    273, 298–299, 321–327
movie reviews, 23–25, 157–160, **160–162**
myths, grammar, 230–232

narratio, 189, 194*t*
narration, 189, 194*t*, 204
NASA Near Earth Object Program, 186–188,
    188, **190**, **191**, **192-193**
Neil, Dan, 153–156, **156–157**
news media, **292**
newspapers, 285, **288**
non sequitur arguments, 100, 102*t*

Obesity in America, 251–258
observation, 151*t*, 151–152, **152**, **156**
On Rhetoric (*The Art of Rhetoric*; Aristotle), 6,
    122, 150
On the Ideal Orator (Cicero), 164
One in Four in U.S. Are Solidly Skeptical of
    Global Warming, 302–306, **313**
one-time pairs, 26
ongoing small groups, 26
Op-Ed arguments, 168-170, **170–174**
Open Directory, 286, 290, 291*fig*
open questions, 280
opposing arguments, answering, **190**, **192**,
    194*t*, **203**, **212**
    see also counterargument
oral media, 69–70

outlines, 60, 61, **66**, 294

page design, 206–208
paragraph development, 237–238
parenthetical documentation, 326–327, 332
partition, 189
passive voice, 226, **228**
pathos, 1, 13, 14*fig*, **23**, 27, 83, **92**, 93, 103–
    104, **109**, **113**, 113–114, **114**, **115**,
    116, **118**, **119**, 174
patterns of development, 204
PDFs, 321, 327
peer editing groups, 26, 235–236, 237–238,
    238
peer editing samples
    Op-Ed arguments, 242–244
    rhetorical analysis assignment, 238–241
    short research paper, 245–267
People for Sale, 104–108, **109**, 114
periodicals, 285
peroratio, 189, 194*t*
persuasion, 12
photos, 207, 208–209
    see also images
placeholder text, 208
plagiarism, 203, 314–315, 315*t*
Plato, 6, 122
"Point When Science Becomes Publicity, The,"
    62–65, **66**
policy, 127, 129*t*, 130
polishing, 124, 125*t*
"Porsche Macan S," 153–156, **156–157**
position, 191
post hoc, 101, 102*t*, **103**
power, rhetoric and, 3
praxis, defining, 2
preciseness, 222
prewriting stage, 122–123, 125*t*, 144–146,
    147, **150**
proofreading, 230
Public Access Catalogs (PACs), 286–288
*Publication Manual of the American
    Psychological Association*, 329
Purdue Owl, 321, 327
purpose, 93

quality, 127, 128*t*, 130
questions, open and closed, 280
Quintilian, 4, 126
quotations, 202–203, 326–327, 332–333

reading aloud, 216, 230
reading rhetorically, 36, 37, 48–49, 58–61, **81**
rebuttal, 190
red herring arguments, 100, 102*t*
references, documenting, 273

References page, 328–332
reflecting on topic, 59, 61
refutatio, 189, 194*t*
rereading, 216–217
research
    inartistic proofs and, 150, 270–271
    overview of, 121, 269
    plan for, 293–295, **314**
    primary and secondary, 272–273, **279,**
        314
    resources for, 271–272, **279**
    secondary sources, 273, **279**, 284–286,
        314
    synthesizing, 312–313
research-based argument essay, 174–175,
    193, 212–213
reviews of your work
    independent, 236–237
    peer editing and, 235–236
revising, 124, 125*t*, 215, 216–217
Rheingold, Howard, 224–225
rhetoric
    canons of, 122–123, 123*t*, 125*t*, **125**
    classification of, 122
    contemporary usage of, **7**
    defining, 1–3
    effective use of, 3–4
    historical usage of, **5**
    reasons for studying, 27–28
    selected definitions of, 4
    training in, 5–6
    use of, **28**
    visual, 29–30, **31–33**, 70–72, **72–73, 75,**
        114, **115–118**
    word map for, 7, **7**, 8*fig*
Rhetorica ad Herennium, 122
rhetorical analysis, 68, **118–119**
Rhetorical Analysis of President Reagan's
    "Challenger Speech," 238–241
rhetorical argument, 11–13, 28
rhetorical judgments, 1
rhetorical situation, 165–166, **171**, 174
rhetorical stance, 93
rhetorical triangle, 66–67, 67*fig*, **67**, 93
Richards, I. A., 4
Rogerian argument, 13, 190–191, **191**, 195*t*
Rogers, Carl, 13, 190
Roose, Kevin, 15–19, **20**
Rosen, Jeffrey, 51–57, **57**
Rosenblatt, Louise, 48–49, **81**
running heads, 327–328

Saad, Lydia, 302–306, **313, 314**
Salinas, Brenda, 8–11, **11**
sample essays
    Op-Ed arguments, 242–244
    rhetorical analysis assignment, 238–241
    short research paper, 245–267
Sarkar, Christian, 133, 138–140, **143, 144**
Schalet, Amy, 20–22, **23**
Scham, Sam, 233–234, **235**
scholarly journals, 285, 291–292, **292**, 323–
    324, 329–330
Scientists Warn of Rising Oceans as Antarctic
    Ice Melts, 310–313, **313, 314**
Scout Report, 296
search engines, 289–290
senses, 152, 222
sentence structure, 238
Shea, Danny, 68
Shelley, Percy Bysshe, 5
Shemtob, Zachary B., 94–96, **96**
Shitty First Drafts, 217–220, **220**
shock value, 73–74, **75**
simplicity, 220–221
skimming text, 59, 61, 207*fig*
Skinner, E. Benjamin, 104–108, **109**, 114
Sky Is Falling casebook, 180–188, **188**, 190,
    191, 192–193
Sleepover Question, The, 12, 20–22, **23**
slippery slope argument, 101, 102*t*, **103**
social media, 165, 166–167, **167, 168**
song lyrics, 69, **70**
Sophists, 6
source materials
    citing, 314–315, 320–333
    electronic format of, 323
    evaluating, 295–296, **297**
    missing information for, 335
    research plan and, 293–295
    support from, 202–203
    synthesizing, 312–313
space, use of, 206
speaking directly, 225–226
special interest publications, 285
speeches, 325, 331
Srivastava, Rahul, 133, 135–137, **143, 144**
stasis questions, 127–131, 128–129*t*, **132,**
    143
stasis theory, 126–128, 131–132, **132, 143,**
    294
stated position, 49, 50, **58**
strategies, 204
straw man fallacy, 101, **103**
strong argument, 99
style, 122–123, 123*t*, 125*t*
subject, 66–67
subject searches, 287
summaries, 61, **68, 80**
supporting your argument, 202–203
supporting your thesis, 203
surveys, 283, **283, 314**

syllogism, 97–98

Take a Leap into Writing, 147–149, **149**
task groups, 26
television programs, 326, 332
Tham, Jason, 209–211
"there is" constructions, 223
thesis, 49, 50, **58**
     working, 196, 294, **313**
thesis statements, 193, 196
$300 House: A Hands-On Approach to a
     Wicked Problem, The, 13, 138–140
$300 House: A Hands-On Lab for Reverse
     Innovation? The, 133–135
$300 House casebook, 13, 133–143, **143–
     144**
$300 Idea that Is Priceless, A, 141–143
timeliness, 84–85
title page, 328
title searches, 287
Top Ten Distractions for Writers, 233–234
topoi, 144
Toulmin, Stephen, 189
Toulmin model, 189–190, **190**, 195*t*
transitions, 204–205, 205*t*
truncated syllogism, 97–98
Truth about Writer's Block, The, 199–201,
     202

Understanding the Effects of Mass Media's
     Portrayals of Black Women and
     Adolescents on Self-Image, 174–180,
     180
URLs, 320–321, 328, 329

validity, 98

verbs, action, 224–225
Vindication for Entrepreneurs Watching Sky,
     181–184, **188**
visual media, 68–70
visual rhetoric, 70–72, **72–73**, **75**, 114,
     115–118
voice
     passive, 226
     strengthening, 226–227

Wade, Lisa, 73–74, **75**
warrant (bridge), 189
Web Means the End of Forgetting, The, 51–57,
     57–58
web pages/websites
     documentation for, 320–321, 325, 327,
          328, 329–331, 333
     evaluating, 295–296, **297**
     as source material, 286
"What Does It Mean to Drink Like a Woman?,"
     270, 275–278, **279**, **281**
What Marriage Means to Me, 242–244
Why Has Godzilla Grown? 73–74, **75**
Wikipedia, 271–272, 285–286, 293–294
word choice, 221–225, **229**, 238
word of mouth, 68
wordy expressions, 223–224
working thesis, 196, 294, **313**
works cited page, 322–326
writer, 66–67
writing process, steps in, 163–164
Writing Program Administrators (WPA), 314
Writing without Teachers (Elbow), 144
Wynne, Craig, 147–149, **149**

Zepeda, Isidro, 35